# Chichester Excavations VIII

Roy and Sheila Morgan, to whom this volume is presented, in appreciation of their work over twenty-five years on the documentary history of Chichester

# Chichester Excavations VIII

by

## Alec Down FSA, MIFA    and
## John Magilton BA, M.Phil., FSA, MIFA

*with specialist contributions by*
P. Armitage M.Sc., Ph.D., M.I.Biol., E.W. Black, MA, FSA, R.G. Browse Cert.Arch., AIFA,
H.E.M. Cool BA, Ph.D., G.B. Dannell FSA, B. Dickinson BA, C. Edwards BA, AIFA,
R. Foden BDS, LDS, RCS, Dip.F.Odont., K. Hartley FSA, J.A.P. Kenny BA, AIFA, R.J. Lintott,
S. Morgan, D. Neal FSA, J. Price BA, Ph.D., FSA, V. Rigby BA, D. Williams BA, Ph.D., FSA, P. Wilthew

Published by
Chichester District Council

Published by
CHICHESTER DISTRICT COUNCIL
East Pallant House, East Pallant, Chichester

ISBN 0 85017 004 4

The Chichester District Council acknowledges with gratitude the technical assistance given by John Wiley & Sons Ltd in the publication of this volume and seeing it through the press.

Printed by Henry Ling Ltd., Dorchester - 2374

# Preface

This volume chronicles a range of archaeological activity extending from 1982 to 1991 at locations in and around Chichester. The policy of investigating and recording all sites within the historic core of the city has again paid dividends, not least in the discovery of a hitherto unknown Roman inhumation cemetery outside the Westgate, and a series of small investigations at points around the defences has resulted in some new thinking about when the Roman wall and rampart were constructed.

We owe much to the devoted work of members of the archaeological team, both professional and voluntary, who have worked long hours, often in foul conditions, to record Chichester's past. We also gratefully acknowledge the help given to us by various landowners, architects and builders who went out of their way to be helpful.

It is impossible, for reasons of space, to mention by name everyone who took part in the fieldwork over the last ten years, but the supervisors during this period were Tim Appleton, Mark Beaton, John Bowen, Robbie Browse, Chris Down, Damian Goodburn, James Kenny, John Piper, Frances Raymond, Brenda Ware, John Wildman and Sue Woodward. Max Wholey drew the small finds, the samian ware and Roman glass, John Piper the Roman fine wares, and John Bowen and Robbie Browse most of the plans and sections. Conservation of the finds was carried out by Carol Edwards, assisted by Graham Langford.

Finally, we wish to thank Pat Livitt and Kitty Grove who put the whole volume on the word processor and assisted in the editorial work, and Dennis Chaplin, formerly of John Wiley and Sons, for seeing the book through the press.

ALEC DOWN
JOHN MAGILTON

# Acknowledgements

The Chichester District Archaeological Advisory Committee and the authors gratefully acknowledge the financial assistance given by the undermentioned organisations towards the funding of the excavations and the publication of the results.

For excavation:
  Abbey Housing Ltd
  Chichester District Council
  Chichester Theological College Ltd
  English Heritage
  London and Manchester Securities plc
  The Manpower Services Commission
  Oakhurst Developments Ltd
  G. Oliver (Footwear) Ltd

For post-excavation work:
  Chichester District Council
  English Heritage

Thanks are also due to Dr Simon Esmonde Cleary for reading and commenting on an earlier draft of the Westgate Cemetery report.

# List of Abbreviations

| | |
|---|---|
| AML Rep. | Ancient Monuments Laboratory Report |
| Ant. J. | Antiquaries Journal |
| Arch. Ael. | Archaeologia Aeliana |
| Arch. J. | The Archaeological Journal |
| BAR | British Archaeological Reports |
| BM | British Museum |
| Brit. Mon. Ser. | Britannia Monograph Series |
| CBA Res. Rep. | Council for British Archaeology Research Report |
| CW | Transactions of the Cumberland and Westmorland Antiquarian and Archaeological Society |
| HBMC (E) | Historic Buildings and Monuments Commission (England) |
| JRS | Journal of Roman Studies |
| LAMAS | London and Middlesex Archaeological Society |
| MPBW | Ministry of Public Buildings and Works |
| PPS | Proceedings of the Prehistoric Society |
| RCHM | Royal Commission on the Historical Monuments of England |
| ROB | Berichten van de Rijksdienst voor het Oudheidkundig Bodemonderzoek |
| RRSAL | Research Report of the Society of Antiquaries of London |
| SAC | Sussex Archaeological Collections |
| VCH (Sx) | Victoria County History (Sussex) |
| WSRO | West Sussex Record Office |

# List of Contents

# List of Level 3 Reports in Archive

Note: These are stored on disks, and print-outs can be obtained for a small fee on application to the Chichester District Museum, Little London, Chichester. A duplicate set of disks is lodged with the West Sussex Record Office, County Hall, Chichester.

All the finds from these excavations have been deposited in the Chichester District Museum.

| | |
|---|---|
| P.L. Armitage | Notes on the skull of a 17th-century horse from 14–15 East Street, Chichester |
| | The cattle horn cores from Greyfriars, Chichester. Tables 4 and 5 and Appendix |
| Justine Bayley | A note on a lead fragment from Chapel Street 1984 |
| E. Black | Catalogue of Roman keyed tiles from Greyfriars |
| H.E.M. Cool & J. Price | Catalogues of Roman glass from Greyfriars, Theological College and Chapel Street sites |
| A. Down | The small finds from Theological College (complete list) |
| | The small finds from Chapel Street 1984 (complete list) |
| | The small finds from Greyfriars (complete list) |
| G. Dannell | Chichester 1987–8, decorated samian report |
| J.A.P. Kenny | Finds from West Walls 1987–8 and St Peter's 1987 |
| | Catalogue of unpublished copper alloy finds from West Walls 1987–8 |
| | Catalogue of unpublished tile, copper alloy and iron finds from St Peter's 1987 |
| R.R. Morgan | Granada Cinema—documentary notes |
| V. Rigby | Catalogue of Roman fine wares from Greyfriars |
| | Catalogue of Roman fine wares from the Theological College |
| D.F. Williams | Iron Age/Roman pottery from Chapel Street, Chichester 1984 |
| | A note on the petrology of a medieval roof tile and a jug from the Theological College, Chichester |
| | Report on petrological examination of certain sherds from the Chapel Street and Theological College sites |
| | Roman amphorae from the 1987–8 excavations at West Walls, Chichester, West Sussex |
| | Roman amphorae from Chapel Street, Theological College and Greyfriars sites |

# List of Plates in the text

## Acknowledgements to Plates

12 A and B       R. Foden
13 and 14        R. Foden
23               English Heritage
The remainder, Chichester District Archaeological Unit

# List of Figures in the text

## 5 St Peter the Great, West Street, 1982

## 6 Recent investigations of the city walls

## 7 Granada Cinema, East Street, 1984

## 8 The post-medieval pottery from 14–15 East Street

## 9 A group of medieval pottery from 74 South Street

## 10 A selection of late/post-medieval pottery from 24 South Street

# CHICHESTER

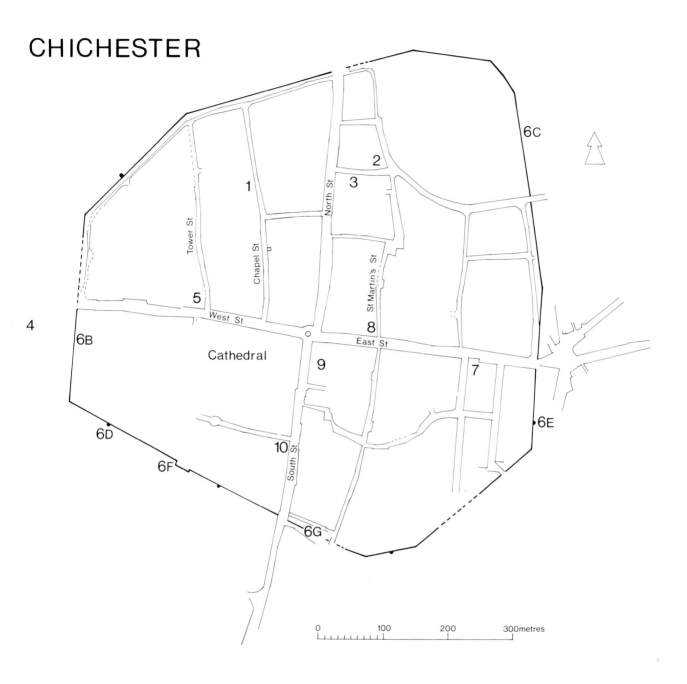

6C

2

3

North St

1

Tower St

Chapel St

St Martin's St

5

West St

4

6B

8

East St

Cathedral

9

7

6E

6D

10

6F

South St

6G

0        100        200        300metres

Location map for all sites

1   Chapel Street 1984
2   Greyfriars 1984
3   St Peter's North Street 1987
4   Theological College 1985 and 1987
5   St Peter the Great 1982
6B  West Walls 1987–88
6C  Jubilee Park 1991
6D  Palace bastion 1985

6E  Pine's Yard bastion 1991
6F  Deanery bastion 1991
6G  Southgate 1960
7   Granada Cinema 1984
8   14–15 East Street 1984
9   74 South Street 1984
10  24 South Street 1984

# Part 1—The archaeology

# 1

# Chapel Street 1984 (Fig. 1.1)

## by Alec Down

### INTRODUCTION

From 1968 to 1978 the Excavation Committee carried out a programme of work in advance of development on both sides of Chapel Street (*Chichester Excavations 3*; *Chichester Excavations 5*). In 1984 an opportunity to examine the small area left undug between the earlier excavation sites presented itself and as the previous excavations had produced evidence of the early military occupation of the site and the subsequent development of the Roman town, followed by settlement in the late Saxon period, the main object of the 1984 project was to re-examine the earliest phases and in particular to try and locate another early Roman pottery kiln thought to be in the vicinity. Two had been found previously and appeared to have started production in the early Neronian period, producing distinctive fine wares of a very high quality as well as the native coarse wares (*Chichester Excavations 3*, 56–7 and figs. 10.3–5).

The work was funded by grants from the Department of the Environment and the developers, Glenlion Consultants Ltd.

The northern edge of the cutting was placed within 0.25 m of the southern edge of the 1977 excavation (Trench X) and for the sake of consistency the excavation was treated as an extension of the earlier site and the same phasing has been used. In view of the limited time available the top 0.75 m of black topsoil was removed mechanically.

The Chapel Street sites were originally classified as follows:

Period 0   Pre-Conquest
Period 1   Claudian
Period 2   Claudius/Nero
Period 3   Early Flavian to late 1st, early 2nd century
Period 4   2nd century
Period 5   Early to mid 4th century
Period 6   Late 4th century
Period 7   c. early 5th century
Period 8   Saxon; c. 9th–11th century
Period 9   Medieval; 12th–15th century
Period 10  Post-medieval, 16th–18th century

No features could be assigned to Periods 0–2. A few residual Early Iron Age sherds were found, but no pre-Conquest Roman fine wares, although these were well attested in the earlier excavations. The hoped-for Period 2 kiln site had been completely destroyed by a medieval well.

Period 3   Flavian–early 2nd century.
Part of a timber building (Pl. 1) alongside a narrow street metalled with gravel and bounded on either side by a timber-lined drain which aligned with the same feature identified first in 1977 (*Chichester Excavations 5*, fig. 8.5, and this volume, Fig. 1.2).

Period 4   No features could be assigned.

Period 5   Early to mid 4th century.
House 2 (Fig. 1.3)
A metalled area west of the Roman street (Street 1) was identified as part of the courtyard or metalled service area excavated in 1977 (*Chichester Excavations 5*, fig. 8.7) and the south end of the timber-revetted latrine pit (X10 in 1977; Pit X14 in 1984) was located and excavated. At the south end, part of the masonry foundation of House 2 was recorded.

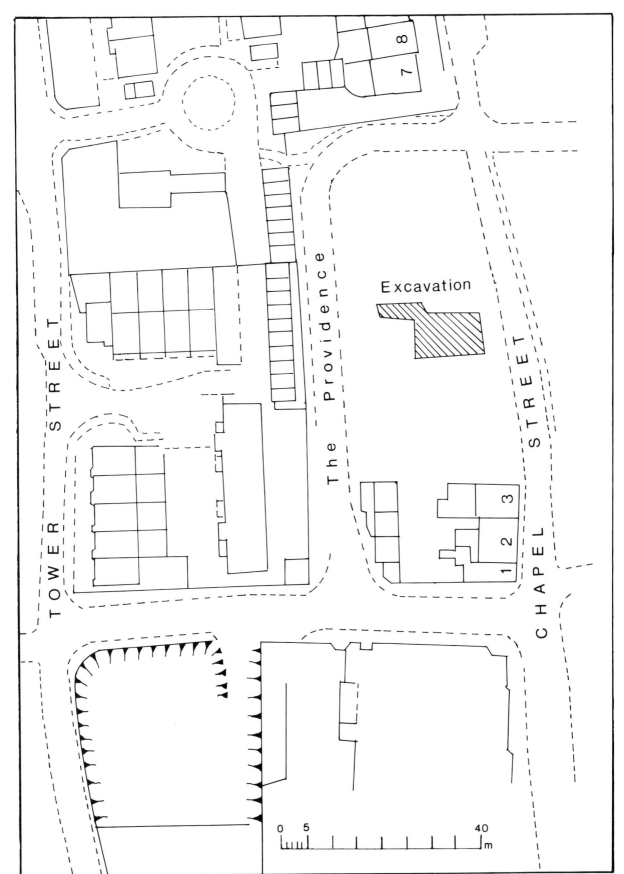

Fig. 1.1  Chapel Street 1984. Location plan

Plate 1    Chapel Street 1984, Trench X, looking north, showing section through Roman street 1

Periods 6 and 7    Late 4th–early 5th century.
In the south-east corner of the trench, and partly in the section, were the remains of a hearth or oven constructed of Roman *tegulae* which was dug into the edge of the Roman street metalling. It was opposite the corner of the range of rooms belonging to House 2, and 10 metres to the east of it. (Fig. 1.3).

Reference to fig. 7.20 in *Chichester Excavations 3* shows a group of hearths on the east side of the north–south street (Street 1). These were also constructed of *tegulae* and assumed by this writer (*op. cit.* p.82) to be of late Roman date. They were within the angle formed by the junction of Streets 1 and 3 and there was no sign of any structure to which they might be related, although one might have existed further to the east, outside the limits of the excavation.

It is likely that the hearth in Trench X belongs to the same period, in which case it would be late 4th–early 5th century in date and the postholes shown in the updated version of fig. 7.20 (Fig. 1.4 this volume) may now be re-interpreted as part of a timber structure on the north-east angle of Streets 1 and 3 and the hearth might well relate to it.

Period 8    Late Saxon.
Two late Saxon pits, one cut through the Roman street and the other through the service area belonging to House 2 were identified.

Period 9    Medieval, 12th–15th century.
A stone-lined well (Pit X13) (Plate 2) and a number of pits (see Fig. 1.5) were dug through the Roman street and the service area to the west of it. The well had some sherds of 15th century painted wares in the construction pit, but earlier medieval wares, some probably dating from the 13th century, were present in the fill, and it is clear from the earlier excavations that occupation on that part of the site was fairly continuous from the late Saxon period at least. The documentary sources are sparse, but a tenement belonging to William Wroth or Adam le Ber was recorded on or near to the excavation site in 1250 (see *Chichester Excavations 3*, fig. 5.2) with other land and buildings to the south owned by John de Beauchamp and Matilda his wife. The well discussed above was probably one of a series dug near the later properties on the site and it appears to have been backfilled at some time after the late 15th century.

## REFERENCES

Down, A., 1978. *Chichester Excavations 3* Phillimore.
Down, A., 1981. *Chichester Excavations 5* Phillimore.

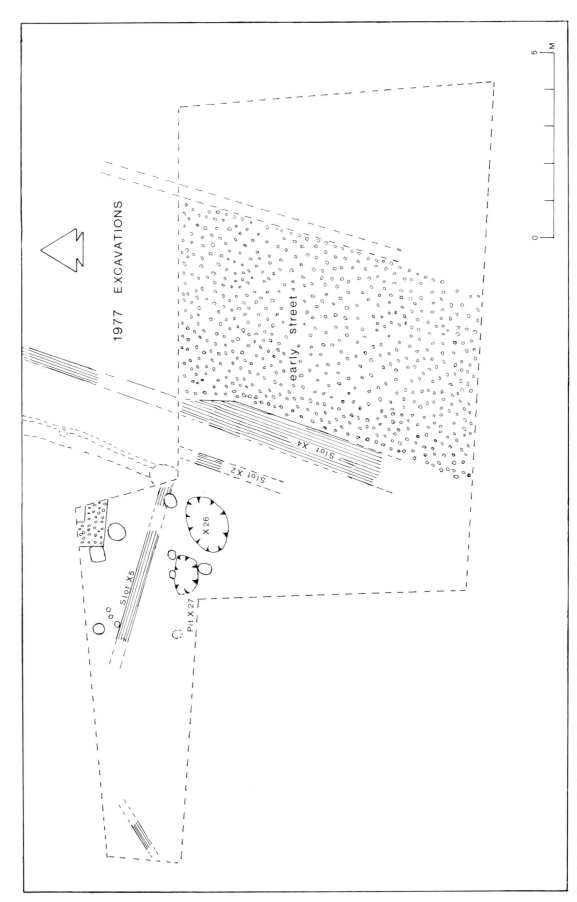

1977 EXCAVATIONS

early street

Slot X4

Slot X2

Slot X5

X 26

Pit X27

0                    5
                          M

Fig. 1.2    Roman, Period 3, Flavian to early 2nd century. Scale 1:100

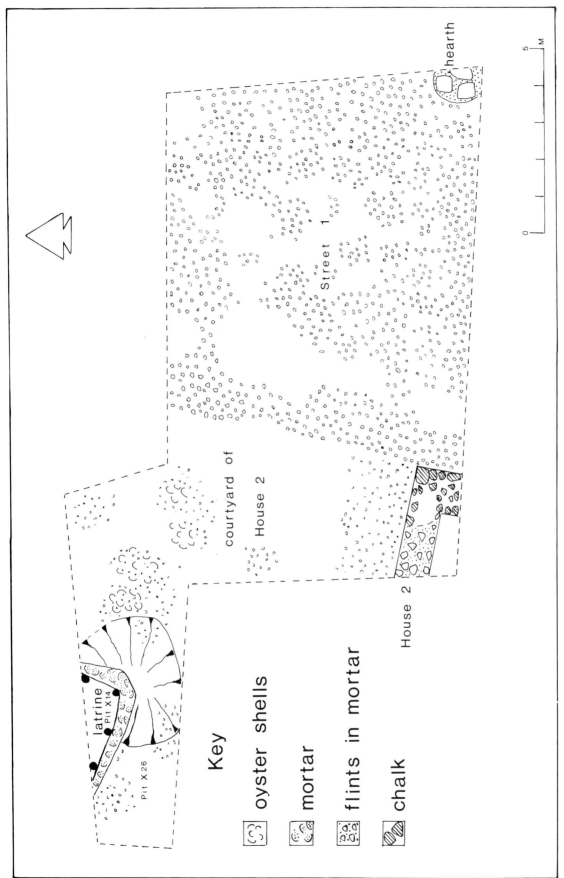

Key

oyster shells

mortar

flints in mortar

chalk

hearth

Street 1

courtyard of House 2

House 2

latrine

Pit X 14

Pit X 26

M

5

0

Fig. 1.3   Roman, Periods 5–7, c. early–mid 4th to early 5th century. Scale 1:100

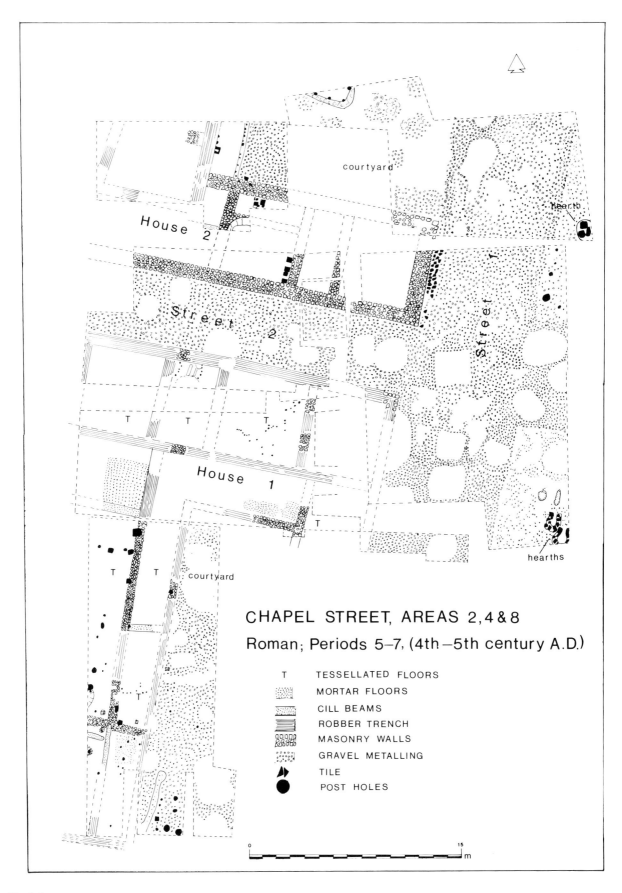

courtyard

hearth

House 2

Street 2

Street 1

T    T    T

House 1

T

T    T

courtyard

T

hearths

CHAPEL STREET, AREAS 2, 4 & 8
Roman; Periods 5–7, (4th–5th century A.D.)

| T | TESSELLATED FLOORS |
| | MORTAR FLOORS |
| | CILL BEAMS |
| | ROBBER TRENCH |
| | MASONRY WALLS |
| | GRAVEL METALLING |
| | TILE |
| | POST HOLES |

0    15
m

Fig. 1.4

Plate 2   Chapel Street 1984, excavating medieval well

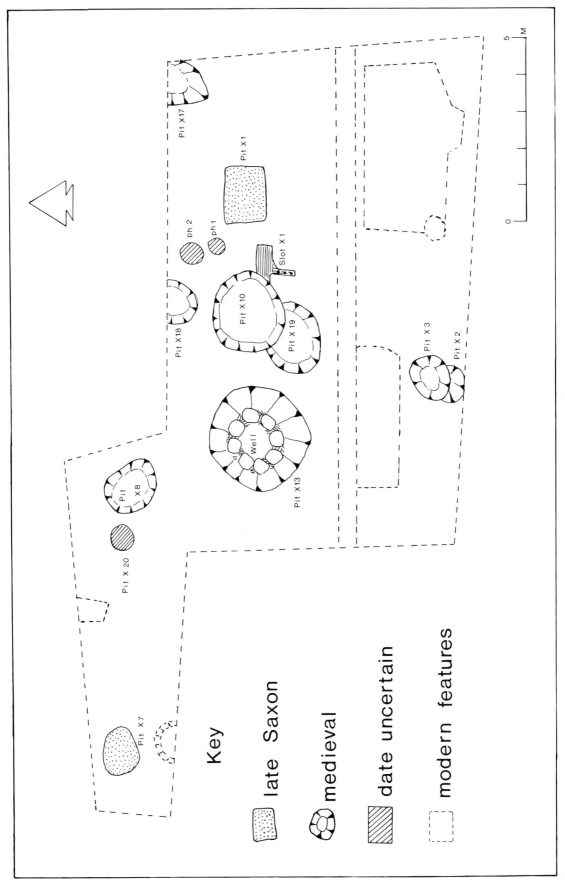

Fig. 1.5 Late Saxon, Period 8, 9th–11th century, Medieval, Period 9, 12th–15th century. Scale 1:100

Pit X17

Pit X1

ph 2

ph 1

Slot X1

Pit X18

Pit X10

Pit X19

Pit X3

Pit X2

Well

Pit X13

Pit X8

Pit X 20

Pit X7

Key

late Saxon

medieval

date uncertain

modern features

0

5

M

# Excavations at Greyfriars, North Street, Chichester, 1984

## by Alec Down

### INTRODUCTION

Greyfriars, No 61 North Street, was previously the offices of the Chichester City Council and became surplus to requirements after local government reorganisation, when the personnel were relocated in East Pallant House. The District Council took the decision to sell the building and also release the land at the rear for building development. In view of the archaeological importance of the site a six-month excavation was launched, funded jointly by the District Council and the Ancient Monuments Division of the Department of the Environment.

### PREVIOUS WORK

Excavations to the south of the site in 1958–9 (Cunliffe and Murray 1962, 93–110) and Fig. 2.1 this volume, showed that there had been Roman occupation there from the Flavian period up to the late 3rd century AD. A total of six phases of Roman occupation were noted, the final phase being a house of masonry construction, and a 7th phase was seen at the western end of the site, where the foundations of an early medieval building was found, fronting on to North Street.

### Site History

(Compiled from notes supplied by Mr R.R. Morgan of the Documentary Research Group; the site numbers are shown on Fig. 2.2).

I  *Greyfriars, No 61 North Street*
   The present mansion dates from about 1755. Previously there was another large house on the site (six hearths in 1670) and an earlier house is mentioned in 1534 when it was in the occupation of Richard Bartram. It was probably in the ownership of the Friars Minor and was seized at the Dissolution. The wealthy Exton family (butchers, merchants and aldermen) had the house in the late 16th and the 17th centuries and in 1684 it was described as 'house and malthouse'. Harry Peckham left it to his father in 1784 and a decade later it went to his sister Sarah Farhill.

II  Was combined with I.

III  *No 62 North Street*
   Timber-framed and jettied; probably 16th century. It is mentioned in 1534 as 'the great house of John Hardham,' who was a butcher. The house had probably belonged to a Chantry up to 1550 and thence passed to the Crown at the Dissolution, being finally acquired by the City. In 1585 it was held by William Comber, a blacksmith. He leased it out, first to his son-in-law, John Carpenter, and then to others during the 17th century. Four hearths were recorded in 1670. It was variously used as one house or sub-divided into two or three. In 1699, when it was briefly used as a Meeting House by the Quakers, it is recorded as being one house with malthouse and stables.

IV  The garden behind 4 Guildhall Street and Priory Road belonged to No 61 North Street and was in the ownership of the Exton family in the 16th and 17th centuries. They also had the lease of VII (see below). The large number of cattle horn cores recovered from Pit A50 in Trench A (Fig. 2.8) may be linked with the Exton's butchery trade, possibly in the 16th century (Armitage, this volume, pp. 211–13.) The garden was in existence for at least four centuries and latterly was always part of No 61.

V  The garden to the east of No 62 belonged to it in the 16th and 17th centuries, but recently has been part of No 61.

VI  Recorded as a barn belonging to John Hardham in 1534 which was still there in 1597. It was in the east (rear) of No 62 North Street and part of that property.

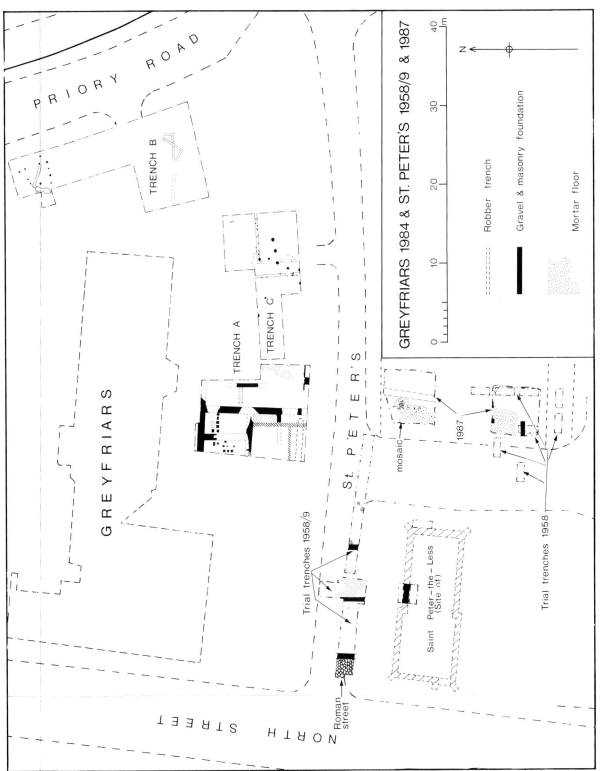

GREYFRIARS 1984 & ST. PETER'S 1958/9 & 1987

Robber trench

Gravel & masonry foundation

Mortar floor

PRIORY ROAD

TRENCH B

GREYFRIARS

TRENCH A

TRENCH C

St. PETER'S

Trial trenches 1958/9

Roman street

NORTH STREET

mosaic

1987

Saint Peter-the-Less
(Site of)

Trial trenches 1958

Fig. 2.1

12

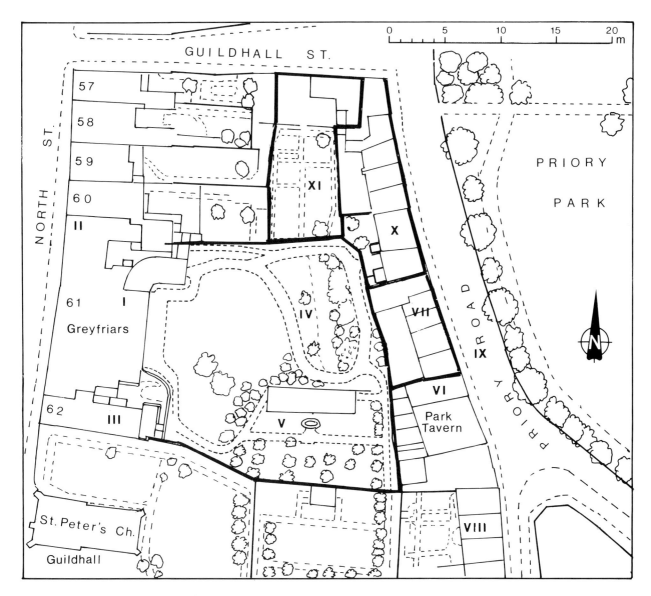

Fig. 2.2   The Greyfriars area in 1875, based on the 1:500 OS plan. The locations referred to in the documentary notes are shown in Roman figures

VII The five dwelling houses in a terrace shown on the 1875 1/500 OS Map had been demolished by 1898 to create a rear access for No 61 North Street. They were owned by the Vicars Choral. Some of the foundations can be identified in Trench B, Period 3 (Fig. 2.11).

In 1851 (1) the occupants included a whitesmith, carpenter, grocer and shoemaker. In 1804 (2) there were two tenements and a storehouse. These were all brick built and the roofs were tiled.

In 1786 (3) the description is 'limehouse and houses'. The reference to a limehouse may be connected with the discovery during excavation in Trench A of the bases of barrels which appeared to have been used for mixing lime (p. 31, Fig. 2.10 and Plate 5). The houses mentioned in 1786 can be seen on the Gardner Map of 1769 and they are described in 1756 (4) as 'Garden with small tenements or dwellinghouses'. The house is mentioned in the Rental for 1660–1760 as a 'house in Vintree' (i.e. St Martin's Lane). The annual amount of the rent (2s. 4d.) suggests that the property was a modest one.

In 1649 (6) the Parliamentary Survey describes it as 'a house or tenement being nigh unto the house called Greyfriars consisting of three low rooms and three chambers over said low rooms and a small yard and well of water and all the little garden plot belonging to the said house containing together 6 roods'. The lessee (Nicholas Exton, a merchant) was required to keep the premises in good repair and hedge the moats and bounds thereof. The Norden Map of 1595 shows a house in this position and on the Priory Road frontage. The earliest reference to VII is 1520 (7) 'item of Vicars for a tenement'.

13

VIII Property of St Mary's Hospital. More recently part of Greyfriars (1).

IX Priory Road is thought to be on the line of the outer bailey of the castle and in the 13th century may have been no more than a footpath along the outside of the wall around the Greyfriars.

X These properties were not demolished with VII. They were also small dwellinghouses. The description in 1749 (8) is, 'two messuages with brewhouse and wash-house and garden belonging'.

XI *No 4 Guildhall Street*

This has an 18th century front to a timber-framed building. It was built about 1676 (9) and is then described as 'a hall, a little room at the end of the hall, chimney, two chambers over the hall with closet belonging to them, one garret over the chambers and all the *old* kitchen and lean-to buttery adjoining it and lying on the east side of the messuage, with the chimney and oven in the said kitchen, and all that backside and two gardens lying against the said new built messuage and old kitchen'. There was also the free use of a well in the fence of the garden and free use of the 'house of office' at the south end of the said garden.

Up to 1716 the owner of the property was Henry Coombes, a cutler. He lived in that part of South Street (Cooper Street) where the shops were and it is possible that he used the rear of his premises in Guildhall Street for manufacturing or processing and the premises in South Street for sales.

Reference to the 1875 map (Fig. 2.2) shows a pump set against the south-east angle of the garden wall and another one further north on the east side. A pump implies a well, and either of the two shown on the map may have been the well mentioned in the description of 1676. The 'house of office' referred to might well have been on the same site as the small building in the south-east corner of the garden shown on the map.

### References

(1) Census
(2) Phoenix Fire Insurance Add. Mss. 17008
(3) Land Tax
(4) Lease Book, Vicars Choral
(5) Cap III/5/1:
(6) Cap I/30/1
(7) Cap I/26
(8) City Deed no 73
(9) Add. Mss. 19648-50
(nos 1–7 and 9 in WSRO)

## THE EXCAVATIONS

The site investigation was confined to the rear of No 61 (see Fig. 2.1) and the excavation plan was considerably restricted by the need to preserve a number of mature trees which were the object of some concern to local amenity groups. In the event, this proved to be no more than a cosmetic exercise, as all the trees were later removed when building works started, with the exception of one near the Park Tavern.

Three trenches were dug, A, B and C, and in view of the short time available to us the top metre of garden soil was removed by machine. Most of it had been made up within the last century.

### Synopsis

### Period 1—Roman, Phase 1; c. mid 1st–mid 2nd century

*Evidence for occupation of the site from Claudian to mid 2nd century was present in later pits, but no structural features survived.*

Phase 2, c. mid 2nd century+ (Figs. 2.3–2.4)

*Phase 2 represents a period of clay-pit digging in Trenches A and B, into which the Phase 1 rubbish was tipped.*

Phase 3a and 3b, c. mid to late 2nd century (Figs. 2.5–2.6)

*Slots and postholes of two or more phases of timber structures, some being built over the fill of the Phase 2 clay-pits in Trenches B and C were noted.*

Phase 4a, c. late 3rd–mid 4th century (Fig. 2.3)

*A building with narrow wall foundations of gravel was constructed above a backfilled clay-pit in Trench A.*

Phase 4b, post-mid 4th century (Fig. 2.7)

*The Phase 4a building was enlarged and a hypocaust was constructed. The house probably extended as far west as the street and the fragments of the masonry house found in 1987 were probably part of the same building. The date for this rebuilding must be after the middle of the 4th century as two mid 4th century coins were found in the gravel foundations of the Phase 4b house. The coin sequence in the destruction layers ends with Gratian (AD 367-83), and the absence of any late colour-coated wares may suggest that occupation had ceased before the turn of the century.*

### Period 2, medieval, c. 11th–15th centuries (Figs. 2.8 and 2.9)

*Late Saxon occupation is represented by a pit (A9) in Trench A and 7 large cess-pits along the frontage with Priory Road. This latter group may have belonged to tenements along a north–south Saxon street, perhaps the northern part of St Martin's Street, which was partly overlain by the outer bailey of the Norman castle.*

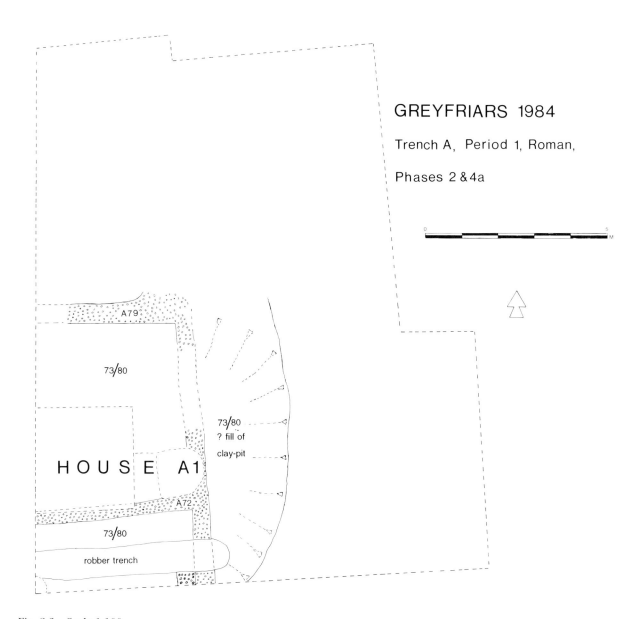

GREYFRIARS 1984

Trench A, Period 1, Roman,

Phases 2 & 4a

A79

73/80

73/80
? fill of
clay-pit

HOUSE A1

A72

73/80

robber trench

Fig. 2.3    Scale 1:100

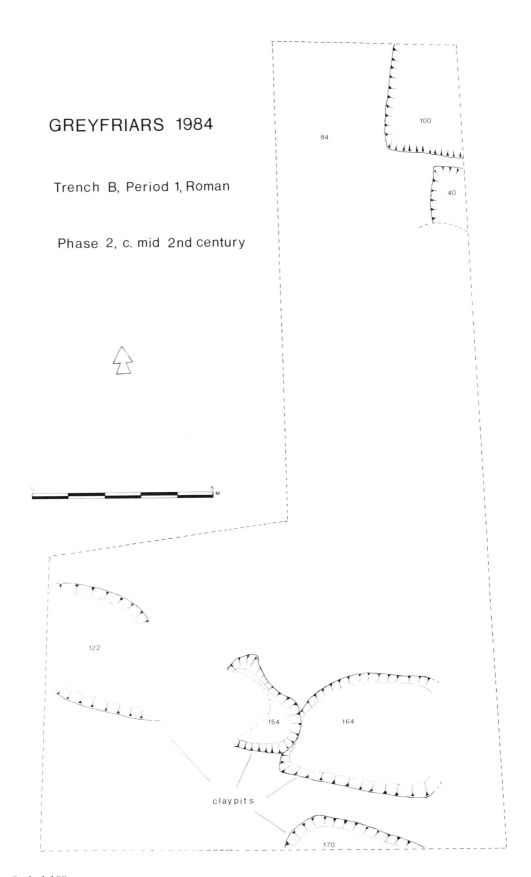

GREYFRIARS 1984

Trench B, Period 1, Roman

Phase 2, c. mid 2nd century

84

100

40

122

154

164

claypits

170

Fig. 2.4   Scale 1:100

16

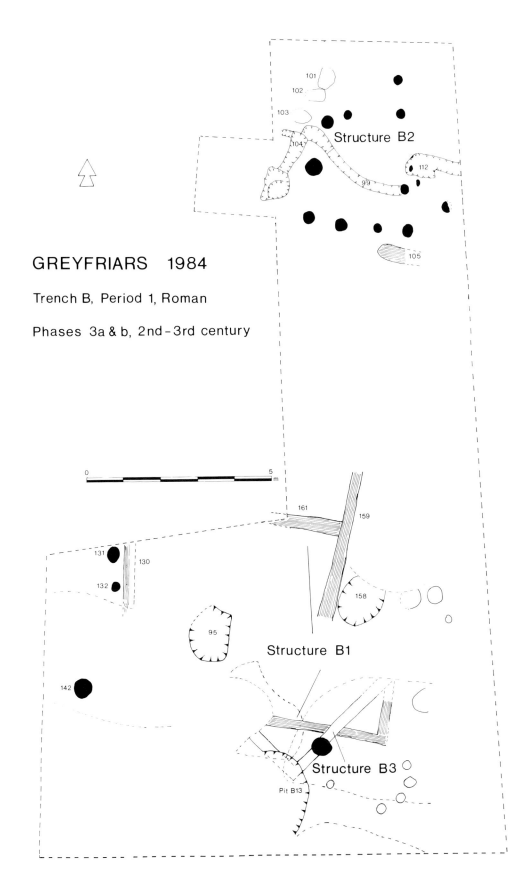

GREYFRIARS 1984

Trench B, Period 1, Roman

Phases 3a & b, 2nd–3rd century

Structure B2

Structure B1

Structure B3

Pit B13

0              5
m

Fig. 2.5    Scale 1:100

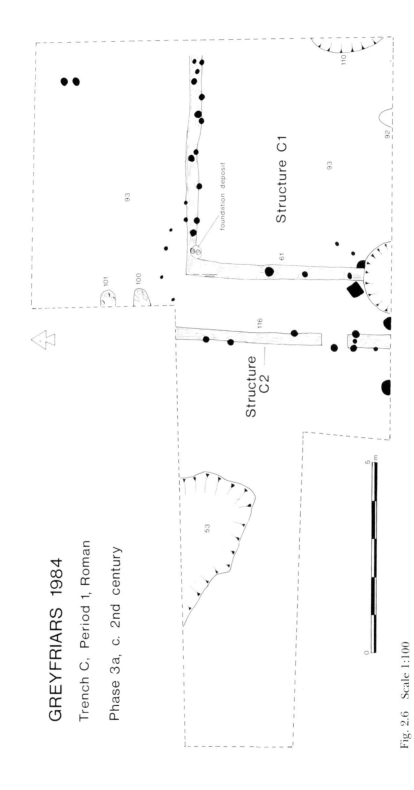

GREYFRIARS 1984

Trench C, Period 1, Roman

Phase 3a, c. 2nd century

Structure C1

Structure C2

foundation deposit

93

93

101

100

110

92

61

116

53

Fig. 2.6   Scale 1:100

5 m

0

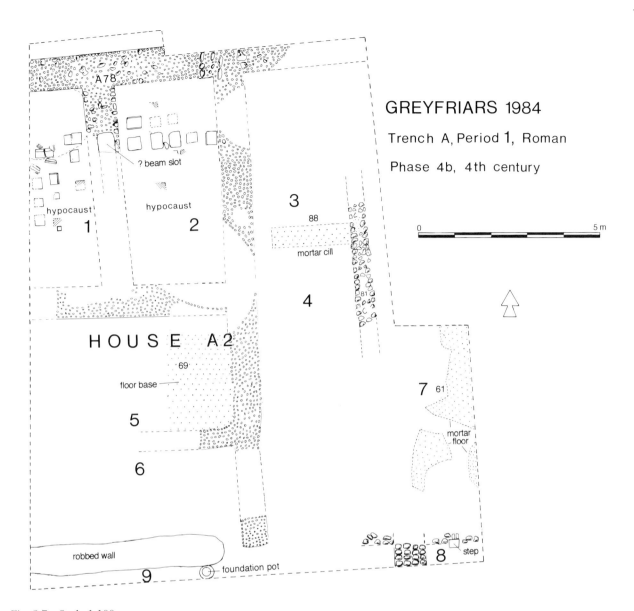

A78

? beam slot

hypocaust 1

hypocaust 2

3

88

mortar cill

4

81

0                    5 m

H O U S E   A 2

69

floor base

5

6

7 61

mortar floor

robbed wall

9

foundation pot

8 step

Fig. 2.7    Scale 1:100

*In the later medieval period, pits and a group of postholes testify to continuous occupation of properties fronting on to North Street and Guildhall Street.*

### Period 3, post-medieval, c. 17th–19th centuries (Figs. 2.10–2.14)

*Throughout the post-medieval period much of the excavated area was within the large pleasure garden at the rear of No 61 North Street while the eastern side (Trench B) was occupied from the 18th century onwards by houses, the latest of which were demolished to allow rear access to Greyfriars.*

### DISCUSSION BY PERIODS

### Period 0, pre-Conquest

There was no structural evidence for the presence of any occupation on the site prior to the invasion of AD 43 (designated as Period 0 in Chapel Street (Down 1978, 52) but a few sherds of Early Iron Age pottery and a silver minim of Verica (p. 182) were recorded. There was also an absence of late Augustan Arretine and imported fine wares to match that found at the Theological College (this volume, p.54; Chapel Street, Dannell 1978, 225–7; Dannell 1981, 263–4).

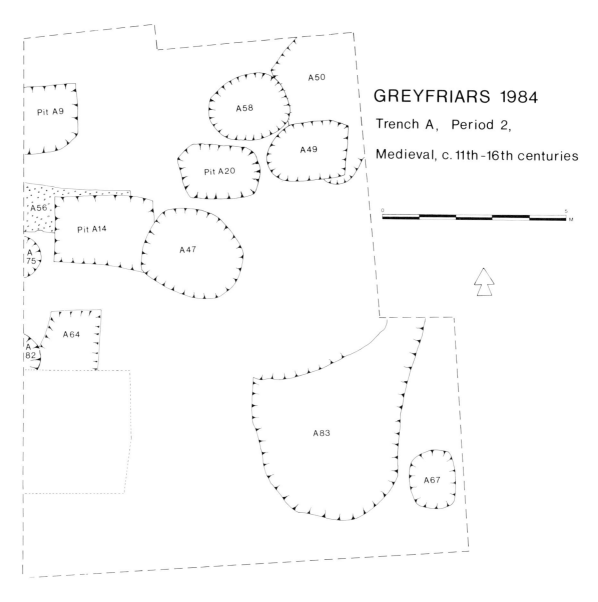

GREYFRIARS 1984

Trench A, Period 2,

Medieval, c. 11th–16th centuries

Pit A9

A50

A58

A49

Pit A20

A56°

Pit A14

A47

A 75

A64

A 82

A83

A67

0    5
              M

Fig. 2.8    Scale 1:100

**Period 1, Roman, Phase 1, Claudian to c. early 2nd century (Figs. 2.3-2.4)**

The evidence for this phase of occupation is almost entirely contained within later pits. Pre-Flavian fine wares, both imported from Gaul and local imitations made in the Chapel Street kilns were identified, together with samian ware of Claudian date and a number of items of 1st-century military equipment (Fig. 20.1, 7). Some of the contexts in which this material was found (Trench A, 73/80 and 96; Trench B, 122) were the earliest features dug into natural clay and the latest dated pottery indicates that they were not backfilled until c. early 2nd century.

**Phase 2, c. mid 2nd century or later (Figs. 2.3–2.4)**

This phase is represented by the pit-digging activity recorded in Trenches A and B, which must have taken place at some time after the early 2nd century. The pits were almost certainly dug for clay, being typically shallow and irregular in shape, and it is likely that the clay was intended for the construction of wattle and daub structures or for use in ovens or kilns making pottery and/or tiles. There was no sign of any residual Phase 1 occupation in the areas between the pits and this must mean that the holes left by the extraction of the clay must have been filled with material brought in from elsewhere. This included demolished building material (i.e. roof tiles and mortar debris) as well as the pottery described above.

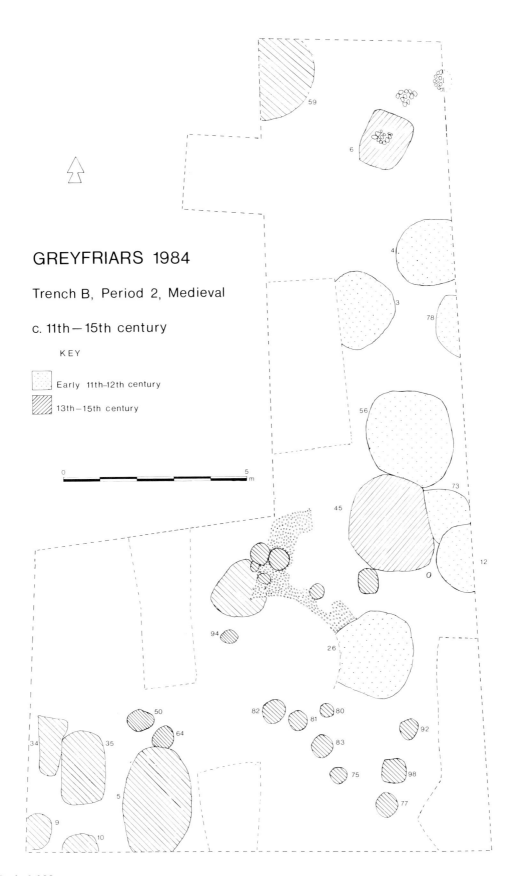

GREYFRIARS 1984

Trench B, Period 2, Medieval

c. 11th — 15th century

KEY

Early 11th–12th century

13th–15th century

0                                                    5
                                                     m

Fig. 2.9   Scale 1:100

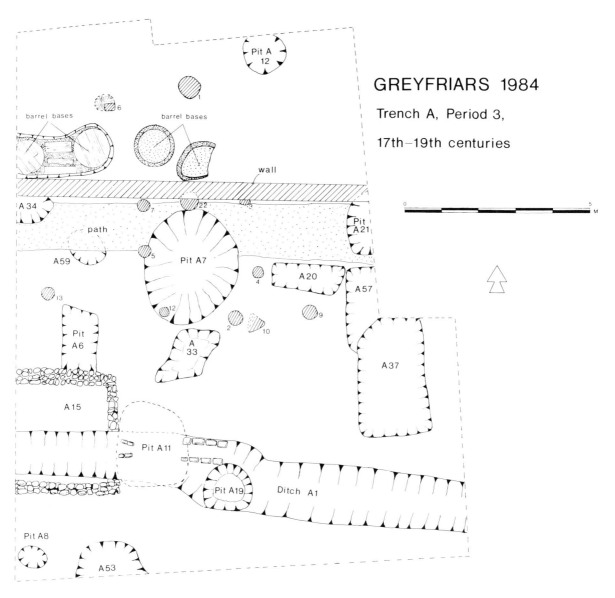

GREYFRIARS 1984

Trench A, Period 3,

17th–19th centuries

Pit A 12

barrel bases

barrel bases

wall

A 34

path

A 59

Pit A7

Pit A6

A 15

Pit A11

Pit A19

Ditch A1

Pit A8

A 53

A 20

A 57

A 37

A 33

Pit A21

0             5 M

Fig. 2.10  Scale 1:100

## Phase 3a and 3b (Trenches B and C and Figs. 2.5–2.6); c. mid 2nd century plus

At some time after the clay-pits were backfilled, a series of timber structures were erected on the site and traces of these were discovered in Trench B (Structures B1–B3), and Trench C, (Structures C1 and C2). In Trench B, only discontinuous lengths of beam slots and some postholes survived in the southern half of the trench, while at the north end an arrangements of postholes (Structure B2) appeared to have two drains below, B122 and B99. B122 drained eastwards and had no datable finds, while B99 drained north-west and joined B104, which terminated in a sump filled with potsherds. This may possibly have been intended as a soakaway, although it was scarcely large or deep enough to have functioned effectively. The arrangement of postholes, which is not very convincing as a domestic building, may have served to support the roof of an open-sided structure. The sump (B104) had a collection of fine and coarse wares including several complete vessels, with a date range of c. pre-Flavian to Antonine, which indicates a date of mid–late 2nd century for the deposit. Amongst the pottery was an almost complete lead-glazed jar, with part of a second one that was probably a waster (Fig. 22.1, 4 and 5) and a complete crucible (Wilthew, this volume, p. 209 and Plate 23, p. 210).

Examination of the residues from the crucible shows that a gunmetal (copper–zinc–tin alloy) was being melted, which may be an indication that metal working was taking place on or near the site in the mid–late 2nd century.

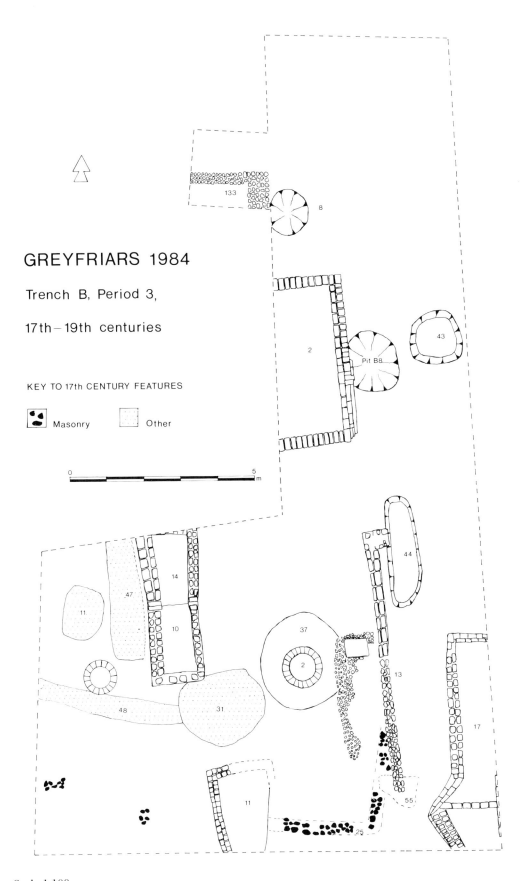

GREYFRIARS 1984

Trench B, Period 3,

17th−19th centuries

KEY TO 17th CENTURY FEATURES

Masonry          Other

0                                    5
                                     m

133

8

2

Pit B8

43

14

47

11

10

37

2

44

13

48

31

17

11

55

25

Fig. 2.11    Scale 1:100

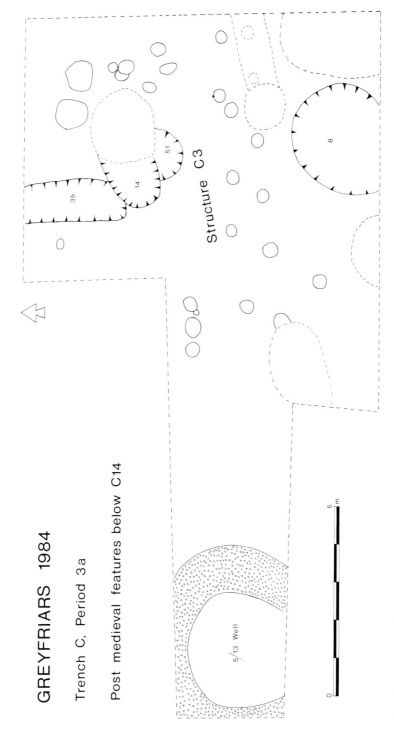

GREYFRIARS 1984

Trench C, Period 3a

Post medieval features below C14

Structure C3

35

14

51

8

5/13 Well

Fig. 2.12   Scale 1:100

5 m

0

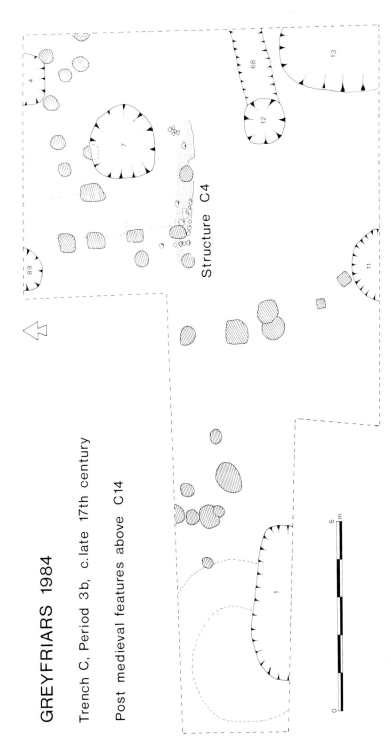

GREYFRIARS 1984

Trench C, Period 3b, c.late 17th century

Post medieval features above C14

Structure C4

Fig. 2.13   Scale 1:100

25

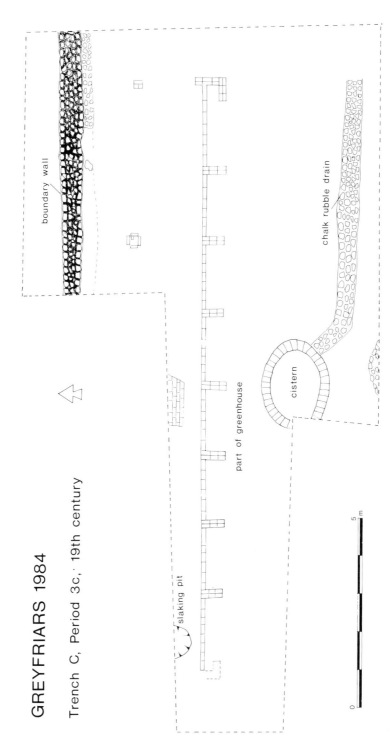

GREYFRIARS 1984

Trench C, Period 3c, 19th century

boundary wall

chalk rubble drain

cistern

part of greenhouse

slaking pit

0                    5 m

Fig. 2.14   Scale 1:100

*Structure B1*

Two sections of beam slot (shown shaded on the plan) seem to make up part of the ground plan of a building, with the lower part built out across the fill of two clay-pits, B154 and 164. The short length of slot (B130) with two postholes alongside (131 and 132) *may* be part of the same structure, but the angle is not quite right and, although it appears to be dug into the top of pit B122, the ground was so badly disturbed that it was impossible to be sure. Although neither of the clay-pits cut by Structure B1 can be closely dated, B122, which is just west of them, and is almost certainly contemporary, had a large group of pottery with a date range of c. Claudian to 2nd century, and a date somewhere towards the middle of the 2nd century is proposed for this building.

*Structure B3*

Only two short lengths of slot, joining at right-angles, survived later pit-digging. It was cut through Structure B1, and assuming that these timber-framed buildings had a fairly short life, at the most probably not more than 20–25 years, then a date of c. late 2nd century for Structure B3 to replace it might be feasible.

Plate 3   Greyfriars, Trench C, looking west, postholes of structures C1 and C2

*Trench C (Structures C1 and C2) (Fig. 2.6 and Plate 3)*

The slots of two timber structures (61 and 116, Structures C1 and C2) could be recognised, cut into context 93. Only the bottom few centimetres survived later cultivation of the area (see below) and they were difficult to define in some places. Whilst Structure C1 can be safely predicted in part, Structure C1, with only part of the east wall visible, is conjectural and it is assumed that the north–south slot 116 is likely to have turned westwards outside the excavated area and any traces of the west wall would have been destroyed by the construction pit for the post-medieval well (Fig. 2.12). The discovery of a foundation deposit consisting of two complete vessels (Fig. 2.6 and 22.1, 1 and 2) in the north-west corner of Structure C1 is evidence that the buildings belong in the Roman period, and although close dating is lacking, they are likely to post-date the early–mid 2nd century. They were both cut into context 93, but must have been dug from the level above (B31/41), which had been heavily churned up by later cultivation. This layer had no later pottery than Trajanic samian, with the remainder of the fine wares being of Claudio-Neronian date.

Plate 4    Greyfriars, Trench A, part of House A2, looking south

*Discussion*

There were few traces of anything which might have been interpreted as domestic occupation. Food bones and shellfish were sparse, as were domestic hearths or ovens. It seems likely that the structures were storebuildings of some kind. There was evidence that the daub walls had been plastered or whitewashed, and the absence of any large amounts of tegulae or Horsham stone tile suggest that the roofs were wooden shingles or thatched.

**Phase 4a, Trench A, House A1, c. early–mid 4th century (Fig. 2.3)**

Phase 4a was discernible only in Trench A, where two rooms of a house with narrow foundations of gravel were seen cutting the fill of the clay-pit A73/80. The latest dated wares in the pit indicate that it was filled at some time after the mid–late 2nd century and there was nothing in the fill of the foundations to indicate a later date. Only a small part of the house extended into Trench A and although the area to the east of the east wall was very heavily disturbed, it would be surprising if no trace of the gravel footings had survived and it is assumed that the east wall shown on the plan marks the boundary. This implies that most of the house must lie to the west, north and south of the excavation. No relationship could be established with the timber structures in Trench C; they could be earlier or perhaps contemporary storebuildings, but the absence of later Roman building development east of the house may be an indication, to some extent borne out by the soil layers above the timber structures, that the whole area to the east of House A1 was garden from the 3rd century onwards.

The narrow wall foundations must have been designed to carry timber framing, and some of the gravel had been used before as A72/79 contained pottery, tegulae and flue tiles; debris from an earlier building, either on or near the site. The construction details may be compared with those in Period 5 in House 2 in Chapel Street (Down 1981, fig. 8.7, 128–134). There, the coin evidence showed that the building was not erected until some time after AD 341–6, with a final reconstruction on a much larger scale taking place towards the end of the 4th century. The similarity of construction techniques between the two sites prompts the speculation that the same firm of builders were involved and although there is an absence of dating evidence for House 1a it may well be that it was built at some time in the first or second quarter of the 4th century. The narrow foundations (0.5 m at the most) indicates that it was a single-story building.

**Phase 4b, c. AD 360 onwards (Fig. 2.7 and Plate 4)**

At some time after the middle of the 4th century a larger and more substantial house (House A2) replaced House A1. This also had some foundations of compacted gravel, re-used from elsewhere, and built to a width of 0.85 m. Two coins were found in the north wall (A78), one of 4th century date and the other of the House of Constantine (AD 341–6). The degree of wear on the coins could not be assessed as both were heavily corroded, but if a period of 5 years is estimated for the coins to be struck, circulated and then lost, the very earliest date for the construction of House A2 would have been c. AD 351.

*The extent of House A2 (Figs 2.7 and 2.1)*

Elements of perhaps 9 rooms can be seen on the plan, with 2 hypocausts at the north end, the most easterly being at a lower level. The north wall may have been the outside wall of the house. It was one metre wide, with the gravel footings ending at ground level, and the wall above ground level being constructed of flints, part of one course remaining in position. A small extension was cut on the north side of the wall, but no trace of other rooms was seen. This, plus the fact that the hypocaust would be fired from the outside of the building, makes it a strong possibility that it was the northern boundary.

The eastern limits must remain conjectural. There was no sign of large amounts of building debris in Trench C and the fragments of mortar floor along the eastern edge of Trench A must be very near to the outside wall, which would have been destroyed by the post-medieval well. If the mosaic and fragments of wall foundations found in the 1987 excavations (Fig. 2.1) are part of the same house, then the building found by Cunliffe and Murray in 1958/9 must also be the same one. This would give a building measuring 43.5 m north to south (from the north wall in A to the most southerly wall found in 1987) and c. 34 m east to west (if measured from the wall alongside the Roman street; Cunliffe and Murray 1962, Phase VI;) to the north–south robber trench east of the mosaic in the 1987 excavations. The trial trenches of 1958 dug by Mr Collins (Fig. 2.1) produced no signs of any masonry walls and fragments of masonry walls recorded in the 1987 excavation may be the southern boundary of the house.

It is clear that House A2 and its predecessor did not extend across the area covered by Trenches B and C and the impression gained is that at some time after the 2nd century most, if not all of the land at the rear of the house was cultivated. In Trench B, contexts B28/30 and 39, and Trench C, C31/41 and 93 were tentatively identified as garden soils, being mid/grey to brown loams which extended across and partly eroded the earlier features.

Apart from the two hypocausts, very little remained of the fabric of the building, due to extensive disturbance by later pit and drain digging and some robbing of foundations. There appears to have been at least one phase of internal alterations, with an east–west masonry wall, later robbed, being inserted (Fig. 2.7). This may have been contemporary with the north–south flint wall on the east side of the excavation.

**Description by rooms (Fig. 2.7)**

*Room 1*, north–south dimension 5.25 m; east–west dimension unknown. Only the base of the hypocaust survived, together with the remains of eight stacks of pilae tiles. A late Saxon pit had been dug through the north-east corner of the wall and the outline of what may have been a beam slot was cut into the top of the north–south wall which suggests that part of the internal wall may have been timber framed.

*Room 2*, east of Room 1; dimensions 2.6 m east–west by 5.5 m north–south. Only the base of the hypocaust floor survived in patches, and for some reason, the floor was 0.24 m lower that that in Room 1.

*Rooms 2 and 3*. The area to the east of Room 2 seems to have been a corridor c. 2.2 m wide originally, bounded on the east side by a dwarf wall constructed of flints. Later, it was subdivided, possibly by a timber partition resting upon a mortar cill which did not appear to extend right across the corridor, leaving a small opening c. 0.5 m wide, possibly as a doorway. Both rooms would have been c. 2.2 m east–west, with Room 3 having a length (north–south) of c. 4.2 m.

*Room 5* (3 m north–south and in excess of 5.5 m east–west). Only part of the base of the white mortar floor survived.

*Room 6*. South of Room 5 and separated from it by a wall foundation of gravel, which may have supported a timber-framed partition wall. The east–west robber trench may mark the position of the south wall of the room and in view of the fact that the robbing took place in the later medieval period, it is likely to have been a flint foundation since a gravel footing would hardly have been worth the trouble to excavate.

*Rooms 7 and 8.* The line of flints two courses thick shown on the plan at the south end of Room 7 is interpreted as the remains of a dwarf wall aligned east–west with a north–south wall joining it just within the limits of the excavation. It served as the southern wall of Room 7 and there is a step set in it at the junction of the two walls, indicating a doorway into the next room (Room 8) of which almost nothing was within the trench.

No limits can be set to Room 7 on the north and east sides, but the north–south wall bordering rooms 3 and 4 on the east side, probably served as the west wall of the room. Little survived of the white mortar floor due to pit and well digging.

*Room 9.* Only a narrow strip along the south side of the robbed wall was within the trench. A complete grey ware vessel (Fig. 2.7) had been inserted beside the wall but it was not clear, due to the robbing, whether it was intended as a foundation deposit for House A2 or for its predecessor.

### The end of House A2

House A2 probably went out of use as a substantial urban residence at some time in the last quarter of the 4th century AD. The latest coins to reach the site and end up in the destruction layers were those of Gratian (AD 367–83), and coins of Valentinian and Valens (AD 364–78) were recovered from the post-Roman levels above. With the exception of a bronze of Arcadius from the Cattlemarket (Down 1989) and the unstratified gold solidus of Valentinian III (Down 1989, 11, 139/77) this is as late as the issues reaching Chichester go. The case for the continuation of some level of town life into the first half of the 5th century has been discussed elsewhere (Down 1981, 95; Down 1988; 100–104) and need not be repeated here, but the absence of Oxford wares and locally made later red wares in the excavations of 1958–9, 1984 and 1987 may well indicate that occupation on this particular site did not continue past the end of the 4th century. It is true that New Forest 'purple' wares were present in small numbers, but these can have a long life which extends from the end of the 3rd century to the late 4th, and their presence, unsupported by the later colour-coated wares, is not conclusive evidence for a 5th century date.

### Period 2, medieval, c. early 11th–16th century

Trench B; Phase 1; c. 11th/12th century (Fig. 2.9)
The earliest medieval occupation that could be identified was a number of late Saxon cess-pits. Seven pits (3, 4, 12, 26, 56, 73 and 78) could be identified as 11th/12th century in date. They all contained large amounts of the typical heavily gritted late Saxon wares designated as Group 3 in the Chichester series (Down 1978, fig. 11.3). One pit, (B12), was timber-lined. The position of the pits, clustered along the eastern frontage of Priory Road, suggests that they may have been originally at the rear of late Saxon holdings fronting on to the north–south Saxon street which was partly destroyed by the outer bailey of the Norman castle.

Only one other pit (Trench A, Pit A9) could be identified as late Saxon. This had been dug through the Roman hypocaust and probably related to a tenement fronting on to North Street.

*Phase 2, c. 13th–16th century*

Trench A
Pits 14, 20, 47, 49, 50, 58 and 64 formed a group of medieval pits, mainly 14th/15th century in date. Pit A50 contained a large number of cattle horn cores, probably a deposit from the Extons' butchery business at some time in the 16th century (Armitage, this volume pp. 211–18) and see also documentary notes, p. 13.) The pottery from A47 is of particular interest, with a group which contained painted wares, clay peg tiles, imported stonewares and roofing slates. The earliest date of deposition might be late 15th century, with the narrowest bracket for the imported stonewares being c. 1450–1490 (p. 220). The roofing material in the pit probably derived from No 62 North Street.

Trench B
Two pits (6 and 59) were dug. B6 contained Saxo-Norman and later medieval coarse wares and is no earlier in date than 13th century. It had a concentration of flint and tile at the centre, either as a consolidation layer or, having regard to the two other groups of flints in line to the north, possibly a post pad. Pit 59 had painted ware sherds in it and is no earlier than 15th century.

At the south end of the trench was a group of pits which have medieval pottery as the latest dated material, although they could be later in date. To the north and east of the pits was a number of postholes, two of which cut a medieval pit, and one posthole is cut by B5. They seemed to belong within Period 2 but not enough of the postholes had survived to enable a convincing reconstruction to be attempted.

## Period 3, post-medieval, c. 17th–19th century

Trench A (Fig. 2.10 and Plate 5)

At the north end were the remains of four barrel bases, two with duckboards between. The bases had a deposit of caked lime in the bottom and two of them were set in a shallow pit which was lined with Reading Beds clay, presumably to catch any spillage. The bases were set against the north side of an east–west boundary wall, which extended into Trench C (Fig. 2.14). The barrels may well have belonged to the 'limehouse' referred to in 1786 (p. 13).

Plate 5    Greyfriars, Trench A, barrel bases and duckboards belonging to 18th century limehouse

On the south side of the wall was a gravelled path aligned east–west. This was cut by four postholes which appeared to form part of a series which may have been intended for some later trellis work, after the path had gone out of use.

At the south end, a flint-lined garderobe pit was cut through by a later drain (Ditch A1) which provided the sanitary arrangements for No 62 North Street. This was filled in with large amounts of pottery which had a date range of c. 17th–19th century.

Trench B

Fragments of a masonry wall of probable 17th century date were recorded in the southern part of the trench, together with several cess-pits and an east–west drain discharging into a sump. Other features were mainly 18th and 19th century in date and, with the exception of B17, which was a cellar, appeared to be settlement pits constructed of flint or brick.

Trench C (post-medieval features below C14) Period 3A (Fig. 2.12)

C14 was a layer of mid-brown clay which covered the eastern part of the trench up to the well pit. It contained Graffham 17th century wares and sealed pits 8, 14, 35 and 51 and the group of postholes designated Structure C3 which may have been a barn or shed aligned roughly north–south.

Pit C5/13 was the top fill of a well which could not be completely excavated. The top stonework had been robbed out and the pit backfilled at some time during the 17th century. The fill of the construction pit for the well was gravel and it contained fragments of post-medieval tile which makes it likely that the well was constructed in the late 16th or early 17th century and had a relatively short life.

**Period 3B, c. late 17th century; (post-medieval features above C14) (Fig. 2.13)**

By the late 17th century the well appears to have gone out of use and Structure C4 had replaced Structure C3. All the pits shown in Fig. 2.13 as cutting C14 had post-medieval wares and at least three of them (4, 7 and 11) postdate Structure C3. C68 appeared to be a robber trench cut at the west end by a small pit (C12), which may have been a post socket. These two features may relate to another more substantial building adjacent to the excavations.

**Period C 3, c. 19th century**

By the late 19th century the excavation site had assumed the aspect that was recorded on the 1875, 1/500 Ordnance Survey Map (Fig. 2.2). In Trench C the earlier post-medieval building had been replaced by a large brick greenhouse with a cistern. This was demolished at some time later, possibly at the same time as the properties to the north of the Park Tavern were knocked down to create a rear access for No 61 North Street.

**BIBLIOGRAPHY**

Cunliffe, B.W., and Murray, K.M.E., 1962. 'Excavations at a site in North Street Chichester. 1958-9' *SAC* 100, 93–110.
Dannell, G.D., 1978. 'The Samian pottery' *Chichester Excavations 3*, 225–7.
Dannell, G.D., 1981. 'The Samian ware', *Chichester Excavations 5*, 263–4 (Phillimore).
Down, A., 1978. *Chichester Excavations 3*.
Down, A., 1981. 'Excavations in the N.W. Quadrant', *Chichester Excavations 5* (Phillimore).
Down, A., 1988. *Roman Chichester*, 100–104.
Down, A., 1989. *Chichester Excavations 6* (Phillimore).

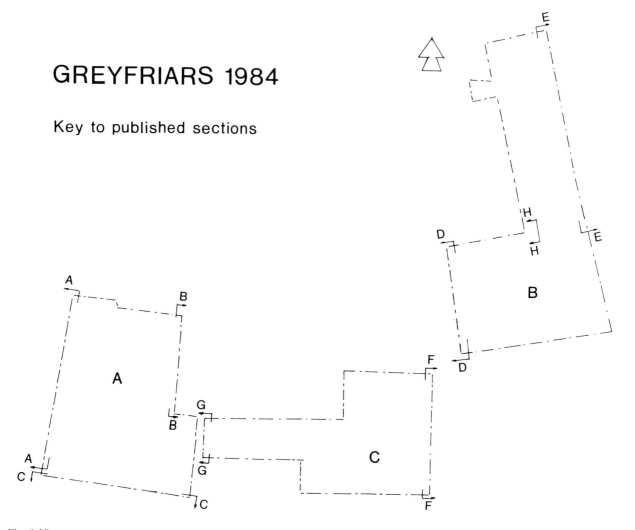

Fig. 2.15

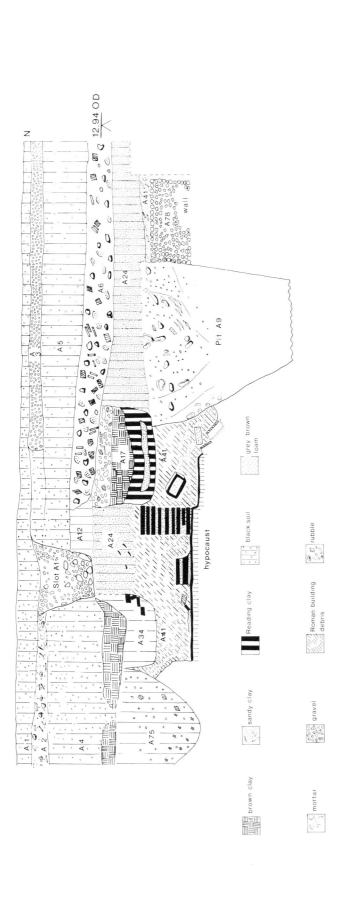

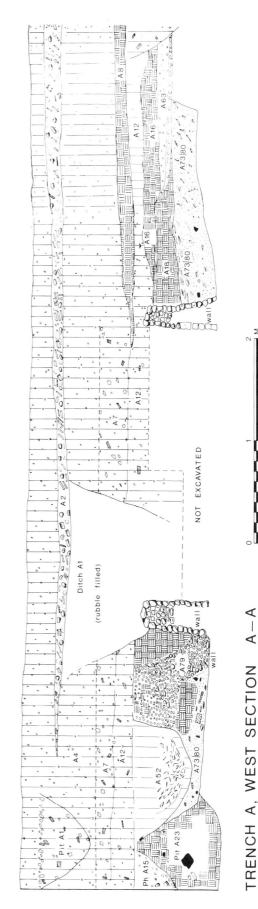

TRENCH A, WEST SECTION A–A

Fig. 2.16

34

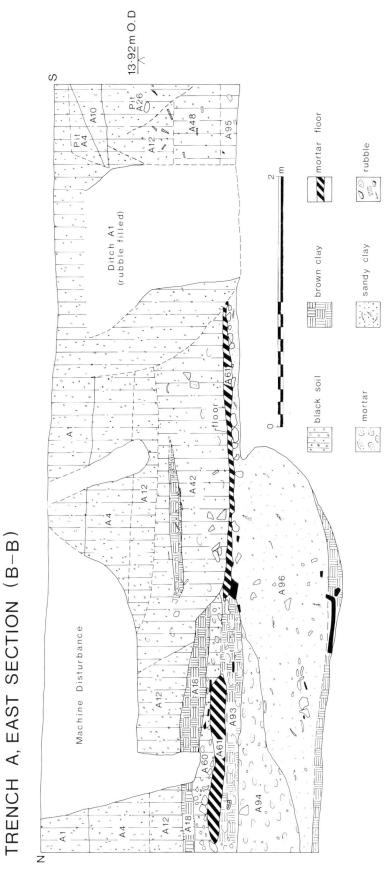

TRENCH A, EAST SECTION (B–B)

13·92m O.D

mortar floor

rubble

brown clay

sandy clay

black soil

mortar

Ditch A1
(rubble filled)

Machine Disturbance

Fig. 2.17

TRENCH A, SOUTH SECTION (C–C)

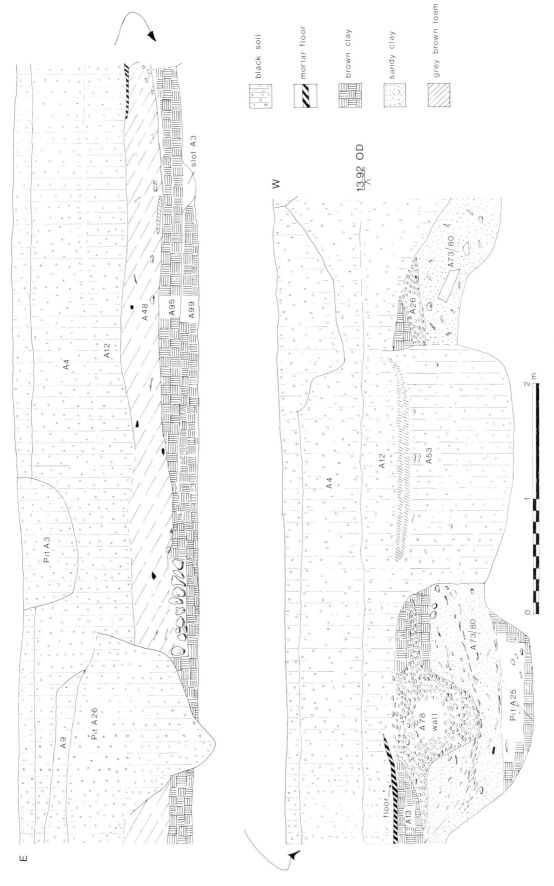

black soil

mortar floor

brown clay

sandy clay

grey brown loam

13.92 OD

Fig. 2.19

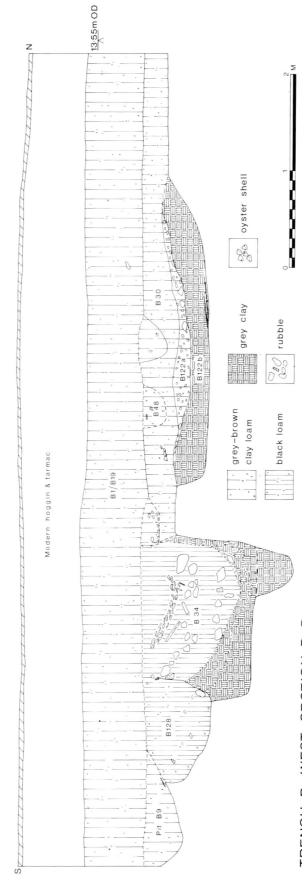

N

13·55 m OD

Modern hoggin & tarmac

B1/B19

B 48

B 30

B122 a
B122 b

B 34

B128

Pit B 9

S

grey-brown
clay loam

black loam

grey clay

rubble

oyster shell

0       1       2
                M

TRENCH B, WEST SECTION D-D

Fig. 2.18

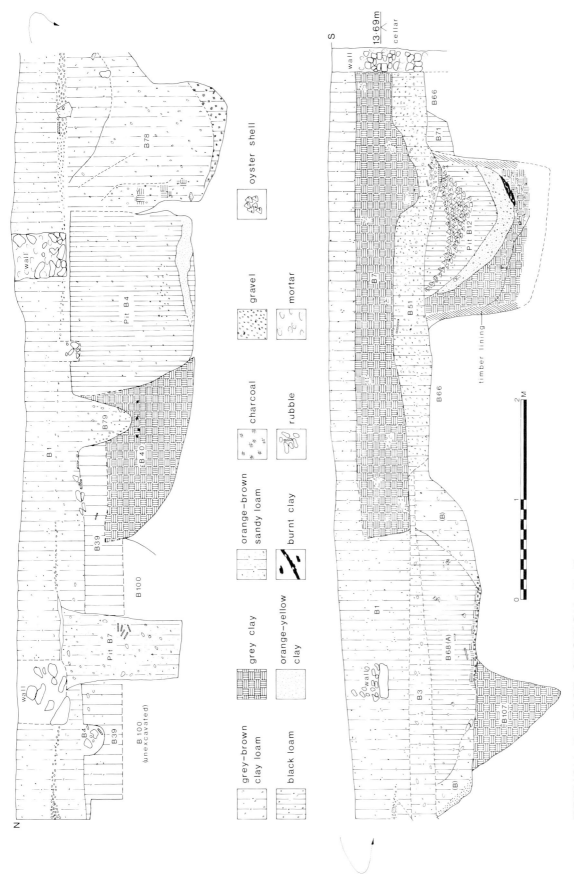

N

S

13.69m

wall

cellar

B66

B71

Pit B12

B7

B51

timber lining

B66

(B)

B1

B68(A)

B3

wall

B107

(B)

wall

Pit B7

B100
(unexcavated)

B4

B39

B100

B39

B1

B79

B40

Pit B4

wall

B78

grey-brown
clay loam

grey clay

orange-brown
sandy loam

gravel

charcoal

oyster shell

black loam

orange-yellow
clay

burnt clay

mortar

rubble

TRENCH B, EAST SECTION E–E

Fig. 2.20

37

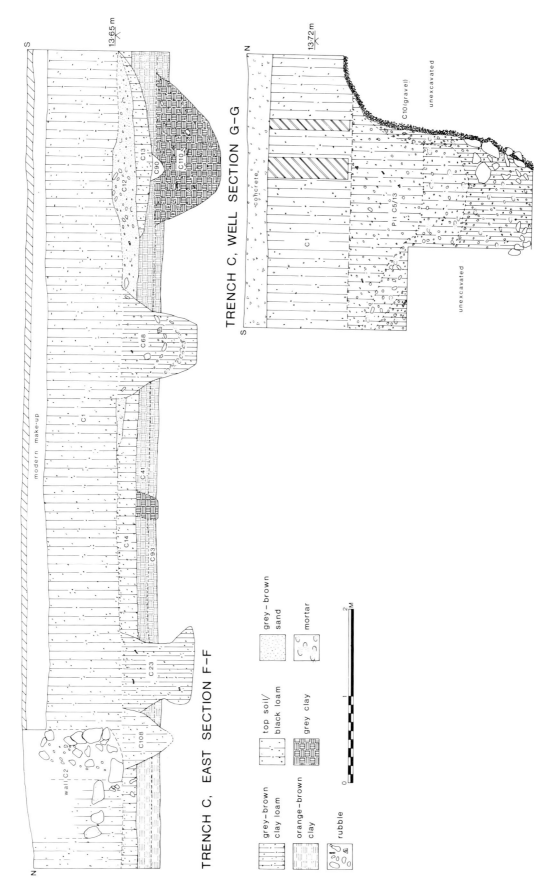

TRENCH C, EAST SECTION F-F

TRENCH C, WELL SECTION G-G

grey-brown
clay loam

orange-brown
clay

rubble

top soil/
black loam

grey clay

grey-brown
sand

mortar

Fig. 2.21

# Pit B6, Section H-H

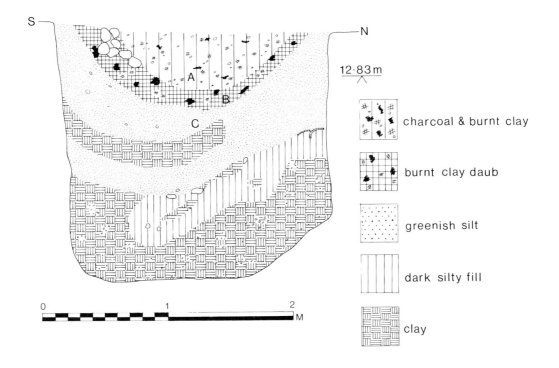

12·83m

| | | |
|---|---|---|
| charcoal & burnt clay | | |

burnt clay daub

greenish silt

dark silty fill

clay

Fig. 2.22

**3**

# St. Peter's, North Street, 1987

## 3A   Excavations in St Peter's, North Street, 1987

by J.R. Magilton

### SUMMARY

*Two small areas were investigated south of the street called St Peter's on the east side of North Street. Both had been damaged by medieval and later pits, and the southern area had suffered additional disturbance from excavations in 1958. Roman features in the northern area included a corridor mosaic of late 3rd or 4th century date, aligned north–south, to the west of a robbed wall. The southern area contained a possible hypocaust sub-floor and related features. The building or buildings may be part of those at Greyfriars (this volume, pp. 11–39) and/or of those investigated in 1959 (Murray and Cunliffe 1962).*

### INTRODUCTION

Excavations south of the street called St Peter's, on the east side of North Street, were carried out in spring 1987 in response to development proposals submitted in the previous year. Most of the fieldwork was paid for by Mr P.H. Blake of Oakhurst Developments Ltd following an informal agreement with Chichester District Council. The site was supervised by Mr R.G. Browse for Chichester District Archaeological Unit, and the Unit's conservator, Mrs C. Edwards, lifted and consolidated the mosaic. Post-excavation and publication costs have been borne by Chichester District Council following an unsuccessful request to English Heritage for grant-aid.

### THE BACKGROUND

The site lies due east of the former medieval church of St Peter the Less, demolished in 1957. In 1958 and 1959 excavations took place to the north of the church, in an area now partly beneath the modern street called St Peter's, to the south-east, and on part of the church site (Murray and Cunliffe 1962, Fig. 1). The trench north of the church revealed, amongst other features, part of the street surface of the Roman precursor of North Street and the remains of a Roman building fronting onto it. The 1958 trial trenches south-east of the church were considered 'too disturbed by post Roman pits to warrant further excavation' (*op. cit.* p.93).

### THE 1987 EXCAVATIONS

The 1986 development proposals involved the construction of two houses linked by car-ports, one house lying adjacent to St Peter's and the other overlying some of the 1958 trial trenches south-east of the church site. As the construction of the car-ports was likely to cause minimal damage to any surviving archaeological deposits, excavation was confined to the house sites. Recording was on standard record cards; plans were drawn at 1:20 and sections at 1:10 on plastic film. The mosaic was drawn *in situ* by Mr D.S. Neal FSA. Finds and original records are lodged at Chichester District Museum, and the mosaic is displayed at Fishbourne Roman Palace.

#### The northern trench

The trench was roughly square, measuring a maximum of 6 × 6.8 m. Because of the constraints of time and resources, it was excavated by machine to a depth of about a metre, just above the latest surviving Roman deposits. Recent damage to the archaeology consisted of a machine-cut trial trench measuring about 1.7 × 0.5 m near the centre of the excavation, dug by the developer to determine the depth of 'made ground'.

*Roman features*

Surviving Roman features were confined to the western half of the excavation, the eastern part having been cut away by a succession of medieval and later pits. The features belong to two phases: those beneath a mosaic floor and its bedding, and those associated with the floor.

*Early Roman features*

Because of the unexpected discovery of the mosaic floor and the decision to lift it for conservation and display there was little time for a detailed investigation of the earliest surviving Roman features, although it is fairly certain that all were located and most were sampled. None was obviously the remains of a structure.

Towards the centre of the trench were two intersecting pits (Fig. 3A.1, 43 and 40), both cut on the east by the robber trench of a later Roman wall. The earlier, 43, was perhaps originally roughly circular, containing oyster shell, tile and pottery and several other items in a filling of grey-brown silty loam. It was cut on the south by a more irregular pit (40) with a similar filling. To the north-west was a further pit (45) which again had a similar filling. This was dug into an earlier pit (48), containing much pottery, which was not satisfactorily defined in plan although it appears in section (Fig. 3A.3, section A). Probable post-pits consisted of, from north to south, 38, 103 and 115, all roughly in a line and two further pits (105, 49) to the west. All these features were dug into a layer of grey-brown earth (42) which yielded an *as* of Antoninus Pius. The only feature which may pre-date this layer was a small pit (107) in the north-west corner of the trench surviving in the base of a large post-medieval pit (101).

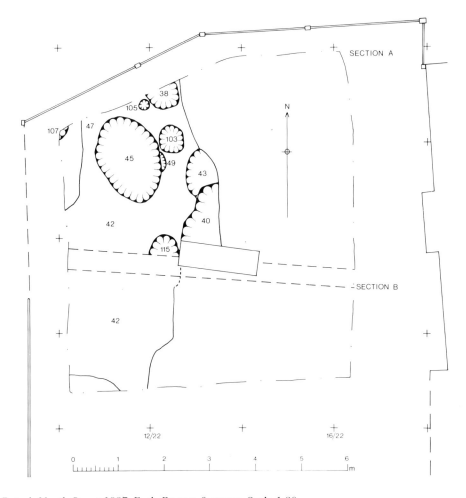

Fig. 3A.1   St Peter's North Street 1987. Early Roman features. Scale 1:80

Plate 6   St Peter's 1987, the mosaic from the south

*Later Roman features*

These consisted principally of a polychrome geometric mosaic (4) bounded on the east by a robbed wall (113) which ran the length of the trench from north to south, and perhaps by a parallel wall on the west, the mosaic probably forming a corridor about 3.25 m wide (Plate 6).

The robbed wall (113) was about 0.6 m wide and filled predominantly with creamy-yellow mortar (114) containing many flint nodules. Its base was about 0.7 m below the top of the mosaic. It may have acted as a retaining wall, since in section (Fig. 3A.3, section B) it appears that the ground-level to the east of the wall may have been lower than the floor-level within the building. Alternatively, there may have been a wall alongside and east of 113, both walls having been robbed simultaneously. The upper filling of the robber trench 18 extended for at least 1.05 m beyond the eastern edge of the wall trench, where it was cut by a number of later pits.

Evidence for the western wall was slight, consisting of two mortared stones in the base of a much later pit (101) in the north-west corner of the excavation. Such a wall, if it did exist, would have been mostly just beyond the western edge of the excavation. The scheme of the mosaic provides some circumstantial evidence that there may have been such a wall. The surviving fragments of mosaic are described below (p. 48) and the details need not be reiterated here. The overall scheme is not uncommon, its execution in coarse tesserae throughout suggests a corridor and its date is probably late 3rd or 4th century. The orientation of a stylised cantharus may indicate that it was intended to be viewed from the north, but is inconclusive.

If it is assumed that the mosaic and the robbed wall (113) were contemporary, the eastern edge of the pavement, where it met the wall-face, would have been composed of rectangular boxes each half the width of those containing the cantharus and other motifs. If the scheme is extended westwards, the corridor may have consisted of another row of complete boxes followed by a row of half-boxes. This takes it precisely to the largely hypothetical wall glimpsed in the base of pit 101, and indicates a corridor about 3.25 m wide. The southern edge of the mosaic was indicated by a small fragment of a border (A on Fig. 3B.1), beyond which was probably an area of coarse red tesserae; two small clumps of tesserae were found here, but they had become detached from their bedding material and cannot, strictly speaking, be regarded as *in situ*. There may have been an east-west wall just beyond the southern edge of the excavation, although the only evidence for it is the southern limit of the pavement. The northern limit of the mosaic cannot be determined, but it must have been at least 5 m long on the basis of surviving fragments.

**The southern trench**

This area had been very badly damaged, not least by the 1958 excavation trenches which had cut away the archaeology in its eastern half to a depth below that of the lowest Roman layer, and by post-Roman pits in the south-west corner. Although the northern and southern trenches were over 7 m apart, there are grounds for believing that surviving Roman features in the southern trench could form part of the same late Roman building as that encountered to the north.

*Roman features (Fig. 3A.2)*

A layer of gravel and mortar (61) initially interpreted as a hypocaust sub-floor occupied the north-west quadrant of the trench. To the north, partly beneath the side of the trench, were two wall-fragments (59, 62) and in the north-east corner was a tile-lined ?flue (60). To the south was a possible robbed wall (58). It is uncertain whether all these features were contemporary, and, if they were, how they should be interpreted.

Layer 61 lay at a depth of about 0.7 m below that of the mosaic in the northern trench and its relative depth supports its interpretation as the sub-floor of a hypocaust, although there was an almost complete lack of charcoal or evidence for burning. Alternatively, it may have been the floor of an ancillary room which was unheated and deliberately constructed below the contemporary ground surface, perhaps to store products best kept in a cool place.

In the north-east corner of the trench was a (?) flue (60) made of tile and mortar. It had been badly damaged, the intact portions consisting of a line of tiles aligned south-west/north-east and a line of mortar, perhaps the bedding for displaced tiles, at right-angles to it. The feature was originally interpreted as part of a channelled hypocaust in the corner of a room but an absence of charcoal or other evidence of burning is against the theory and would seem to rule out the alternative explanation that it was part of an oven. On the western side of the excavation, partly beneath the section, was a square tile initially interpreted as a *pila* base. It appeared to have been *in situ* before the mortar floor was laid down, and was capped by a layer of mortar, suggesting that there had been at least one further tile stacked on top of it. Other *pilae* should have been visible as palimpsests in layer 61 if a hypocaust had been constructed, but no trace survived.

Of the two wall fragments at the northern end of the excavation, 62 appeared to be the southern face of an east–west wall constructed after layer 61 had been laid down. Context 59 was originally thought to be part of the same structure, but examination of the section (Fig. 3A.3, section C) indicates that it may not have been constructed until later, and that the fragment may be a cross-section of a north–south wall, the remainder of which had been destroyed. It is on the same line as the robbed wall (113) in the northern trench, although 113, from the debris in its robber trench, was of flint construction whereas 59 was built of Greensand. The construction trenches for both walls were of a similar depth of c. 13.00 m OD.

Feature 58, interpreted as a wall foundation, extended for about 1.8 m eastwards from the southern side of the trench. It was composed of a mass of small flints and mortar, damaged on the south side by a number of post-Roman pits and partly collapsed on the north side where it had tumbled into the hole cut into the natural brickearth which was lined by floor layer 61.

The only feature possibly pre-dating 61 was a small pit (63) in the north-west corner of the excavation. According to notes, this was cut through layer 61 but the drawn section (Fig. 3A.3 section C) shows no such relationship, and it is more likely that the pit was sealed by the floor, being detected in plan as a slight dip and discoloration in the surface.

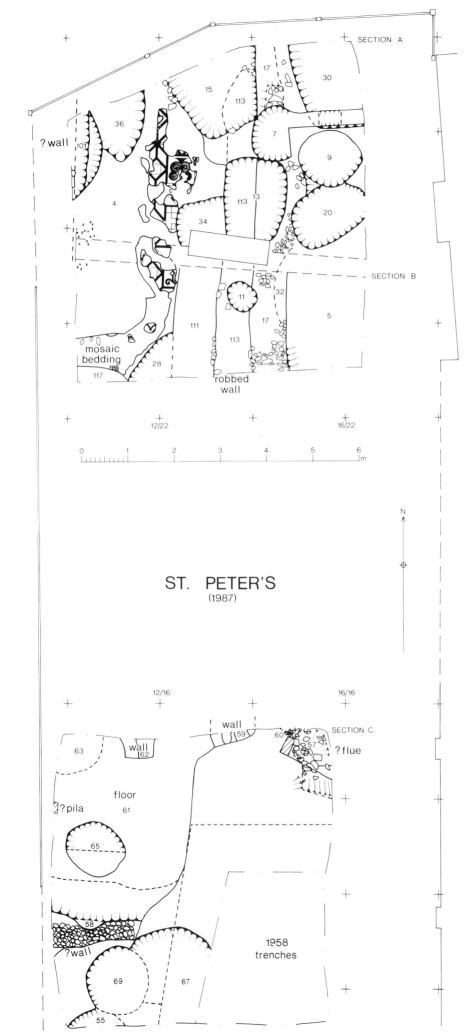

SECTION A

?wall
101
36
4
15
113
17
30
7
9
113 13
20
34

SECTION B

11
32
111
17
5
113
mosaic
bedding
117 28
robbed
wall

12/22                                16/22

0   1   2   3   4   5   6
                              m

Fig. 3A.2  St Peter's
North Street 1987.
Roman and later features.
Scale 1:80

N

ST.  PETER'S
(1987)

12/16                    16/16

wall
wall         59
63      62                60    SECTION C
                              57   ?flue
floor
?pila    61
65
58
?wall
1958
trenches
69      67
55

45

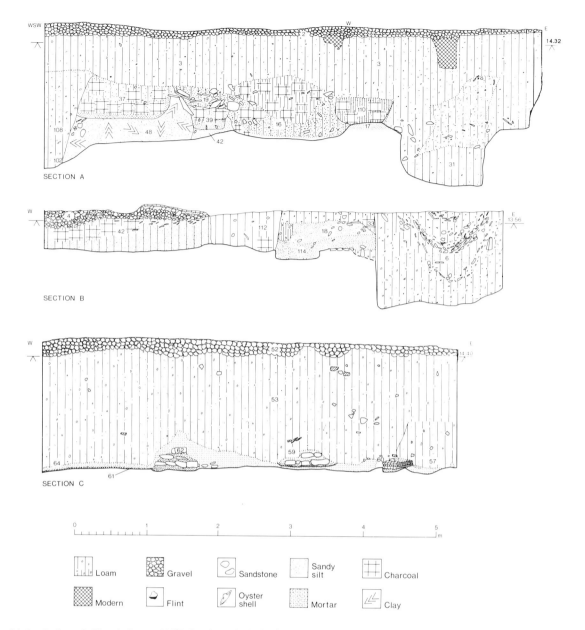

SECTION A

SECTION B

SECTION C

| | | | | |
|---|---|---|---|---|
| Loam | Gravel | Sandstone | Sandy silt | Charcoal |
| Modern | Flint | Oyster shell | Mortar | Clay |

Fig. 3A.3   St Peter's North Street 1987. Sections A–C. Scale 1:50

## Discussion

The very fragmentary nature of the remains renders any attempt at overall interpretation tentative. The two broad phases represented are (i) features earlier than the mosaic floor and (ii) those contemporary with it. Features thought contemporary with the floor include the certain and probable north–south walls in the northern trench, and the fragment of a north–south wall 59 in the southern trench. All the other features described above—the pits and post holes in the northern trench, and the floor, remaining walls and other features in the southern trench—should pre-date this phase, although they need not be, and are not likely to be, contemporary. If this is correct, we have the remains of two buildings, the earlier consisting of walls 58 and 62, the ?flue 60 and the floor 61, all surviving in the southern trench, and the building with the mosaic floor, most of which is represented by features in the northern trench.

In general, the St Peter's site conforms to a pattern of late Roman redevelopment seen elsewhere in Chichester (Chapel Street: Down 1978; 30 East Street: Magilton and Wildman 1987) and in other Roman towns (Esmonde Cleary 1989) whereby well-appointed dwellings, characterised by stone foundations, tessellated floors, mosaics and hypocausts are constructed in the late 3rd and early 4th century, presumably by the villa-owners of the hinterland as town houses. The Chapel Street houses, facing east and ranged around three sides of a courtyard bounded on the fourth side by a street, both had corridors giving access to a range of rooms, and the northern corridor of House 1 was of comparable width to the St Peter's example (Down 1978, fig. 7.20).

If the later phase of occupation at St Peter's represents a fragment of a house of similar plan, as seems likely, there is, unfortunately, little more which may be adduced about it. The building is too distant from Roman North Street to have faced onto it, and there is no known north–south street east of North Street onto which the building could have faced. There are hints that the robbed wall east of the mosaic was an exterior wall; if so, there should have been a range of rooms west of the corridor. It cannot be convincingly demonstrated that the fragments are part of either the North Street buildings (Murray and Cunliffe 1962) or those at Greyfriars (Down this volume p. 11–39).

## The medieval background

The church of St Peter's North Street, usually dated to the 13th century (Fleming 1957) but which may have been older, was one of several small churches in Chichester (the surviving St Olave's, and the mostly demolished St Martin's are two other examples) occupying burgage plots little wider than those allowed for houses. Although burials took place within the church, there is no record of an attached burial ground. By 1898 there was open ground to the north and east of the church (OS 1:2500 plan) but Gardner's map (1769) shows an adjoining building to the north, the church occupying a little over half the length of its burgage plot. According to Fleming (1957, 4) the building adjoining the church on the north side had been medieval and timber-framed. The foundation of its west wall was probably that encountered in 1959 (Murray and Cunliffe 1962, 101).

St Peter's church, usually called St Peter the Less, is also known from 1304 onwards as St Peter by the Guildhall, and is so described down to 1553 (Salzman 1935, 93), by which time the corporation had acquired the chancel of the Greyfriars' church for their deliberations. It is now reasonably certain that the former guildhall adjoined the church on the south side. This is based on the grant of a tenement to provide for the celebration of the soul of Bishop John Arundel (WSRO Cap 1/17 Ancient Charter no 73 of 1.3.1520-1) which is described as abutting 'Gilden Hall or Common Hall' to the north. This became a city property as a result of the Reformation (R.R. Morgan pers. comm.).

This digression on St Peter's is relevant to the 1987 excavations in that both excavated areas appear to lie west of the eastern boundary of the plot occupied by St Peter's and adjoining properties to the north and south (Fig. 2.1). If the line of the north wall of the church is projected eastwards, it runs across the middle of the northern trench, whereas the southern trench lies mostly in the property south of the church (i.e. behind the former guildhall), and perhaps partly in the plot south of that (the Arundel tenement). These considerations are of potential relevance to the interpretation of the medieval archaeology although, in practice, no physical trace of property boundaries was noted.

## The northern trench—medieval features

Given the constraints of time and resources post-Roman features had to be dealt with fairly rapidly, and the decision to excavate the upper levels of both trenches by machine meant that the contents of the upper portions of several features were lost. Most of the post-Roman features consisted of pits, either dug for rubbish disposal or finding a secondary use as such.

Stratigraphically amongst the earliest post-Roman activity in this trench was the robbing of wall 113; had it not been for the presence of three probable medieval sherds from the upper fill, this activity could have been assigned to the late Roman period.

Of the features at the northern end of the trench, 36 and 15 may have been roughly contemporary. The bases of both features contained much charcoal, and the sides and bottom of 37 had been lined with red clay which had been burnt. A specialised function is indicated but its nature is uncertain. Context 36 was partly cut away by a deep post-medieval pit (101) and both lay mostly beyond the northern edge of the trench. Part of the upper filling of 15 on the west side was a spread of stone rubble (19) omitted for the sake of clarity on the plan, but shown on section A, Fig. 3A.3 which could have been derived from its superstructure; if so, it may have been part of a bread or malting oven. The other side of the feature was cut by a small pit (section A, layer 110; also omitted from the plan, Fig. 3A.3). Other features in the western part of the trench included two pits, 117 and 28, in the south-west corner. The latter had been cut by a straight-sided linear feature (111) parallel to and west of the robbed Roman wall 113 which cut through both the robber trench and the mosaic (Fig. 3B.1, section B). Its interpretation is uncertain. An initial suggestion that it represented a robbed medieval wall, the northern end of which had been cut away by later features, does not seem to be borne out by its filling of red-brown clay, silt and sand containing few stones and no mortar. At the northern end of the feature was a small pit (34), but the relationship between the two, if any, was undetermined. Context 34 was cut by a shallow pit (13) on the east.

The eastern part of the trench, beyond the robbed Roman wall, was mostly occupied by a deep late or post-medieval trench (5; filling 6) which ran the length of the excavation from north to south. Beneath it was a deep pit (20) containing layers of mortar and a quantity of flints in its upper filling, material presumably derived from the robbing of the Roman wall (113), and to the west of (5) was part of a small clay-filled pit (32, filling 33).

Few features appeared to post-date feature 5. Of those which did, pit 30 (fill 31) in the north-east corner of the trench was the largest, and this in turn was cut by a post-medieval ?soakaway (7) consisting of a gully leading to a roughly circular pit. South of this was a circular pit (10) containing many oyster shells. All the above features were sealed beneath a layer of very dark grey soil containing tile and stones which covered the whole site to a depth of up to a metre. The only feature cut through this layer, apart from demonstrably modern features, was a post-pit (11) lying in the centre of the southern part of the excavation.

### The southern trench

Only the deepest post-Roman features survived, and these were confined mainly to the western part of the trench. In the south-west corner were three intersecting pits (55 and 67, both cut by 69), all of which could be Roman on the basis of the pottery recovered from them. Pit 68 contained crucible fragments of probable Iron Age date (p. 228, Fig. 27.1). In the north-east corner a pit (57) apparently cut into the Roman ?flue 60 contained two skull fragments, presumably derived from disturbances during a refurbishment of St Peter the Less. Alternatively, it is just possible that feature 60 should be interpreted as the north/west end of a tile-lined grave of medieval or later date. The only other feature thought to be of medieval date is a roughly circular pit (65), about a metre deep dug into the Roman floor 61. No post-Roman material was recovered from the pit and it is possible, as with the three pits to the south, that it should be attributed to the late Roman period.

### BIBLIOGRAPHY

Down, A., 1978. *Chichester Excavations 3* (Phillimore).
Esmonde Cleary, S., 1989. *The Ending of Roman Britain.*
Fleming, L., 1957. 'The little churches of Chichester' *Chichester Papers* 5.
Magilton, J.R., and Wildman, J., 1987. '30 East Street (Mothercare)' *The Archaeology of Chichester and District 1987*, 16–19.
Murray, K.M.E., and Cunliffe, B.W., 1962. 'Excavations at a site in North Street, Chichester 1958–9' *SAC* 100, 91–110.
Salzman, L.F., 1935. *VCH (Sx)* 3.

## 3B    The St Peter's mosaic

**by David S. Neal (Fig. 3B.1)**

The mosaic, discovered in February 1987 and inspected and drawn *in situ* by the writer, consists of a fragmentary strip of pavement approximately five metres long by one metre wide, constructed in coarse tesserae throughout with nine tesserae in a width of 200 mm. The range of colours is limited to three—a creamy white limestone used in the backgrounds, grey tesserae for the structure of the pattern and red brick tesserae used in the motifs.

### The scheme

Although fragmentary, the basic design of the pavement can easily be identified. It is based on a scheme of large squares (about 600 mm wide internally) at a tangent to smaller tilted squares (250 mm wide internally) with eight lozenge stars filling the interspaces (Neal 1981, 22 D).

### The motifs

Of the large squares a row of three survives. Working from left to right, only about one-quarter of the first square survives but contains what was possibly a heart-shaped bud with a pointed excrescence at the axis and, on either side, two curled shoots. The second large square has a pattern of red T-shapes forming a quincunx arrangement of white squares with single white squares in each corner. The third panel has a stylised scroll motif, worked in grey and red, springing from a grey triangular pedestal and with a pointed excrescence on top. The triangular pedestal would suggest that the form of the motif is based on a cantharus the handles of which have become increasingly stylised as scrolls at the expense of the body of the vessel which is absent.

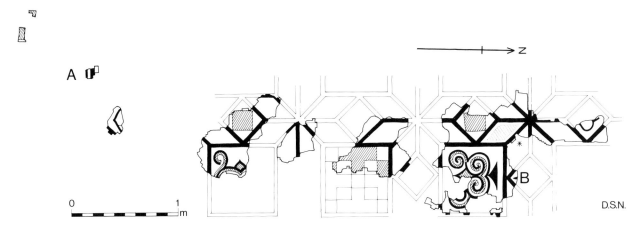

Fig. 3B.1    The St Peter's mosaic (drawn by D.S. Neal)

### The tilted squares

Of the tilted squares parts of seven survive and appear to have contained an alternating arrangement of red squares, set tangentially, and heart-shaped leaves (the individual motifs are in rows when at 45 degrees to the design). On the left a triangular fragment outlined in grey is almost certainly the tip of a leaf or bud similar to another leaf or bud with a stalk to the right. Evidence for them having alternated can be found in a third square (at B) where just the tip of a leaf survives.

### Interpretation

The large tesserae used in the construction of the pavement might possibly suggest that the mosaic decorated a corridor which usually have coarse workmanship. This interpretation is perhaps further supported by the position of the heart-shaped leaves which all seem to point to the left, suggesting that the mosaic was intended to be viewed from the right or from the north end (reservations regarding this interpretation, however, are expressed in the discussion). With the lack of surviving walls it is not possible to confirm this, nor to suggest the overall size of the pavement since the repeating design can be increased in multiples of about one metre. Nevertheless, at point 'A' are four grey and white bands possibly forming part of a border on the south side. Close by, two small fragments of mosaic in coarse red tesserae were also found but they are not believed to have been *in situ*.

### The workmanship

It is not worthwhile to comment on the quality of the workmanship since corridor pavements are usually coarse. However, the method of infilling the lozenges is somewhat unusual; they have been infilled with a single 'row' of white tesserae placed parallel to the grey lozenges and further infilled with white tesserae set at 'right angles'. This may have been a deliberate attempt to create a rhomboid by changing the plane of the interstice of the tesserae; usually rhomboids are depicted in colour.

### Dating and discussion

Although the basic scheme is very common and can be found on mosaics throughout Britain in all periods, the developed and stylised spiralled form of the 'cantharus' would indicate a late third or fourth century date. It further indicates the influence of local mosaicists whose repertoire favoured spiralled forms which are particularly common in central southern England. Even though the work is not sufficiently distinctive to date from parallels, it can be compared closely to another pavement found in Chichester—a mosaic from the Morant's site discovered in 1960 (Holmes 1965, fig. 6). It has the same scheme, also with squares set tangentially in the smaller tilted squares. This mosaic was also constructed in coarse tesserae but appears to have paved a bath-house which would suggest therefore that the mosaic under discussion need not necessarily have paved a corridor.

### BIBLIOGRAPHY

Holmes, J., 1965. 'Chichester, the Roman Town' *Chichester Paper No 50*, Chichester City Council.
Neal, D.S., 1981. 'Roman Mosaics in Britain', *Britannia Monograph Series 1*.

# 3C   The conservation of the mosaic

by Carol Edwards

Development within the city walls has caused the surviving Roman mosaics to be few and fragmentary. Where possible these have been conserved *in situ*, as in the case of the mosaic fragments under Morant's West Street, now the Army and Navy Stores (Down and Rule 1971, 15 and 129; Down 1988, 36) and in Chichester Cathedral (Down and Rule 1971, 132). Where this was not practicable they have been lifted for display, as in the case of the David Greig mosaic (Johnston 1974, 155).

The St Peter's mosaic, excavated in 1987, survived as five separate fragments which had subsided down the centre along the line of brownish grey tesserae at the bottom of the box section design. The foundation consisted of a base of large flints in soil, on top of which was a 30–70 mm layer of creamy-white mortar with small pebbles and stones. This was followed by a skim 2–4 mm thick of *opus signinum* and an off-white setting bed. Very little of the white grouting survived. The mortar was generally in a poor condition.

The mosaic was recorded photographically and traced onto polythene sheeting. When clean and dry it was faced up for lifting using a water-soluble PVA adhesive and two layers of cotton butter muslin cloth. Lines connecting all five fragments were marked across the cloth at relevant points to allow for accurate repositioning. The fragments were lifted by undercutting below the mortar layer and then supported on a board and removed. Problems were caused by the subsidence and the intermittent survival of the mortar. The largest fragment was cut into three parts to allow easier detachment and the fragments were placed upside-down into prepared boxes so that the mosaic lay flat. It was then transferred to the work room.

Soil and mortar were removed from the backs of the tesserae. When clean, PVA adhesive was applied to the tesserae to assist in bonding them to the next layer, consisting of lime putty, silver sand and brickdust. This formed a separating layer between the tesserae and the main supporting layer of epoxy resin and vermiculite (Bradley *et al.* 1983, 161–70; Munday 1986, 47–55). This was reinforced with galvanised steel weld mesh and incorporated nut and bolt fittings. The largest fragment was rejoined into one piece.

The fragments were reversed and water applied to their facing up cloths to soften the adhesive so that the cloth could be removed. Excess adhesive was cleaned from the surface and the lacunae were infilled with lime mortar.

The fragments were mounted on sloping panels and are displayed at Fishbourne Roman Palace.

## The sizes of the tesserae

After the soil and mortar were removed from the backs of the tesserae their size and shape could be seen. The measurements for the tesserae are taken from the largest fragment. They are roughly cut with uneven sides.

| White | Face | 10 × 16 mm to 20 × 30 mm |
| | Back | 14 × 15 mm to 23 × 27 mm |
| | Depth | 10 to 31 mm with straight or slightly tapering sides |
| | | Some of the tesserae tapered to a point or chisel edge. |
| Red | Face | 13 × 20 mm to 23 × 25 mm |
| | Back | 11 × 13 mm to 25 × 27 mm |
| | Depth | 13 to 20 mm with mainly straight sides |
| Brown/grey | Face | 15 × 16 mm to 22 × 25 mm |
| | Back | 13 × 16 mm to 23 × 25 mm |
| | Depth | 13 to 21 mm sides straight or slightly tapering |

The tesserae which are white in colour are hard chalk, as are the slightly yellow ones, some displaying small borings made by molluscs or worms. The yellowish colour is probably natural and not due to burning.

The dark brownish/grey tesserae are a hard silty shale.

## Acknowledgements

I would like to thank Christopher Smith of Art Pavements and Decorations Ltd for information on lime mortars as reversible separation layers. I especially acknowledge the assistance and advice given by the late W.E. Novis O.B.E., mosaic consultant, during the application of the support backing. Thanks also to Dr D. Williams FSA for identification of the tesserae.

## BIBLIOGRAPHY

Bradley, S.M., *et al.*, 1983. 'A modified technique for the lightweight backing of mosaics' in *Studies in Conservation* 28, 161–70

Down, A., 1988. *Roman Chichester* (Chichester).

Down, A., and Rule, M., 1971. *Chichester Excavations 1* (Phillimore).

Johnston, D.E., 1974. 'The David Greig mosaic' in A. Down *Chichester Excavations 2*, 155–8 (Phillimore).

Munday, V.W., 1986. 'Experience with a conservation technique at the British Museum' in *Mosaicos no 4, Conservacion in "situ"*, Soria, 47–55.

# 4

# The Theological College 1985 and 1987

## 4A   Excavations at the Theological College in 1985 and 1987

by Alec Down

### SUMMARY

*A few sherds of late Iron Age pottery , late Augustan Arretine and other fine wares, and sherds from a Dressel 1–Pasqual 1 amphora, present in later clay pits, are indicative of pre-Conquest trade between the local Atrebates and Rome. The earliest feature on the site was a V-shaped ditch aligned north-south, possibly a defensive ditch connected with the military phase of AD 43–4. This is supported by the presence of early imported fine wares of Claudian date and some fragments of military equipment, all residual. The site was on the western edge of the early Roman town and a well and beam slots belonging to timber structures were found on the eastern side of the excavation. These were probably demolished when the defences were constructed. At some time later, probably in the 4th century, the land became a cemetery. Excavations in 1987 exposed further Roman burials, and pits and gullies dug behind the houses fronting on to the south side of Westgate. The pottery from these features points to occupation from the late Saxon through to the post-medieval period. At the southern end of the site in the post-Roman periods the presence of field drainage ditches indicates that that part of the land formed part of the Dean's Farm.*

### INTRODUCTION

The building of the new College in 1985/6 was preceded by an archaeological excavation carried out by the Chichester Excavation Unit. Trial trenching followed by a detailed examination of the area shown on the plan (Fig. 4A.1) was carried out over seven weeks and a watching brief was maintained on the building works, when a number of additional Roman burials were recorded.

In 1987 the Chichester Archaeological Unit under the direction of John Magilton carried out further work to the north of the original excavation, on the site where new garages were planned.

The excavation projects were funded by Chichester Theological College Ltd and Abbey Housing Association, with assistance towards post-excavation costs being provided by HBMC (E) and Chichester District Council. Previous work by J. Holmes for the Chichester Excavation Committee in 1959 (Holmes 1962, 80–82) showed that the late 2nd-century Roman defensive ditches on the west side of the town had cut through the remains of buildings which had been left outside the new defensive perimeter, and it could be seen that the earlier town extended westwards below the College lawns and playing field. Work started in May 1985.

A series of trial trenches (A–E) were dug by machine. Of these, trenches A and B were expanded to examine features, trenches C, D and E being barren. Trench F was later dug to the east of A, being eventually combined with it, whilst Trench G was dug in 1987 on the site where additional garages were planned.

### Documentary history of the site (compiled from notes prepared by Mr R.R. Morgan)

Before the Civil War there was a row of buildings along the south side of the road outside the West Gate, which extended from the City wall to the church of St Bartholomew, also known as St. Sepulchre's. It was a round church, one of only nine known in England, built on a similar plan to the Church of the Holy Sepulchre in Jerusalem. Both the Church and the houses were demolished by the Royalist defenders during the siege of the town in 1642. The whole frontage at that time was owned by the Dean of Chichester and formed part of the Dean's Manor.

Occupation on the excavation site is recorded from the 13th century onwards. There was a substantial house on the site later occupied by the Theological College, leased by the Dean to John Tolpet, a clothier, up to 1598, after which it was bequeathed to his son. It was re-built after the Civil War and subsequently, in the early 19th century, a new house was erected which was acquired by the Theological College in 1919 when they moved from Cawley Priory.

## THE EXCAVATIONS (Fig. 4A.1)

At the south end of the site three narrow trial trenches (B1–3) were dug to examine the ground for traces of occupation. Trenches B1 and B2 struck a large feature which was probably a gravel pit, and a half section was cut across it by machine (Fig. 4A.11, section C–C).

The shape of the feature suggests that it was dug to extract gravel and although finds were sparse, only Roman pottery was found. An almost complete greyware vessel was found in the bottom and the samian ware found in the primary silt (B4) ranges in date from Augusto-Tiberian Arretine to early Antonine. The section indicates that the feature remained open for some time and it seems certain that it was dug during the Roman period and that it was out of use by the middle of the 2nd century.

## DISCUSSION BY PERIODS

**Period 0,** *pre-Conquest c. mid -late 1st century BC to AD 43*

No features can be assigned to Period 0 but the presence of pottery which can be confidently attributed to pre-Conquest trade with Rome reinforces the evidence from other Chichester sites (Dannell 1978, 225–7; Dannell 1981, 263–4; Williams 1989, 127–131; this volume, p. 56). Most of the pottery came from Trench A/F and was in the bottom of a series of shallow pits which were probably dug for clay and which cut the side of a V-shaped ditch which may have been of military origin (Figs. 4A.3 and 4A.10, sections A–A and B–B). The pottery is divided into two groups.

Group 1:  Identified as late Augustan and traded in before the Conquest.
Group 2:  (in brackets alongside Group 1)—Augusto-Tiberian and *probably* arriving before AD 43.

| Arretine | Pompeian red | Gallo-Belgic | Other | Amphorae |
|----------|--------------|--------------|-------|----------|
| 8 (—) | — (1) | — (11) | 1 (—) | 1 |

This brings the total to date for all the recently excavated sites in Chichester (Chapel Street, County Hall, Cattlemarket and Fishbourne, as follows:

| Arretine | Pompeian red | Gallo-Belgic | Other | Amphorae |
|----------|--------------|--------------|-------|----------|
| 174 * | 2 (2) | 38 (49) | 6 (—) | 6 |

* 104 of this total are sherds from Chapel Street. All others are vessel counts.

This adds up to a significant and growing amount of pre-Conquest material which will be discussed in greater detail in a future publication. What is lacking at the moment is an assemblage of pre-Conquest traded wares uncontaminated by post-Conquest material and in association with pre-Conquest Atrebatic pottery. So far it has always occurred in post-Conquest deposits, usually in areas where there is evidence for military occupation. The pottery fragments are usually small and heavily abraded, as might be expected of material which had been around for a long time (see Fig. 4A.2 for distribution).

**Period 1,** *Phase 1, Roman, AD 43 plus (Trench A/F)*

This period is represented by a V-shaped ditch running north–south across the site. It was probably c. 1.4 m deep when originally dug and might have been either a temporary 'marching camp' defence or a drainage ditch. It was backfilled with re-deposited brickearth and the sides showed no signs of weathering. The fill (A65) contained a number of sherds of Roman grey and black wares which cannot be dated closely; a sherd of samian of Claudian date and a number of sherds of Terra Nigra, all pre-Flavian, the majority being pre-Claudian.

*Trench G*    No Phase 1 features were found. The alignment of the ditch meant that it just missed the eastern side of the trench, if it did not turn before. The 'early' pottery from the trench (all residual) may be summarised as follows:

samian—Claudian and earlier—5; pre-Flavian—9.
TN—pre-Flavian—1

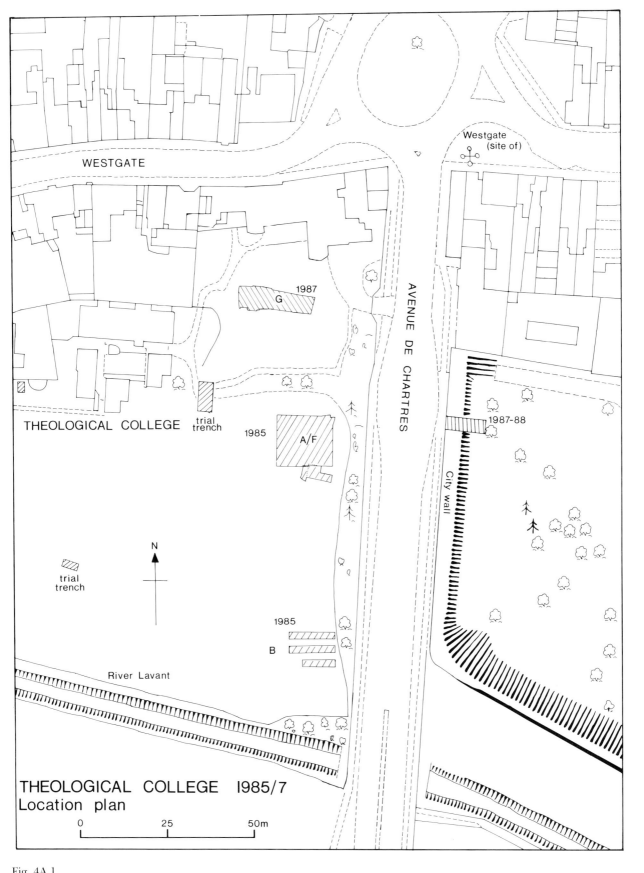

WESTGATE

Westgate
(site of)

AVENUE DE CHARTRES

1987
G

trial
trench

THEOLOGICAL COLLEGE

1985
A/F

City wall

1987-88

trial
trench

N

1985
B

River Lavant

THEOLOGICAL COLLEGE 1985/7
Location plan

0       25       50m

Fig. 4A.1

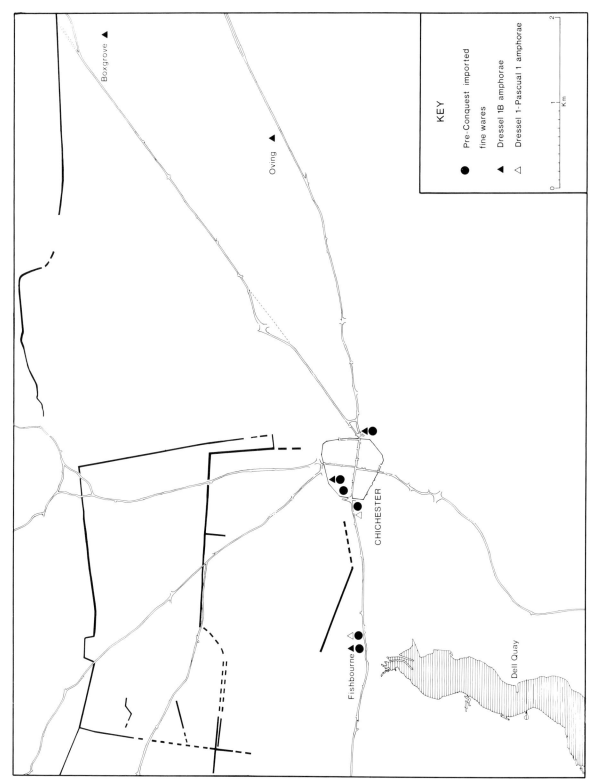

Fig. 4A.2  The distribution of pre-Conquest imports of amphorae, Arretine and Gallo-Belgic fine wares

In the north-east corner of the trench were the shallow beam slots and post-holes belonging to a timber-framed structure. This had been partly destroyed by clay-pits which are early in date and the structure, which appears to be similar in plan to those found in 1st-century levels in Chapel Street (Down 1981, fig. 7.6) might perhaps belong to the legionary phase.

*Phase 3, Trench A/F (Pits A52/61 and A9)*

At some time in the 1st century a series of pits was dug at the north end of Trench A/F. They cut away part of the Phase 1 ditch and the Phase 2 structure and were shallow and irregular in shape. They were probably dug

# THEOLOGICAL COLLEGE 1985
## Trench A/F
Period 1, Roman – Phases 1 – 3, c. AD 43 +

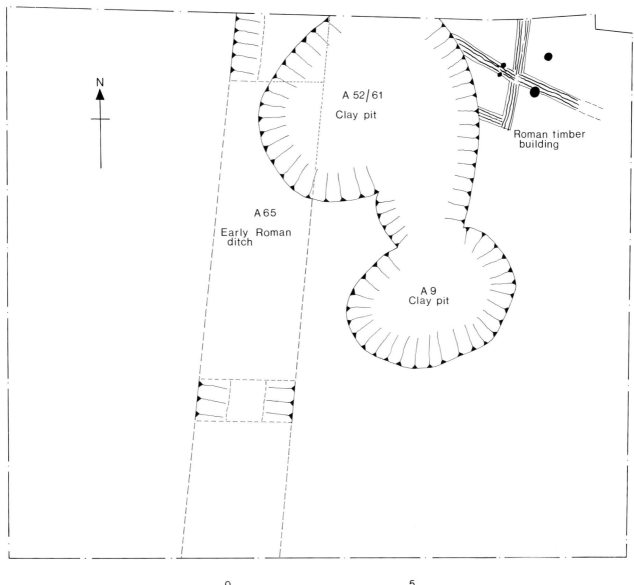

Fig. 4A.3    Scale 1:100

Plate 7   Theological College 1985, Trench A/F, looking east, slots of 1st century AD timber buildings

for clay, either for building wattle and daub houses or, perhaps less likely, for making pottery. It was evident that the pit digging had disturbed earlier Roman rubbish dumps belonging to the military occupation of the area as a considerable amount of early pottery dating from late Augustan to Claudian was present, together with scraps of metalwork which are probably military. One sherd of samian dated to the Flavian period suggests that A52/61 was backfilled after AD 70, while Pit A9 had 5 sherds of medieval ware in the top which must represent later contamination; otherwise the imported fine wares are no later than Tiberio-Claudian. Baked clay daub with white plaster applied to it was present in the fill of A52/61, indicating that the pit diggers had dug through a demolished clay building, possibly the superstructure of the Phase 2 building discussed above.

*Phase 4, Trenches A/F and G; c. late 1st–2nd century, (Fig. 4A.4)*

*Trench A/F*    Along the east side of the trench and cut into A2, which was the top of the Roman horizon below the plough-soil, were the beam slots of possibly two structures. These represent the backs of buildings further to the east which were excluded from the town when the defences were constructed c. late 2nd or early 3rd century. A well (F8) on the west side of the buildings was probably contemporary. Time did not permit the complete excavation of the well, which had a burial (Grave 15) placed across the top.

# THEOLOGICAL COLLEGE 1985

Trench A/F

Period 1, Roman – Phase 4, c. late 1st – 2nd century.

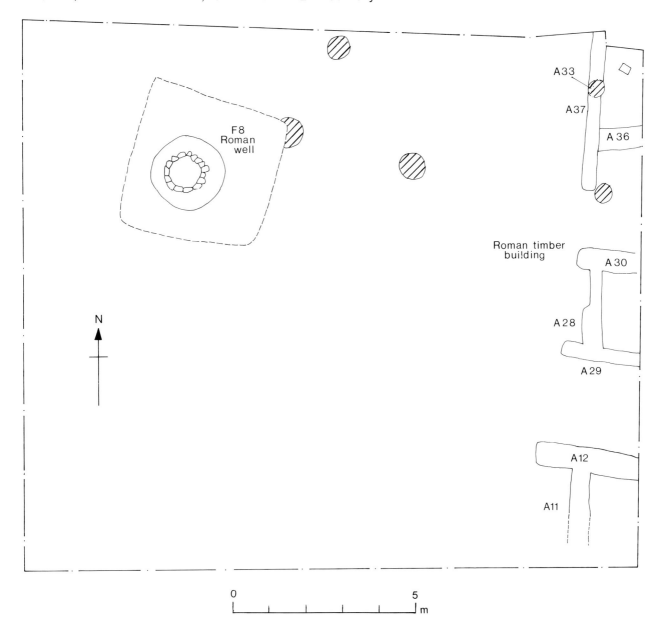

Fig. 4A.4   Scale 1:100

The dating of the beam slots is complicated by the fact that two slots (A12 and A30) had abraded sherds of post-Roman pottery in the top, but it seems reasonable to consider these to be intrusive, and that the structures *are* Roman and are the western end of the house or houses noted by Holmes in his report (*op. cit.* p. 82).

*Trench G (Figs 4A.5 and 4A.12)*   Two pits (119/68 and 109/108) were the earliest features and may well belong to Phase 4 as the latest datable pottery in the earliest pit is Hadrianic. Both pits were cut by a ditch (65/104), aligned north-west–south-east which, on the evidence of the pottery, was backfilled towards the end of the 2nd century or perhaps even later. Alongside the ditch and possibly replacing it as a boundary was a flint wall (12) which was partially robbed and had a grave (72) cut through it. It is possible that both were intended to mark the northern boundary of the cemetery, with the wall replacing the ditch, but equally it could be argued that both features mark the southern boundary of a property fronting on to Westgate. Certainly, the wall must have been demolished and forgotten when Grave 42 was dug through it and this would be consistent with structures which had been left outside the town limits when the defences were constructed and which had become derelict.

The interesting thing about both wall and ditch is the alignment. They are not in conformity with the modern road issuing from Westgate, which is itself of some antiquity. It has long been realised that the original Roman road could not have run on the modern alignment, since to do so would take it through the middle of the Roman Palace at Fishbourne. The logical course for the road-builders would be to take it out of the Westgate in a north-westerly direction, passing to the north of the palace more or less on the line of the railway. If this is so, then the wall and ditch (whether they delimit the cemetery or an earlier property) may well follow the line of the road. Nothing is known of the line between the West Gate and the Palace and much more fieldwork is needed, especially on the line of one of the Chichester Dykes (Bradley's east–west c), which appears to be aiming towards the Westgate and might be the agger of the road, with a ditch on both sides, (Bradley 1971, fig. 6).

*Phase 5, c. late 3rd–4th century, Trenches A/F and G (Figs. 4A.5 and 4A.6)*

At some time after the defences had been constructed the site became a cemetery. The remains of 62 inhumations were recorded and it is certain that many more await discovery. The burials are the subject of a detailed report by John Magilton (pp. 72–94 and Figs. 4A.5 and 4A.6 and Plate 8), but it would seem from the absence of any firm evidence for cremation burials that the cemetery is a late one and probably dates from the late 3rd–early 4th century onwards.

## Period 2, medieval c. late 10th–16th century (Fig. 4A.7)

*Trench G*   Most of the evidence for medieval occupation comes from Trench G where an east–west ditch (59/102) and a number of pits were dug and backfilled in the late medieval period. These features were at the rear of the premises fronting on to Westgate and the ditch must have drained into the Lavant which then flowed northwards a few metres away, up to Squitry Bridge where it turned south-west to drain into the harbour (see Gardner Map, Fig. 4A.14). A selection of pottery published from the site indicates a date range of c. late 10th to 16th century (this volume, Fig. 31.1, nos 1–10).

## Period 3, post-medieval c. 17th–19th century, (Fig. 4A.7)

*Trench G*   A second ditch (24/26) was dug on the same alignment as the medieval ditch, but south of it. It appeared to turn southwards and may have ended in a soakaway. The latest pottery in the backfill was 17th century in date but the feature might well be later. It was cut by 18th and 19th century pits and two brick settlement tanks which represent part of the early domestic sanitary arrangements for the present building.

*Trench A/F (Fig. 4A.8)*   This area was probably part of the Dean's Farm and the two ditches (A10 and F3) are late medieval field boundary or drainage ditches which were still open in the 17th century.

## BIBLIOGRAPHY

Bradley, R., 1971. 'A survey of the Chichester Entrenchments' in B. Cunliffe, 'Excavations at Fishbourne 1961–69' Vol. 1, *RRSAL* XXVI, 17–36.
Dannell, G., 1978. 'The Samian pottery' in A. Down, *Chichester Excavations 3* (Phillimore).
Dannell, G., 1981. 'The Samian ware', in A. Down, *Chichester Excavations 5* (Phillimore).
Down, A., 1981. *Chichester Excavations 5* (Phillimore).
Holmes, J., 1962. 'The defences of Roman Chichester' *SAC* 100, 80–92
Williams, D.F., 1989. 'The amphorae from the sites' in A. Down, *Chichester Excavations 6* (Phillimore).

THEOLOGICAL COLLEGE 1987

Trench G

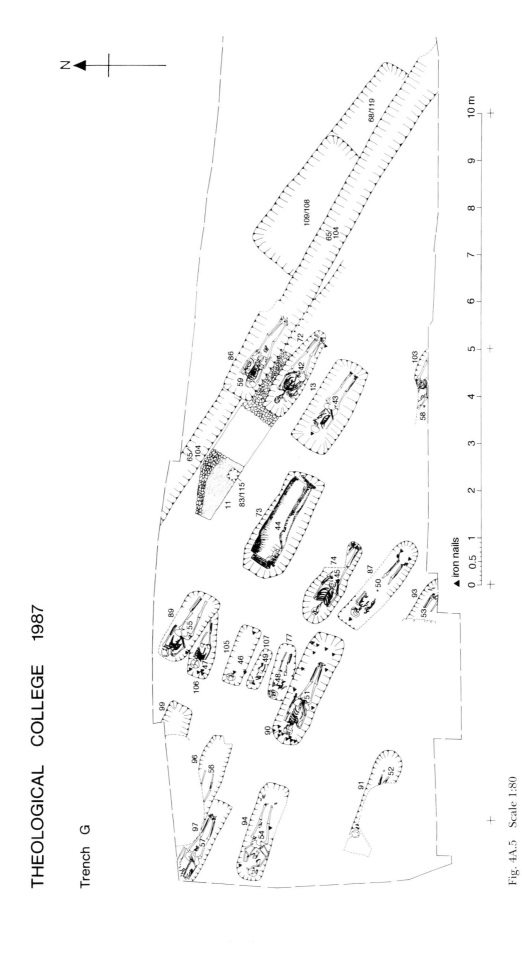

Fig. 4A.5   Scale 1:80

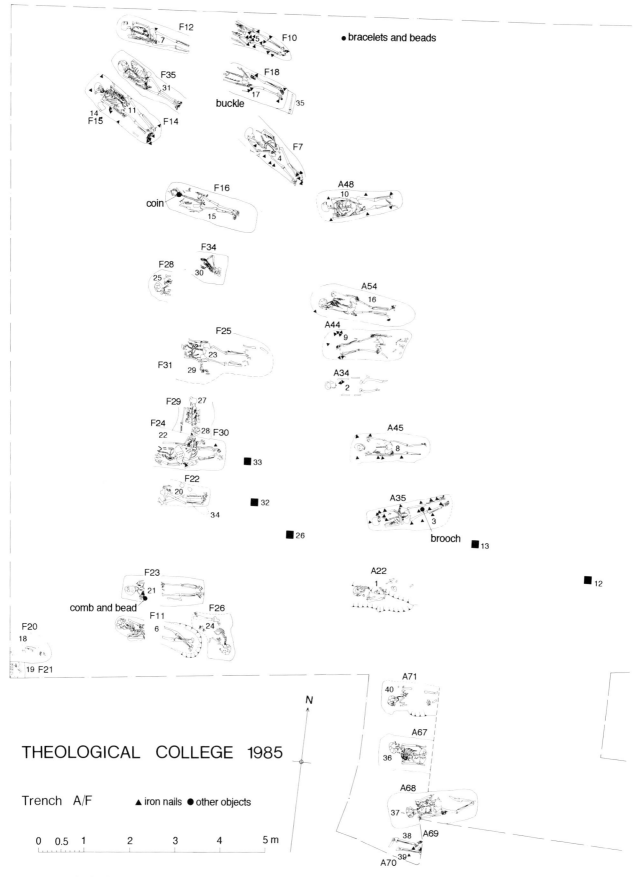

● bracelets and beads

buckle

coin

THEOLOGICAL COLLEGE 1985

Trench A/F     ▲ iron nails ● other objects

0  0.5  1      2      3      4      5 m

Fig. 4A.6   Scale 1:80

Plate 8   Theological College 1985, Trench A/F, general view looking east

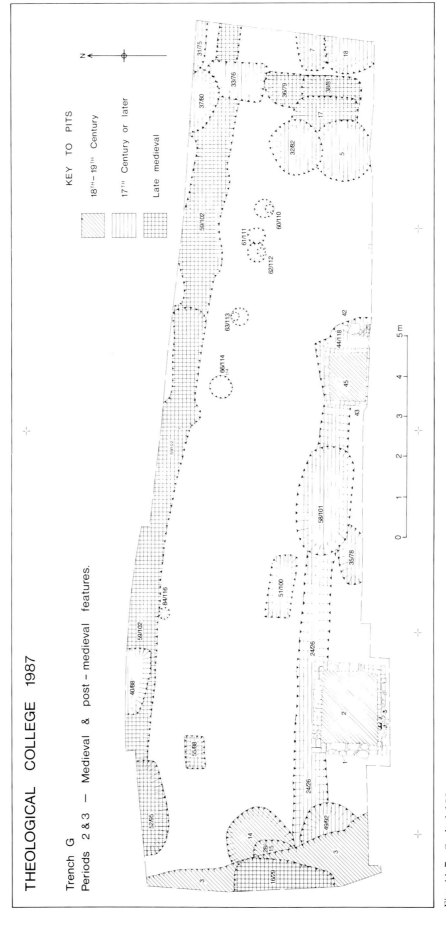

THEOLOGICAL COLLEGE 1987

Trench G

Periods 2 & 3 — Medieval & post – medieval features.

KEY TO PITS

18ᵀᴴ–19ᵀᴴ Century

17ᵀᴴ Century or later

Late medieval

Fig. 4A.7   Scale 1:100

# THEOLOGICAL COLLEGE 1985
Trench A/F
Late and post-medieval

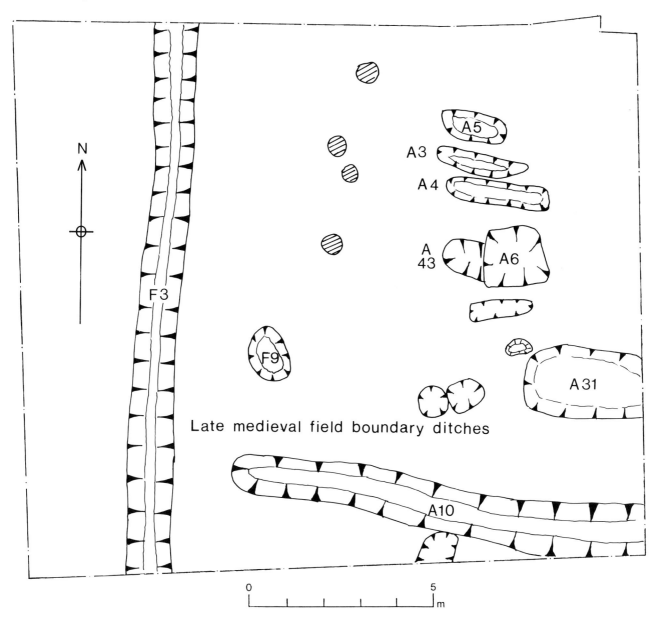

N

F3

A5

A3

A4

A
43

A6

F9

A31

Late medieval field boundary ditches

A10

0                    5
|_|_|_|_|_|          |
                     m

Fig. 4A.8   Scale 1:100

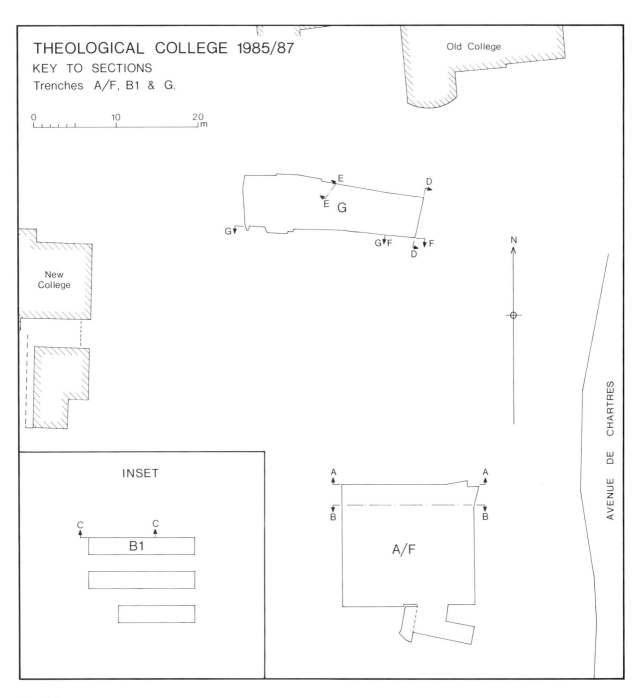

THEOLOGICAL COLLEGE 1985/87
KEY TO SECTIONS
Trenches A/F, B1 & G.

Old College

New College

INSET

B1

A/F

AVENUE DE CHARTRES

Fig. 4A.9

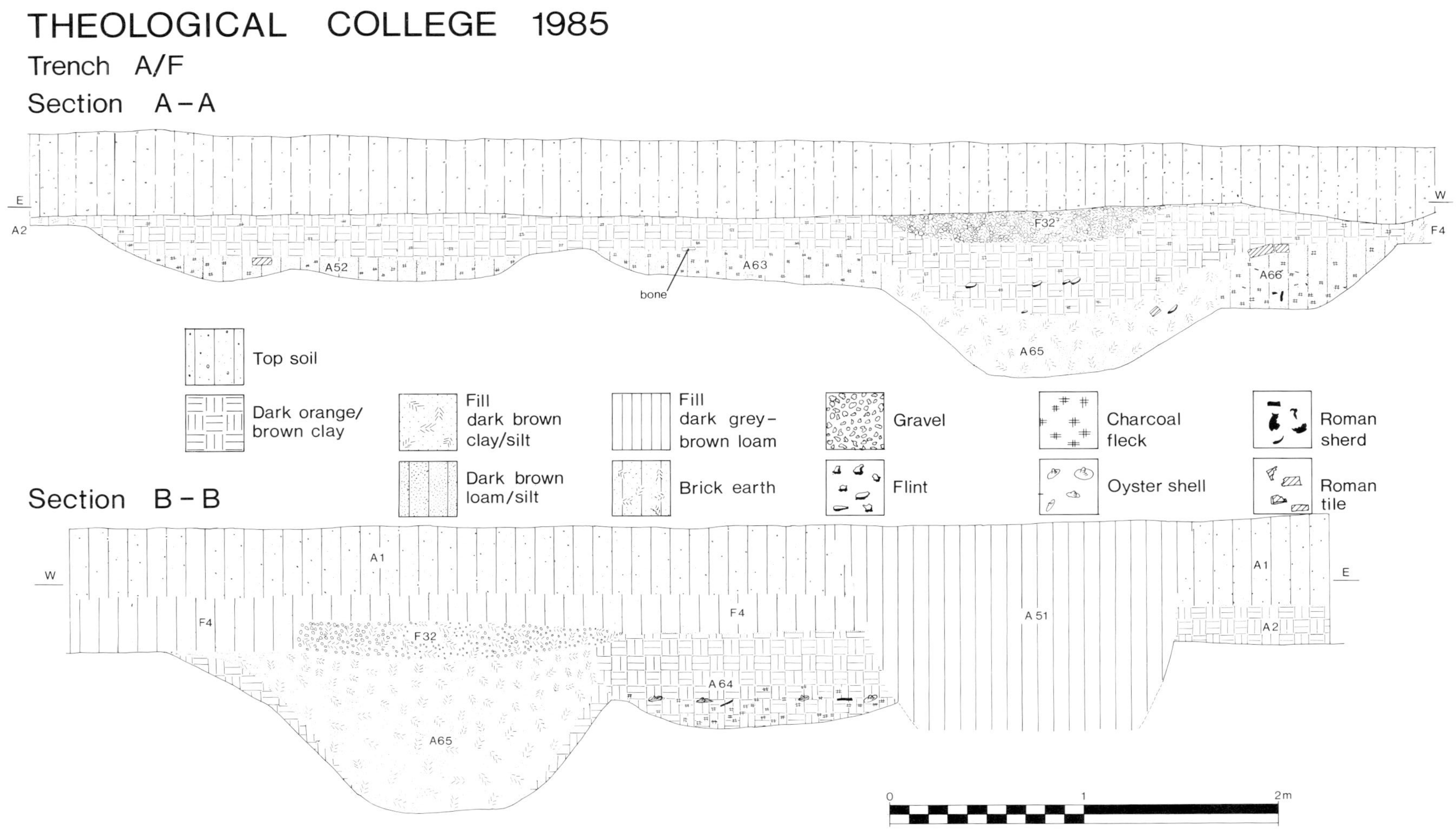

# THEOLOGICAL COLLEGE 1985

Trench A/F

Section A–A

Section B–B

**Legend:**

Top soil

Dark orange/brown clay

Fill dark brown clay/silt

Dark brown loam/silt

Fill dark grey-brown loam

Brick earth

Gravel

Flint

Charcoal fleck

Oyster shell

Roman sherd

Roman tile

A2, A52, A63, A65, A66, F32, F4, W, E

A1, A51, A64, F4, F32

0 1 2m

Fig. 4A.10

67

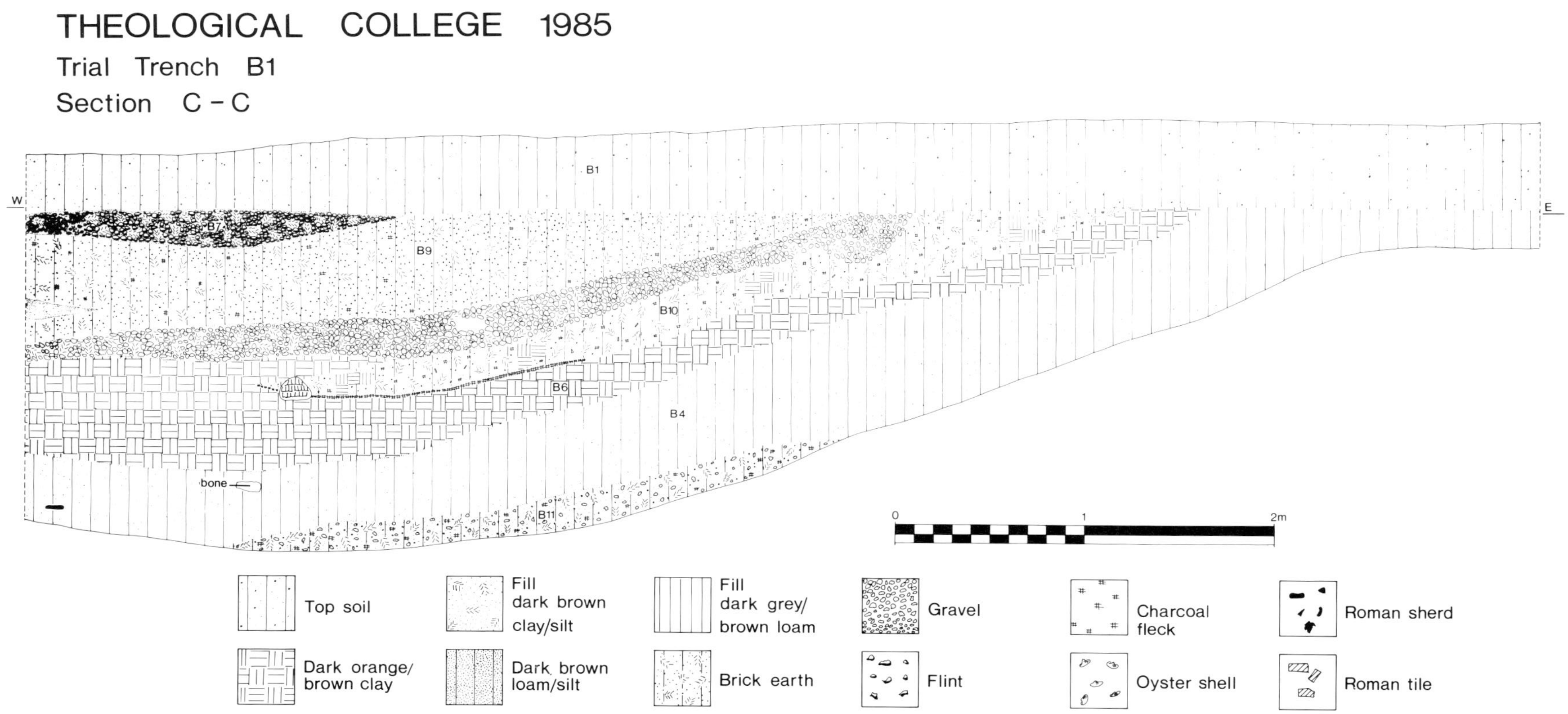

68

THEOLOGICAL COLLEGE 1985
Trial Trench B1
Section C – C

Fig. 4A.11

# THEOLOGICAL COLLEGE 1987

Trench G

Sections D – D, E – E & F – F.

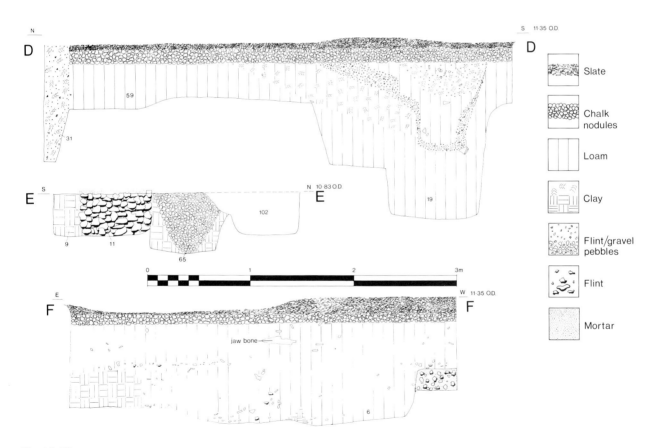

Fig. 4A.12

# THEOLOGICAL COLLEGE 1987

Trench G

Section G – G.

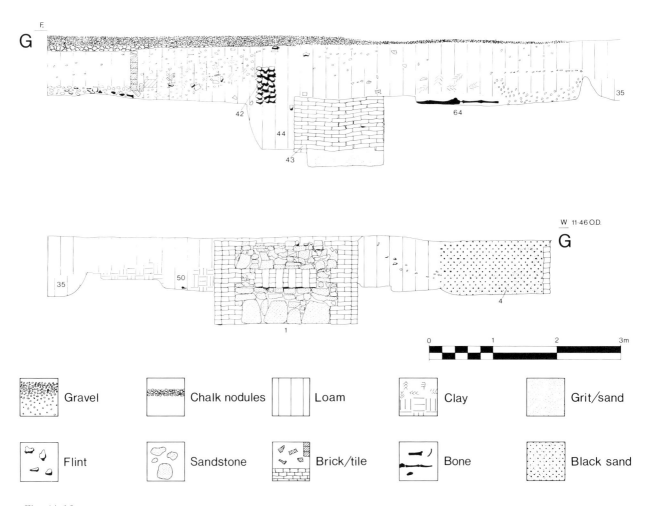

Gravel  Chalk nodules  Loam  Clay  Grit/sand

Flint  Sandstone  Brick/tile  Bone  Black sand

Fig. 4A.13

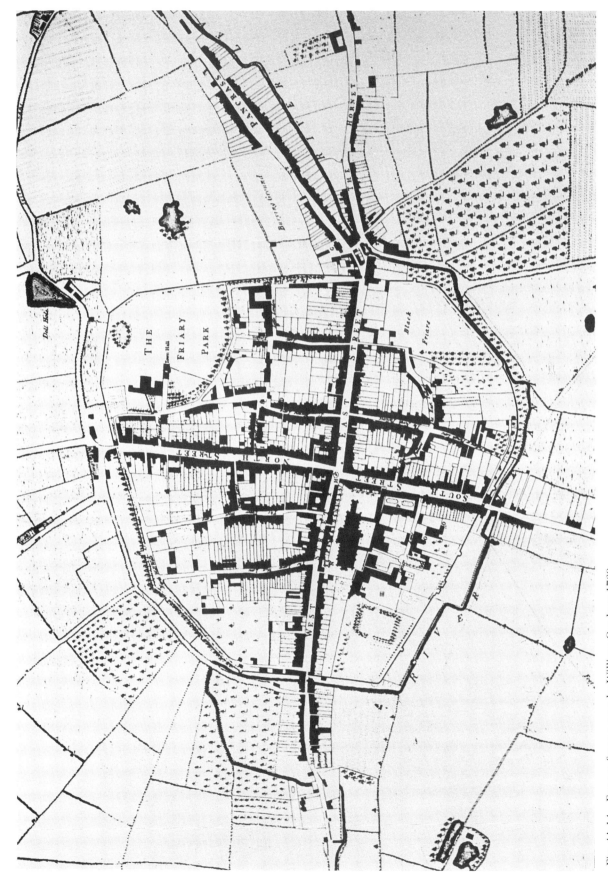

Fig. 4A.14  Extract from a map by William Gardner 1769

# 4B   The Westgate Roman inhumation cemetery

**by J.R. Magilton**

## SUMMARY

*Excavations in 1985 and 1987 in the former grounds of the Theological College west of the walled city revealed 62 burials of a late Roman cemetery of predominantly west–east graves. Two burials were in lead coffins. Most graves were of adults with males twice as frequent as females. There was virtually no evidence for grave goods. As there were no positive indicators for Christianity, the cemetery is assumed to have been pagan.*

## INTRODUCTION

Excavations (site code CHT) within the former grounds of Chichester Theological College in 1985 and 1987 revealed 62 burials of a late Roman inhumation cemetery (Figs. 4A.1, 4A.5 and 6). Investigations were prompted by redevelopment proposals, since carried out, to construct blocks of flats in the eastern part of the grounds (now Tollhouse Close) next to the Avenue de Chartres. The first season of excavations, directed by Alec Down and supervised by Mark Beaton, took place in the spring of 1985 and was entirely funded by the developers. It had been understood that English Heritage were to contribute a similar amount in grant-aid, but as this was not forthcoming only half of the projected programme of work could be carried out. In the autumn of 1985, observations and salvage recording during construction work revealed further burials, including one in a lead coffin, the first from Chichester. The 1987 excavations to the north stemmed from a modification to the development scheme and took place on the site of a proposed garage block. Work was funded by the developers and the Manpower Services Commission and supervised by John Wildman. Post-excavation and publication of the site has been funded by English Heritage and Chichester District Council.

   Prior to the 1985 excavations, Roman inhumation burials were known on Stane Street outside the east gate of Chichester (Down and Rule 1971, 53–126; Down 1981, 77–118), outside the walls to the east of the north gate (Down 1978, 7–9) and perhaps south of the city, in the vicinity of the canal basin (Salzman 1935, 15–16; Fig. 4B.4). Neither antiquarian sources nor earlier excavations outside the west walls of the city (Holmes 1965) had indicated the presence of Roman burials in the former grounds of the College.

## RECORDING METHODS

### (i) Planning and surveying

The 1985 excavations were planned at 1:50 by triangulation from a series of fixed points and individual skeletons were drawn at 1:10 in site notebooks with the aid of a planning frame, the corners of which were triangulated to the survey pegs. The 1987 excavations were surveyed from grid-pegs at 5 m intervals and skeletons were recorded at 1:20 on plastic drawing film. In order to standardise the cemetery archive, the 1987 grid has been projected southwards and imposed on the 1985 site and site plans for the latter have been redrawn at 1:20 on plastic film from data recorded in the notebooks.

### (ii) Contexts and recording

The 1985 skeletons were numbered from 1 to 35 and the sequence was continued during salvage recording and for the 1987 site, so that each skeleton has a discrete number. The orientation of the burials has been recorded in such a way that the first compass reading marks the anterior end of the body. In 1985, each grave pit was assigned a number prefixed by either A or F according to its position within the area excavation, but the numerical sequences overlap (F22 is the grave pit for skeleton 20, whereas A22 is the pit for skeleton 1). Pottery and other finds were marked with the site code (CHT) followed by the year (85) and the grave pit number. Context descriptions were recorded in the site notebooks.

   The 1987 site was recorded on standard context cards and skeleton forms, using a continuous numerical sequence. All contexts, including grave pits and grave fills, were assigned different numbers (skeleton 42 occupied grave pit 72, the fill of which was 9) and the pottery and other finds have been marked with the fill number. Again in order to standardise the archive, data from the 1985 site notebooks have been transferred to the card system.

Small finds and photographs were numbered consecutively during each season, each series starting at 1. CHT 85.43, for example, is a coin from grave pit F16, whereas CHT 87.43 is a bronze needle from grave pit 73.

## DESCRIPTION

### (i) The 1985 site (area A/F)

The 1985 site was rectangular, measuring roughly 17 m from east to west by 14 m from north to south. The burials lay in its central and western areas. Thirty-five skeletons or parts of skeletons were identified, of which five assemblages (12, 13, 26, 32, 33) were isolated fragments most probably disturbed from nearby articulated but incomplete burials. Their find spots are represented by numbered black squares on Fig. 4A.6. Two other assemblages (14, 34) consisted of disturbed skeletal fragments within the grave pits of articulated burials. The remaining skeletons were all articulated and *in situ*, although some were very fragmentary. Most of the burials were west–east supine inhumations. Of the seven exceptions, burial 9, an east–west skeleton in a wooden coffin, may have been accidentally interred the wrong way round. Three burials (19, 27 and 28) were on a north–south alignment, one (35) was a south–north burial of which only parts of the legs survived and one (24) was a crouched burial. All five were either cut or sealed by west–east burials and there was no evidence from the grave pits in the form of nails or other iron fittings that any had been in coffins. Burial 30 was prone and aligned roughly east–west.

The west–east burials, which tended towards a north-west/south-east alignment at the northern end of the site, plainly formed part of an organised cemetery. Burials 10, 16, 9, 2, 8, 3 and 1 were more or less in a row, as were 15, 25, 23, 22, 20, 21 and 6 to the west. Burials in the north-west corner (7, 31, 11, 5, 17 and 4), forming a separate group, tended towards a north-west/south-east alignment. Iron nails were recovered from the fills of fourteen graves and their find- spots, where recorded, are indicated by triangles in Figs. 4A.5 and 6). Other finds from grave pits included potsherds, found with nine burials and almost certainly accidentally redeposited. Burial 3 had an Aucissa-type brooch in its filling and burial 17 a buckle from a *lorica segmentata*, both finds (p. 230 3 and 6 and Fig. 28.1) again presumably accidentally incorporated. A bone comb fragment (p. 231 2 and Fig. 28.6) and a glass bead (sf no. 85.82 not illustrated) from burial 21 may also have been accidentally redeposited. The only find perhaps deliberately placed in a grave pit was a bronze coin of the 'falling horseman' type (p. 182 TC7) found near the base of the skull of burial 15, which provides a *terminus post quem* of c. AD 350 for the grave. It may be concluded that grave goods, unless of a perishable nature, were not normally deposited with west–east burials in this cemetery. The position of the body within the grave exhibits a number of variations, although there is no apparent difference between burials known or thought to have been in coffins and the remainder. Of the coffined burials, 6 is unusual in that the lower legs were crossed. Two of the coffined burials (3 and 7) were interred with the arms or wrists crossed and two others (10 and 4) with the hands side by side over the pelvis. Others lay with arms at their sides. The crossed femurs of burial 20, which was not demonstrably in a coffin, are a result of disturbance after burial.

Of the skeletons which were examined, twelve were probably or certainly male, seven probably or certainly female and all were adults. Their distribution appears to be random, although men appeared to be marginally more likely to have been in coffins than women. The ages at death were determined with varying degrees of probability for thirteen skeletons, nine male and four female (Table 4B.1). Given the very small size of sample, no valid conclusions may be drawn, although a tendency for women to die younger than men seems apparent.

Finally, a group of artefacts—an inlaid glass bead, a melon bead and three linked bronze bracelets—must be mentioned. Although not found in a grave fill, they all occurred together and could have been deposited ritually (see p. 82).

### (ii) The 1985 salvage recording

In the autumn of 1985 four more burials (36–38 and 40) were excavated south of area A/F and four additional graves were found during construction work. Three burials south of area A/F were extended inhumations (36, 37, 40) with heads to the west. Nails were found in the fills of 36 and 40, suggesting that they had been in coffins. Burial 38 consisted only of the flexed legs of a skeleton and could represent a crouched inhumation similar to 24 in area A/F. The rest of the skeleton had been cut by the northern edge of a feature (A70), almost certainly a further west–east grave, although circumstances did not permit it to be excavated.

To the north and west of area A/F three burials were observed in a 2 m wide construction trench but there was no opportunity for a proper record to be made (Figs. 4B.1–3). The westernmost (62) had been very badly disturbed by a mechanical excavator, but enough survived *in situ* to indicate that it had had a north-west/south-east orientation. Burial 61 was a west–east extended burial. Little of it survived apart from the legs and an outline of the position of the right arm, which was extended alongside. Burial 60, north of area A/F, was aligned north-west/south-east and appeared to be the skeleton of a juvenile. The lower part of the body had been removed by machine, and the skull lay beyond the trench limit. The position of the skeleton was curious, with the right arm bent at 90 degrees and the hand resting on the hip, but may be paralleled by the articulated fragment burial 30 in area A/F. There were almost certainly other burials which were not observed during the machining of the construction trench.

To the west of area A/F, building workers discovered burial 41 in a lead coffin. It was aligned north-west/south-east and contained the body of an adult male. The coffin is described and discussed on p. 88, together with the second lead coffin from the 1987 site. A partial excavation of the grave pit revealed a greyware sherd, a nail and a tessera in a loose fill containing much mortar.

### (iii) The 1987 site (area G)

The remains of a further eighteen burials were excavated at the western end of area G, together with part of a probable grave pit (feature 99) which contained no bones. All were supine extended inhumations aligned north-west/south-east and one (44) was in a lead coffin (Plates 10 and 11).

As in area A/F to the south, there was evidence for cemetery organisation and four rows of burials may be discerned (from west to east 59, 42, 43; 44, 45, 50, 53; 55, 47, 46, 49, 48, 51; 54, 56, and ? feature 99) (Plate 9). Burials 58, 52 and 57 do not conform to this pattern. The alignment of the burials may have been determined by a ditch (65/104) containing 2nd century pottery, replaced by a stone wall (11), which had been robbed to foundation level and perhaps succeeded by a fence (posthole 83/115) before burials 42 and 59 were interred (Plate 10). These features may represent a long-established property boundary which was perpetuated into the 4th century; this is discussed on p. 60. No burials were found north-east of the line of the ditch. Iron nails were recovered from twelve grave pits, including feature 73 which contained the lead coffin, a reminder that lead on its own would have lacked the necessary rigidity for a coffin which must have been wooden with a lead lining. Three of the grave fills from which coffin nails were absent (52, 57 and 58) do not fall within the pattern of

Plate 9   Theological College, the Westgate cemetery 1987, from left to right, child burials 48, 49, 46 and 47, from the south-east

Plate 10   Theological College, the Westgate cemetery 1987. In the foreground, burials 43 (l) and 42 (r), the latter cut through wall 11. In the background is burial 45 (l) and 44 in the lead coffin. Camera looking north-west

graves suggested above and the other two (48 and 49) were children's graves. The explanation may be partly chronological, in that 52, 57 and 58 could pre-date the majority of the interments; 57 pre-dated 56, by which it was cut, in a cemetery where intersections between graves were rare.

The depth of the grave pits below natural varied from 0.29 m to 0.69 m. The average depth of graves known or thought to have contained coffins was 0.51 m contrasted with an average of 0.38 m for the others. Of the four non-adult burials, two were in coffins and two were not, so the figures are not distorted by the fact that non-adults tended to be buried in shallower graves. Some graves (for example, skeleton 55) seemed scarcely large enough for the skeleton which they contained. Others were apparently excessively long. Skeleton 51, for example, occupied only 67% of the length of the grave pit, but in this instance the reason seems to have been that the coffin was considerably longer than the body which it contained.

Apart from nails, finds from the grave pits are all likely to have been redeposited. Grave 44 yielded a bronze strip, a further fragment of bronze (sf nos. 87.41, 87.42, not illustrated) and a bronze needle (sf no. 87.43, not illustrated) but as these lay outside the lead coffin they cannot be considered as grave furniture. A bronze stud from grave 51 (sf no. 87.47, not illustrated) is also likely to have been fortuitous. The only coin recovered was a *dupondius* of Vespasian from grave 59 (p. 182 TC2), again likely to have been redeposited.

## THE EXTENT OF THE CEMETERY

The southernmost burial of the 1985 excavations and the northernmost of the 1987 excavations lay about 54 m apart. There were indications from the 1987 site that the northern limit of the cemetery may have been a wall (11) (Fig. 4A.5, and Plate 10) replacing an earlier ditch (104) although burials had been cut into both of them, indicating that the wall had been reduced to foundation level before the cemetery went out of use. Little of the 1987 excavation lay north of the possible limit of the cemetery and there may be graves beyond this line. The southern boundary of the cemetery was undetermined, although no graves were found in the three trial trenches cut in 1985 opposite the south-west corner of the city walls (Fig. 4A.1, Site B).

The easternmost of the burials from the 1985 site lay about 37 m away from the city walls and those of the 1987 site were about 50 m from the wall-line. No physical boundary on the east side of the cemetery was identified on either site. However, as no burials were reported during the construction of the Avenue de Chartres, it is unlikely that they extended as far east as the outer lip of the late Roman town ditch. The westernmost burials, from the 1987 excavation and from salvage work in autumn 1985, lay about 65 m west of the city wall line and may extend beyond, towards the new buildings of the Theological College. In all, the burials recovered in 1985 and 1987 appear to be a small sample of an extensive cemetery, but the available data do not permit an estimate of its extent to be made.

## CEMETERY ORGANISATION

### (i) Burial alignment

All the burials excavated in 1987 and most of the 1985 burials were supine extended inhumations with the head to the west or north-west. Orientations, to the nearest 5 degrees, are given in Table 1. The 1987 burials (Fig. 4A.5) all lay north of west, more or less parallel with the robbed wall 11 and the ditch 104 which pre-dated it, suggesting that these features or a similar feature on the same alignment had influenced the layout of the cemetery, perhaps causing a deviation from an intended west–east orientation. A tendency for inhumation burials to be influenced in alignment by nearby linear features has been noted elsewhere (Dawes and Magilton 1980, 13). A mathematical study of Roman and post-Roman burial orientation in Southern Britain (Kendall 1982) has failed to reach any convincing conclusions and no further analysis of the Chichester burials is attempted here.

The 1985 burials fall into two groups: those which lay roughly west–east or north-west/south-east and a minority of burials on a different alignment. Of the former group, many burials were within few degrees of true west–east, but some burials in the north-west corner of the excavated area were aligned considerably north of west, like the burials from the 1987 site. The reason for the misalignment, if it was not merely the result of carelessness, may have been a feature lying beyond the excavated area, possibly a linear feature to which they lay parallel, or they could have been arranged radially around a focal point, perhaps a 'special' burial. Two of the burials noted during construction work in autumn 1985 also lay north-west/south-east.

The other burials from the 1985 site consisted of three with heads to the north (Fig. 4A.6, nos 19, 27 and 28), an articulated fragment (35) of a possible south–north example and a crouched burial (24). Of the north–south burials, 19 in the south-west corner of the site, lay mostly outside the limits of excavation. The skull and shoulders had been cut away by a west–east burial (18), and 27 and 28 intersected one another. Most of 27 from the pelvis downwards had been cut away when 28 was interred and 28 was in turn overlaid by a west–east burial (22). The crouched burial 24 lay in an irregularly shaped grave with the skull at the southern end. It had been cut by a west–east grave (6). The articulated fragment 35 appeared to be the right leg of a burial with its head to the south and had been cut by a west–east burial (17). One further unusual burial was 9, which lay with its head to the east, but this may have been accidental, due to its coffin having been lowered into the grave pit the wrong way round. The similarly orientated prone burial (30) is more likely to have been deliberately interred on this alignment. Despite the fact that some graves appeared excessively long for the skeleton which they contained, whereas other graves were only just adequate, the pits were not necessarily excavated much in advance of the interment and cannot be explained by the grave-digger's ignorance of the size of coffin or corpse which the grave was to hold. With coffined burials the size of the grave pit required was determined by the length of the coffin, not the length of the corpse within it, and the four children's graves in area G lying between burials 51 and 55 are appropriate for the sizes of the bodies (Plate 9). The average length of adult grave pit in area G was 2.27 m, but the range was from 1.64 to 2.8 m. Where the probable length of the coffin could be determined from the position of nails, the pits appeared to be 0.36 to 0.58 m longer than required. In area A/F the average grave pit was 1.96 m long (range 1.72 to 2.28 m) and in the only instance where both the length of the grave pit and the probable length of the coffin could be determined, the difference was 0.23 m. These figures seem to exclude the possibility that standard-sized graves were dug for adults, leaving the burying party to use them as best they could.

### (ii) Cemetery management

There was fairly clear evidence from the 1987 site and more ambiguous indications from the 1985 site that graves had been dug in rows. From the 1987 excavations, three rows could be defined from east to west although at the western end of the site the pattern was less obvious. Intersections between graves were relatively rare, again perhaps as a result of cemetery planning. At the 1987 site, the grave pits for burials 48 and 51 intersected, as did 56 and 57, but in neither case did the later interment cause displacement of the earlier skeleton. The only example of this was between 55 and 47. Much the same was true of the 1985 site, where all the intersections were either of the west–east burials cutting earlier burials on a different alignment or in one case a north–south burial (28) cutting an earlier north–south one (27). Disarticulated bones (29) within the grave pit of burial 23 may represent the remains of a further north–south burial, as may fragments of human bone (34) in a small pit partly sealed by burial 20.

As there was no evidence of grave markers it must be assumed that the mounds covering graves were sufficient to distinguish their locations. Whether cemetery planning was a responsibility of the civic authorities, burial societies, which may have held discrete blocks within the cemetery, or simply private professional undertakers, is unclear. There is no evidence for clusters of graves with gaps between which could have hinted at private burial plots. Burial enclosures of the type attested at Dorchester (Chambers 1988), Lankhills (Clarke 1979) and elsewhere are not evident in Chichester.

### (iii) Coffins and burial rites (Fig. 4B.1)

Many of the west–east skeletons from both the 1985 and 1987 sites but none of the north–south burials or the crouched burial had been encoffined. Remains consisted of nails within the grave fill but the outline of the coffin in no case survived as a stain in the ground. The absence of nails in some grave fills need not imply the lack of a coffin, since six sides of a timber box could easily have been held together with wooden pegs. Arras-culture burials at Burton Fleming had coffin stains but no metal fittings (Whimster 1981, 43) and an early post-Conquest burial at Worth Maltravers, Dorset, was similarly coffined (*op. cit.* 271).

Conversely, the presence of one or two nails in the grave fill, particularly on the 1985 site, need not imply a nailed coffin; they might be residual from earlier phases of occupation. There may also have been nails in some graves which did not survive or were not recovered. Nevertheless, the evidence indicates that burial in a wooden coffin was normal when west–east inhumations became the predominant custom. The lead coffins found are described below on p. 88.

The layout of bodies within the coffins and graves, where it could be determined, was fairly consistent. The 'normal' position, represented by eleven examples, seems to have been with the arms straight beside the body. The next most frequent attitude (five examples) was with the arms slightly bent and the hands resting above the pelvis. There were eight burials where one arm was bent with the hand above the pelvis and the other lay beside the body, perhaps due to displacement during or after interment. If these had been originally laid out with both arms bent and the hands resting in the pelvic region, such burials would have been slightly more frequent than those with straight arms. Women were more than twice as likely to be buried with straight arms as men. In area A/F, nine of the fifteen burials for which the attitude could be determined were buried with their arms straight, as opposed to three out of ten in area G, but this apparent difference is due to the majority of the female burials occurring in A/F. There seems to have been no difference in layout between burials known or thought to have been buried in coffins and the few for which evidence of a coffin is lacking.

The skull, where it was not supine, lay almost equally often on the right side as on the left, and it may be assumed that displacement from a supine position had occurred during or after burial. In almost all cases the legs of burials were straight.

### (iv) Distribution of burials by age (Fig. 4B.2)

The excavated parts of the cemetery must represent only a small fraction of its total area and to look at distribution patterns is therefore of doubtful validity. There is nevertheless an apparent difference between the ages at death of individuals in the northern part of the cemetery (area G) and those to the south (area A/F). Of the eleven adult burials in area G, nine have been assigned to the 45+ age group (82%) whereas in area A/F the figure is two (12.5%). The apparent difference between the two areas could reflect chronological or social factors.

The number of burials for which both sex and age at death can be determined is too small for meaningful comparisons and includes one uncertain individual from each sex. The figures are as in Table 3. As seven out of the 22 skeletons are female, it could be argued that women are over-represented in the 17–25 age group, under-represented in the 25–35 age group and at about the expected level in the other two categories, but, given the sample size, such a conclusion would be unjustifiable. Children and juveniles were under-represented throughout the excavated parts of the cemetery.

**Table 1**
**The burials from the Theological College Westgate Cemetery**

| Skel no | Sex | Age | Skull position | Arm position Rt | Arm position L | Leg position Rt | Leg position L | Grave pit | Grave fill | Relationships | Orient. | Coffin nails | Pot | Assoc. SFs | Skel no |
|---|---|---|---|---|---|---|---|---|---|---|---|---|---|---|---|
| 1 | M | 33–45 | ?Supine | Pelvis | — | — | — | A22 | — | — | W–E | — | Y | — | 1 |
| 2 | M | 25–35 | Supine | Str. | Str. | ?Str. | Str. | A34 | — | — | 0 | 2 | Y | — | 2 |
| 3 | F | | Left | Rt angle | Pelvis | Str. | Str. | A35 | — | — | –10 | Many | Y | 85.22 (brooch) Illus. Fig. 28.1.3 | 3 |
| 4 | M | 33–45 | Right | Pelvis | Pelvis | Str. | Str. | F7 | — | — | +45 | 8 | Y | — | 4 |
| 5 | ?M | — | — | Str. | Str. | Str. | Str. | F10 | — | — | +25 | Many | N | — | 5 |
| 6 | M | 17–25 | Supine | Indet. | Indet. | Crossed | | F11 | — | ?Cuts 24 | +20 | Yes | Y | — | 6 |
| 7 | M | 45+ | Left | Str. | Pelvis | Str. | Str. | F12 | — | — | +20 | Yes | Y | — | 7 |
| 8 | F | 17–25 | Right | Str. | Str. | Str. | Str. | A45 | — | — | 0 | 6 | Y | — | 8 |
| 9 | M | 25–35 | — | Str. | Indet. | Str. | Str. | A44 | — | — | 180 (E–W) | 7 | Y | — | 9 |
| 10 | M | 25–35 | Left | Pelvis | Pelvis | Str. | Str. | A48 | — | — | –5 | 7 | N | — | 10 |
| 11 | M | 45+ | Supine | Str. | Pelvis | Str. | Str. | F14 | — | Contains 14 | +40 | 10 | N | 85.32 (fe object) 85.35 (part bone pin) | 11 |
| 12 | Isolated skull fragments, not studied | | | | | | | | | | | | | | 12 |
| 13 | Isolated skull fragments, not studied | | | | | | | | | | | | | | 13 |
| 14 | Fragments only, not studied | | | | | | | F15 | — | With 10 | — | — | N | — | 14 |
| 15 | F | ?33–45 | Supine | Str. | Str. | Str. | Str. | F16 | — | — | +20 | — | N | 85.43 (coin c. AD 350) p. 182 | 15 |
| 16 | F | 25–35 | Right | Str. | Str. | Str. | Str. | A54 | — | — | +10 | 1 | N | — | 16 |
| 17 | Not studied | | — | Str. | Pelvis | Str. | Str. | F18 | — | ?Cuts 35 | +20 | 5 | Y | 85.73 (lorica) Illus. Fig. 28.1.6 | 17 |
| 18 | Lower legs only | | — | — | — | ?Str. | Str. | F20 | — | Cuts 19 | W–E | — | N | — | 18 |
| 19 | Fragments only | | — | — | Chest | — | — | F21 | — | Cut by 18 | N–S | — | N | — | 19 |
| 20 | Fragments only | | — | — | Str. | Str. | Str. | F22 | — | Seals 34 | W–E | — | N | — | 20 |
| 21 | F | 17–25 | Supine | Str. | — | Str. | Str. | F23 | — | — | 0 | Yes | N | 85.81 (bone comb) Illus. Fig. 28.6.2 85.82 (glass bead) | 21 |
| 22 | ?F | — | — | Str. | Str. | Str. | Str. | F24 | — | Cuts 28 | 0 | 1 | N | — | 22 |
| 23 | F | — | — | Str. | Str. | Str. | Str. | F25 | — | Contains 29 | +10 | — | N | — | 23 |
| 24 | ?M | — | Left | Rt angle | (Crouched burial) | | | F26 | — | ?Cut by 6 | Crouched | — | N | — | 24 |
| 25 | ?M | 25–35 | Right | — | — | — | — | F28 | — | — | W–E | — | N | — | 25 |
| 26 | Jaw only, not studied | | | | | | | | | | | | | | 26 |
| 27 | Not studied | | — | Str. | — | Str. | Str. | F29 | — | Cut by 28 | +90 (N–S) | — | N | — | 27 |
| 28 | M | 25–35 | Right | — | — | Str. | Str. | F30 | — | Cuts 27; cut by 22 | +75 | — | N | — | 28 |
| 29 | Feet only, not studied | | | | | | | F31 | — | With 23 | W–E | — | N | — | 29 |
| 30 | Prone articulated fragment | | | — | Rt angle | — | — | F34 | — | — | E–W | — | N | — | 30 |

| No. | Assoc. | Illus. | Orient. | Sfs | Relationship | Context | Skel. no. | Pos. 1 | Pos. 2 | Pos. 3 | Pos. 4 | Posture | Sex | Age |
|---|---|---|---|---|---|---|---|---|---|---|---|---|---|---|
| 31 | — | N | +40 | — | — | — | F35 | Str. | Str. | Pelvis | Str. | Supine | — | — |
| 32 | Disturbed fragments, not studied | | | | | | | | | | | | | |
| 33 | Skull fragments, not studied | | | | | | | | | | | | | |
| 34 | Fragments, not studied | N | ?S–N (Legs only) | | Below 20 | | — | | | | | | — | — |
| 35 | Legs only, not studied | | | | Cut by 4, ?17 | | — | | | | | | — | — |
| 36 | Ae stud nearby | Y | +10 | 1 | | — | A67 | Str. | Str. | Str. | Str. | Left | — | — |
| 37 | — | Y | –10 | — | | — | A68 | Str. | Flexed | Indet. | Str. | Supine | — | — |
| 38 | — | N | — | — | Relationship uncertain | — | A69 | Flexed | Flexed | — | — | — | — | — |
| 39 | — | N | — | — | | — | A70 | Skeleton not exposed | | | | | — | — |
| 40 | — | Y | W–E | Yes | | — | A71 | — | — | Str. | Str. | Supine | F | 35–45 |
| 41 | — | Y | +35 | 1 (Pb c) | — | — | A72 | Str. | Str. | Indet. | Str. | — | M | (Adult) |
| 42 | 87.99 (Fe object) | Y | +35 | 8 | — | 9 | 72 | Str. | Str. | Pelvis | Str. | Supine | ? | 45+ |
| 43 | — | Y | +35 | 1 | — | 25 | 13 | Str. | Str. | ?pelvis | Pelvis | Left | F | 45+ |
| 44 | 87.40,41,43 (Ae fragments) | N | +30 | 2 (Pb c) | — | 10 | 73 | Str. | Str. | Str. | Str. | — | ? | 45+ |
| 45 | 87.92 (glass fragment) | Y | +35 | 4 | — | 10 | 74 | Str. | Str. | Pelvis | Pelvis | Indet. | M | 45+ |
| 46 | — | N | +25 | 2 | — | 69 | 105 | Indet. | — | — | — | Indet. | ? | ? |
| 47 | — | Y | +15 | 11 | Cut by 55 | 70 | 106 | Str. | Str. | Str. | Str. | Left | — | 8/9 |
| 48 | — | N | W–E | — | Cut by 51 | 34 | 77 | Flexed | Str. | Indet. | Indet. | Indet. | ? | 5 |
| 49 | 87.158 (Fe fragment) | N | +25 | 6 | — | 71 | 107 | Str. | Flexed | Indet. | Indet. | Indet. | — | 33–45 |
| 50 | — | N | +45 | — | — | 39 | 87 | — | Str. | Indet. | Indet. | Left | M | — |
| 51 | 48.77 (Ae stud) | Y | +25 | 25 | Cuts 48 | 47 | 90 | Str. | Str. | Str. | Pelvis | Left | M | 25–35 |
| 52 | — | Y | +25 | 1 | | 48 | 91 | ?Str. | Str. | — | — | — | ? | 45+ |
| 53 | — | N | NW–SE | 1 | | 50 | 93 | Str. | Str. | Pelvis | Pelvis | — | — | — |
| 54 | 87.150 (Fe object) | Y | +20 | 4 | Cuts 47 | 51 | 94 | Str. | Str. | Str. | Pelvis | Right | M | 45+ |
| 55 | — | N | NW–SE | 2 | ?Cuts 57 | 41 | 89 | Str. | Str. | — | — | Left | F | 45+ |
| 56 | — | N | W?E | 1 | ?Cut by 56 | 53 | 96 | Str. | — | — | Pelvis | — | — | — |
| 57 | — | N | +35 | 1 | | 54 | 97 | Str. | Str. | Str. | Pelvis | — | M | 45+ |
| 58 | — | N | +25 | — | | 64 | 103 | Str. | — | — | — | — | — | — |
| 59 | 87.84 (coin c. AD 74) p. 182 | Y | +35 | — | | 85 | 86 | Str. | Str. | Str. | Str. | Right | M | 45+ |
| 60 | — | N | NW–SE | 1 | — | — | A73 | — | — | — | Rt angle | — | — | — |
| 61 | — | N | W–E | 2 | — | — | A74 | Str. | Str. | — | Str. | — | — | — |
| 62 | — | N | NW–SE | — | — | — | A75 | — | — | — | — | — | — | — |

Abbreviations: Assoc., associated small finds; Illus., Illustrated in text; N no; Orient. orientation (see below); Pb c, lead coffin; Pot, associated pottery; Str. straight; Y yes.

Orientation: The figures give the variation from Ordnance Survey west–east to the nearest 5 degrees. +15 means a burial was aligned 15 degrees north of west: –5 means a burial was aligned 5 degrees south of west. [A compass bearing (e.g. NW–SE) means that circumstances did not permit the orientation to be determined accurately.] Readings were taken from the site plans.

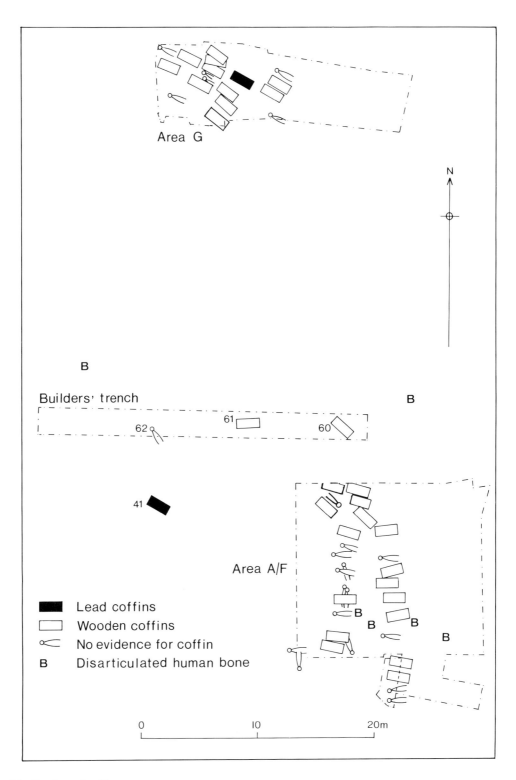

Area G

B

Builders' trench

B

62    61    60

41

Area A/F

B

B    B

B

■ Lead coffins
☐ Wooden coffins
⚲ No evidence for coffin
B Disarticulated human bone

0          10          20m

Fig. 4B.1   Distribution of coffins

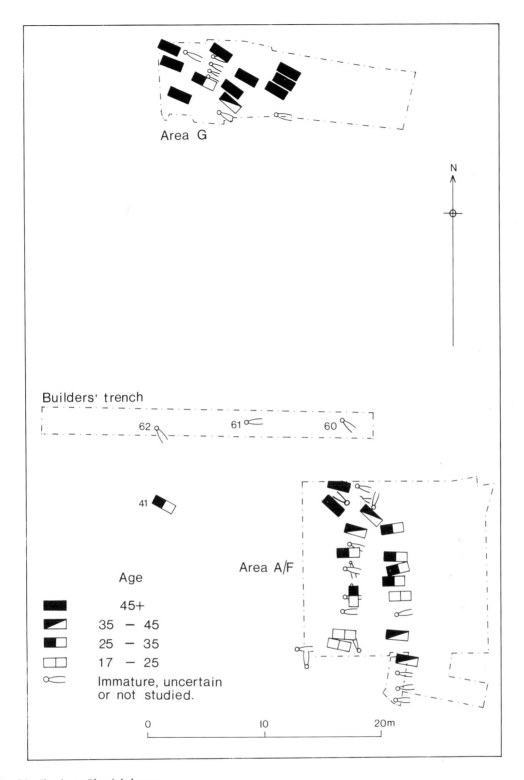

Fig. 4B.2   Distribution of burials by age

**Table 2**

| Age of adults: | | 45+ | 35–45 | 25–35 | 17–25 |
|---|---|---|---|---|---|
| Area G | (%) | 9 (82) | 1 (9) | 1 (9) | — |
| Area A/F | (%) | 2 (12.5) | 4 (25) | 7 (43.75) | 3 (18.75) |
| Totals | (%) | 11 (40.74) | 5 (18.52) | 8 (29.63) | 3 (11.11) |

**Table 3**

| Age of adults: | 45+ | 35–45 | 25–35 | 17–25 |
|---|---|---|---|---|
| Area G (male/female) | 4/2 | 1/0 | 1/0 | 0/0 |
| Area A/F (male/female) | 2/0 | 2/?2 | ?4/1 | 1/2 |
| Totals | 6/2 | 3/?2 | ?5/1 | 1/2 |

### (v) Distribution of burials by sex (Fig. 4B.3)

The cemetery contained nineteen certain or probable male burials and ten certain or probable female burials. All the burials for which a sex could be adduced were adult, but not all could be assigned to a specific age at death category. Although it is unclear why male burials should constitute nearly twice the female total, the male and female burials appear to be evenly scattered throughout the cemetery; there was no hint that specific areas had been set aside for the exclusive use of members of either sex. Of the two prestige burials in lead coffins, one was an adult male and the sex of the other was undetermined. Burials apparently in wooden coffins where the sex of the skeleton could be adduced numbered twenty, twelve being male and eight female. A similar preponderance of males to females was found at Cirencester Bath Gate, where the ratio was 2.5:1 (McWhirr *et al.* 1982, 109–11), and West Tenter Street, London (Whytehead 1986, 102), where the ratio of inhumations was 2.2:1, compared with 1.9:1 at Chichester. The cultural explanation at Cirencester proposed by the late Calvin Wells—that Cirencester became a home for military veterans and other retired officials who lacked wives—is even less convincing when applied to Roman Chichester.

## ARTEFACTS FROM GRAVE PITS

Many graves contained a few sherds of pottery, but there is no reason to conclude that their incorporation was other than fortuitous and some sherds are demonstrably earlier than the likely date of the cemetery.

The most frequent non-ceramic finds were iron nails, found in 29 grave pits, which in most cases may be interpreted as components of wooden coffins. There were no nails associated with the north–south burials from the 1985 site (nos 19, 27 and 28) or, as would be expected, associated with the crouched burial (24). As each of the four burials was demonstrably earlier than a west–east burial, the absence of nails may have chronological implications. It could be concluded that burial in nailed wooden coffins was unusual before west–east burials became the norm, or that coffins were not often used by those who practised north–south burials. The explanation could be religious. Modern Jews and Muslims, for example, transport the body to the burial ground in a coffin but then inter the corpse simply in a shroud. Alternatively, it could reflect the relative poverty of the deceased. At the St Pancras cemetery (Down and Rule 1971) nails were found with only one of the nine inhumation burials and at Needlemakers (Down 1981) four of the six west–east burials had nails or iron spikes in their fills, against only two of the other eight burials. At this site, the west–east burials lie north or east of those with different alignments, perhaps indicating that they were later interments peripheral to the original core of the cemetery.

Two burials had coins in their fill (see p.182). The only secure example of a coin associated with an inhumation in Chichester comes from Needlemakers, where a west–east burial (13) had a coin of Constantine in the skull. The pit of burial 9 from the same site contained a number of late 3rd to 4th century coins, but these are interpreted as a hoard scattered when the grave pit was dug (Down 1981, 90–95).

A brooch of Aucissa type was recovered from the fill of grave 3 but it is unlikely to have been a deliberate deposition (p. 230, 3 and Fig. 28.1). A buckle from a *lorica segmentata* came from the fill of grave 17 (p. 230 and Fig. 28.1) and it is also likely to have been redeposited. Fragments of a double-sided bone comb and a bead from burial 21 (sf 85, 81 and 82, not illustrated) are less easily interpreted but again may have been accidentally incorporated in the filling. The only secure examples of inhumations from Chichester with grave goods are from the St Pancras cemetery (Down and Rule 1971) where three of the nine burials contained finds.

Finally, there is the group of finds from the 1985 site. It comprised an inlaid glass bead, a melon bead (Fig. 15.1, TC13 and TC12) and three linked bronze bracelets (Fig. 28.1, 13) lying on the old ground surface and not apparently connected with a burial. They may have been associated with a shallow inhumation which had been ploughed away, or even a cremation. A similar group of jewellery is known from Ancaster (Lincs), a cemetery where grave goods are otherwise absent (Watts 1991, 67).

Note. Small finds not illustrated are in the level 3 archive.

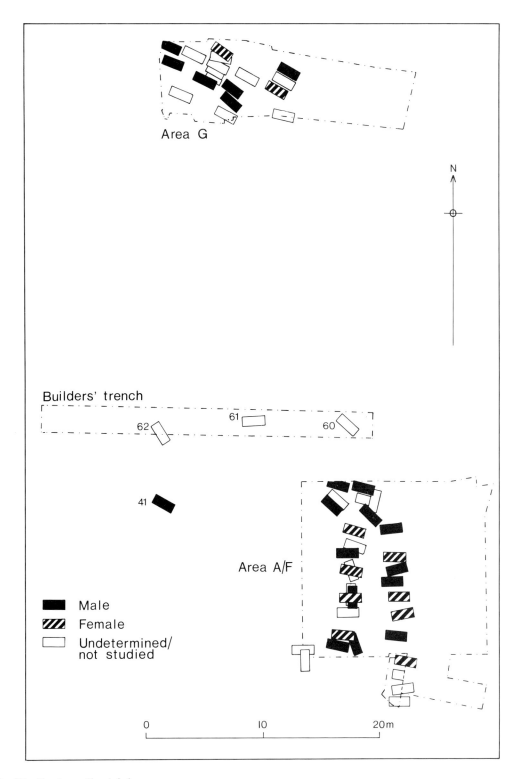

Fig. 4B.3   Distribution of burials by sex

## DISCUSSION

### (i) The date of the cemetery

The 1985 site indicates that there were at least two broad phases of use. To the later phase belong the west–east or north–west/south-east burials which were usually in coffins. The earlier phase is characterised by seven inhumations which were on a different alignment (north–south or south–north) buried in a crouched position

83

or prone; six of these are known or thought to have been cut by a west–east burial. There are at least two crouched burials at St Pancras (nos 185 and 271) which pre-date 200, but this practice in a regional context is not an Iron Age survival (Philpott 1991, 57). Such burials could be low-status or reflect a family tradition of incomers to the region. The cemetery organisation present in the later phase appears to have been lacking in this initial phase, since the grave pit for the later of two of the north–south burials was dug through the lower part of the earlier burial. An absence of grave markers may be inferred.

The relative dates of the west–east burials in area G and area A/F cannot be established. It is possible that those in area A/F were the earlier, the west–east interments taking place in an area which had already been set aside as a cemetery and which later expanded northwards. Alternatively, the west–east cemetery may have been initially established to the north of area A/F and have expanded southwards into the old cemetery at a time when the positions of the earlier graves were no longer visible or remembered. Absolute dates for the cemetery cannot be determined. Burial 15 in area A/F cannot be earlier than c. AD 350 on the evidence of its filling. No other grave can be adequately dated either by finds from the grave pit or by finds from earlier features cut by the grave pit which could provide a *terminus post quem*. As the Westgate cemetery is the only example so far known of a predominantly west–east inhumation cemetery in Chichester, it cannot be dated by analogy. However, a coin of Constantine (AD 330–337) from burial 13 at Needlemakers (Down 1981) reinforces the likelihood that west–east burials in general belong to the 4th century. At Ospringe, Kent (Whiting *et al.* 1931) the west–east burials seem to be mainly later than those on other alignments (Black 1986, 217).

## (ii) Religion

In a wider context, the Westgate cemetery belongs to the category of 'managed' cemeteries (Thomas 1981, 232) which are found in the 4th century at the urban centres and small towns of Roman Britain, characterised by west–east graves with few intersections and few or no finds (Philpott 1991, 226–7). Whilst it is fair to assume that inhumations aligned other than west–east are likely to be pagan, west–east burials in what became the Christian tradition cannot be assumed to be Christian without supporting evidence and at Chichester Westgate this was lacking. At Poundbury, Dorchester (Dorset), one of perhaps three cemeteries in Roman Britain containing demonstrably Christian graves (Green 1982) the west–east burials avoided an area of north–south inhumations with grave goods, perhaps because these overtly pagan graves were regarded as a source of ritual pollution. According to Irish legend, there was a cemetery full of saints in County Wexford which moved overnight to the opposite side of the river when a rogue was buried amongst them, leaving the rogue-corpse in solitude (Yeats n.d., 214). At Chichester there seems to have been no objection to the continued use of an area containing a few north–south and other burials in the pagan tradition, although it is possible that these graves were unmarked and had been forgotten by the time the west–east interments took place.

An increased concern for preserving the physical integrity of the body is characteristic of late Roman 'managed' cemeteries, and is reflected in the widespread use of coffins. This process starts at too early a date for Christian influence to be suspected, although Christian belief in a physical resurrection may have accelerated the trend (Philpott 1991, 238). Resources which had previously been used for the provision of grave goods may have been switched to the coffin itself. At Poundbury, for example, there is a clustering of stone and lead coffins around the mausolea (Green 1982, 65), so there is an apparent correlation between the nature of coffins and status. At Chichester Westgate, the lead coffin found in 1987 appeared to be simply one of a row of burials and, apart from its container, the burial had no distinguishing characteristics. The dentition of the skeleton in the 1985 lead coffin, however, distinguished it from the other burials, and is very likely a reflection of status (see below, p. 91).

With a very few exceptions burials give few clues to the specific pagan beliefs of the deceased (Alcock 1980). This is not surprising, given the amalgam of Roman, native and more exotic creeds available to the citizen of late Roman Britain, but it must also be suspected that burial customs reflect an evolving local tradition as much as more widespread religious practices. This certainly seems to be true of Lankhills cemetery, Winchester (Clarke 1979), where the evolution of established burial rites can be seen throughout the 4th century. Burial customs may even reflect religious beliefs which are no longer current, as in late 20th century Britain, where secular burials retain Christian elements. Thus the coin found at the base of the skull of burial 15 at Chichester Westgate, even if originally placed in the mouth as Charon's fee, need not indicate any literal belief in an afterlife crossing of the Styx, and it must be remembered that Celtic gods as well as Graeco-Roman deities had an interest in money (Ross 1967, 138, fig. 96; Brunaux 1988, 92–3); to interpret the practice solely in the context of classical mythology (*pace* Down and Rule 1971, 72) may be misleading. It may represent a local or even family tradition, the religious significance of which had been forgotten by the mid 4th century.

The custom is also attested at Chichester Needlemakers (burial 13; Down 1981, 77–118) where a coin of Constantine was found in the skull of a south-west/north-east inhumation with a radiocarbon date of AD 320 ± 65; the coin was a worn Constantinopolis issue of 330–337 which may have been in circulation for some time before deposition. In an earlier period the custom was uncommon. Only six of the 326 burials from the St Pancras cremation cemetery had coins with them (Down 1988, 59).

Elsewhere in later Roman Britain the tradition appears to have been equally unusual (Alcock 1980, 57–9). At Cirencester (McWhirr *et al.* 1982, 129) only two inhumations had coins in their mouths and at Winchester Lankhills the practice is recorded three times (Clarke 1979, 174). There are only five known from Trentholme Drive, York (Wenham 1968) out of at least 350 inhumations.

The custom, however, persisted throughout the Roman period. The cemetery at Snell's Corner, Hants (Knocker 1955) yielded three coins with a *terminus post quem* of AD 388. Early coins no longer in common use were sometimes saved for burial (for example, the Lankhills graves 336 and 437 (Clarke 1979, 204–5) so the *dupondius* of Vespasian from grave 59 at Chichester Westgate cannot be dismissed entirely as having been disturbed from an earlier deposit, although its date of minting is much earlier than the date of the grave compared to the Lankhills examples.

All the other finds from graves, as suggested above, may be fortuitous, with the exception of coffin nails. The only case where there is cause to doubt is grave 21, the burial of a young woman, where a fragment of a double-sided bone comb and a glass bead were found together by the right shoulder of the skeleton. These could be interpreted as favourite personal possessions intended for use in the afterlife, or as divine offerings. As the skeleton had been disturbed, they could have been items worn at the time of burial. Similar double-sided bone combs are known from Cirencester (McWhirr *et al.* 1982, 129, fig. 80) and Lankhills, Winchester (Clarke 1979) and are dated to the late 4th century. Combs are generally uncommon as grave goods, but careful arrangement of the hair, attested by hair-pins and, less frequently, hair rings, seems to have formed a part of Romano-British funerary customs (Philpott 1991, 181). Beads, often present singly, are perhaps token offerings removed from a necklace (*op. cit.* p. 130).

The occurrence of an inlaid glass bead, melon bead and three linked bronze bracelets together, although not apparently associated with a grave, could be a third example of a ritual deposit with a skeleton. The difficulties of interpretation are as for grave 21. After brooches, bracelets form the commonest class of personal items found in graves. Bracelets in general became especially popular in the late 3rd and 4th centuries, and wearing groups of thin bangles was a late Romano-British fashion (Philpott 1991, 129–30). It is noteworthy that the coin and the two possible examples of grave goods all occur in area A/F. If burials here are slightly earlier than those in area G it could be suggested that the custom of placing coins and other artefacts in graves had almost ceased when the earliest burials were dug and had lapsed entirely by the time burials in area G took place.

Prone burials and other unusual rites have been discussed by Harman *et al.* (1981) and most recently by Watts (1991) and Philpott (1991, 71–76). Prone burial is found throughout the Roman period in Britain, but is commonest in the 4th century. Although some such burials are undoubtedly the result of carelessness and some betray signs of coercion, the practice should perhaps be recognised as a minority custom in its own right. At Cirencester Bath Gate, for example, a third of all female burials were prone (Watts 1991, 58) and it is difficult to attribute such a high percentage to either carelessness or to the theory that they were religious or social outcasts, although at other cemeteries (e.g. Lankhills: Clarke 1979, fig. 105) such burials were clearly peripheral to the main area. At Chichester Westgate skeleton 30 was both prone and aligned the opposite way to most of the burials, so in this instance it must be regarded as, in Philpott's term, 'non-normative', although the alignment may not be significant if the burial belongs to an early phase in the cemetery before west–east burials predominated. From folklore it is clear that prone burial was reserved for those who were feared or despised (Hirst 1985, 36–7) and, according to Lady Wilde, it was believed in 19th century Ireland that the dead would turn over on their faces if a suicide were to be interred amongst them (Yeats n.d., 147). Prone burial for such individuals and similar offenders against moral or religious codes may have prevented this.

**(iii) The site in its local context**

A number of the larger towns of late Roman Britain have extensive new cemeteries established in the 4th century and the Chichester Westgate cemetery may be interpreted as a further example, albeit that its extent is unknown. The creation of new inhumation cemeteries may be merely a belated response to the practical difficulties in attempting to fit inhumations into cremation-sized plots at existing sites, as illustrated at Trentholme Drive, York (Wenham 1968), rather than reflecting a more widespread campaign of urban reorganisation, but it does confirm that the civic authorities were still functioning.

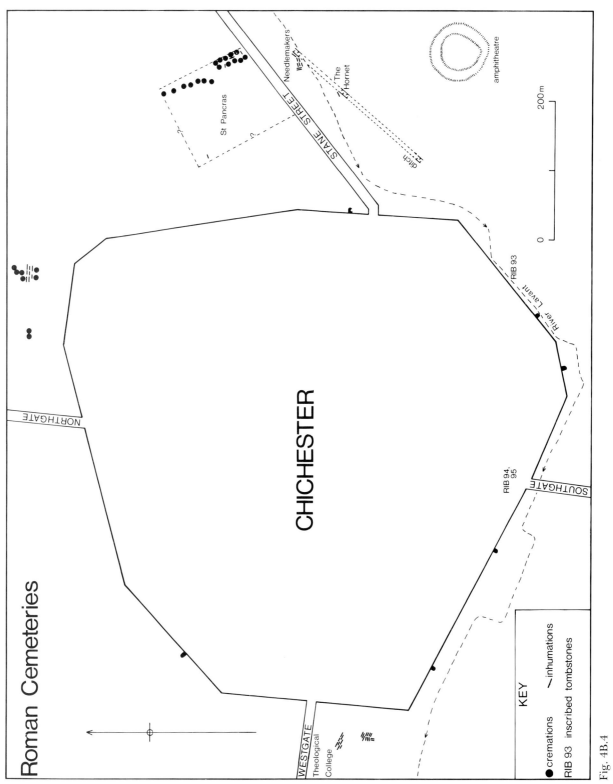

# Roman Cemeteries

CHICHESTER

St Pancras

STANE STREET

Needlemakers

The Hornet

ditch

amphitheatre

200 m

0

RIB 93

River Lavant

RIB 94, 95

NORTHGATE

SOUTHGATE

WESTGATE

Theological College

KEY

● cremations

⟋ inhumations

RIB 93 inscribed tombstones

Fig. 4B.4

It has been remarked of Roman Winchester that the 4th century cemeteries are larger than those for the other three centuries combined (Esmonde Cleary 1989, 80), but this is far from true of Chichester on present knowledge. To the 62 Westgate inhumations may be added six from the Northgate, nine from St Pancras, fourteen from Needlemakers and two from recent excavations in The Hornet (Magilton 1988), a total of 93, contrasted with 317 cremations from St Pancras alone dating to the period c. AD 70 to perhaps the early 3rd century. The Northgate cemetery, consisting of six inhumations and eleven cremations, may be contemporary with the last phase of use of the St Pancras cemetery, and the Needlemakers cemetery, of which the two burials from The Hornet may be a part, seems to belong to the 4th century. If it is valid to assume from the Westgate cemetery that burials aligned approximately west–east are later than those on other alignments, the Needlemakers cemetery, where roughly half the burials were aligned other than west–east, may be slightly earlier than the Westgate, although the excavator (Down 1981, 95) has proposed a date at the very end of the 4th century for the cemetery. The extent of the Needlemakers cemetery is unknown. The two burials at The Hornet are now separated from the Needlemakers site by the culverted River Lavant, but its Roman course is undetermined. The burials on both sites lie north of the same late Iron Age or early Roman defensive ditch aligned north-east/south-west which may have been perpetuated as a feature of the late Roman landscape to define the southern edge of the cemetery. Its northern boundary could have been either Stane Street itself or the backs of properties fronting onto it. It is significant that there was open ground at The Hornet available for use as a cemetery in the 4th century since the site lies within 150 m or so of the city's east gate, but the same phenomenon may be observed at Colchester, where the late Roman inhumation cemeteries lie closer to the walled circuit than the earlier cremation cemeteries.

## BIBLIOGRAPHY

Alcock, J.P., 1980. 'Classical religious belief and burial practice in Roman Britain' *Arch. J.* 137, 50–85
Black, E.W., 1986. 'Romano-British burial customs and religious beliefs in South-East England' *Arch. J.* 143, 201–39.
Brunaux, J.L., 1988. *The Celtic Gauls: Gods, Rites and Sanctuaries.*
Chambers, R.A., 1988. 'The late and sub-Roman cemetery at Queenford Farm, Dorchester-on-Thames, Oxon.' *Oxoniensia* LII, 35–69.
Clarke, G., 1979. *Pre-Roman and Roman Winchester.* Part II. *The Roman Cemetery at Lankhills.*
Dawes, J.D., and Magilton, J.R., 1980. *The Cemetery of St Helen-on-the-Walls, Aldwark* Archaeology of York, 12/1.
Down, A., 1978. *Chichester Excavations* 3 (Phillimore).
Down, A., 1981. *Chichester Excavations* 5 (Phillimore).
Down, A., 1988. *Roman Chichester.*
Down, A., and Rule, M., 1971. *Chichester Excavations* 1.
Esmonde Cleary, A.S., 1989. *The Ending of Roman Britain.*
Green, C.J.S., 1982. 'The Cemetery of a Romano-British Community at Poundbury, Dorchester, Dorset' in S.M. Pearce (ed.) *The Early Church in Western Britain and Ireland, BAR* 102, 61–76.
Harman, M., *et al.*, 1981. 'Burials, bodies and beheadings in Romano-British and Anglo-Saxon cemeteries' *Bulletin British Museum of Natural History (Geology)* 35 (3), 145–88
Hirst, S.M., 1985. *An Anglo-Saxon inhumation cemetery at Sewerby, East Yorkshire* York University.
Holmes, J., 1965. *Chichester the Roman Town,* Chichester Papers 50.
Kendall, G., 1982. 'A study of grave orientation in several Roman and post-Roman cemeteries from southern Britain' *Arch. J.* 139, 101–23.
Knocker, G.M., 1955. 'Early burials and an Anglo-Saxon cemetery at Snell's Corner near Horndean, Hampshire' *Papers and Proceedings of the HFC* 19, 117–65.
Magilton, J., 1988. '23–35 The Hornet' in *The Archaeology of Chichester and District 1988*, 10–11.
McWhirr, A., *et al.*, 1982. *Romano-British Cemeteries at Cirencester,* Cirencester Excavations II.
Philpott, R., 1991. *Burial Practices in Roman Britain, BAR* 219.
Ross, A., 1967. *Pagan Celtic Britain.*
Salzman, L.F., 1935. *VCH (Sx), 3.*
Thomas, C., 1981. *Christianity in Roman Britain to AD 500.*
Watts, D., 1991. *Christians and Pagans in Roman Britain.*
Wenham, L.P., 1968. *The Romano-British Cemetery at Trentholme Drive, York,* MPBW Archaeological Reports 5.
Whimster, R., 1981. 'Burial practices in Iron Age Britain: A discussion and gazetteer of the evidence c. 700 BC–AD 43, *BAR* 90, parts i and ii.
Whiting, W., Hawley, W., and May, T., 1931. *Report on the Excavation of the Roman Cemetery at Ospringe, Kent,* Society of Antiquaries of London (Oxford).
Whytehead, R., 1986. 'The excavation of an area within a Roman cemetery at West Tenter Street, London E1' *Trans. London and Middlesex Archaeol. Soc.* XXXVII, 23–124.
Yeats, W.B., (ed.) n.d. *Irish Fairy and Folk Tales* Walter Scott Ltd, London.

## 4C   The Roman lead coffins from the Westgate cemetery

by J.A.P. Kenny

*Coffin I* CH.T.85, grave pit/fill A72 , skeleton 41
The coffin base, sides and ends are of one piece with sides and ends folded up (Toller 1977, type 2). The edges of the sides and ends were joined by crudely hammering them together. The coffin is 2040 mm long, tapering from 460 mm to 430 mm in breadth and from 300 mm to 210 mm in height. The lid, which is incomplete, is in a single piece 1700 mm long, tapering from 590 mm to 540 mm in breadth and with folded down sides from 60 mm to 120 mm in height. There are no nail holes, no sign of wooden structure and no decoration. The coffin contained an adult inhumation with the head orientated to 315 degrees (north-west).

*Coffin II* CH.T.87, grave pit 73, grave fill 10, skeleton 44 (Plate 11)
The coffin base and sides are of one piece with sides folded up (Toller 1977, type 3). Separate ends were attached by hammering small fillets of lead between the top 140 mm of the sides and the edges of the ends and over the edges of the base and bottom edges of the ends. The coffin, which is incomplete, is 1800 mm long, tapering from 460 mm to 350 mm in breadth and from 320 mm to 290 mm in height. The lid (also incomplete) is a single flat piece 1800 mm long and tapering from 590 mm to 550 mm in breadth. The foot end of the base and both sides and both ends of the lid were extended by the addition of puddles of hot lead beaten together and onto the existing lead sheet. There are no certain nail holes, the many holes, particularly in the lid, are probably the result of natural oxidization. There is no decoration and no sign of wooden structure, two nails found in the grave pit were probably residual. The coffin contained an adult inhumation and was buried in a grave pit 2400 mm by 1000 mm and 940 mm below the present ground surface with the head orientated to 306 degrees (slightly west of north-west).

   Though no trace of a wooden structure survived in either example, the sizes of both lids and lack of decoration on the lead indicate that both had external wooden casing. The lids were presumably heavy enough not to need securing.

   These are the first two Roman lead coffins to have been recorded from Chichester and, until more are discovered, it is hard to draw any conclusions about their typology. In comparison with other examples from elsewhere in Roman Britain they seem quite crude, and may have been constructed by unskilled craftsmen, to fulfil special requirements.

### BIBLIOGRAPHY
Toller, H., 1977. 'Roman lead coffins and ossuaria in Britain' *BAR 38.*

Plate 11    Theological College, the Westgate cemetery 1987. The lead coffin of burial 44 from the south-east

# 4D    A report on the human skeletal remains

**by Ronald D. Foden**

The bones in some cases were considerably decayed and friable and all the skulls and pelvic bones were fragmented to varying degrees, which posed practical problems of reconstruction in order to be able to assess overall morphology for sex determination. I have carried out a general survey of the bones as stored, with my objective being to determine, wherever possible, the sex and age at death of each individual, together with any relevant observations.

Very few bones were completely intact, these being for the most part the femur, tibia and humerus; not one box yielded an intact skull or pelvis. Most of the bones still had adherent soil. This caused problems with skull fragments, which were often covered with a concretion of soil, the removal of which required great care in order to avoid further fragmentation. The examination of the bones was carried out systematically using a prepared report sheet which was completed for each box. The individual bones and fragments were cleaned and examined in turn and when (or if) identified, assigned to and arranged in one of nine specified groups:

*Skull*
1. Cranial fragments
2. Elements of facial skeleton and maxillary dentition
3. Mandible and dentition

*Post-cranial*
4. Cervical vertebrae
5. Thoracic skeleton (including pectoral girdle, ribs, sternum and vertebrae)
6. Lumbar vertebrae and sacrum
7. Pelvis (or more correctly the innominate bones)
8. Upper limb
9. Lower limb

On completing this initial survey a clear impression was gained of the quantity and state of preservation of the bones from each grave, a summary of which is set out in Table A. It was clear at this stage that the material in some of the boxes was too sparse and poorly preserved to provide any useful evidence and so these were eliminated from further study.

The variation in content of the boxes as illustrated by Table A for the most part reflects the 'geographic' distribution of the graves, in that some features of the site (e.g. ditches) post-dating the cemetery had resulted in more damage to some areas than to others. However, there was also variation in the physical state of preservation of the bones from different graves.

## Method adopted for sex determination

The bone fragments previously allocated to each anatomical grouping were now examined for morphological characteristics indicative of the sex of the individual. In view of the fragmentary and incomplete nature of most of the remains, a systematic approach was adopted which it was felt would render as much evidence as possible from each group; this centred on the use of a check-list of features to be searched for in each group. In compiling this check-list only those features that were held to be generally applicable to this sample were included. The literature on sexing criteria is very comprehensive, but for the most part assumes that specimens are intact and well-preserved. This is particularly the case with the skull and pelvis, the two most important sources of evidence.

The criteria included in the check-list were by no means exhaustive, but provided a useful framework of reference for this sample. In compiling the list the recommendations of a working party of European anthropologists regarding sexing criteria was also referred to (*Journal of Human Evolution* 1980, 9, 517–49). In applying the criteria to each set of remains a system was adopted whereby the features observed were categorised and scored on a scale:

| Hyperfeminine | Feminine | Indeterminate | Masculine | Hypermasculine |
|:---:|:---:|:---:|:---:|:---:|
| −2 | −1 | 0 | +1 | +2 |

This enabled the variations in the features displayed in each anatomical group to be equated so that an assignment of sex could be made on the accumulated evidence. Using this procedure the assessments given in Table B were made.

## Age estimation

The preliminary survey of the remains established that nearly all were adult specimens. Age estimations for adult skeletons cannot be made with the degree of precision that it is possible to attain with the remains of immature subjects, where the age-specific indicators of epiphyseal union and dental development enable an accuracy of plus or minus 1 year to be claimed.

The teeth are considered to be by far the most important indicators of age in the skull, and, as is the case with this sample, often provide the only consistent source of evidence throughout a series in which decay and fragmentation have reduced the number of skeletal indicators available for assessment. Age-related changes which occur in the mature dentition enable estimates of age of plus or minus 10 years to be made.

The preliminary survey revealed that varying amounts of the dentition were present in the remains from 29 of the excavated graves. It was decided that the pattern of attrition in the molar teeth would provide a comprehensive means of age assessment in this sample. A classification chart compiled by Brothwell was used for the comparisons. This chart is based on the molar wear patterns which have been observed in various series of British skulls, ranging from the Neolithic to the medieval period. In using this system the broad assumption has to be made that rates of molar wear have been similar throughout all of the

## Table A

Anatomical groupings used as headings:
1. Cranial fragments
2. Elements of facial skeleton and maxillary dentition
3. Mandible and dentition
4. Cervical spine
5. Thoracic skeleton (inc. pectoral girdle, sternum and vertebrae)
6. Lumbar vertebrae and sacrum
7. Innominate bones
8. Upper limb
9. Lower limb.

| Grave no | Anatomical grouping | | | | | | | | |
|---|---|---|---|---|---|---|---|---|---|
|  | 1 | 2 | 3 | 4 | 5 | 6 | 7 | 8 | 9 |
| 1 | R | $\frac{1}{2}$ | R | R | R | ? | $\frac{1}{2}$ | R | M |
| 2 | R | M | M | ? | R | R | $\frac{1}{2}$ | R | R |
| 3 | R | ? | $\frac{1}{2}$ | ? | R | R | R | R | R |
| 4 | R | R | $\frac{1}{2}$ | ? | R | ? | $\frac{1}{2}$ | R | R |
| 5 | $\frac{1}{2}$ | ? | ? | ? | R | ? | ? | R | R |
| 6 | R | R | R | R | R | ? | ? | $\frac{1}{2}$ | $\frac{1}{2}$ |
| 7 | R | R | $\frac{1}{2}$ | ? | ? | ? | $\frac{1}{2}$ | $\frac{1}{2}$ | R |
| 8 | R | ? | $\frac{1}{2}$ | ? | R | R | R | R | R |
| 9 | R | ? | $\frac{1}{2}$ | ? | ? | $\frac{1}{2}$ | $\frac{1}{2}$ | $\frac{1}{2}$ | R |
| 10 | R | R | R | R | R | $\frac{1}{2}$ | $\frac{1}{2}$ | R | R |
| 11 | R | $\frac{1}{2}$ | R | $\frac{1}{2}$ | R | R | R | R | R |
| 12 | — | — | — | — | — |  |  |  |  |
| 13 | — | — | — | — | — | — | — | — | — |
| 14 | — | — | — | — | — |  |  |  |  |
| 15 | R | ? | $\frac{1}{2}$ | R | $\frac{1}{2}$ | $\frac{1}{2}$ | R | R | R |
| 16 | R | R | $\frac{1}{2}$ | $\frac{1}{2}$ | $\frac{1}{2}$ |  | R | R | R |
| 17 | — | — | — | — | — |  |  |  |  |
| 18 | — | — | — | — | — | — | — | — | — |
| 19 | — | — | — | — | — |  |  |  |  |
| 20 | $\frac{1}{2}$ | ? | ? | ? | ? | ? | $\frac{1}{2}$ | ? | $\frac{1}{2}$ |
| 21 | R | $\frac{1}{2}$ | R | $\frac{1}{2}$ | $\frac{1}{2}$ | M | M | $\frac{1}{2}$ | $\frac{1}{2}$ |
| 22 | ? | $\frac{1}{2}$ | $\frac{1}{2}$ | $\frac{1}{2}$ | $\frac{1}{2}$ | $\frac{1}{2}$ | $\frac{1}{2}$ | $\frac{1}{2}$ | $\frac{1}{2}$ |
| 23 | $\frac{1}{2}$ | ? | ? | ? | $\frac{1}{2}$ | ? | $\frac{1}{2}$ | $\frac{1}{2}$ | $\frac{1}{2}$ |
| 24 | $\frac{1}{2}$ | $\frac{1}{2}$ | ? | $\frac{1}{2}$ | $\frac{1}{2}$ | $\frac{1}{2}$ | $\frac{1}{2}$ | $\frac{1}{2}$ | $\frac{1}{2}$ |
| 25 | R | $\frac{1}{2}$ | R | ? | $\frac{1}{2}$ | M | M | $\frac{1}{2}$ | M |
| 26 | — | — | — | — | — | — | — | — | — |
| 27 | — | — | — | — | — |  |  |  |  |
| 28 | R | $\frac{1}{2}$ | R | ? | $\frac{1}{2}$ | $\frac{1}{2}$ | $\frac{1}{2}$ | $\frac{1}{2}$ | $\frac{1}{2}$ |
| 29 | — | — | — | — | — | — | — | — | — |
| 30 | — | — | — | — | — |  |  |  |  |
| 40 | R | $\frac{1}{2}$ | R | $\frac{1}{2}$ | $\frac{1}{2}$ | M | M | $\frac{1}{2}$ | $\frac{1}{2}$ |
| 41 | $\frac{1}{2}$ | $\frac{1}{2}$ | $\frac{1}{2}$ | ? | ? | R | ? | $\frac{1}{2}$ | $\frac{1}{2}$ |
| 42 | R | R | R | R | $\frac{1}{2}$ | R | $\frac{1}{2}$ | R | R |
| 43 | $\frac{1}{2}$ | $\frac{1}{2}$ | R | $\frac{1}{2}$ | $\frac{1}{2}$ | ? | ? | R | R |
| 44 | ? | ? | $\frac{1}{2}$ | ? | ? | $\frac{1}{2}$ | ? | — | — |
| 45 | R | ? | $\frac{1}{2}$ | $\frac{1}{2}$ | $\frac{1}{2}$ | ? | $\frac{1}{2}$ | R | R |
| 46 | ? | — |  |  |  | — |  | — | — |
| 47 | R | R | R | R | ? | R | R | R | R |
| 48 | R | $\frac{1}{2}$ | $\frac{1}{2}$ | ? | ? | $\frac{1}{2}$ | $\frac{1}{2}$ | ? | ? |
| 49 | ? | M | M | M | ? | M | R | $\frac{1}{2}$ | R |
| 50 | ? | $\frac{1}{2}$ | ? | ? | ? | — | M | — | — |
| 51 | R | $\frac{1}{2}$ | R | R | R | R | R | R | R |
| 52 | $\frac{1}{2}$ | ? | $\frac{1}{2}$ | — | — | — | — | — | — |
| 53 | — | — | — | — | $\frac{1}{2}$ |  |  |  |  |
| 54 | $\frac{1}{2}$ | $\frac{1}{2}$ | ? | ? | ? | $\frac{1}{2}$ | ? | ? | ? |
| 55 | ? | ? | ? | $\frac{1}{2}$ | $\frac{1}{2}$ | $\frac{1}{2}$ | $\frac{1}{2}$ | $\frac{1}{2}$ | $\frac{1}{2}$ |
| 56 | M | M | M | M | M | M | M | M | $\frac{1}{2}$ |
| 57 | ? | ? | $\frac{1}{2}$ | R | R | R | ? | R | R |
| 58 | M | M | M | M | M | R | R | R | R |
| 59 | ? | $\frac{1}{2}$ | R | R | R | R | R | R | R |

*Key*: R = good representation of group recognised; 1/2 = a few fragments of the group recognised; ? = greatly decayed and fragmented, difficult to identify; M = not represented, presumed to be missing; — = not examined or eliminated from study.

90

**Table B**

| Grave no | Overall assessment | Grave no | Overall assessment | Grave no | Overall assessment |
|---|---|---|---|---|---|
| 1 | M | 20 | — | 46 | — |
| 2 | M | 21 | F | 47 | O |
| 3 | F | 22 | F | 48 | O |
| 4 | M | 23 | F | 49 | O |
| 5 | M | 24 | M | 50 | M? |
| 6 | M | 25 | M? | 51 | M |
| 7 | M | 28 | M | 52 | — |
| 8 | F | 40 | F | 53 | — |
| 9 | M | 41 | M? | 54 | M |
| 10 | M | 42 | M | 55 | F |
| 11 | M | 43 | F | 56 | — |
| 15 | F | 44 | — | 57 | M |
| 16 | F | 45 | M | 58 | — |
| | | | | 59 | M |

*Key*: M = determined as male on 3 or more criteria; F = determined as female on 3 or more criteria; M?/F? = sex determined on basis of single feature; — = insufficient evidence available; O = juvenile remains.

earlier British populations. On this basis estimates of age are made which assign the individual to one of four age categories (Brothwell 1981) (Table C). The age estimate for grave no 15 is tentative as the evidence available could not be considered conclusive; the assignment represents the minimum age category. Age estimates were made using other methods for the juvenile remains in graves nos 48 and 49. Age estimates for other remains have not been made as they would for the most part be purely conjectural in the absence of specific skeletal or dental indicators.

**Table C**
**Age assignments using Brothwell's chart**

| Grave no | | Grave no | | Grave no | |
|---|---|---|---|---|---|
| 1 | 33–45 | 16 | 25–35 | 47 | 8–9 |
| 2 | 25–35 | 21 | 17–25 | 48 | 5[a] |
| 4 | 33–45 | 25 | 25–35 | 49 | 2 months[b] |
| 6 | 17–25 | 28 | 25–35 | 50 | 33–45 |
| 7 | 45+ | 40 | 33–45 | 51 | 25–35 |
| 8 | 17–25 | 4. | 45+ | 52 | 45+ |
| 9 | 25–35 | 42 | 25–35 | 54 | 45+ |
| 10 | 25–35 | 43 | 45+ | 55 | 45+ |
| 11 | 45+ | 44 | 45+ | 57 | 45+ |
| 15 | (33–45?) | 45 | 45+ | 59 | 45+ |

[a] Age assignment by dental development.
[b] Age assignment by length of femur (Krogman 1962).

**Conclusions**

The fragmented nature of the skeletons and general state of preservation made observations of bony pathology difficult. As far as could be reliably ascertained no evidence of ante-mortem fractures was seen in any specimen nor any signs of traumatic injury other than grave no 51 (p. 93). Most skeletons in the 33–45 age bracket and above exhibited osteoarthritic changes of varying degrees, particularly of the vertebral bodies.

Dental attrition was marked, and some specimens showed signs of having had chronic infections associated with particularly worn and broken teeth. Dental caries when present was of the type due to stagnation around the cervical margins of lower premolar teeth, and is associated with the breakdown of teeth due to high rates of attrition rather than the primary decalcification and penetration of enamel, which is seen in the modern-day population. Overall, the pattern of tooth loss, caries and attrition was similar to that reported for other Romano-British population groups (Whittaker *et al.* 1985).

The dentitions from graves nos 4 and 40 had gross depositions of calculus, to a degree that would not normally be consistent with the consumption of a diet which required vigorous use of the dentition, as manifest by the amount of tooth loss due to attrition. This calculus deposition could perhaps be interpreted as being due to a change in diet as a consequence of a febrile terminal illness extending over weeks or a few months.

In conclusion, to continue in a speculative vein, the remains from grave no 41 were of interest. This was a lead coffin burial, the coffin having been flattened to encase the bones by the weight of the overlying soil. The skeleton had been crushed, and was comminuted when separated from the coffin. However, from an examination of the bone fragments as stored at the depot the indications were that the remains were those of a male, in the 45+ age category. There was evidence of considerable osteoarthritic lipping of vertebral bodies, an indication of advanced years. This was not borne out by portions of the dentition that were examined. The wear on the surfaces of the upper second molars had not begun to eliminate the

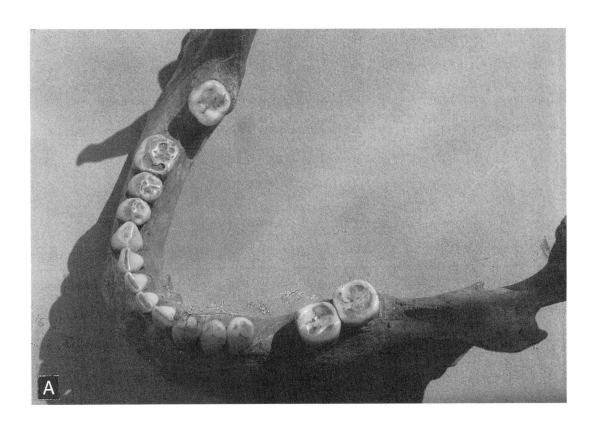

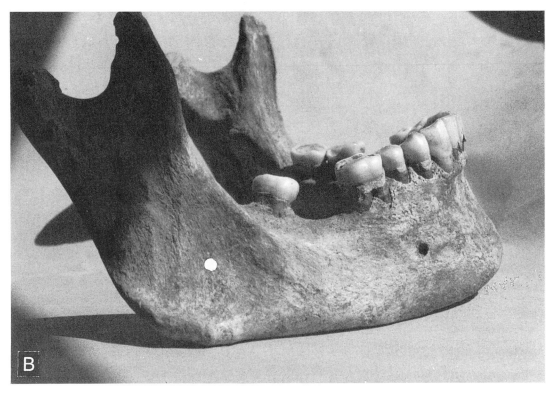

Plate 12A and B   Photograph of mandible of burial 42

natural fissure pattern, these teeth being comparable with those of individuals aged at 25–35 years. Such minimal wear in a person of advanced years could be accounted for by the early loss of the lower molars (these were not found with the stored remains). Alternatively it could denote the fact that the dentition had not been subject to the rigours of a coarse diet throughout the lifetime of the individual, indicative perhaps of a cultural divide. Examination of remains from similar burials at other sites would be interesting in this regard.

The bones from grave no 42, although fragmented, were in a good state of preservation. The mandible was particularly well preserved and remained intact. The teeth are free from dental caries and moderately attrited, (Plates 12A and B). What is of great interest is the loss of two molar teeth from this jaw. The left first molar and the right second molar are both missing.

It is not unusual to find broken-down molar teeth among the dentitions of the Romano-British population, or indeed missing teeth, particularly in the older age groupings. Teeth subjected to a high degree of attrition are susceptible to coronal fractures with subsequent decay resulting in total destruction of the crown of the tooth. In all such cases, however, the roots of the affected teeth usually remain in the jaw and are exposed above the surface of the alveolar bone. In the case of the mandible from grave no 42 no roots are visible. A radiograph (Plate 13) of this jaw reveals that nothing remains of the lower left first molar; but the outline of the lamina-dura of the healed socket is plainly visible. Of the lower right first molar, part of the mesial root remains within the jaw and has been covered by a layer of remodelled bone. There can be very little doubt that these teeth were surgically extracted—the radiographic appearances are classically those of healed extraction sockets—and in the context of this particular individual's dentition, no other explanation for the absence of these teeth is more likely. The presence of the retained root apex of the lower right first molar with an overlying layer of bone indicates that the main body of the tooth was forcibly removed leaving behind the root fragment in the socket (Plate 14—radiograph).

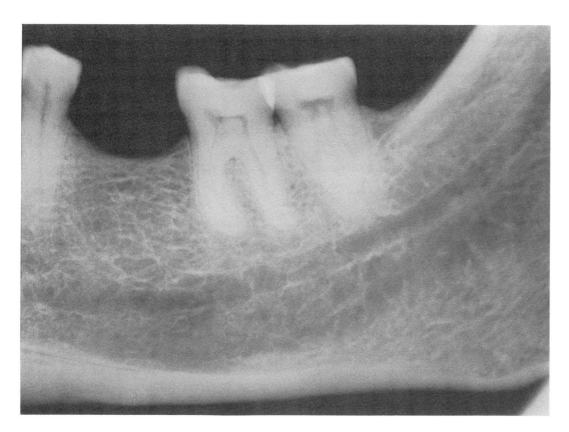

Plate 13    Radiograph of left body of mandible, burial 42

Tooth extraction forceps have been found in Roman settlements, although they do not appear to have been discovered in Britain. There is a report of a site excavated in Rome which has been interpreted as having been used by a tooth drawer, large numbers of extracted teeth (many fractured) having been found in an associated drainage channel (Weinberger 1940). Studies of large series of Romano-British skulls, which have included the taking of radiographs, have not produced reports of anything comparable to the findings described above (Whittaker *et al.* 1985).

Grave no 49. These few fragmented bones were the remains of a baby. The length of the intact femur (86 mm) indicates that the death occurred within two months of birth.

Grave no 51. These bones were fragmented but generally well preserved. Of particular interest were the left tibia and fibula which were intact and both showing evidence of a well-united, old fracture.

Grave no 52. The cranial fragments of this individual showed considerable thickening characteristic of Paget's disease of bone. (This has an estimated incidence of 3% in a modern-day elderly population.)

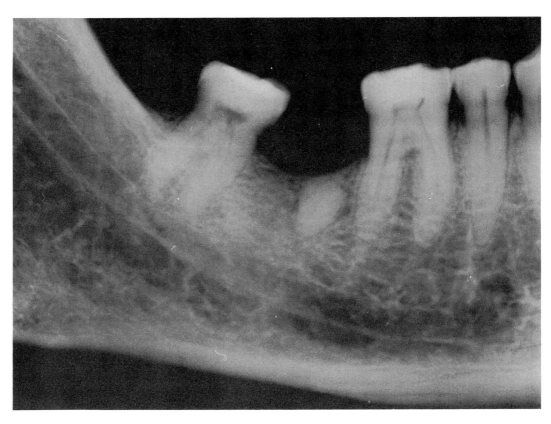

Plate 14    Radiograph of right body of mandible, burial 42

**BIBLIOGRAPHY**

Brothwell, D.R., 1981. *Digging up bones*, 72, British Museum (Nat. Hist.), Oxford University Press.

Goodyear, F.H., 1971. *Archaeological Site Science*, 146–9, Heinemann (London).

Krogman, W.M., 1962. *The Human Skeleton in Forensic Medicine* Thomas, USA.

Weinberger, B.W., 1940. 'Did dentistry evolve from the barbers, blacksmiths or from medicine?' *Bull. Hist. Med.* 8, 965–1011.

Whittaker, D.K., *et al.* 1985. 'Quantitative assessment of tooth wear, alveolar crest height and continuing eruption in a Romano-British population' *Archs. Oral Biol.* 30, 6, 493–501.

# St. Peter the Great, West Street, 1982 (Fig. 5.1)

## by Alec Down

This redundant church was converted to secular use by Housetrend Ltd in 1982. The site is of particular interest as it lies near the presumed western boundary of the Roman public baths complex (Down 1978, 145 and fig. 7.3), and three trial holes were dug within the building to assess the archaeological potential in advance of excavating nineteen column base holes. In the event, the development was subsequently modified to avoid disturbance of the features below ground.

Observation during the digging of the trial holes was carried out by Frances Raymond and Brenda Ware and thanks are due to Mr Barry Motion of Housetrend Ltd for his co-operation.

### Trial Trench 1 (Figs. 5.1 and 5.2)

Dug from the level of the church floor to a depth of 2.2 m, it cut through a partially robbed Roman foundation aligned north–south, built of flints in creamy mortar. It was in excess of 0.70 m wide. West of it was the remains of a floor of *opus signinum* which had been laid above a dump of dirty yellow clay which in turn sealed the base of an earlier hypocaust. This consisted of a hard clay floor, baked by the heat to a depth of 150 mm and below this was a layer of dirty brown clay which rested on natural undisturbed clay.

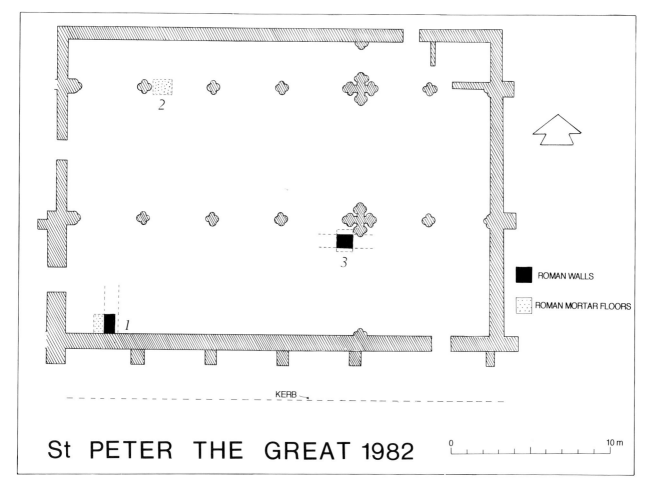

ROMAN WALLS

ROMAN MORTAR FLOORS

KERB

St PETER THE GREAT 1982

0          10 m

Fig. 5.1

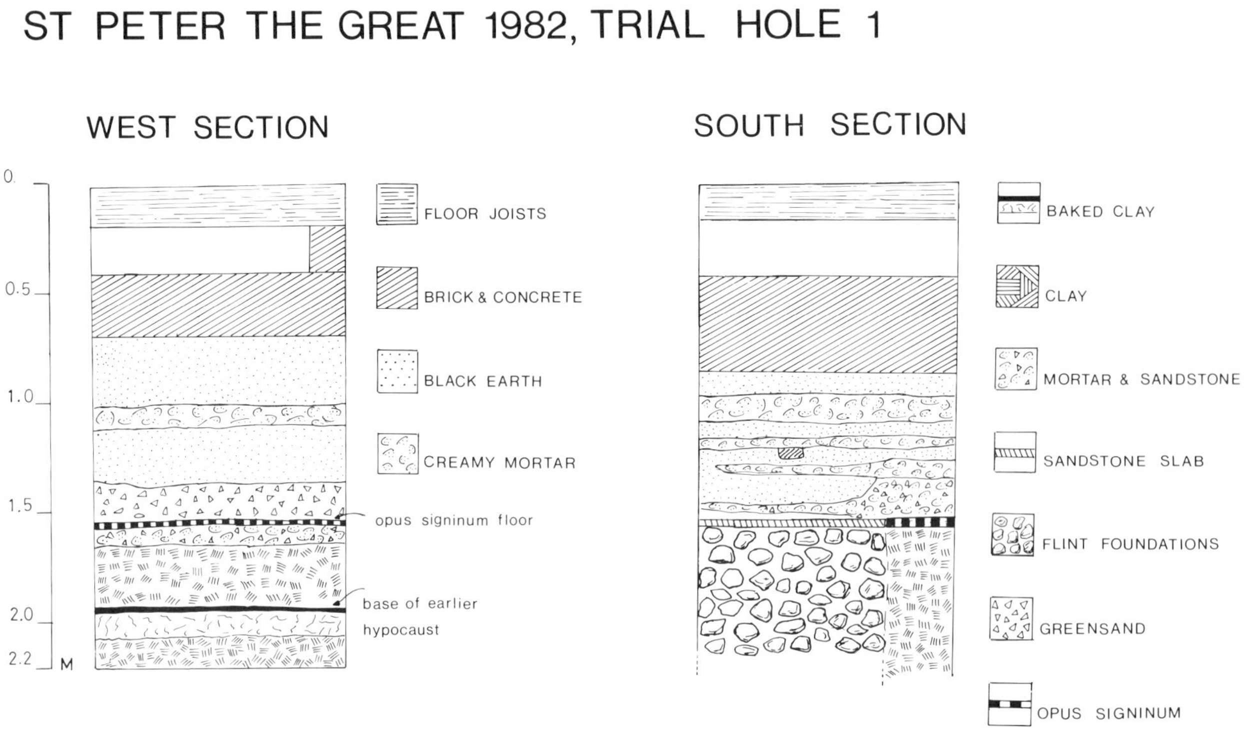

# ST PETER THE GREAT 1982, TRIAL HOLE 1

## WEST SECTION

0

0.5

1.0

1.5

2.0

2.2 M

FLOOR JOISTS

BRICK & CONCRETE

BLACK EARTH

CREAMY MORTAR

opus signinum floor

base of earlier
hypocaust

## SOUTH SECTION

BAKED CLAY

CLAY

MORTAR & SANDSTONE

SANDSTONE SLAB

FLINT FOUNDATIONS

GREENSAND

OPUS SIGNINUM

Fig. 5.2

## Trial Trench 2

At 1.6 m below the church floor were the remains of a white mortar floor which was 140 mm thick in places. This rested on a layer of dirty brown clay, similar to that in Trial Trench 1. The fill above the floor was black earth and it was clear that the top surface of the floor had been eroded by pit digging.

## Trial Trench 3

A Roman wall foundation of similar construction to the wall in Trial Trench 1 was found. It was aligned east–west, was 0.83 m wide and the top of the surviving foundation was 0.45 m below the church floor.

## Site history (compiled by Mr R.R. Morgan)

Sub-deanery (St Peter's Church) was built in 1852. Previously, the eastern half of the site was the city Custom House in 1790 and, before that, the corner house, which was a substantial freehold, was occupied by various families, of whom two are recorded: Crosweller (1534) and Bellingham (1580–1620). The western half of the site, which also included No 21 West Street, was owned by the Dean and Chapter. Four houses are recorded in 1521 and four cottages from 1563. The Norden Map of 1595 shows the north side of West Street completely occupied by houses and it is likely that there has been nothing other than domestic occupation on the site for most, if not all, of the post-Conquest period. Domesday gives eleven haws on the north side of the street.

## Discussion

There seems little doubt that the Roman features seen in the three trial trenches belong to the public baths and it is likely that the western end of the church might be near, if not on, the western limits of the baths. Trial Trench 1 shows that the room had been converted from a hot room to cold and the fact that the hypocaust floor had been subjected to considerable heat suggests that it was part of a *caldarium*, which would have been fired from a stokehole outside the building and almost certainly on the west side of it.

The subsequent history of the site, with the evidence for continuous domestic occupation over a long period suggests that the Roman levels are heavily disturbed by cess-pit digging in the areas where the gardens were. Below the frontages some robbing of the wall footings might have taken place during the period that the Cathedral was being built in the late 11th century, but the chances of recovering the plan of that part of the baths are quite good and should further development take place within the church in the future it should be preceded by archaeological excavation on as wide a scale as possible.

**REFERENCE**

Down, A., 1978. *Chichester Excavations 3* (Phillimore).

# 6

# Recent investigations of the city walls

## 6A    Introduction

Most of the observations, investigations and trial excavations reported on in this section stem from the programme of restoration and repairs to the walls carried out by a team from T. Couzens and Sons, builders, on behalf of Chichester District Council. In several instances the need to investigate was recognised by the builders themselves, and the authors are grateful to them for having drawn attention to features which might otherwise have gone unrecorded. One exception was the trial excavation at Pine's Yard bastion, which was undertaken to test a hypothesis about the age of the tower prior to a refurbishment of the yard and its buildings by the District Council. The other arose from damage resulting from the storm of October 1987 which brought down a section of the wall south of the site of the West Gate. The work was funded mainly by Chichester District Council, with some assistance from English Heritage for the last-named site. The authors are grateful to Bert Bridges and his successor John Bacon, the Council's Principal Surveyor responsible for the maintenance of the walls, for their co-operation and encouragement.

## 6B    A section through West Walls 1987–8

by J.R. Magilton

### SUMMARY

*In 1987–8, following damage to the rampart from a falling tree, a section was cut through the defences south of the west gate. Four main periods of activity were identified: (1) a uniform layer of soil pre-dating Roman occupation of the site, (2) features pre-dating the defences, including a street or lane and timber-framed buildings, (3) the Roman rampart and wall and (4) later features. The rampart and wall are considered to be contemporary and are dated to the late 3rd century.*

### INTRODUCTION

One of the many victims of the gales of October 1987 was a large tree which had been growing on the ramparts, next to the inner face of the city wall, about 75 m south of the site of the West Gate (Fig. 4A.1). The tree fell eastwards, into the garden, but as it fell the roots caused a considerable portion of the wall, which is brick-faced at this point, to collapse, revealing the flint and mortar core of its Roman precursor. In view of the damage already caused, and the further disturbance which would result from rebuilding the wall, the District Archaeological Unit was invited to cut a section through the defences at this point. There had been no investigation of the ramparts since 1959, when Holmes, in a section in the grounds of Cawley Priory in the south-east corner of the city, had recognised that at this point the rampart and wall were not contemporary (Holmes 1962). One objective of the 1987–8 excavation was to recover artefacts from the rampart in the hope of dating it more securely. Like many Romano-British urban earthwork defences, Chichester's rampart is conventionally dated to the later 2nd century and, as in many other instances (Crickmore 1984), the evidence is far from conclusive.

### THE EXCAVATIONS

The excavation (Site code CHW) was 10 m long and originally 4 m wide, later reduced to 2 m wide for operational and safety reasons. Work began in December 1987 and was completed early in the following year. Recording was carried out using the Unit's card index system. The sections were drawn at a scale of 1:10 and plans at 1:20. Original records and finds have been deposited with the Chichester District Museum. The fieldwork was funded by Chichester District Council and English Heritage, and jointly supervised by John Bowen and Christopher Down.

# WEST WALLS

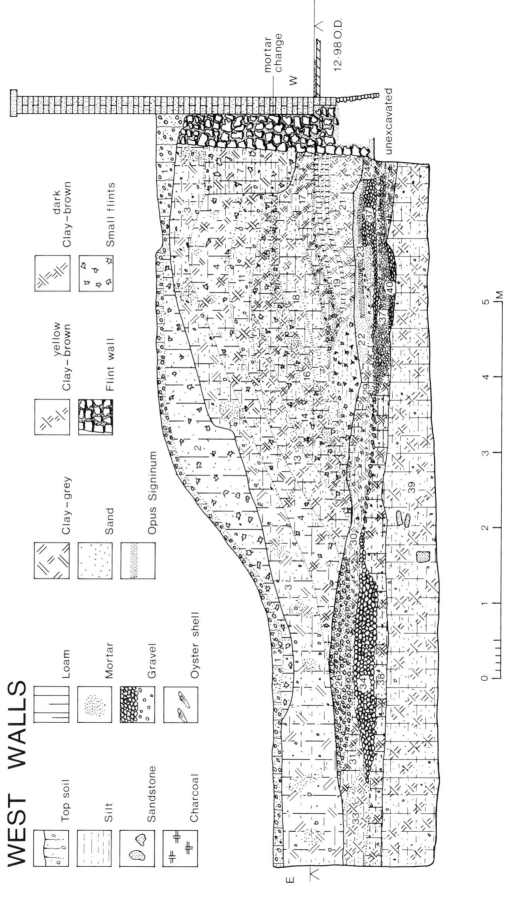

Fig. 6B.1   North-facing section through the city walls 1988. Scale 1:50

## DESCRIPTION

### Phase 1

The earliest layer encountered (Fig. 6B.1, 39 and Plate 15) was of light brown soil overlying natural at the base of the trench to an average depth of 0.65 m, becoming deeper towards the east. It contained pottery and a number of artefacts, including a bronze brooch (Fig. 33.1, no 4), and may be interpreted as a cultivation soil of early Roman and perhaps Iron Age date, pre-dating the earliest occupation in this area. There were no hints of the method of cultivation in the top of the underlying natural.

Plate 15    West Walls 1987–8, the north-facing section of the rampart

### Phase 2

The main features were two superimposed layers of gravel (34, 26) at the east end of the excavation, interpreted as a north–south lane which had been resurfaced, and the more complex remains of a timber-framed building at the west end of the excavation.

The earlier of the gravel layers 34 (Fig. 6B.1), over 3 m wide and 0.3 m thick at its deepest point, partly sealed a thin layer (38) of dark brown loam which extended across much of the site. Two linear indentations, interpreted as wheel-ruts (Fig. 6B.2A and Plates 16, 17 and 18), were visible on the surface of the gravel. They lay about 1.4 m apart. The gravel layer dipped to the east to produce a cambered surface. On this side a light brown clay layer (33) accumulated which seems to have been contemporary with the use of the gravelled surface. It contained an *as* of Domitian, AD 91–96. This layer was cut by two intersecting postholes (27, 35) and by a shallow linear feature (31), perhaps a roadside ditch.

The filling of 31 was a green silt layer (30) containing a large number of oyster shells which, at the western end of the trench, sealed two layers which must have been roughly contemporary with the road surface. The later of these was a layer of compact gravel and white mortar (37), partly sealed by a thin layer of dark grey silt, which incorporated, amongst other material, painted wall plaster, and this sealed a lens of hard-packed gravel (40)

Plate 16    West Walls 1987–8 during excavation. Roman street and wheel-ruts in foreground. Camera looking west

which appeared to have been cut into, or laid on, the general pre-occupation layer 39. Layer 37 is interpreted as debris from the destruction of a timber-framed building. Layer 40, if part of a linear feature, could be a metalled path pre-dating the creation of the lane to the east.

The later gravel layer 26 was of similar composition and dimensions to 34 and may be interpreted as a re-metalling after the earlier surface had become rutted and covered in silt. Unlike the original surface, 26 was cambered on both sides and showed no signs of wear. West of the lane was a layer of black soil and charcoal (29) which, to the west, was partly sealed by the remains of a building.

The principal feature at the western end of the excavation was a floor of *opus signinum* 23, found across the width of the trench, which extended about 2.7 m eastwards from the point where it was cut by the construction trench of the city wall (Fig. 6B.2,A). Its eastern edge formed a straight line which was not quite parallel with the lane and there was no trace of a wall foundation or construction trench to mark its limits. Beneath the floor were mortar lenses, presumably relating to the construction of the building of which it formed a part, and it was sealed by similar lenses (22) relating to the demolition of the building, which incorporated a quantity of *tesserae.*

Plate 17    West Walls 1987–8, the inside face of the Roman town wall viewed from the east

Plate 18    West Walls 1987–8, the Roman street surfaces sealed beneath the tail of the later rampart, seen from the north

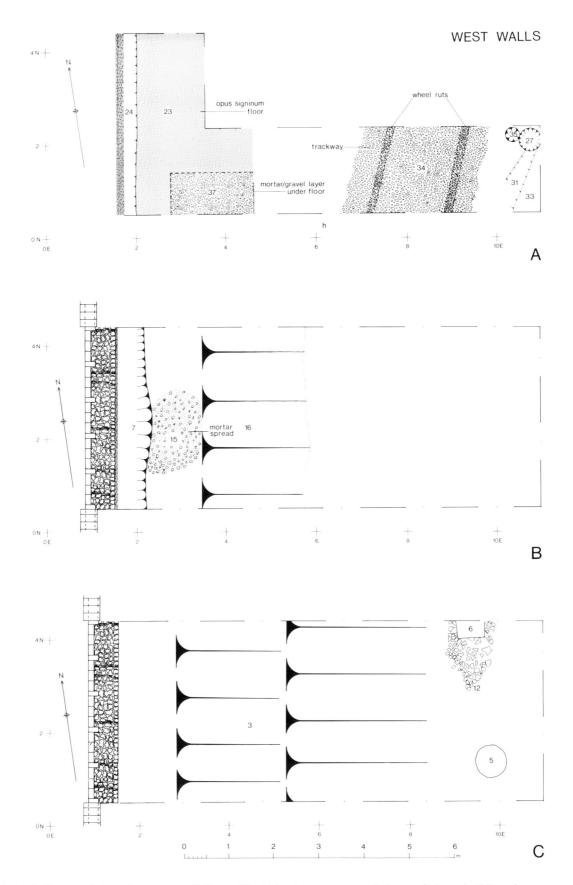

Fig. 6B.2 A. Features below the rampart. B. Layer 15 within the rampart, and the cut 7 for rebuilding the upper wall. C. Late features at the foot of the rampart. Scale 1:80

## Phase 3: the wall and rampart

The third phase of activity is represented by the construction of the wall and rampart over what had formerly been an area of settlement, even if peripheral to the main concentration of occupation. The building of the wall at this point pre-dated the rampart. The inner edge of its construction trench 24 was cut through layer 22 and earlier features. It had been backfilled with dark brown clay and large flints. The wall, of mortared flints, survived to a height of 2.5 m and was at least 0.8 m wide (its outer face was not found). It had no proper foundations and its base was about 0.8 m above the undisturbed natural clay. The inner face of the wall was made of carefully coursed large flints. At about 1.3 m above foundation level the flints were bonded by a mortar differing slightly in colour from that used in the lower part but despite this the wall appeared to be of uniform construction.

The rampart, or at least its lower portion, had been piled against the wall. The lowest level (21) was of yellow brown earth, almost certainly redeposited natural. Immediately on top was a layer (19) composed predominantly of yellow clay and lenses of what appeared to be dark loam which could represent decayed turf. This was capped by a layer of black soil (17), sandwiched between two narrow layers of mortar, clay and small flints. Both 17 and 19 contained material which was paralleled in the layers below 21, and could be explained if the layers had been derived from digging an associated ditch through the remains of demolished buildings. Successive layers were relatively 'clean'. Layer 18 is probably to be equated with layer 39, below the buildings, and layers 16, 14 and 13 may all represent redeposited natural for the most part, although some contained artefacts. Layer 11 contained some fragments of painted plaster and mortar, as did layer 4 forming the top of the original bank, which was roughly 2.2 m high at its maximum and at least 6.5 m wide.

As indicated above, the material for the rampart was almost certainly derived from the digging of an associated ditch. If, as Holmes (1962) has suggested, there were two V-shaped ditches outside the early defences, the sequence of deposits on this site suggests that the inner ditch was dug first, through layers of occupation, and the outer ditch, beyond the area of early settlement, supplied material for the upper rampart. This is a seemingly illogical order of events, since it would involve taking material across the top of (or perhaps round the end of) the inner ditch in order to complete the rampart. The material attributed to the inner ditch (layer 18 and those below it) would not have provided a wall-walk of suitable height on its own.

The rampart may have been built in two stages, the first consisting of layer 16 (i.e. the top spit from the outer ditch, if the sequence outlined above is correct) and those below it, the lower stage forming a platform at a height of about 1.5 m above the foundation trench from which the upper part of the wall was constructed. This was indicated by a large oval spread of clean mortar (15) incorporated within the rampart (Fig. 6B.2,B), interpreted as the remains of mortar mixed for wall construction.

The upper part of the wall seems to have been rebuilt on the east side, above the point where the change of mortar was noted, from a narrow platform (7 on Figs. 6B.1 and 6B.2,B) cut into the upper face of the rampart. This may have followed a localised collapse as no similar feature has been recorded elsewhere in Chichester. It is possible that the wall was essentially of a single phase of construction, that the rampart was for some reason heaped up higher than the wall and then cut back so that its upper part could be built, but this seems unlikely. Feature 7 was filled with light grey silt barely distinguishable from layer 3, the final Roman augmentation of the rampart.

## Phase 4: post-Roman activity

### The wall

The surviving stretch of wall south of the site of the West Gate is now fronted with 19th century red bricks. At the point where the excavations took place, an investigation of the area below the pavement in front of the wall revealed that, at foundation level, the wall was only one brick thick and rested on an earlier wall-face of small mortared flints traced to a depth of about 0.55 m. This may have been the wall-face in the Middle Ages; if so, the Roman wall had been reduced to less than half its original width by that date.

### The rampart

Post-Roman additions are represented by layer 2 on Fig. 6B.1. It must be suspected, in retrospect, that this layer incorporated several features which were not properly recognised in the course of excavation. The current uniform profile of the rampart, thought to be the result of 18th or 19th century landscaping, may have caused the truncation of post-Roman deposits although the Roman layers survive relatively intact despite disturbance from tree roots etc.

Late features within the rampart were discovered at the east end of the excavation. These included a spread of loose flints (12) capped by a small patch of mortared flints (6) which could be late Roman since they were directly sealed by layer 2, and a circular patch of chalk filling a pit or posthole cut into layer 2 (Fig. 6B.2,C).

## A SUMMARY OF THE DATING EVIDENCE (see Table 1)
**by J.A.P. Kenny**

### Phase 1 (pre-occupation)

Most of the finds from layer 39 (and from 38) indicate a 1st to early 2nd century date, and both yielded significant quantities of pre-Flavian samian and other fine wares. This material may, however, be residual, since layer 39 also apparently yielded a late 2nd century/early 3rd century colour-coated beaker and a small quantity of Trajanic samian. If this later pottery is regarded as intrusive, a mid 1st century date would be possible for layer 39 and a later 1st century/early 2nd century date for layer 38.

**Table 1**
**West Walls: dating evidence**

| Context | Samian | Other fine wares | Amphorae | Coins | Brooches | Coarse wares | |
|---|---|---|---|---|---|---|---|
| 1 | late 1st | | | | | post–med. –modern | |
| 2 | mid–late 2nd | 4th | | | | post–med. | |
| 3 | late 1st– early 2nd | mid 2nd– early 3rd | | | | 2nd–3rd | |
| 4 | mid–late 2nd | | 1st | | late 1st | late 3rd– mid–4th | |
| 8 | late 1st– early 2nd | | | | | 2nd–3rd | |
| 11 | mid–late 2nd | | | | | 2nd–3rd | |
| 12 | early–mid 2nd | | | | | 2nd–3rd | Bank |
| 13 | mid–late 1st | | | | | 2nd–3rd | |
| 14 | mid–late 2nd | | | | | 2nd–3rd | |
| 16 | mid 1st | | | | | 2nd–3rd | |
| 17 | late 1st– early 2nd | | | | | 2nd–3rd | |
| 18 | mid–late 2nd | | | | 1st | 2nd–3rd | |
| 19 | mid–late 2nd | | | | | 2nd–3rd | |
| 20 | late 1st– early 2nd | late 1st– mid 2nd | | | | 2nd–3rd | |
| 21 | mid–late 1st | | | | | 2nd–3rd | |
| 22 | mid late 2nd | | 2nd | | mid 1st– mid 2nd | 2nd–3rd | |
| 23 | 2nd | | | | | 2nd–3rd | |
| 26 | early–mid 2nd | | | late 4th | | 2nd–3rd | |
| 28 | early 1st | | | | | 2nd–3rd | Occupation Levels |
| 29 | late 2nd | | | | | 2nd–3rd | Below Bank |
| 30 | late 2nd | mid 2nd | 3rd | | | 2nd–3rd | |
| 33 | mid–late 1st | | | late 1st | | 2nd–3rd | |
| 37 | early 1st | | | | | 2nd–3rd | |
| 38 | late 1st– early 2nd | mid 2nd | | | 1st | 2nd–3rd | |
| 39 | late 1st– early 2nd | late 2nd– mid 3rd | 1st | | 1st | late 1st– early 2nd | |

## Phase 2 (occupation)

Layers 37 to 22 contained late 1st to early 3rd century material. Layer 38 was distinguishable from the others by its quantities of pre-Flavian pottery. If the floor layer 23 was laid immediately after the loss of the latest pottery sealed beneath it, and if the building which it represents had a fairly short life, the construction and destruction of the building may both be attributed to the early 3rd century.

## Phases 3 and 4 (rampart and wall)

Layers 21 to 1 have a mixture of earlier 1st century material, presumably derived from layers like 38 and 39 and of late 1st to 3rd century material like that in layers 37 to 22. In addition there are some later 3rd or 4th century sherds in layers 1, 2 and 4. The initial construction of the bank (represented by layer 4 and the layers below it) cannot have occurred before the early 3rd century on the basis of the *terminus post quem* provided by Phase 2 finds, and unless the coarse wares recorded from layer 4 are regarded as intrusive, a later 3rd century date would seem to be indicated for the rampart and wall.

Layer 3 may well represent an accumulation rather than a deposition of material, and a late 4th century coin, wrongly attributed to layer 26, may have come from layer 3. If, however, layer 3 was deposited, the coin may date the rebuilding of the upper part of the wall since the layer was distinguished only with difficulty from the fill of feature 7.

Layers 2 and 1 are respectively post-medieval and modern on the basis of coarse pottery recovered.

## A summary of the coarse pottery from West Walls

Almost 52 kg of coarse pottery were recovered from the West Walls excavation. Of this, 59% came from the bank (20% from layer 4, 8% each from layers 2, 14 and 18), 31% from the occupation levels below the bank (15% from layer 38 and 5% from layer 22) and 10% from layer 39 below the occupation levels. The majority of sherds are of unidentified local greyware fabrics, which though often similar to some of the Alice Holt/Farnham wares are probably more likely to have come either from the Rowlands Castle kilns some 15 km away or from an unknown local source. Small quantities of Black-Burnished ware are also present.

More than 180 individual diagnostic sherds have been identified with reference to published material from local sites, particularly Fishbourne Palace (Cunliffe 1971, II). The main forms are a group of dishes and platters, jars and bowls with quite a wide potential date range. Though many, especially the jars, may continue through the 3rd century, the majority probably date from the late 1st and 2nd centuries. Large numbers of imitation Gallo-Belgic beakers and platters and some bowls or dishes in the local Atrebatic tradition may not outlive the 1st century. Only one rimsherd of a flanged bowl (Fishbourne type 356) from layer 4 may be of later 3rd or even 4th century manufacture.

Though accurate dating of the coarse wares is impossible, the general indications are that layer 39 is mid 1st to early 2nd century, the occupation levels below the bank are 2nd to early 3rd century and the layers within the bank are a redeposited mixture of the two, perhaps with some later intrusions.

A full catalogue of the sherd by sherd identifications is included in the Level 3 archive.

## Roman brick and tile

Almost 65.5 kg of Roman brick and tile was recovered together with about 3 kg of medieval or post-medieval roof tile (all the latter from contexts 1, 2 and 3). Each fragment was examined to identify fabric, form and any surface impressions. Samples of each fabric have been retained, together with every fragment of flue tile and other tile with unusual impressions. The complete tile record, including drawings of all markings and impressions and the results of analysis will form part of the level 3 archive.

Analysis of the quantities of tile by layer is limited by the small size of the sample; however, if the bank (contexts 3–21) was constructed from material derived from ditches cut through layers of occupation similar to those beneath the bank then it should be possible to relate layers in the bank to those beneath it. Thus layer 4, containing 32% of all tile, is possibly a reflection of layers 26, 29 and 30 (23% of all tile), while layers 7, 16 and 21 (1% of all tile) may reflect layer 39 (3.5% of all tile from a layer with a volume 20% of the total).

The types of tile are as follows: 48.7% tegula and 6.5% imbrex (ratio 7.5:1), 35.9% brick, 5.2% flue tile and 3.7% water pipe. Almost all the fragments showed only minor variation on a single basic fabric which is presumably based on a fairly local clay source. Typically it has small, medium, large and very large ferruginous inclusions and an even spread of very fine micaceous inclusions, sometimes with blobs and streaks of white clay. Occasionally the fabric is tempered by the addition of sand or grog, sometimes in large quantities. Colour can vary greatly, depending on firing, from buff-orange to blue-grey. Other fabrics, notably one with large white inclusions, possibly limestone, occur in such small quantities that it is hard to explain their relevance. It is tempting to note that there seems more variation in the flue tile fabrics than generally, perhaps implying the specialist manufacture of these more complex forms. Three of the fragments of flue tile are relief-patterned, the largest having Lowther's Die 20, and date from the late 1st or early 2nd centuries AD.

## DISCUSSION
### by J.R. Magilton

### The early buildings

The only comparable material to the remains of buildings beneath the ramparts comes from Holmes' 1959 trench outside the walls to the south, where fragments of structures survived between the town ditches (Holmes 1962). In both instances the area which survived and was examined is so small that no detailed discussion is possible, beyond pointing out that both sites produced evidence indicating high-quality buildings with mosaics, tessellated floors and walls of painted plaster. These may have been the homes of Chichester's wealthier citizens who preferred to live at a distance from the commercial centre but, if so, it is surprising that they apparently lacked the political influence to have their houses enclosed within the city defences. Settlement outside the north walls was recorded in Franklin Place, where two Roman wells were examined in 1967 (Down and Rule 1971, 9) but their dates relative to the establishment of the defences is unknown. Further to the east, where New Park Road joins the ring-road, 1st century pits were recorded in 1973-4 (Down 1978, 7–9) but these need not indicate settlement. Beyond the east gate, at the Needlemakers site, evidence for early settlement was discovered in 1976–8 (Down 1981) but this is so distant from the walled city that the nature of occupation may be classified as suburban, if not rural. In brief, other than on the west side, there is no evidence that areas of occupation were excluded when the defences were erected.

### The wall and rampart

The traditional date for the origin of Chichester's defences is the later 2nd century (Down 1988, 53–6). It has been assumed that the first phase consisted of two V-shaped ditches and a rampart. The wall belonged to a secondary phase, when the face of the rampart was cut back and the wall built, and the bastions belonged to a final phase (traditionally after the 'barbarian conspiracy' of AD 367) when the original ditches were replaced by a wide flat-bottomed ditch.

The relative dates of the wall and rampart were determined by one section cut by Holmes in 1959 (Holmes 1962) and apparently confirmed by analogy with Silchester and elsewhere. The implicit assumption is that earlier excavators had simply failed to notice a cut-back in the face of the rampart for the insertion of a wall. Although some of the earlier section drawings (e.g. Wilson 1957a fig. 3) show a sequence which is stratigraphically impossible, they appear to indicate that the bank was piled up after the wall was built; on balance, it is Holmes' section which is the odd one out. This does not cast doubts on the accuracy of Holmes' drawing but simply implies that by chance he excavated a section where the original wall had been totally rebuilt. It has been suggested above that at West Walls only the bottom 1.3 m of the original wall survived, so there is nothing improbable in the total rebuilding of portions of the enceinte.

The nature of the wall excavated by Holmes differs from that in other sections. Holmes shows an offset between the inner face of the wall and the wider foundations, whereas Rae's nearby section (Rae 1951–2, fig. 17) shows the wall and its foundation without an offset, as does Wilson at Priory Park (Wilson 1957a, fig. 3). Excavations by Down just north of the west gate through the levelled defences (Down and Rule 1971, 143–7) revealed only the foundations of the wall which at this point were 1.8 m (6 Roman feet) wide. This corresponds to the width of the wall recorded by Holmes in 1959 (the foundations were wider) and suggests that there was no offset immediately above the foundations. The implication would appear to be that where the wall needed to be entirely rebuilt it was reconstructed on broader foundations, at least in the Cawley Priory area. Additional confirmation that stretches were rebuilt comes from examination of the bastions. The wall face behind the Palace bastion (Down, this volume) was of flints, whereas behind the Friary Close bastion it was of small dressed stones (Wilson 1957a, 10–11).

Parallels for the contemporary construction of walls and ramparts at urban sites can be found at Caistor St

Edmund, Ancaster, Cambridge, Godmanchester and Canterbury (Johnson 1983, 131–2). In military architecture the provision of an earthen rampart was becoming archaic at the time when the first Saxon Shore forts were built, and the presence of a bank has been used as a criterion in defining early forts within the system (Johnson 1976, 102–3). The advantages of bank and wall construction were twofold. Firstly, constructing a rampart solved the problem of disposal of soil from the digging of ditches and, second, the retaining wall could be narrower than a free-standing wall, an important consideration where good building materials were scarce. The construction of the walls of Chichester without tile-courses is paralleled at Canterbury and the Saxon Shore fort at Dover (Johnson, *loc. cit.*) and is another feature indicating a relatively early date, suggesting that all three may have been contemporary.

## The date of the defences

As stated in the introductory section, one of the main purposes of sectioning the rampart was to recover a large sample of material in order to reassess its date. This was not because the 'traditional' late 2nd century date was considered unlikely, but because it was felt that the information from earlier excavations was insufficient to justify it.

Unless an improbably large quantity from the 1987–8 excavation is dismissed as intrusive in the layers to which it has been ascribed, the rampart cannot be as early as the traditional date demands. The discrepancy is almost certainly due to the past practice, exemplified by Wilson (1957a) in particular, of relying on samian ware, with all the associated heirloom problems, as the main dating medium. It is noteworthy that a reliance on samian and other early fine wares alone would have allowed the 1987-8 site to fit into the traditional dating scheme. On the other hand, the more numerous and potentially more useful coarse wares have not yet received the detailed local study which would enable them to be dated with precision, and it must be suspected that, even when such work has been done, it will be found that many forms remained in production over long periods.

For the 1987–8 site there are two possible chronologies. The more compressed assumes a very short-lived occupation period but still cannot allow the construction of the wall and rampart much before the middle of the 3rd century. This involves dismissing the late 3rd to mid 4th century coarsewares in layer 4 as intrusive, or postulating that layer 4 represents a late augmentation of the bank.

Material in ramparts is inevitably in a secondary context, and what the pottery is able to date is not so much when the rampart was built as the last occupation of the buildings from which the rampart material was derived. However, in this instance, the last phase of use of the buildings seems to have immediately preceded the rampart's construction, so the problem does not arise. If the pottery ascribed to layer 4 is accepted as belonging to that layer, and if it is accepted that the earliest date for the diagnostic sherds cannot be earlier than the late 3rd century, and if it is accepted that layer 4 formed the top of the original bank, this allows an extended occupation period but puts the first phase of defences up to a century later than the traditional date.

The nature of Chichester's defences (wall without string courses but with a rampart) is of some additional help in dating the enceinte, since, as noted above, it is stylistically linked with both the Saxon Shore fort at Dover and Canterbury's city defences. Coin evidence supported by coarse pottery dates the the latter to AD 270–90 (Frere 1982, 51–6) and its construction may be seen in the context of Germanic piracy in the Channel. Chichester, virtually a coastal town, would have been even more under threat.

# 6C   Jubilee Park 1991

by R.G. Browse and J.R. Magilton

## INTRODUCTION (Fig. 6C.1)

Much of the face of the city wall north of Priory Lane along the eastern defences was renewed in the 1950s, but sections of an older facing which had then been sound had deteriorated by 1991. Two portions were removed in preparation for rebuilding, but the face of an older wall was revealed behind each, and the archaeological unit was asked to investigate in the hope that the date of the wall-face could be ascertained. Some additional work was carried out on the north-east corner of the defences, where the core of the Roman city wall was exposed, and two small trenches were dug to the south on the supposed sites of bastions. The better-preserved portion of the early wall-face has been consolidated and left exposed.

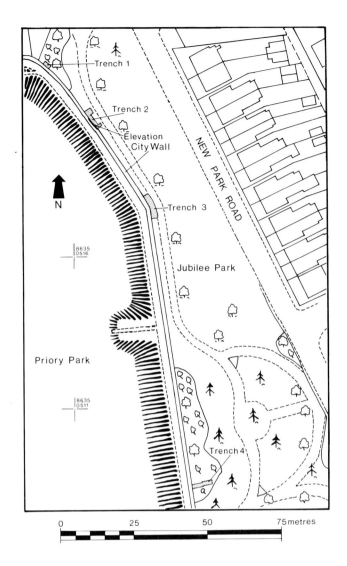

Fig. 6C.1   Jubilee Park 1991 location plan

## THE EXCAVATIONS

### Trench 1 (Fig. 6C.1)

A rectangular trench 2.4 × 1.0 m, situated at grid reference SU 86342/05222, 2.5 m south of the north-east corner of the city wall, where a mound occurred. On excavation the remains of a Roman wall footing (20) and a Victorian rubbish pit (21) were discovered.

The wall footing comprised four Greensand facing stones set in mortar on a layer of redeposited brickearth. This layer is either part of the original earth defences or a feature pre-dating the defences.

Just south of Trench 1 the core of the Roman wall had been exposed when an unstable recent facing was removed in readiness for rebuilding. All that survived was a thin skim representing the inside of the back face of the wall. However, there were two horizontal layers of silt incorporated in the core, one at a metre above ground-level and one at 1.5 m. These presumably represent material washed from the rampart at the conclusion of a period of building.

### Trench 2 (Fig. 6C.2)

Grid reference SU 86357/05205. Initially a rectangular trench 2.7 × 1.75 m, dug to investigate the relationship of the early wall face discovered by contractors to the foundations, but on discovery of a wall foundation another

110

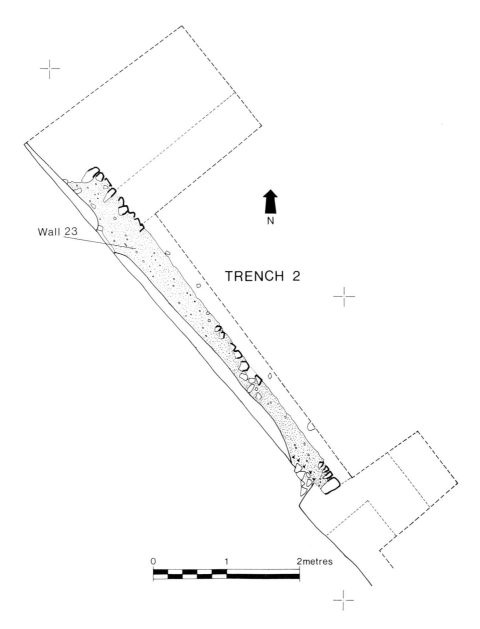

Fig. 6C.2  Jubilee Park 1991. Scale 1:50

small rectangular trench 1.8 × 0.9 m was excavated 4.5 m south of the initial trench and the intervening gap was excavated to a distance of 0.7 m from the face of the city wall.

The early wall face, composed of flints, Greensand and occasional pieces of Roman tile, survived as a narrow band of material roughly halfway up the existing city wall (Fig. 6C.3 and Plate 19). There was no post-Roman material incorporated in it. Below the wall-face the core of the Roman wall was exposed, and a band of silt separating two phases of construction was again noted. Above the wall-face the flint and mortar core of a later, probably modern, phase of the wall was recorded.

The foundation (23), on a north-west/south-east alignment, ran for the whole of its length of about 5.5 m partially under the existing city wall. At the north end the wall consisted of three courses of flint, with the top course protruding approximately 40 mm, tapering at its northern extreme to one course. Its southern end consisted of one course of flint. The wall is presumably the foundation of the original Roman city wall. The foundation appears to have survived within the trench, although not to the north or south of it, because it was dug to a greater depth at this point. Elsewhere in Jubilee Park the presumed base of the Roman foundations lies at or above the modern ground surface outside the city walls. Excavation did not reveal why a deeper foundation was thought necessary here. A pre-existing archaeological feature beneath the foundation which could have needed excavating and consolidating, or a dip in the natural, must be assumed.

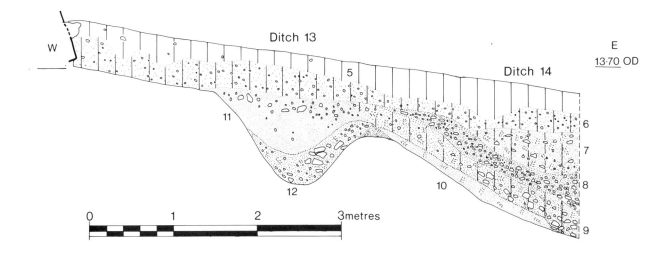

SECTION.
Trench 4

CH CW JP 91

W

Ditch 13

5

E
13·70 OD

Ditch 14

11

12

10

6

7

8

9

0    1    2    3metres

ELEVATION.
City Wall

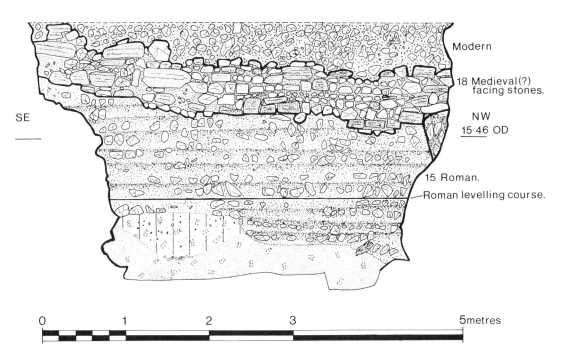

SE

Modern

18 Medieval(?)
facing stones.

NW
15·46 OD

15 Roman.
Roman levelling course.

0    1    2    3    5metres

Fig. 6C.3    Jubilee Park 1991

## Trench 3 (Fig. 6C.1)

This was 7.9 × 1.6 m and formed a dog-leg running parallel to the city wall at SU 86376/05175. It was excavated because a bastion was suspected at this point. After removal of the topsoil, a row of flint and sandstone facing stones (24) became visible at the southern end of the trench, approximately 0.6 m from the city wall and running more or less parallel with it. On examination they appeared to be kerb stones, perhaps for a path. On the east side, butted against (24), was a layer of mortar and gravel, possibly metalling. Cut by a tree hole, the edging stones disappeared and only the gravel and mortar layer continued to the north end of the trench.

Plate 19   Jubilee Park, the outer face of the city wall looking west, showing the earlier wall face

## Trench 4 (Figs. 6C.1 and 6C.3)

This was 6.4 × 1.0 m on an east–west alignment at SU 86394/05084, the supposed site of another bastion.

After removal of scrub and topsoil, two ditches were discovered. The smaller ditch (13), 1.7 m east of the city wall, was U-shaped with a rounded bottom, and was cut away by a larger ditch (14) only partially excavated because its outer edge lay beyond the limit of the trench. An assemblage of medieval and post-medieval pottery and tile was found in the upper layer of ditch 14, but the lower levels of ditch 13 contained an Iron Age sherd, and those of 14, 1st century AD pottery. In profile the ditches are remarkably similar to those examined in 1959 at West Walls (Holmes 1962, 80).

## DISCUSSION

Trenches 3 and 4 were placed to test the theory that bastions should exist at 96 m intervals around the wall. No traces of bastion footing were discovered, but more surprising was the lack of foundations for the wall itself, with only a very shallow footing surviving in Trench 2. This absence of foundations can be explained by the possibility that a general lowering of ground levels outside the wall had taken place (the ground surface outside the wall is as much as 0.8 m lower than that inside), presumably when the medieval defensive ditch was back-filled. Alternatively the ground may have been lowered in the Middle Ages as a means of increasing the relative height of the Roman walls without recourse to building. This may be thought improbable because instability would result, but it seems to be attested at Doncaster (Buckland, Magilton and Hayfield 1989, 76). The two ditches sectioned in Trench 4 probably represent one of the original Roman ditches (13) and a medieval re-cut (14). The fact that the medieval ditch is within 3 m of the wall indicates that no bastions survived when it was dug and that any bastion foundations would have been destroyed by its construction, if not by the deliberate lowering of the ground level.

The two newly discovered areas of wall facing were constructed on top of the Roman rubble core, presumably to replace sections of the wall which were in bad repair. The rebuilding may have taken place at at any time in the Middle Ages, though it is most likely that it was as part of the construction of the Norman castle in the late 11th century. According to the contractors, nothing similar had been found elsewhere during the repair of the walls. Layers of silt within the core of the Roman wall had been noted elsewhere by the contractors, but have not been recorded before. The same phenomenon was seen west of the Palace bastion.

## 6D    The Palace bastion 1985 (Fig. 6D.1 and Plates 20 and 21)

**by Alec Down**

Repairs to the City walls by contractors working for the Chichester District Council involved the stripping and replacement of the top 'skin' of flintwork which covered the original core of the Roman wall, and which had been added at various times since the late 19th century. Recent frost damage had resulted in considerable areas requiring replacement to the wall and surviving bastion in the south-west corner of the city.

   The following notes were compiled during an archaeological survey of the bastion following the discovery of a large 'void' below it.

1. The original face of the Roman wall was 1 m forward of the present line (see Fig. 6D.1, west elevation) and it is clear that this is due to weathering over the last 1600 years. Although this has been noted before from an examination of the foundations in various parts of the town, it is the first time that it has been possible to see an upstanding face of the Roman wall as it would have been in the late 4th century AD.

   It was noted that the flints were pointed with pink *opus signinum*, but whether this was done when the wall was originally constructed or whether it was added in the late 4th century when the bastion was built, is impossible to say. From an examination of the exposed face in the void below the bastion there did not seem to have been much, if any, erosion between the construction date and the late 4th centuries unless the face of the wall had been repaired before the bastion was built up against it.

2. At a point 1.68 m up from modern ground level there was a change in the mortar. Below the line, which was clearly defined, the mortar was a yellowish mix, while above it and extending up to 2.75 m, it was greyish in colour.

   This change in colour might indicate that the bastion had been rebuilt from that point, or that, for some reason, a different mortar mix was used. If the bastion had been rebuilt, the likeliest times would have been when Alfred the Great re-fortified the town against the Danes in the late 10th century or in the 14th century when King Richard II ordered the Mayor and the citizens to repair the defences. In either case, it could be expected that there would have been some erosion of the face of the wall above the point where the mortar changes; but there is no sign of this. The flintwork seems to have been laid in the same fashion and up to the same wall face—only the mortar is different.

3. The line of demarcation between the wall and the bastion ends at a point 2.75 m up from ground level. From this point upwards there is no change and both structures appear to have been incorporated up to the present top, which is 3.4 m above modern ground level.

4. On the north side of the bastion–wall interface, and about 1.65 m up from ground level there is a horizontal layer of dirt in the flintwork. This was also clearly seen in the face of the wall to the west of the bastion after the modern flintwork had been stripped off. It therefore seems to run through the Roman wall at that height and is likely to represent trample by the feet of the wall builders. Sections cut through the bank at the rear of the wall have shown layers of mortar trampled by the builders, who apparently built as high as they could reach and then raised themselves by increasing the height of the rampart. The line of trampled earth noted above probably derives from one of these operations.

5. Removal of the facing along the base of the east side of the bastion showed that there was a void existing below it at the point where the bastion is butted up to the face of the wall (Plate 21). A close examination of this, and reference to the 1959 excavations (Holmes 1962) suggests the following sequence of events which may have caused the void to appear.

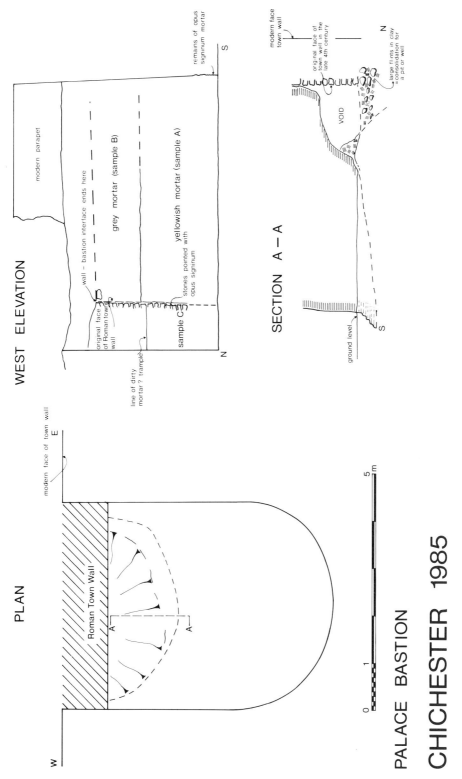

PLAN

W

E
modern face of town wall

Roman Town Wall

A          A

WEST ELEVATION

N

S

modern parapet

wall – bastion interface ends here

grey mortar (sample B)

line of dirty
mortar ? trample

original face
of Roman town
wall

yellowish mortar (sample A)

stones pointed with
opus signinum

sample C

remains of opus
signinum mortar

SECTION A – A

N

modern face of
town wall

original face of
town wall in the
late 4th century

VOID

large flints in clay
= consolidation for
a pit or well

S

ground level

0          1          5 m

PALACE BASTION

CHICHESTER 1985

Fig. 6D.1   Scale 1:80

115

Plate 20   A and B, Palace bastion, west side. A—showing the surviving face of the Roman wall and bastion after removal of the 19th century facing. B—Close-up showing the bastion–wall interface

Plate 21　A and B, Palace bastion, east side. A—The void below the bastion. B—Looking west, below the bastion, showing the face of the Roman wall

(a) The front edges of the bastions around Chichester are built out over the inner Roman defensive ditch which Holmes thought was probably dug at the end of the 2nd century AD. During the 1959 excavations, in which the present writer participated, it was noted that there was an earlier ditch present on the north side of the defensive ditch and Holmes concluded that this was a local ditch, probably not defensive and probably 1st century in date. The sections show that this ditch had been re-cut on one occasion, but this was not commented upon by the excavator.

(b) It is known that the original 1st century town extended beyond the limits of the later walls and that when these were built, parts of the earlier town (notably on the south-west and north-east sides) were cut off and levelled.

(c) There is evidence of subsidence below the bastion foundation which can hardly be accounted for by the presence of the earlier ditch. There was a soft spot present which the original wall builders were aware of and which they backfilled with clay and large flints. It appeared to be of little concern to them. The wall was in any event about 2.4 m thick at that time and the soft spot did not threaten the stability of the structure. But by the time the bastion came to be built in the 4th century some considerable settlement had taken place and it seems that this was backfilled, and clay (probably derived from the digging of the new flat-bottomed defensive ditch) was piled up over it. The bastion foundation of mortared flints was then laid across it and in the succeeding fourteen centuries further sinkage occurred, leaving the void we have today. It is likely that the cause of the subsidence was the presence of the 'core' of a robbed-out Roman well, dug at some time after the middle of the 1st century AD after the earlier ditch had been backfilled. Two others have been found in the grounds of the Theological College nearby, one in 1959 (*op. cit.* 81–2 and section) and the other in 1985 (this volume p. 58).

## 6E   Pine's Yard bastion 1991

by J.A.P. Kenny

### INTRODUCTION

In August 1991 a trial trench was dug against the north side of the bastion in Pine's Yard south of the site of the East Gate (Fig. 6E.1 and Plate 22). This was the only surviving bastion not to have been examined by excavation, and the work was carried out to test a hypothesis, subsequently confirmed, that the tower did not form part of the system of Roman defences but was a post-medieval folly constructed in imitation of surviving Roman examples. The timing of the excavation was dictated by a District Council proposal to refurbish the yard and its buildings later in the year, and this has since been carried out.

### THE EXCAVATIONS (SITE CODE CH.91 SE6A) Figs. 6E.1-3)

A trench 4 m by 1.4 m was excavated in the angle between the north side of the bastion and the boundary wall at the west end of Pine's Yard. Layers of modern concrete and topsoil and disturbed flinty brickearth were removed to reveal the shallow foundations of the bastion and boundary wall, which were of flint and gravel and apparently contemporary (layer 14). The east end of the bastion had more substantial footings of large flints in compacted chalk (6). From a point about halfway along the bastion, where it starts to curve, its wall is much deeper and has a pronounced batter with repointing in sandy mortar (2). Where the change in depth occurs a butt-joint is visible in the superstructure, indicating that the original square tower was given a semi-circular facade to imitate the known Roman bastions. A large pit (7), which caused the deeper foundations to be built, contained a single sherd of green glazed medieval or post-medieval pottery. No trace of the Roman city wall was found; presumably it lies further east or west of the line of the later boundary wall. Possible Roman features included pits 9 and 11 and layer 4, any of which may be associated with the city defences or earlier occupation.

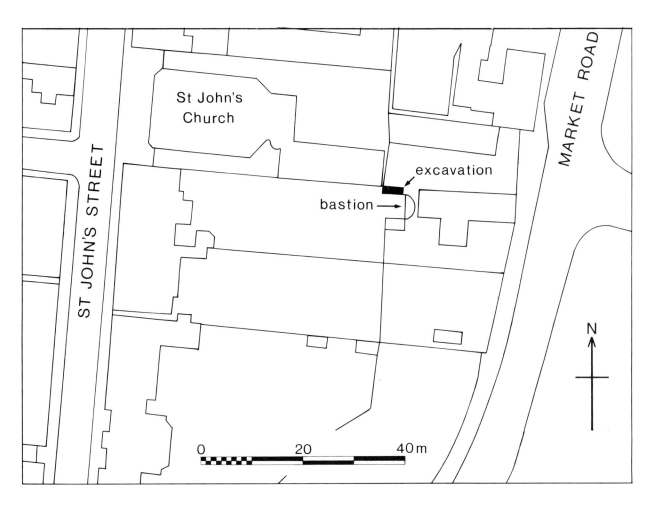

Fig. 6E.1   Pine's Yard bastion 1991 location plan

Plate 22   Pine's Yard bastion during excavation, looking south

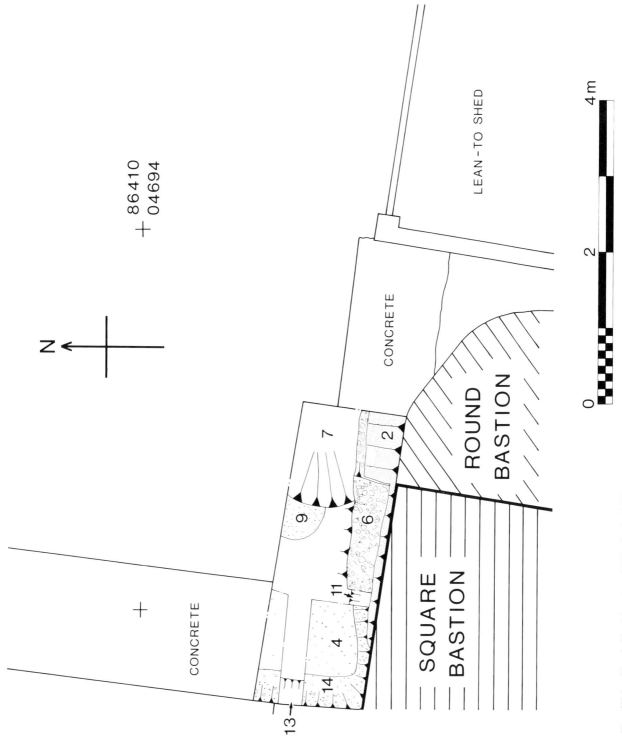

86410
04694

N

CONCRETE

CONCRETE

LEAN-TO SHED

7

9

11

4

14

13

2

6

SQUARE BASTION

ROUND BASTION

0          2          4 m

Fig. 6E.2  Pine's Yard bastion 1991. Scale 1:50

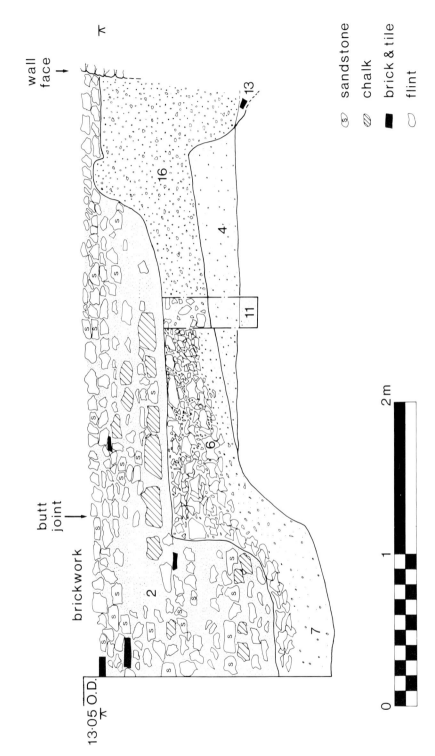

wall face →

brickwork

butt joint →

13·05 O.D.

sandstone
chalk
brick & tile
flint

0    1    2 m

Fig. 6E.3   Pine's Yard bastion 1991. Section and elevation. Scale 1:50

## 6F    A resistivity survey of the Deanery bastion 1991

by J.R. Magilton

A resistivity survey was carried out in September 1991 by R.G. Browse and S. Woodward to try to locate a supposed bastion sited mid way between the Residentiary and Palace bastions. An area of 402 m $^2$ was examined, just west of the point where the southern part of the old Deanery projects beyond the line of the city wall (Fig. 6F.1). The very high readings noted at the eastern end of the survey area (Fig. 6F.2) most probably reflect the course of a 19th century pathway which led from a gate in what is now the south-east corner of the Bishop's vegetable garden to a footbridge over the Lavant roughly opposite the present pavilion. The site of the supposed bastion appeared to be indicated by a series of high readings at the expected location. Occasional high readings to the west may reflect the positions of two buildings, perhaps a garden shed and a sty, indicated on the 1875 1:500 plan of Chichester.

If the bastion has been correctly located, this would appear to contradict Salzman's statement (1935, 88) that the 'old Deanery...in spite of protests in the Middle Ages, had been built upon one of the bastions of the wall...'. The earliest map of Chichester, Norden's 1595 plan (Butler, 1972, 4) shows the old Deanery part-way between the Residentiary bastion and the one located by resistivity survey, although closer to the latter. Neither Norden nor Speed (1610) shows the deanery projecting beyond the wall line, and it is possible that the surviving structure south of the wall represents an extension to the medieval building constructed at some time between 1610 and its partial destruction in 1642 during the siege of Chichester.

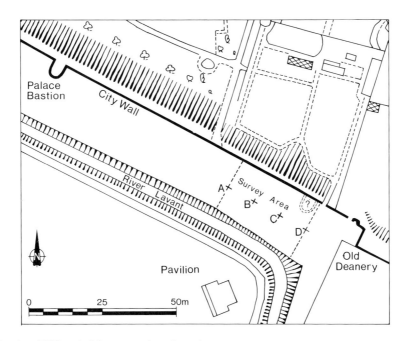

Fig. 6F.1    Deanery bastion 1991 resistivity survey location plan

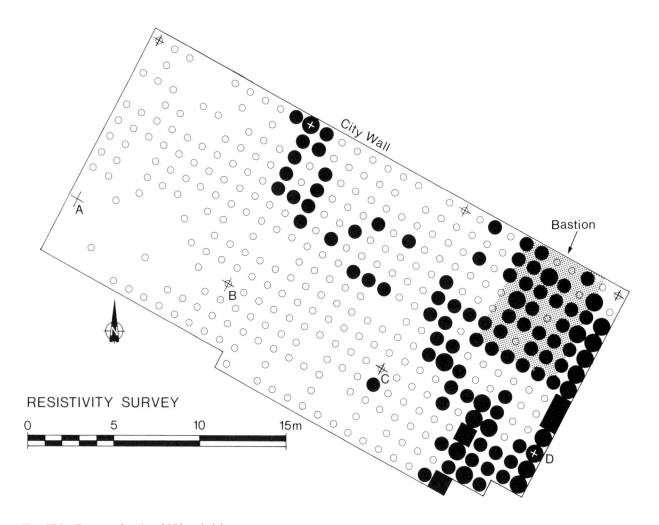

Fig. 6F.2   Deanery bastion 1991 resistivity survey

## 6G   Excavations at Southgate 1960

**by J.R. Magilton**

The site of the Catholic Church and presbytery was investigated in 1960 by John Holmes FSA in advance of redevelopment, but details were never published. Mr Holmes has recently given one of the authors (J.M.) a plan of the excavations, redrawn as Fig. 6G.1, and, as this has implications for the defences and topography of Roman Chichester, it is reproduced here with a brief account based on a note supplied by the excavator.

The site lies to the east of South Street, between Theatre Lane and Old Market Avenue. The South Street frontage is currently occupied by Rumbelow's. Nine trenches were dug.

The three trenches closest to South Street had been disturbed by cellars, and no archaeological features were recorded. The fourth and fifth trenches revealed a gravel layer, apparently cambered to the west and east, into which a number of features had been cut. The sixth trench contained no archaeological features, but the easternmost three contained the inner face of the foundations of the city wall with remains of the Roman bank behind. If, as seems probable, the gravel layer is to be interpreted as a Roman street, the results of the excavation indicate that the medieval south gate lay to the west of its Roman precursor. This implies that the Roman equivalent of South Street was on approximately the same line as medieval and modern North Street, which is known from excavations in 1958–9 to be on the line of a Roman street (Murray and Cunliffe 1962). Such a conclusion would not conflict with Down's (1978, 20) observations in a service trench at Southgate, except insofar as what he interpreted as the east guard-room of the Roman gate would become the west guard-room. It would also explain the location of the otherwise anomalous tower designated SE1 on Fig. 6H.1, which could be interpreted as an extra bastion inserted to lie the same distance east of the gate as the regularly spaced SW6 is to the west of it.

It is difficult to understand why the medieval gate apparently lay to the west of its Roman precursor. One possibility is that, as at Caerwent in the late Roman period, the south gate was walled up, and it was as easy to create a new gap in the curtain wall as to unblock the Roman gate. This may have been made just to the east of bastion SW6, the bastion forming the west tower of the medieval gate.

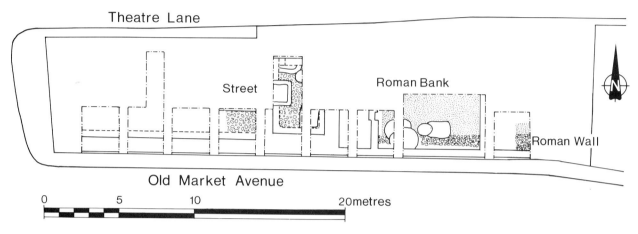

Fig. 6G.1    Excavations at Southgate 1960. Roman features and intrusions (after J. Holmes)

## 6H    The positions of the Roman bastions

### by J.R. Magilton

The walls of Chichester currently have five projecting towers or bastions (Fig. 6H.1). From the south-west corner of the city, going anti-clockwise, these are known as the Palace bastion, the Residentiary bastion, Market Avenue bastion, Pine's Yard bastion and Orchard Street bastion. The last-named is now a large lump of flints and mortar detached from the wall-face. Prior to 1991, all but the Pine's Yard bastion had been examined by excavation, some of them on more than one occasion, and shown beyond reasonable doubt to be Roman. All are conventionally dated to the mid 4th century, although the evidence from Chichester is inconclusive. Two further bastions are known from excavations, but do not survive above ground. These are the Friary Close bastion in the south-east quadrant, cut away to make a garden house in the early 19th century, the remains of which were excavated in 1956 (Wilson 1957a, 10–11; Wilson 1957b, 123–5) and the Eastgate bastion, excavated in 1972, in the north-east quadrant (Down 1974, 59–72).

It was noted that the distance between the Palace and Residentiary bastions was exactly twice that between the Market Avenue and Friary Close bastions, and from this it was deduced that the original intention had been to augment the Roman city walls with projecting towers at intervals of approximately 96 m (about 325 Roman feet) or conceivably at intervals of half that distance. Of the five known bastions in the southern half of Chichester, all but the Pine's Yard example fitted in with this notional spacing, and in the northern half of the city there were ten notional towers at this spacing between the East Gate and Orchard Street bastions. This theoretical scheme produced some anomalies. For example, one of the hypothetical bastions occurred on the supposed site of the Roman north gate, and on the west side of the city the gap between the first hypothetical tower of the south-west quadrant and the last of the north-west quadrant was considerably less than would have been predicted.

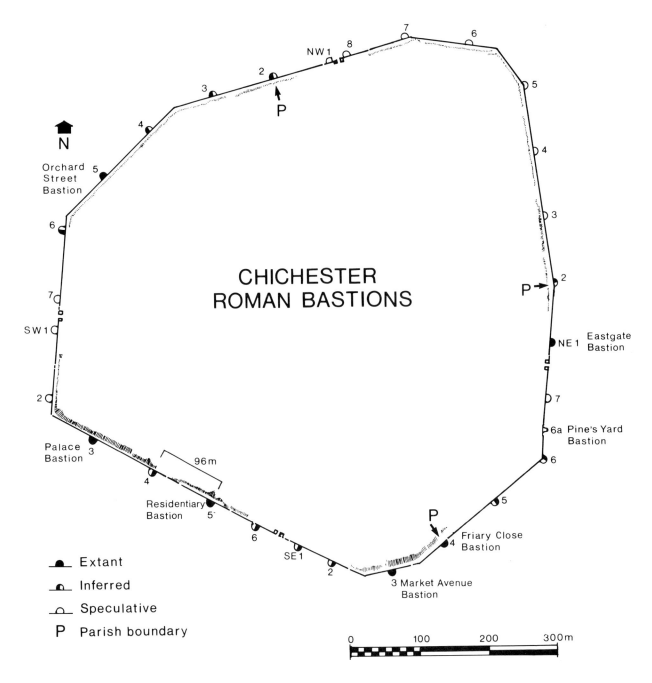

CHICHESTER
ROMAN BASTIONS

Orchard
Street
Bastion

SW 1

Palace
Bastion

Residentiary
Bastion

SE 1

3 Market Avenue
Bastion

Friary Close
Bastion

Market Avenue
Bastion

NE 1  Eastgate
Bastion

6a Pine's Yard
Bastion

96 m

- Extant
- Inferred
- Speculative
P Parish boundary

0      100      200      300m

Fig. 6H.1

Many of the early maps of Chichester (Butler 1972) show the walled circuit to have had more projecting towers than survive to the present day, and an attempt (Table 1) has been made to correlate these with the hypothetical bastions described above. This was successful in that maps from Norden (1595) onwards appear to show bastions at the predicted points, although it must be admitted that in some cases the maps are so inaccurate that an element of subjectivity is involved. The results were most impressive for the north-west quadrant, where only the Orchard Street bastion survives today. Again, some anomalies were noted. There is good cartographic evidence for a bastion just east of the south gate, now beneath buildings on the south side of Theatre Lane, which is not at the expected spacing. Two maps appeared to show a gate in the north-west quadrant between the northern ends of Tower Street and Chapel Street which is otherwise unattested. The Pine's Yard bastion, which does not occur at the predicted interval, seems not to be depicted on any map before 1749, and is shown as square on the first reasonably accurate map of Chichester, Gardner's 1769 plan.

126

**Table 1**
**Cartographic evidence for bastions**

| Bastion | Date of map | | | | | | | | | | Remarks |
|---|---|---|---|---|---|---|---|---|---|---|---|
| | 1595 | 1610 | 1723 | 1749 | 1764 | 1769 | 1812 | 1820 | 1822 | 1898 | |
| SE1 | X | X | | | | | X | | | | |
| SE2 | X | X | X? | X? | X | | | | | | See note (a) |
| SE3 | X | X | X | X | X | | X | X | X | X | Market Ave—extant |
| SE4 | X | X | X | X | X | X | | X | X | X | Friary Cl.—parish boundary |
| SE5 | X | | X | X | X | | | | | | |
| SE6 | | | X | X | X | | | | | | |
| SE6a | | | | X | X | X | X | X | X | X | Pine's Yard—post medieval |
| SE7 | | | | | | | | | | | |
| SW1 | | | | | | ? | | | | | |
| SW2 | X? | X? | | X | X | | | | | | See note (b) |
| SW3 | X | X | X | X | X | X | X | X | X | X | Palace—extant |
| SW4 | X | X | X | X | X | | | | | | |
| SW5 | X | X | X | X | X | X | X | X | X | X | Residentiary—extant |
| SW6 | X? | X? | | | | | | | | | Doubtful—see below |
| NW1 | | | | | | | | | | | See note (c) |
| NW2 | | | | | | | | | | | Parish boundary |
| NW3 | X | X | XG | X | X | X | | | | | |
| NW4 | XG | | | | | | | | | | |
| NW5 | X | X | | | | X | | | | X | Orchard St—extant |
| NW6 | | | | | | X | | | | | |
| NW7 | | | | | | | | | | | |
| NE1 | | | | | | | | | | | Excavated 1972 |
| NE2 | | | | | | | | | | | Parish boundary |
| NE3 | X? | | | | | | | | | | |
| NE4-8 | | | | | | | | | | | See note (d) |

*Key*: X = bastion shown; XG = bastion shown as gate; X? = bastion possibly shown.
*Notes*:
(a) It is not certain whether the maps of 1723 and 1749 show SE2 or SE1.
(b) As SW2 seems to be indicated in 1749 and 1764, this may be the first bastion shown on Norden's and Speed's maps of 1595 and 1610. If so, they do not illustrate SW6.
(c) The east side of this bastion may have been noted during salvage recording (Down 1981, 11).
(d) All the remaining bastions in the north-east quadrant are speculative. The absence of all bastions in this quadrant from maps of 1610 onwards suggests that they had been demolished by this date.

Further confirmation of the sites of now missing bastions was sought from an examination of ecclesiastical parish boundaries, since it had been noted that the Friary Close bastion, presumably a prominent topographical feature when such boundaries were established, lay at the exact junction between Subdeanery parish and the extra-parochial area formerly belonging to the Dominican Friars. Two further parish boundaries occurred at the predicted sites of two missing bastions. One (NE2) lay north of the excavated East Gate bastion, and the other (NW2) west of the site of the north gate. These are indicated on Fig. 6H.1 by the letter P and an arrow.

As has been noted, the Pine's Yard bastion was the only surviving example not to have been excavated, it was not at the expected spacing, and it did not appear in cartographical sources until the 18th century. All these factors tended to suggest that it was of relatively modern construction. In order to examine it, a small trench was dug in 1991 by the north face of the tower. The results are described in detail above, but it was concluded that the tower was of two broad periods of construction. Part of its foundations could be equated with the square projection shown on Gardner's map and the semicircular front of the tower and most of its superstructure were of later date. It is reasonable to conclude that the bastion is an ornamental garden feature constructed in imitation of surviving bastions at some time after 1769, partly overlying an early 18th century structure.

A further check on the hypothetical spacing of bastions was possible in the area south of the Bishop's Garden, mid way between the Palace and Residentiary bastions where, with the permission of the Dean and Chapter, a resistivity survey was carried out. This is described in detail above but, in brief, an anomaly was located on the supposed site of the intermediate bastion. Ideally, this should be checked by excavation, but it tends to confirm the validity of the supposed spacing.

The distances between bastions of a number of Roman towns and forts are shown in tabular form in Fig. 6H.2 for comparison with Chichester. The forts tended to have regularly spaced bastions, typically with one at some distance from the gate, one on the corner and one halfway between the two. The interval distance is usually between 100 and 200 Roman feet (approximately 30–60 m). Most of the towns appear to have irregularly spaced bastions (though this may be due to a lack of survival) which usually do not occur at corners. Chichester and Colchester may have regular spacing which implies a degree of planning, though with little regard for military effectiveness. The interval distance on towns varies greatly, though most often it is between 200 and 330 Roman feet (approximately 60–100 m).

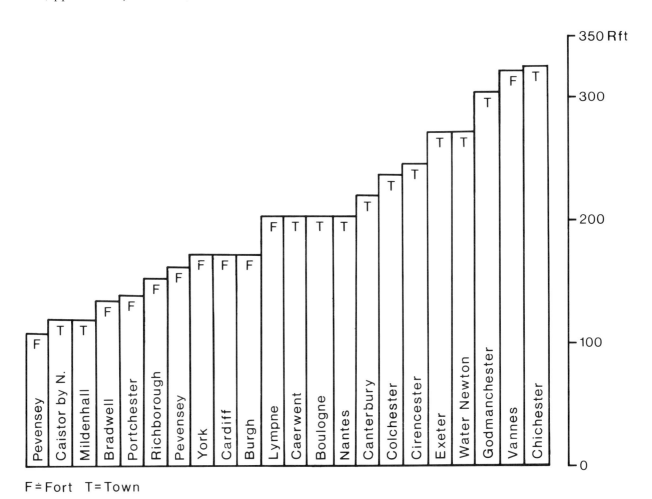

F = Fort    T = Town

Fig. 6H.2    The distances between bastions for selected sites in Britain and Gaul. Pevensey is listed twice as there seem to be two standard distances. Scale in Roman feet (*pes monetalis*)

**GAZETTEER**

Towers in the south-east quadrant

SE1    This is not on the expected site of a Roman bastion. Norden (1595) and Speed (1610) show a tower in this position, but Gardner (1769) is the only 18th century cartographer to indicate a tower here. Loader (1812) and his successors show no trace of one. Speed (1610) indicates that the tower had a cross-shaped arrow loop, whereas the towers to the east all have vertical slits. This may be no more than artistic licence, although it could indicate that the tower was a medieval addition to the enceinte.

SE2    This is the expected distance west of a demonstrably Roman tower (SE 3). It lies directly opposite the southern end of South Pallant, and may have been the feature upon which the street was aligned. It apparently occurs on all maps down to 1764.

SE3  Market Avenue bastion. A surviving example, now within a District Council car park. Excavated by A.E. Wilson in 1956 (Wilson 1957a, 13–15; 1957b, 125–7). Appears on all maps consulted apart from Gardner (1769).

SE4  Friary Close bastion. Survived into early 19th century. Foundations exacavated by A.E. Wilson 1952–3 (Wilson 1957a, 10–11, 14; 1957b, 123–5) and demonstrably Roman. Identified on most maps consulted down to the late 19th century. Marks the boundary between Subdeanery parish and the extra-parochial area formerly belonging to the Dominicans.

SE5  Appears to be shown on all maps, apart from Speed's, until 1769. If both Bowen and Gardner are to be trusted, it must have been demolished in the period 1764–69.

SE6  Sited on an angle in the city wall. Not apparently shown by Norden (and therefore omitted by Speed) but occurs on 18th century maps until 1769.

SE6a  Pine's Yard. First cartographic appearance in 1749, when shown conventionally. Gardner, however (1769) shows it square, whilst his successors always show it rounded. Excavated 1991. Probably 18th century.

SE7  Entirely speculative. Not shown on any maps. Sited the expected distance north of SE6.

Towers in the south-west quadrant

SW1  Entirely speculative, apart from a possible portrayal on Gardner's map.

SW2  Possibly shown by Norden and Speed, and apparently indicated in 1749 and 1764. Lies the expected distance west of the demonstrably Roman SW3.

SW3  The Palace bastion. The most frequently investigated of the surviving towers, dug by I.C. Hannah in 1932, J. Holmes in 1959 and examined by A. Down in 1985 (Hannah 1934; Holmes 1962; Down 1985 and above pp. 114–118). Shown on all maps.

SW4  The Deanery bastion. Appears to be shown on all maps until 1769. Probably located by resistivity survey, 1991 (see above p. 123).

SW5  The Residentiary bastion. Investigated by G.M. Hills in 1885 and I.C. Hannah in 1932–3 (Hills 1886; Hannah 1934). Appears on all maps.

SW6  Speculative, although Norden and Speed may show a bastion in this approximate location. It may have formed the west tower of the medieval south gate.

Towers in the north-west quadrant

NW1  A feature re-interpreted as the east side of this bastion was seen in a gas pipe trench in 1977 (Down 1981, 11). It cannot be part of the north gate unless the gate had towers projecting beyond the wall-line.

NW2  This tower lies at the junction between the parishes of Subdeanery and St Peter's, North Street, but is otherwise unattested.

NW3  A tower at this approximate site is shown on all maps down to 1769. Stukeley's plan (1723) seems to show a gate through the tower. According to Hay (1804, 341, footnote) this tower was built in c. 1643 from the debris of the churches of St Pancras and St Bartholomew, but it is clearly shown by both Speed and Norden, and Hay, if correct, must be referring to a reconstruction. The tower is shown prominently by Stukeley and his successors, but seems to have been pulled down before 1812 since Loader omits it.

NW4  Shown by Norden, apparently as a gate. Lies the expected distance NE of the only surviving bastion in this quadrant, NW5. Also indicated by Gardner (1769).

NW5  The Orchard Street bastion. The only Roman survivor in this quadrant, and now a lump of flints and mortar detached from the wall. Examined by A.E. Wilson in the 1950s and A. Down and F. Aldsworth in the 1980s (Wilson 1957a, 11; Down 1989, 26).

NW6  The expected distance south-west of the Orchard Street tower. Shown by Gardner (1769).

NW7  Speculative, and not shown on any maps. According to Spershott, in 1781 'One round tower of the fortification taken down and quite erased which stood near the West Gate' (Steer 1962, 23). This could refer to SW1 or NW7 (or, conceivably, SW2 or NW6).

Towers in the north-east quadrant

NE1  The Eastgate bastion. Excavated by A. Down, 1972 (Down 1974, 59–74). Found during commercial boring. Tower had been demolished by the early modern period. Not shown by Norden (1595) or his successors.

NE2  Bastion inferred. It lies roughly the expected distance north of NE 1, on the boundary between the parishes of St Pancras and St Andrew Oxmarket, and at a point where there is a bend in the city wall.

NE3 Speculative. It lies the expected distance north of NE1, and may be shown by Norden (1595) although not by his successors.

NE4 Speculative. Unattested by cartographers. No evidence found in 1991 excavations.

NE5 Speculative. Unattested by cartographers, but lies on a bend in the city wall. The 1991 Jubilee Park excavations found no trace of a bastion here (see p. 109) but the modern ground surface is lower than in Roman times.

NE6 Speculative. Not shown on maps.

NE7 Speculative. Not shown on maps.

NE8 Speculative. Its existence is inferred from the slightly better attested NW1.


## 6J Bibliography for the city defences

Buckland, P.C., Magilton, J.R, and Hayfield, C., 1989. *The Archaeology of Doncaster 2. The Medieval and Later Town, Part i, BAR* British Series 202.

Butler, D.J., 1972. *The Town Plans of Chichester 1595–1898* WSCC (Chichester).

Crickmore, J., 1984. *Romano-British Urban Defences, BAR* British Series 126.

Cunliffe, B.W., 1971. 'Excavations at Fishbourne 1961–69' *RRSAL XXVII.*

Down, A., 1974. *Chichester Excavations 2* (Phillimore).

Down, A., 1978. *Chichester Excavations 3* (Phillimore).

Down, A., 1981. *Chichester Excavations 5* (Phillimore).

Down, A., 1985. *Chichester Excavations Committee Report for 1984/5.*

Down, A., 1988. *Roman Chichester.*

Down, A., 1989. *Chichester Excavations 6* (Phillimore).

Down, A., and Rule, M., 1971. *Chichester Excavations 1* (Chichester).

Frere, S.S., *et al.,* 1982. *Excavations on the Roman and Medieval Defences of Canterbury* The Archaeology of Canterbury, Vol. ii.

Hannah, I.C., 1934. 'The walls of Chichester' in *SAC* 75, 107–27.

Hay, A., 1804. *The History of Chichester.*

Hills, G.M., 1886. 'Chichester: the city walls and their Roman form and foundation' in *Journal of the British Archaeological Association* 42, 119–36.

Holmes, J., 1962. 'The defences of Roman Chichester' in *SAC* 100, 80–92.

Johnson, S., 1976. *The Roman Forts of the Saxon Shore.*

Johnson, S., 1983. *Late Roman Fortifications.*

Murray, K.M.E., and Cunliffe, B.W., 1962. 'Excavations at a site in North Street, Chichester. 1958–9.' in *SAC* 100, 93–110.

Rae, A., 1951–2. 'Cawley Priory—wall excavations' in *SAC* 90, 179–200.

Salzman, L.F. (ed.), 1935. *VHC (Sx),* Vol. 3, University of London Institute of Historical Research.

Steer, F.W. (ed.), 1962. *The Memoirs of James Spershott* Chichester Papers 30.

Wilson, A.E., 1957a. *The Archaeology of Chichester City Walls* Chichester Papers 6.

Wilson, A.E., 1957b. 'Roman Chichester' in *SAC* 95, 116–45.

**7**

# The Granada Cinema site, East Street, 1984 (Fig. 7.1)

## by Alec Down

In 1984, the Granada Cinema, formerly the northern end of the old Corn Exchange, was redeveloped by London and Manchester Securities plc, and thanks are due to them and their architects, Roth and Partners, for their co-operation in allowing a watching brief on the excavations inside the building and for providing a grant to cover the cost of having an observer stationed on site.

### SITE HISTORY (FROM NOTES PROVIDED BY MR R.R. MORGAN)

The site of the Granada Cinema abuts the extreme north-west corner of the land originally occupied by the Blackfriars, whose boundary wall ran south from East Street on the east side of Baffins Lane. There is no evidence of Friary buildings and there was a possibility that the cemetery of the friars might have extended westwards as far as the boundary wall.

The friars appeared to have settled there in the mid 13th century. One purchase on 30th April 1286 (1) describes Queen Eleanor as buying 'another area of land with all the buildings' from Sir John the Chaplain, son of Nicholas the Goldsmith. In 1310 (2) a further large area of land was bought. It was contiguous to the friars' homestead, to enable them to enlarge the burial ground and cloister and build a church and houses.

In 1538 the Friary was dissolved and the site was empty for a year. In 1540 (3), the Friars' house and site with belfry, churchyard buildings, gardens and lands were purchased privately. The whole site changed hands a number of times. A 'capital messuage' (i.e. a major dwelling) is recorded in 1600 (4). This building, which was large and had eleven hearths (5), was on the site of the Granada Cinema and eventually came into the Page family. The house changed shape over the years and was pulled down in 1852 (6), to make way for the Corn Exchange.

### THE EXCAVATION

The following notes were compiled by Sue Woodward, who maintained a watching brief on behalf of the Excavation Unit.

The ground inside the old cinema had been excavated so as to slope from north to south, where the screen had been, and at that end no archaeological levels had survived. Excavations for an interior wall footing and two bases uncovered three pits of probable Roman date, one of which contained a complete New Forest folded beaker of 4th century date. Fragments of human skeletal material representing at least three individuals were found in disturbed ground between the two central columns at the north end of the site. These had evidently been disturbed when the Corn Exchange was built in the mid 19th century. No other trace of human burials was found and, bearing in mind the density of the burials a few yards further east, (7), it seems likely that these remains were originally interred near to the western boundary of the Blackfriars cemetery. They may be Blackfriars or possibly members of Catholic families that were placed there after the Dissolution.

Part of a substantial flint-built wall aligned north–south was noted during the excavation of a central north–south wall foundation. It was not Roman, but might well have been part of the 'capital messuage' recorded in AD 1600.

### REFERENCES

1. *SAC* 29, Pat. 18 Ed.2.
2. *SAC* 29, Pat. 4 Ed. 2.
3. *VCH* (Sx) Vol. 2, 94; Vol. 3, 77.
4. Post Mortem Inquisitions 3 and 14, Nos 252, 458, 460.
5. *SAC* 24.
6. City Deed 168.
7. Unpublished rescue excavation in 1966 by Mrs Rule. The density of the burials was considerable and extended from just east of the cinema towards St John's Street. See also *Chichester Excavations 3*, fig. 1.1 and pp. 1–4.

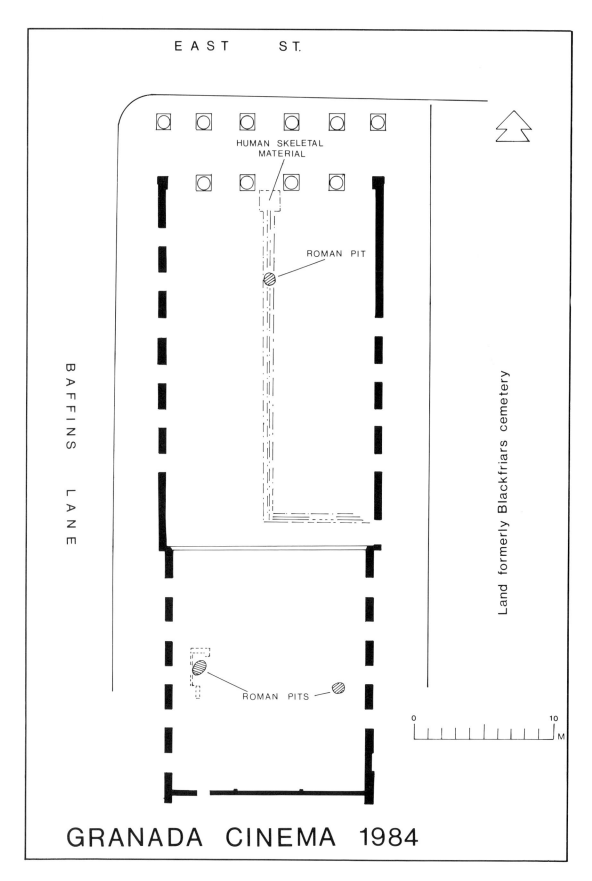

EAST ST.

HUMAN SKELETAL
MATERIAL

ROMAN PIT

BAFFINS LANE

Land formerly Blackfriars cemetery

ROMAN PITS

0                    10
                      M

GRANADA CINEMA 1984

Fig. 7.1

132

# Part 2—The finds

# 8

# The post-medieval pottery from 14–15 East Street (Figs. 8.1–8.4)

## by Alec Down

The area to the rear (north) of the above premises was very restricted and had been subjected to centuries of cess-pit digging which had disturbed the soil to a depth which varied between two and three metres. Whilst digging a soakaway near the northern boundary of the site the machine struck a rich collection of pottery and other debris which was collected by Mrs. Woodward. It was evident that a pit dating to the late 17th–early 18th century had been dug out—much of the pottery being made in the Graffham kilns, and a representative selection is published below. An unusual find was the upper part of a horse's skull which was seen by Dr. Philip Armitage of the Booth Museum of Natural History, Brighton, where it has now been deposited (Armitage, in archive). A crucible containing bronze residues was unearthed by the machine and it was noticed that some of the pottery was flaking as the result of having been heavily burnt since being discarded—pointing to some form of metal working being carried out in the vicinity, before the pit had been dug and filled. The crucible is likely to be late–post-medieval in date (see report by Miss J. Bayley and Fig. 8.3).

### THE POTTERY

1. Dripping pan; mid grey fabric oxidised to a dirty buff, patchy brown/green glaze inside. From Graffham, 17th century, two examples.
2. Rim of a straight-walled dish or pan. The fabric is very hard, sandy and burnt since being broken. Brownish/green glaze inside. Probably Graffham. 17th century.
3. Bowl; fine grey fabric oxidised reddish buff. Internal greenish/brown glaze. Graffham. c. 17th–early 18th century.
4. Base of a large vessel, probably a jar, with a patchy green glaze inside. The fabric is hard, sand-tempered and oxidised to a dirty off-white colour. ?Graffham.
5. Lower part of a jar, heavily flaked on the outside due to heat. The fabric is mid brown and sand-tempered and the vessel is coated internally with an olive-green lead glaze. Graffham. c. 17th century.
6. Jar in a hard, mid grey fabric oxidised buff. Internal olive-green glaze. Graffham. c. 17th century.
7. Jar; dirty reddish buff fabric, internal dark brown glaze. Graffham. c. 17th century.
8. Jar in a hard sandy dirty-grey fabric oxidised to reddish buff. Internal green glaze. Graffham. c. 17th century.
9. Straight-walled bowl; orange-buff ware with internal brownish green lead glaze. Graffham.
10. Small bowl; similar fabric to no 9. Internal brown glaze. Graffham.
11. Straight-walled bowl in a hard white fabric and internal pale yellow/green glaze. ?Graffham or Surrey. c. late 16th–early 17th century.
12. Jar; dark grey fabric, oxidised to dark orange. Internal brown glaze. Graffham. c. late 17th–early 18th century.
13. Base of a ?jug in a hard white fabric with internal dark apple-green glaze inside and a dark brown exterior glaze. Probably a cream jug. ?Crane Street, c. late 17th century.
14. Base of a jug in similar fabric to no 13. Glossy dark brown glaze inside and out. Possibly from the same source as no 13.
15. ?Chamber pot in a fine sandy off-white fabric with an internal 'Tudor' green glaze. Source uncertain but likely to be Graffham or Crane Street. c. 17th century.
16. Chamber pot; dirty buff fabric and green glaze on inside and over rim. Graffham. c. 17th century.
17. ?Chamber pot; sandy orange fabric. Dark green/brown internal glaze. ?Graffham or Crane Street.
18. ?Chamber pot; sandy brown fabric, unglazed. Graffham.
19. Rim of a chamber pot. English Delft, probably Southwark. c. 18th century.
20. ?Porringer; fine off-white fabric, internal 'Tudor' green glaze. ?Surrey. 17th century.
21. Small cup; hard white sandy fabric. 'Tudor' green glaze inside and out. ?Surrey. 17th century.
22. ?Porringer; similar in fabric to no 20, probably from the same kiln. Internal yellow glaze. 17th century.
23. Lid handle and part of a lid; mid grey fabric oxidised buff. Olive-green glaze inside lid. Graffham. ?17th century.
24. Sherd from a large chafing dish. Very hard white sandy fabric with internal pale yellow/green glaze. ?Surrey. c. late 16th–17th century.
25. Lid; English Delft. ?Southwark.
26. Floor tile; pale yellow glaze.
27. Floor tile; patchy green glaze.
28. Peg tile; complete, hard off-white sandy fabric.

### THE CRUCIBLE (Fig. 8.3) BY JUSTINE BAYLEY

Two pieces were submitted for examination, a small body sherd and a substantial fragment of the lower part of a crucible. They do not join, but could come from the same vessel.

The fabric of the crucible was specular dark grey and most probably contains a high proportion of graphite (elemental carbon). This has advantages from the metallurgical point of view as it both helps to maintain reducing conditions as metal is melted (which reduces losses to the crucible slag) and provides a surface which metals do not easily 'wet', so reducing the physical retention of metal when the melt is poured. Graphitic crucibles are a post-medieval development. There are considerable signs of vitrification (slagging) of both inner and outer surfaces on the base but the refractory nature of the fabric means that these changes do not penetrate deeply into the walls which would therefore have retained much of their strength, even at high temperatures. The body sherd is much less affected on the outside, presumably because it was higher up and thus farther from the fire.

The form of the crucible is typical of the late and post-medieval periods. It has a flat base and straight sides that splay out slightly towards the top like a traditional flower pot (Fig. 8.3). This example has a base diameter of about 100 mm which is a typical size. The body sherd is about 10 mm thick and the walls of the base slightly more.

The traces of copper-rich metal on both pieces were analysed quantitatively by energy-dispersive X-ray fluorescence. The metal is best described as bronze (copper + tin) but also contained zinc and lead in significant amounts as well as lower levels of arsenic and antimony.

## REFERENCES

Graffham—Aldsworth F.G. and Down A., (1991) Production of Late and Post-medieval Pottery in the Graffham area of West Sussex', *SAC* 128

Crane Street—Down A., *Chichester Excavations 5* (1981), pp. 197–211 (Phillimore).

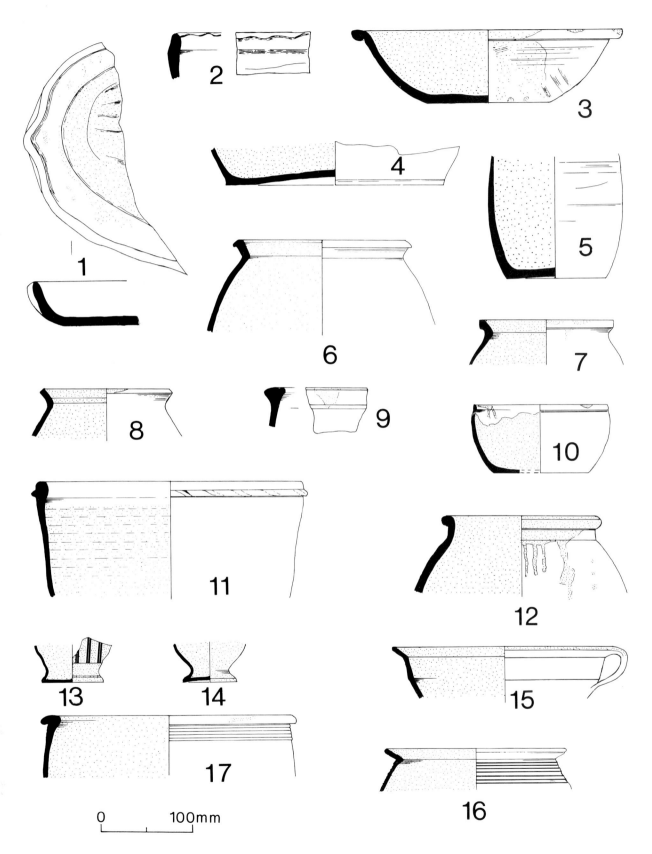

Fig. 8.1   Post-medieval pottery from 14–15 East Street 1984, nos 1–17. Scale 1:4

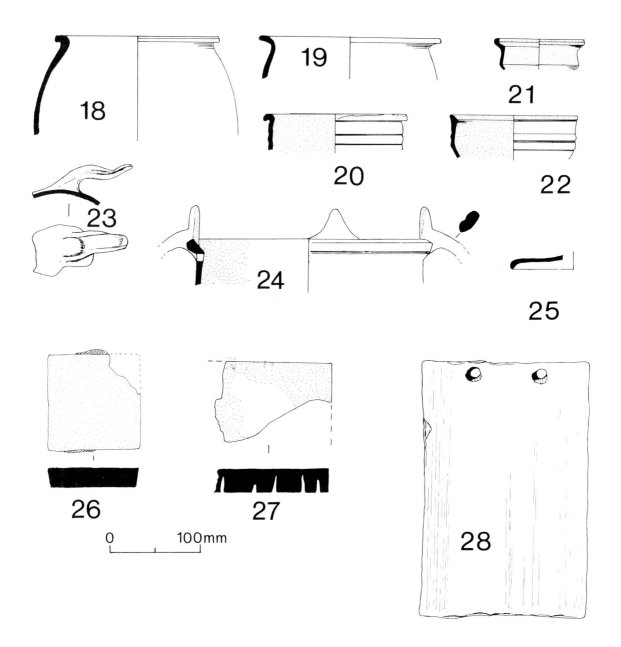

Fig. 8.2  Post-medieval pottery and tile from 14–15 East Street 1984, nos 18–28. Scale 1:4

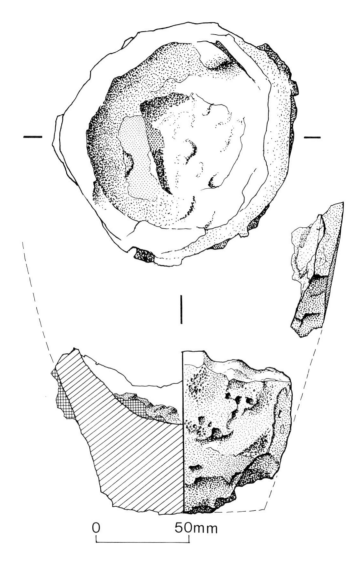

0            50mm

Fig. 8.3   Crucible from 14–15 East Street 1984. Scale 1:2

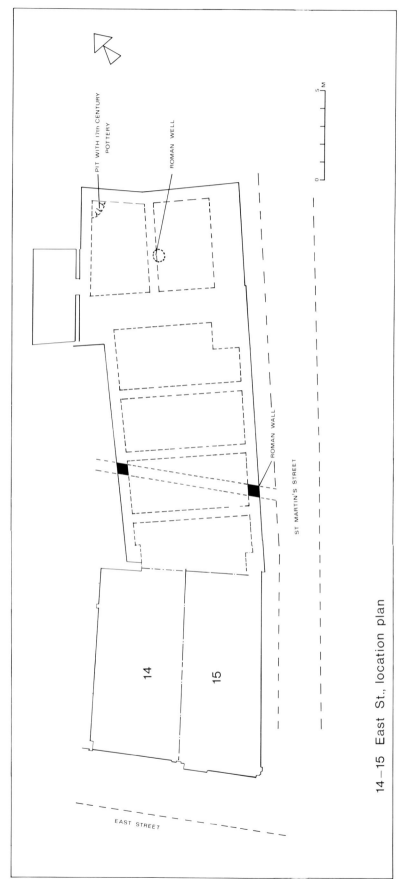

PIT WITH 17th CENTURY POTTERY

ROMAN WELL

ROMAN WALL

ST MARTIN'S STREET

14

15

EAST STREET

0       5 M

14–15 East St., location plan

Fig. 8.4

# 9

# A group of medieval pottery from 74 South Street (Fig. 9.1)

## by Alec Down

In 1984, Hogg Robinson Travel built a small extension at the rear of their premises at 74, South Street, Chichester. As the site is of potential archaeological interest a watching brief was maintained on the site by Sue Woodward.

The present house is probably 17th century in date, but part of it must lie above a large Roman building, known to extend below the Midland Bank, next door to the north. A very deep and narrow excavation by the builders at the rear of the property showed that the 17th century house foundations had been built on the top of a well constructed wall of flint which formed a right-angle with a similar wall below the south wall of the Midland Bank. It was, in fact, two sides of a medieval garderobe pit belonging to an earlier house on the site. A large amount of green-glazed pottery was recovered by Mrs Woodward and from these it was possible to identify elements of at least nine jugs and two cooking pots.

Only part of the north-east corner of the pit could be excavated and it is likely that many more vessels had been dumped there. The fragments were large and unabraded which suggests that this was a primary deposit and that the pit went out of use towards the end of the 14th or beginning of the 15th century.

Three of the jugs were restored to their original form. Two are held by the owners, Hogg Robinson, and the third is in the Chichester District Museum, together with the rest of the vessels. A selection of these is illustrated below.

## THE WARES

1.  Jug with rilled neck and slashed rod handle, with combed vertical decoration below a sparse green glaze. A zone of white paint extends from inside the rim for a distance of c. 35 mm. The fabric is hard fired, sandy, with a pale grey core which is oxidised to a pale buff.
2.  Tall necked jug, neck and rim restored, with vertical combed decoration and three bands of horizontal grooving around the neck and body. The base is heavily thumbed and the body is covered with a patchy green lead glaze. The fabric is dark grey, oxidised to a slightly darker buff than no 1.
3.  Fragment of a similar jug to no 2, with a band of white paint inside the rim.
4.  As no 2, neck and rim restored. (*Not illustrated.*)
5.  Similar in form and fabric to no 2 but without combed decoration. The glaze is dark olive-green.

6 and 7 As no 3. (*Not illustrated.*)

8.  Jug with heavily scored horizontal decoration around the neck, slashed rod handle and white painted decoration below a sparse green glaze. The fabric has a pale grey core, reduced to a very pale buff on the exterior surface. This is the only paint-under-glaze vessel in the assemblage and a date in the late 14th or possibly early 15th century is possible.
9.  Part of the body of a West Sussex ware jug decorated with vertical and zigzag applied strips below an olive-green glaze. Fine sandy fabric reduced to a mid-grey.
10.  Cooking pot in a dark grey sandy fabric with a patchy green glaze over the inside of the base.
11.  Heavily sooted fragment from a cooking pot with scored decoration on the shoulder. Heavily sand-tempered, dirty grey fabric.

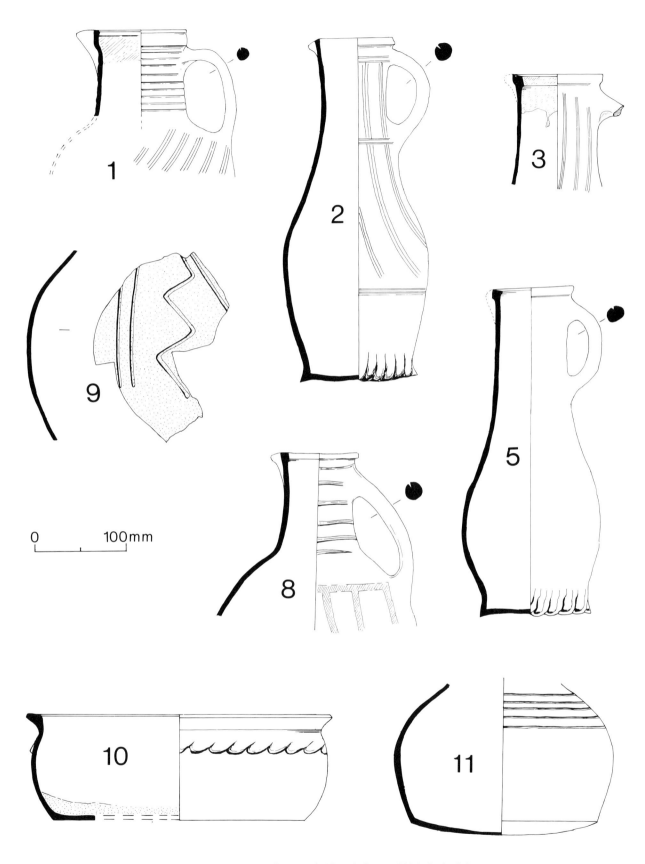

Fig. 9.1    A group of medieval pottery from Hogg Robinson, 74 South Street 1984. Scale 1:4

# A selection of late/post-medieval pottery from 24 South Street (Figs. 10.1–10.2)

## by Alec Down

In July 1984, extensions were carried out to the rear of 24 South Street (now Dillons Book Shop). The property occupies the south-west corner of the junction between Canon Lane and South Street and the land originally belonged to the Cathedral, the frontage on to South Street being leased out as shops, the earliest reference to the site being in the early 15th century.

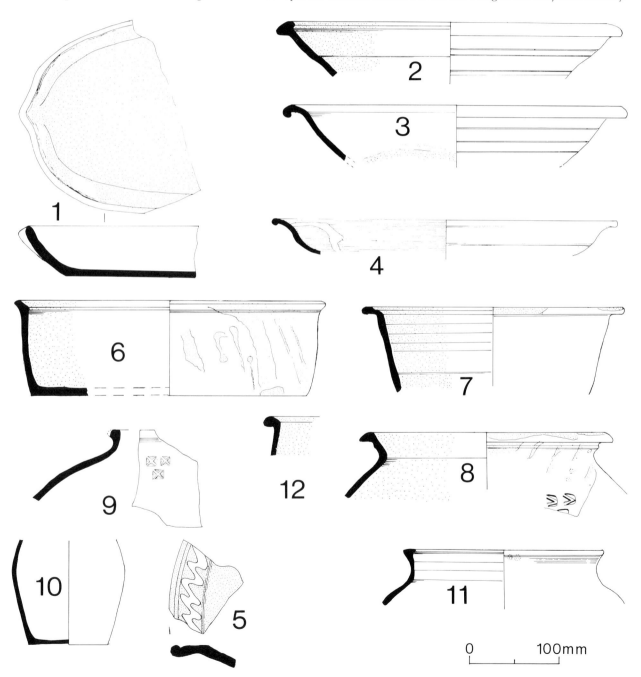

Fig.10.1  Late/post-medieval pottery from 24 South Street 1984, nos. 1–12. Scale 1:4

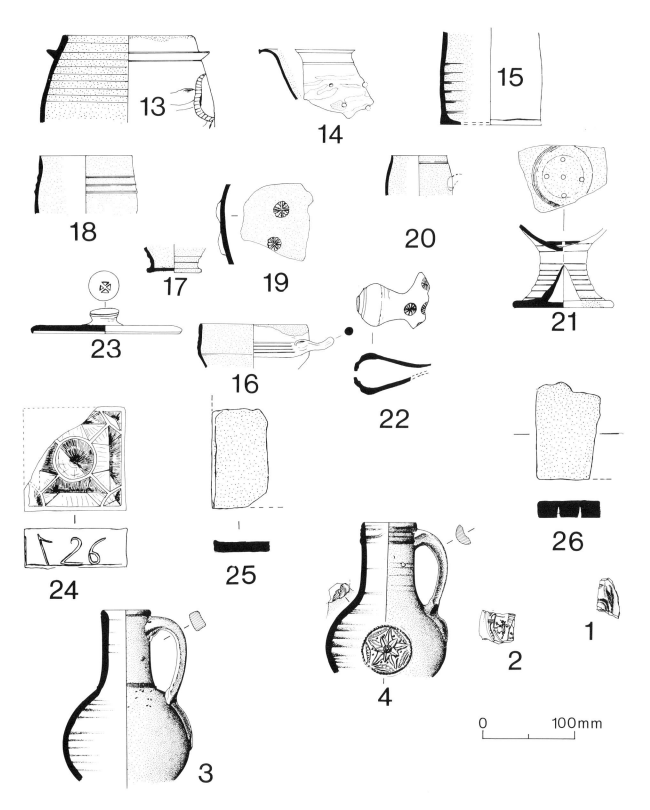

Fig.10.2    Late/post-medieval pottery from 24 South Street 1984, nos. 13–26. Imported German stonewares, nos 1–4. All 1:4

By courtesy of the Architects, Critchell Harrington Partnership, and the contractor, John Snelling Ltd, a watching brief was maintained throughout the foundation work by Sue Woodward and the Writer. The yard at the rear of the shop where the extension was planned had been built over by earlier outhouses in the 17th and 18th centuries and no earlier features had survived with the exception of the area immediately against the west wall of the shop. Here the foundations of the present building, which were only 0.5 m deep, were built over a mass of burnt clay and charcoal which may have been part of a demolished oven.

An interesting group of pottery, with a date range of c. late 14th to 18th century was recovered from the site by Mrs Woodward, and a selection is published below.

1. Small dripping pan; pale grey fabric oxidised buff, internal green lead glaze. Graffham. c. 17th century.
2. Shallow dish; pale grey, sandy fabric oxidised to a pale buff, internal greenish/yellow lead glaze. Possibly Graffham. c. late 16th–17th century.
3. Dish; fine grey fabric oxidised to orange/buff, sand-tempered, brown lead glaze in the bottom. Graffham. c. late 16th–17th century.
4. Dish; similar fabric to no 3 and possibly from the same source, with white painted decoration on the rim.
5. Plate; orange-buff fabric glazed inside with an orange/brown lead glaze with white slip decoration on rim. Graffham. c. 18th century.
6. Bowl; dark grey sandy fabric, oxidised orange-buff with an internal olive-green lead glaze. Graffham. c. 17th century.
7. Steep-sided bowl; hard white sandy fabric with an internal pale yellow glaze. Probably Graffham. c. 17th century.
8. Jar; stamped on shoulder, fine sandy grey fabric, internal olive-green glaze. Graffham. c. 17th century.
9. Jar; stamped below neck, fine dark grey fabric oxidised orange-buff. Internal olive-green lead glaze. Graffham. 17th century.
10. Lower part of a jar; fine sandy orange fabric, possibly Graffham or Crane Street. Date uncertain, but probably late 17th–18th century.
11. ?Cooking pot; hard grey fabric tempered with small flint grits. Medieval, c. 14th–15th century.
12. Steep-sided bowl; similar fabric to no 7, internal pale yellow-green glaze. Probably Graffham. 16th–17th century.
13. Pipkin; similar fabric to no 12, internal pale yellow glaze. Crane Street or Graffham. c. 16th–17th century.
14. Sherd from a colander; fine sandy creamy-white fabric with an internal yellow glaze. ?Surrey. c. 16th–17th century.
15. Butter-pot; hard sandy white fabric, internal pale greeny/yellow glaze. Graffham. c. 17th century.
16. Cup with loop handle in a fine sandy white fabric with an internal 'Tudor' green glaze. ?Surrey. c. late 16th–17th century.
17. Base of a ?jug; similar in fabric to no 16 but with a dark brown glaze inside and out. Dark brown glazed cups and jugs were made both at Graffham and Crane Street, but none have so far been recorded at either site in a white fabric, which appears to have normally been used only for glazes with a relatively poor opacity, e.g. pale green and yellow. This hard sandy white fabric is, however, well attested at Graffham and this piece is tentatively assigned to that source. c. 17th century.
18. Rim of a jug in identical fabric and glaze as no 17, and from the same kiln.
19. Sherd from a jug; dark grey fabric oxidised to orange, and with a dark brown glaze inside and out. ?Graffham or Crane Street. c. 17th century.
20. Cup in identical fabric and glaze as no 19.
21. Base of a chafing dish; fine grey sandy fabric, oxidised orange. Internal brown glaze. Probably Graffham or Crane Street. c. 17th–18th century.
22. Skillet handle; fine sandy orange fabric, with wheel-stamped decoration. Graffham. c. 17th century.
23. Lid; dirty reddish brown fabric with a stamp in the form of a Maltese cross, well attested at Graffham. c. 17th–18th century.
24. Decorative facing brick with the date 1726 cut into one side where it would not be seen when in position. The figure seven is reversed.
25. Fragment from the exposed lower half of a medieval roofing tile, which has been glazed to prevent moisture penetration and subsequent damage by frost in the winter (cf. Down 1978, fig. 3.4 and pp. 13–14).
26. Fragment of glazed floor tile.

## GERMAN IMPORTED STONEWARE FROM 24 SOUTH STREET (Fig. 10.2)

*Note*: numbers in brackets are earlier catalogue numbers.

1. (3) Fragment from a Cologne/Frechen jug; Bartmann type. c. 1550-1575
2. (8) Sherd from a Frechen jug; Bartmann type. c. 1600
3. (12) Frechen jug; Bartmann type. Second half 16th century.
4. (14) Cologne/Frechen jug; Bartmann type. c. 1550–1575

*Not illustrated*

5 . (4) Frechen jug; Bartmann type. c. 1575–1650
6. (5) Bartmann type jug. c. 1575–1650
7. (6) Frechen type jug. Second half 16th century.
8. (7) Raeren mug or jug. c. 1500–1525
9. (9) Jug (as 7).

10. (11) Jug (as 7).
11. (13) Frechen jug; Bartmann type. Mid 16th–17th century.

*Note*: I am indebted to Mr David Gaimster of the Department of Medieval and Later Antiquities, The British Museum, for assistance in dating these pieces.

## BIBLIOGRAPHY

Down, A., 1978. *Chichester Excavations 3*, Phillimore.

# 11

# The samian ware from the sites

## by G.B. Dannell

*Note*: Context numbers in brackets; other figures are form numbers.

### (i) Greyfriars 1984 (Fig. 11.1)

1. (Pit B)    37    Rogers's ovolo B61 with astragalus, R23 and cushion U2. The bird is O.2267A, and the double medallion was used by potter X-5, and the only possibility for the frond is Rogers's K22. c. AD 125–145 CG.
2. (Pit A14.2)    37    This ovolo is known from an f.30 (Museum of London 122296): the core always seems to be squashed to the right, pushing the tongue out to the side. The bird is O.2291, cf. Bushe-Fox 1928, Pl. XXVII.11, stamped by MERCATO. c. AD 75–90 SG.
3. (A49.3)    37    Feet of figure D344; probably in the DOECCVS style, cf. CGP, Pl. 150.41 for the beads, and 147.7 for the foliage. c. AD 160–190 CG.
4. (Pit B12c.4)    37    Small palm leaf used by ALBVS together with his roped column (Mus. de Fenaille, Rodez). c. AD 50–65 SG.
5. (B45)    37    Rogers's ovolo B109, used by BVTRIO, CATVSSA and GRANIO. c. AD 130–160? CG.
6. (A73)    37    Rogers's ovolo B14, used by potter X-14 and SACER. The flattened beads are in the DONNAVCVS/SACER style, cf. CGP, Pl. 84.1. The figures are indistinct. c. AD 125–150? CG.
7. (A96)    37    Possibly the IVSTVS ovolo; there is a similar impression on an f.30 (Mus. of Lond. 117739). c. 75–90 SG.
8. (A73)    37    Probably by BIRAGILLVS, cf. K52, Taf. 6c. c. AD 80–110 SG.
9. (B100)    37    Warrior, D136, with candelabra, Rogers's Q50. c. AD 100–120 M de V.
10. (B93A)    37    PATERNVS style; his use of a small ring in a double medallion, cf. CGP Pl. 108.40. The bird is O.2316. c. AD 160–190 CG.
11. (A50)    37    Rogers's ovolo B12, probably on an Antonine piece; it was used then by CRICIRO, DIVIXTVS and CINNAMVS. c. AD 150–180? CG.
12. (Pit B14)    37    Figure D381, with Rogers's G334?, used by SECVNDINVS and the QVINTILIANVS group. c. AD 125–145 CG.
13. (A49)    37    Very excoriated, but sufficient to suggest the hand of AVSTRVS, cf. CGP. Pl. 21, for the astragali, the acanthus, and the frequent overrun of the laying-out line. c. AD 125–150 CG.
14. (A43)    37    DOECCVS style; his leaf, Rogers's H114, medallion E8 and cushion, U34. c. AD 160–190 CG.
15. (C13A)    37    Lion, O.1445 which is attributed to Banassac. However, this small sherd is almost certainly not from South Gaul. c. AD 100–120 M de V.
16. (A26)    37    Rogers's ovolo B38? c. AD 100–120 M de V.
17. (B50)    72    Figures D382 and D612?. Probably on a Hadrianic piece. CG.
18. (A99)    37    A scrap from Montans. Second century? Mont.
19. (A36)    37    Badly moulded piece in a fabric used by the PATERNVS group. Late Antonine. CG.

### (ii) Theological College 1985/7

20. (B1)    37    An early piece in the CINNAMVS style with a bear, D 820, a demi-medallion, Rogers's F40, and a vine scroll M2. c. AD 145–170 CG.
21. (F2)    37    A very small trident-tipped tongue, with an asymmetric egg. Known so far only from Colchester. c. AD 75–90? SG.
22. (10)    37    Rogers's beaded medallion, C295 used as an ovolo replacement, with column P85, and warrior D136. The fabric is micaceous and GEMINVS is a likely candidate. c. AD 120–140 CG.
23. (A7) (A47)    29    The cordate, stipuled bud was used by GENIALIS, cf. *K52*, Taf. 57.1 and also from La Graufesenque (Mus. de Millau). c. AD 55–70 SG.
24. (F3)    37    Rogers's ovolo B45 attributed to ARCANVS. c. AD 120–140 CG.

Fig.11.1    Figured samian ware from Chichester. Nos 1–19, Greyfriars 1984; nos 20–24, Theological College 1985 and 1987.
Scale 1:2

## ARRETINE AND SOUTH GAULISH (Fig. 11.2)

### Theological College

1. (A13)     Loeschke 2a. This piece looks Italian, but has a Gaulish shape, cf. O and P, Pl. XLII. 9/10. Tiberian. Italian.
2. (A13)     Loeschke 8a. Aug.-Tiberian. Arr.
3. (A13)     Loeschke 14a. Aug.-Tiberian. Italian.
4. (F2)     Loeschke 1a. The profile looks early, but the slip is not Italianate and nearer to SG. The paste is highly calcareous. Tiberian. SG?
5. (A13/F4)     Ritt.5. Tib.-Claud. SG.
6. (A13)     Loeschke 14. Hawkes and Hull, 1947, type A. Probably Italian. Tiberian. Arr?
7. (A13)     Dr. 24/5. Claudian. SG.
8. (A13)     Loeschke 2a. *op. cit.*, type 10, (Fig. 42). Aug.-Tiberian. Arr.
9. (A13)     Dr. 17. Profile as O and P, Pl. XLII.3 but Italian. Aug.- Tiberian. Arr?
10. (A13)     Loeschke 14a. Aug.-Tiberian. Arr?
11. (A13)     Loeschke 8 or 8a, wall. Aug.-Tiberian. Arr.
12. (A13)     Loeschke 14. Tiberian. Italian?

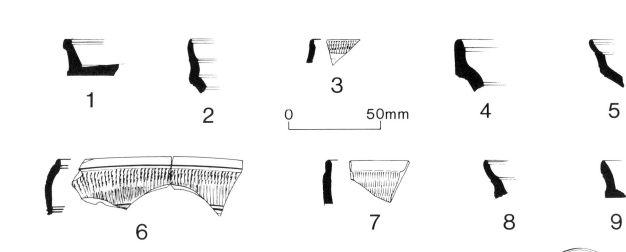

Fig.11.2    Arretine and South Gaulish wares from Theological College 1985. Scale 1:2. Arretine stamp 1:1

### STAMP

*Note*: Number in italics is the small find number.

### Theological College

a.   C.N.ATEI   *58*, (A52/61) on a plate, cf. O-C, 205,312 and 347a by description, with the curious 'division sign' inside the praenomen. It is interesting that 347a comes from Silchester. Tiberian? Arr.

This group of early sigillata complements those previously reported from Fishbourne, Chichester and Selsey. There remain few contacts with Oberaden, and the majority of the finely slipped, well-moulded pieces fall into the range described at Haltern. The series is completed by provincial and Gaulish wares which are eventually overtaken by a standard South Gaulish ware from the late Tiberian period onwards.

The quantities seen are not yet conducive to establishing a reliable population distribution, and this is best seen from the stamps, still less than 20 from the whole area. Those which are identifiable seem to have their connections with Rhine frontier developments. At this point the sourcing is not unlike Camulodunum, the open question being whether the trade route is direct, from the south, or a continuation of coasting from the north. Intuitively, I favour the possibility that the earliest pieces may be the result of direct trade, but that it was later replaced by supplies from traders drawing on Rhineland stocks. Direct trade would be represented by the earliest pieces from Lezoux and Montans. Camulodunum has consistently produced a far larger haul than any other contemporary site, and domination of such a trade may be connected with the expansion of the Catuvellauni, to both the east and west. Control over merchant activity deriving from the rich legionary forts would surely have been a valuable prize for predatory Celtic chieftains, and the stuff of which wars have been made throughout history.

In terms of dating, the lack of two-line stamps, and the small showing for Service 1 indicates that we should be looking to the last decade B.C.E. for a start of substantial trade, and this takes us into the occupation period of Haltern. Can the evidence take us further? Only tenuously, I think. Working from the other end, we do have a 'pre-export' South Gaulish presence (D1002) (Dannell, forthcoming) being a typical example; we have early Montans ware (Chichester Cathedral), we have early Lezoux products. These typically belong to the period c. AD 15–30/5, and can be seen as the intermediate economic phase, which includes La Muette, before the real weight of production passed finally from Italy to the provinces. In quantity these wares are much less than the total of Italian sigillata. Unless we are to postulate a gap in supply or availability, this may help us to see the Italian wares as coming from the first decade AD rather than earlier, but the judgement is subjective and fine.

### Addenda and Corrigenda to Chichester 6

While all samian reports suffer the erosion of the advancement of knowledge, four pieces deserve a prompt updated commentary:

11. May be associated with No 69 from Fishbourne (Cunliffe, 'Excavations at Fishbourne, 1961–9'), as belonging to the series published from the newly postulated production centre at Brive (Moser and Tilhard 1987, ovolo A).
18, 40 and 162. Can now be confirmed as belonging to the CALVVS workshop. The ovolo is the one with the smaller of two rosettes which he used, and much evidence from rubbings made by the Cardiff extra-mural class, led by Dr P.V. Webster, covers the detail. CALVVS was a 'Master Potter' cf. Knorr (Germania, 26) who stamped form 29 in the interior, signed form 37 in the mould, and apparently worked with other potters. A bowl from the same mould as No 49, from Fishbourne, but found at La Graufesenque, has the signature of CALVOS (Gaulish) in the decoration and a plain ware stamp of PATRICIVS on one of the handles (by kind permission of M. Alain Vernhet). A re-assessment of the material is awaited from Miss Brenda Dickinson, who has been very helpful in providing comparative material.

### Abbreviations

| | |
|---|---|
| Arr. | Arretine |
| Asciburgium | Vanderhoeven, M., 1975. *Funde aus Asciburgium*, Duisburg. |
| CG | Central Gaulish |
| CGP | Stanfield, J. and Simpson, G. 1958. *Central Gaulish Potters*, London |
| D | Dechelette, J., 1904. *Les Vases ceramiques ornes de la Gaule romaine*, Paris. |
| K19 | Knorr, R., 1919. *Topfer und Fabriken verzierter Terra-sigillata de ersten Jahrhunderts*, Stuttgart. |
| K52 | Knorr, R., 1952. *Terra-sigillata-Gefasse des ersten mit Topfernamen*, Stuttgart. |
| La Nautique | Fiches, J.L., Guy, M., and Poncin, L. 1978. 'Un lot de vases sigillées de premières années du regne de Neron dans l'un des ports de Narbonne' *Archaenautica* Vol. 2, 1978. |
| Lez. | Lezoux |
| M de V | Les Martres-de-Veyre |
| O | Oswald, F., 1937. *Index of Figure-Types on Terra Sigillata*, University of Liverpool. |
| O and P | Oswald, F., and Davies Pryce, T., 1920. *An introduction to the study of Terra Sigillata*, London. |
| O-C | Oxe, A., and Comfort, H. (eds.), 1968. *Corpus Vasorvm Arretinorvm (A Catalogue of the Signatures, Shapes and Chronology of Italian Sigillata)*, Bonn. |
| Rogers | Rogers, G., 1974. *Poteries sigillées de la Gaule Centrale*, Paris. |
| SG | South Gaulish |

### BIBLIOGRAPHY

Atkinson, D., 1914. 'A hoard of samian ware from Pompeii' *JRS*, 4, 27–64
Bird, J., and Marsh, G., 1978. Report in *Southwark Excavations 1972–4* 1, 96ff.
Boon, G.C., 1967. 'Micaceous sigillata from Lezoux at Silchester, Caerleon and other sites' *Ant. J.* 47, 1, 27ff.
Bushe-Fox, J., 1928. *Second Report on Excavations at the Roman Fort of Richborough, Kent* (London).
Cunliffe, B.W. (ed.), 1968. (ed.) *Fifth Report on the Excavations at the Roman Fort at Richborough, Kent* (Oxford).
Dannell, G.B., (forthcoming) 'The Plain Arretine from Fishbourne (A27)' in A. Down *Chichester Excavations 9*.
Frere, S.S., 1972. *Verulamium* (London).
Hawkes, C.F.C., and Hull, M.R., 1947. *Camulodunum* (Oxford).
Hermet, F., 1934. *La Graufesenque* (Paris).
Hull, M.R., 1958. *Roman Colchester* (Oxford).
Moser and Tilhard, J.L., 1987. 'Un Nouveau Atelier de sigillée en Aquitaine' *Revue Aquitania*, Tome 5
Oswald, F., 1937. 'Carinated bowls (Form 29) from Lezoux', *JRS* 27, 210ff.
Piboule, A., *et al.*, 1981. *Les Potiers de Lezoux du Premier Siècle: Titos* (Avignon).
Stanfield, J., 1935. 'A samian bowl from Bewcastle, with a note on the potters Casurius and Apolauster' in *CW*, 35, 182–205
Stead, I.M., and Rigby, V., 1986. *The Excavation of a Roman and Pre-Roman Settlement, 1968–72*, Brit. Mon. Ser. 7 (London).
Terrisse, J.R., 1968. *Les Ceramiques Sigillées Gallo Romaine des Martres-de-Veyre* (Paris).
Ulbert, 1967. *Novasium* 1, Limesforschungen Band 6.
Van Giffen, 1944. *Jaarverslag van de Vereeniging voor Terponderzoek*, 1940–44, 25/8.
Wacher, J.S., and McWhirr, A.D., 1982. *Early Roman Occupation at Cirencester* (Cirencester)

# 12

# Samian potters' stamps from Chichester

## by Brenda Dickinson

Each entry gives: site code, context number, small find number, potter (i, ii, etc. where homonyms are involved), die number, form, pottery of origin, date. (a), (b) and (c) indicate:

(a)  Stamp attested at the pottery in question.
(b)  Potter, but not the particular stamp, attested at the pottery in question.
(c)  Assigned to the pottery on the evidence of fabric, distribution and, or, form.

Some entries also give published example of type.
   *Note*: see Fig. 12.1 for interpretation of stamps. Underlined letters are ligatured. Small find numbers are in italics.

*Key to sites*:
| | |
|---|---|
| CH/84/CS | —Chapel Street 1984 |
| CH/84/G | —Greyfriars |
| CH/T/85 | —Theological College |
| CH.P.87 | —St Peter's, North Street |
| CH.W.87–8 | —West Walls |

| | | | | | | |
|---|---|---|---|---|---|---|
| 1 | [ADVOC]ISĐ | c.A.D. 160 - 190 | | 24 | [MA]RTIIO | c.A.D. 160 - 190 |
| 2 | ΛΓIIRI. | c.A.D. 160 | | 25 | [O]F .MVRRAN̄ | c.A.D. 50 - 65 |
| 3 | MAND[IMA] | c.A.D. 50 - 65 | | 26 | OFNI[GR] | c.A.D. 60 - 70 |
| 4 | [ΛVITV]S·F·V | c.A.D. 100 - 120 | | 27 | [PATER]NIAF | Late 2nd/early 3rd c. |
| 5 | IINIBI[NHM] | c.A.D. 100 - 120 | | 28 | [QE]CVLIAR·F | c.A.D. 140 - 160 |
| 6 | BIGA[·FEC] | c.A.D. 125 - 145 | | 29 | [PRIM]IGENIM | c.A.D. 140 - 160 |
| 7 | CALVINI | c.A.D. 140 - 170 | | 30 | OFIC·PRI[MI] | c.A.D. 55 - 70 |
| 8 | OFCΛLVI | c.A.D. 65 - 90 | | 31 | [R]OPPI· [RV] | c.A.D. 100 - 120 |
| 9 | CΛ·PI·TV·Γ | Flavian | | 32 | RV [FFI˙M] | c.A.D. 140 - 160 |
| 10 | OFCELADI | c.A.D. 45 - 65 | | 33 | SECVNDI | c.A.D. 70 - 90 |
| 11 | ]DI | c.A.D. 45 - 65 | | 34 | SENISF | Tiberian |
| 12 | CELSIAN[IF] | c.A.D. 170 - 200 | | 35 | SEVE[RIMΛN] | c.A.D. 70 - 90 |
| 13 | COR | Tiberio - Claudian | | | or | |
| 14 | OFCO[IVC] | c.A.D. 80 - 110 | | | SEVE[RIMΛI] | |
| 15 | CRES[TIO] | c.A.D. 45 - 65 | | 36 | SVIIRIV | c.A.D. 70 - 85 |
| 16 | CRICIRONISOF | c.A.D. 135 - 165 | | 37 | VIDVCV[SF] | c.A.D. 100 - 120 |
| 17 | DOCCALI | c.A.D. 130 - 160 | | 38 | [VI]TALI‹S› | c.A.D. 70 - 95 |
| 18 | [DON͡]N͡ΛVCI | c.A.D. 100 - 120 | | 39 | ΛΥNΛI[ | Flavian/Flavian - Trajanic |
| 19 | [FELIC]IONS | c.A.D. 65 - 85 | | 40 | ⅢⅢ[ | Flavian - Trajanic |
| 20 | MΛCRIΛΛ | c.A.D. 125 - 150 | | 41 | ᴖᴖᴖ OᴗΛ | Trajanic ? |
| 21 | M͡ALLVRO | c.A.D. 140 - 160 | | 42 | XXV[ | Flavian - Trajanic |
| 22 | M͡ARCIILLIΛI | Trajanic - early Hadrianic | | 43 | ]I.M | Antonine |
| | or | | | 44 | V[ or ]Λ | Antonine |
| | M͡ARCIILLIΛ | | | 45 | ]IC | Antonine |
| 23 | MΛRTIΛ | c.A.D. 165 - 190 | | 46 | O/\VIΛ | Antonine |

Fig.12.1   Interpretation of samian stamps

1. CH.W.87 30 Advocisus 2a 33 Lezoux (a).
   A stamp used on a wide variety of forms, including some introduced c. AD 160, such as 31R, 79 and Ludowici forms Tg and Tx. c. AD 160–90.

2. CH.W.87 29 Aferus 1a 37 rim.
   A central Gaulish Afer is known, but this is too late to be one of his stamps, and the name Aferus would be grammatically more correct. The decoration is similar to the Paternus bowl from Brigetio (Juhasz 1935) and the fabric and glaze of the Chichester piece make origin at Lezoux virtually certain. Only one other example has been noted, on the rim of a decorated bowl from Rottweil with the same ovolo as this (information from J. Lauber). Antonine, possibly after AD 160, though not necessarily much later.

3. CH.W.87 13 *34* Amandus ii 10b 15/17 or 18 (Paunier 1981, no 60) La Graufesenque (a).
   There is no internal dating evidence for this stamp. Amandus stamped forms 16 and Ritt. 8 and his stamps turn up in a group of samian of c. AD 50–60 at La Graufesenque and in the Cirencester Fort Ditch group of c. AD 55–65. A date c. AD 50–65 is likely, therefore.

4. CH/T/85 A13/F4 *89* Avitus ii 1a 27 Les Martres-de-Veyre (a).
   There are eight examples of this stamp from London Second Fire deposits. The meaning of the final V (cf. Dagomarus at Les Martres) is not obvious. c. AD 100–20.

5. CH/T/85 F1 *91* Balbinus 2a 18/31 Les Martres-de-Veyre (a).
   The die for this originally gave BALBINIM, but damage or inefficient cleaning soon caused it to produce this rather misleading stamp, often attributed to Ainibinus or Enibinus. It occurs in the London Second Fire deposits and occasionally on form 15/17, which was not normally made at Les Martres after the Trajanic period. c. AD 100–20.

6. CH/T/85 U/S *90* Biga 1a 27? Lezoux (a).
   Examples of this in the Rhineland and on Hadrian's Wall suggest that it was in use in the second quarter of the 2nd century. It occurs on forms 18/31, 18/31R, 27, 31, 38 and 42. c. AD 125–45.

7. CH/84/G C53 *228* Calvinus ii 3a 33 Lezoux (b). c. AD 140–70.

8. CH/84/CS X23 *61* Calvus i 5o' 18 La Graufesenque (b).
   No other examples of this stamp have been noted. It comes from a die made by *surmoulage*, from the impression of a longer die on a pot. Stamps from the original die (5o) occur at Flavian foundations, such as Binchester, Caerwent and Rottweil, but also in the pre-Flavian cemeteries at Nijmegen. c. AD 65–90.

9. CH/84/G A96 *109* Capitus ii 2a 15/17 or 18 La Graufesenque (a).
   This occurs at the Nijmegen fortress and Ulpia Noviomagus sites and at the Chester fortress. Flavian.

10,11. CH/84/G A83 *279*; CH/T/85 U/S *93* Celadus 1b 15/17 or 18 (2) La Graufesenque (a).
   Celadus's stamps occur on plain ware in groups of samian of c. AD 50–60 and the early 60s at La Graufesenque and Oberwinterthur (Switzerland), respectively, also on decorated bowls of the period c. AD 45–65.

12. CH/84/CS Pit X14 (B) *59* Celsianus 8a 33 Lezoux (a).
   This stamp occurs at Chester-le-Street (founded in the 160s), at South Shields, in a late-Antonine context at Lezoux and on forms 31R, 79 and 80. c. AD 170–200.

13. CH/T/85 A13 *4* Cor- 1b Ritterling 5 La Graufesenque (b).
   A vessel in coarse, pale orange fabric, with limestone inclusions. Presumably samian, though Arretine stamps in COR are known (Oxe and Comfort 1968, 153, 467). Tiberio-Claudian, though unlikely to be later than c. AD 45.

14. CH/84/G Slot A3 *112* Cosius Iucundus 1b 27 La Graufesenque (b).
   One of the less-common stamps of a potter whose wares turn up at sites such as Catterick, Newstead and the Nijmegen fortress. c. AD 80–110.

15. CH.W.87 38 *115* Crestio 15a 24 (Hermet 1934, pl.110, no43) La Graufesenque (a).
   Crestio's general record suggests Claudio-Neronian activity. This stamp, normally found on cups, often of forms 24 and R.8, will have been in use in the period c. AD 45–65.

16. CH/84/CS Pit X21 *20* Criciro v 7a 18/31R Lezoux (b).
   No other examples of this stamp are recorded. Criciro's wares occur on Hadrian's Wall, but are more common in Antonine Scotland. His forms include 18/31 and 27, and one stamp is known on form 79. c. AD 135–65.

17. CH/84/G A60 *57* Doccalus 5c 33 Lezoux (b).
   There are eleven examples of this stamp in a group of burnt samian of c. AD 140–50 at Castleford. It is also known at Rhineland forts and on forms 18/31, 27 and 81. One of his other stamps is in a pit at Alcester filled in the 150s. c. AD 130–60.

18. CH/84/G A1 *89* Donnaucus 2e 27 Les Martres-de-Veyre (b).
   There is no site dating for this, but vessels with other stamps of Donnaucus occur in the London Second Fire groups and he is known to have made form 15/17, which would be unusual at Les Martres after Trajan. c. AD 100–20.

19. CH/T/85 F4 *87* Felicio i 4a flat base La Graufesenque (b).
   Apart from one example on form 29 (without surviving decoration), all the stamps recorded for this potter are on dishes. This particular stamp occurs at a pre-Flavian cemetery at Nijmegen and another, from a different die, comes from Chester. c. AD 65–85.

20. CH/T/87 65 *75* Macrinus ii 4a 18/31 Lezoux (a).
   Stamps of this potter are common in Hadrianic-Antonine groups at Lezoux and one is known from the lowest level of the Birdoswald Alley. c. AD 125–50.

21. CH/84/G A73 *232* Malluro i 5c 18/31 Lezoux (a).
   Some of Malluro's stamps, including this one, occur at Rhineland forts, suggesting activity in the second quarter of the 2nd century. In view of his frequent use of forms 18/31 and 27, he is unlikely to have worked after c. AD 160, though two (unverified) examples are noted on form 80. c. AD 140-60.

22. CH/84/G B28 *242* Marcellinus i 1c or, more probably, 1c′ 27 Les Martres-de-Veyre (b).
    A stamp from the complete die (1c) is in the London Second Fire deposits, while the shorter version of the stamp occurs on an early variant of form 79. This particular piece seems, on the evidence of the fabric, to be Trajanic or early Hadrianic.
23. CH/84/CS Pit X14 (B) *60* Martinus iii 7a 79R or Ludowici TgR Lezoux (b).
    A stamp noted from Bainbridge, Binchester and Catterick, and on forms 79, 79R and 80. c. AD 165–90.
24. CH.W.87 3 *2* Martio 4a 33 Lezoux (a).
    Stamps from this die occur at forts in the Hadrian's Wall system reoccupied c. AD 160. 4a was used on form 31R and other dies were used on forms 79 and 80. A date c. AD 160–90 is not in doubt, therefore.
25. CH/84/CS X26 Murranus 8a 29 (O) retrograde (from a mould stamped in the decoration) La Graufesenque (b).
    This was used on form 29 both as a mould-stamp and an internal stamp (applied inside the base, after moulding). It also appears occasionally on dishes and on form Ritterling 8. The decorated bowls involved belong to the range c. AD 50–65.
26. CH/T/85 TTB1 B10 *2* Niger ii 4a′ 15/17 or 18 La Graufesenque (a).
    The die from which this stamp comes originally had an O without a stop in it and a frame with squarer ends than 4a′. A stamp from it occurs in the Cirencester Fort Ditch of c. AD 55–65. The modified version was also used in the pre-Flavian period, on form Ritterling 8, but there is an example on a different form from Caerleon. c. AD 60–70.
27. CH/84/CS X22 *63* Paternianus ii 3a 31R Rheinzabern (a).
    The only dating evidence for Paternianus ii comes from his use of forms 32, 36 and, with 3a, 31R. Late 2nd to first half of the 3rd century.
28. CH/T/85 F4 *19* Peculiaris i 5a 27 Lezoux (a).
    A stamp from the earlier of Peculiaris's common dies, used mainly on forms 18/31 and 27 and only occasionally on forms 79 and 80. It occurs at Wallsend and in Antonine Scotland. c. AD 140–60.
29. CH/84/G A41 *71* Primigenius ii 2a 31 Lezoux (c).
    All the stamps recorded from this die are on dishes. There are three examples on form 18/31 in a group of burnt samian of c. AD 140–50 from Castleford and one each from Camelon and Newstead, on forms 18/31R and 31, respectively. c. AD 140–60.
30. CH/84/CS X23 Primus iii 3a 15/17R or 18R La Graufesenque (a).
    A stamp used on form 29 and rouletted dishes, including one example of form 16R. A broken version of the die was also used to stamp form 29s. These are stylistically late for Primus and may belong to the early 70s. The Chichester piece, therefore, will fall into the range c. AD 55–70.
31. CH.P.87 39 *70* Roppus-Rutus 1a″ 18/31 Les Martres-de-Veyre (a).
    The stamp presumably represents the names of two potters, one of whom, Roppus ii, is known to have worked at Les Martres. Rutus is tentatively suggested for the other name. The die originally gave ROPPI.RVT.M, but was shortened after the surface had flaked off after the V. This almost certainly comes from the die in its final form, ROPPI.RV. The only dating evidence comes from the original version, 1a, which occurs in the London Second Fire material. c. AD 100–20.
32. CH.W.88 u/s *136* Ruffus ii 2a 33 (Curle 1911, no 82, which is taken, wrongly, as RVFFI. *MA*) Lezoux (b).
    Ruffus ii's stamps occur in Antonine Scotland, where they are known from Newstead (from two dies, including 2a) and Cappuck. They also turn up in the Rhineland, suggesting that part of his career, at least, was before c. AD 150, after which Lezoux ware scarcely reached the area. He stamped forms 18/31 and 27 with 2a and 18/31R with another die. c. AD 140–160.
33. CH.W.87 23 *82* Secundus ii 22e cup La Graufesenque (b).
    It is possible that Secundus ii began his work in the pre-Flavian period, but most of his output is Flavian. This particular stamp is known from Carlisle. c. AD 70–90.
34. CH/T/85 A9 *37* Senis i 1a Ritterling 5 (with footstand groove) in an internal frame La Graufesenque (c).
    No other stamps have been noted for this potter. Tiberian, on form and fabric.
35. CH/84/CS X23 Severus i 20a or 20a′ 15/17 or 18 La Graufesenque (b).
    Stamps from both the complete and broken dies occur at the Nijmegen fortress and 20a′ is also known from Caerleon, Chester and Catterick. c. AD 70–90.
36. CH/T/87 59 *89* S.Verius 2a 33a La Graufesenque (a).
    With one other exception, all the stamps from this die recorded by us are on form 29s of the early-Flavian period. They include examples from Camelon, Elginhaugh and the Nijmegen fortress. c. AD 70–85.
37. CH/T/87 44 *76* Viducus ii 5d concave base Les Martres-de-Veyre (a).
    There is no site dating for this stamp, but Viducus ii's wares occur in the London Second Fire groups, and he is known to have made form 15/17, which at Les Martres was almost entirely Trajanic. c. AD 100–20.
38. CH/T/85 A13 *67* Vitalis ii 25a′ 27 La Graufesenque (a).
    There is no evidence that this stamp was used in the pre-Flavian period, though Vitalis ii almost certainly began work in the 60s. c. AD 70–95.
39. CH/84/CS U/S *65* on form 15/17 or 18, South Gaulish. Flavian or Flavian-Trajanic.
40. CH/84/CS X16 *46* on form 27g, South Gaulish. An illiterate stamp. Flavian-Trajanic.
41. CH/84/CS X23 *66* and *67*, joining, on form 33a. Probably from Les Martres-de-Veyre, to judge by the pale, evenly speckled fabric and brownish glaze. Trajanic(?).
42. CH/84/G Pit A24 *234* on form 27g, South Gaulish. Flavian-Trajanic.
43. CH/84/G Pit B13 *240* on form 33, Central Gaulish. Antonine.
44. CH/T/87 22 *77* on form 33, Central Gaulish. Antonine.

45. CH.W.87 19 *75* on form 31, Central Gaulish, Antonine.
46. CH.W.87 14 *45*, retrograde, on form 33, Central Gaulish. Antonine.

## BIBLIOGRAPHY

Curle, J., 1911. *A Roman Frontier Post and its People, the Fort of Newstead* (Glasgow).

Dannell, G.B., 1971. 'The samian pottery' in B.W. Cunliffe, 'Excavations at Fishbourne 1961–1969' *RRSAL* XXVII, 260–318.

Delgado, M., 1975. *Fouilles de Conimbriga IV* (Paris).

Hartley, B.R., 1972. 'The samian ware' in S.S. Frere, 'Verulamium Excavations' I *RRSAL* XXCIII, 216–62 (Oxford).

Hartley, B.R., 1985. 'The samian ware' in L.F. Pitts and J.K. St. Joseph 'Inchtuthil: The Roman Legionary Fortress, 314–22, *Britannia Monograph Series No 6.*

Hartley, B.R., and Dickinson, B., 1982. 'The Samian' in Wacher, J., and McWhirr, A. *Cirencester Excavations 1* 119–46, (Cirencester).

Hawkes, C.F.C., and Hull, M.R., 1947. 'Camulodunum' *RRSAL* XIV (Oxford).

Hermet, F., 1934. *La Graufesenque (Condatomago)* (Paris).

Juhasz, G., 1935. *Die Sigillaten von Brigetio* (Budapest).

Knorr, R., 1919. *Topfer und Fabriken verzierter Terra-Sigillata des ersten Jahrhunderts* (Stuttgart).

Oxe, A., and Comfort, H., 1968. *Corpus Vasorum Arretinorum* (Bonn).

Paunier, D., 1981. *La ceramique gallo-romaine de Geneve* (Geneva).

Ulbert, G., 1959. *Die romischen Donau-Kastelle Aislingen und Burghofe* Limesforschungen 1 (Berlin).

# 13

# The Roman imported and local fine and specialist wares from the sites

## by Valery Rigby

The form and fabric classifications adopted for Greyfriars and Theological College sites are those used previously in *Chichester Excavations*, Volumes 3, 5 and 6. The sherd counts are summarised in Tables A–B and C–D respectively. Illustrated and catalogued sherds are confined to types or variants which are not adequately represented in previous volumes.

*Note*: Figures in brackets are context numbers.

### GREYFRIARS (Fig. 13.1)

### A. The Gaulish imports

*(i) Gallo-Belgic wares*

The typology is that published by Hawkes and Hull in *Camulodunum*, whilst the fabrics have been defined and described in Rigby 1973, 8. For the most recent discussion see Rigby 1989, 117–141.

The vessel forms (Table A and Fig. 13.1)

The collection is small, a maximum of 13 vessels has been recorded. The sherds are small and rather abraded, suggesting that they are residual and redeposited. Two large T.R. platters date to the pre-Claudian period, two T.N. platters are definitely post-Conquest in date, while the remainder fall between these two groups, and may have been pre- or post-Conquest imports.

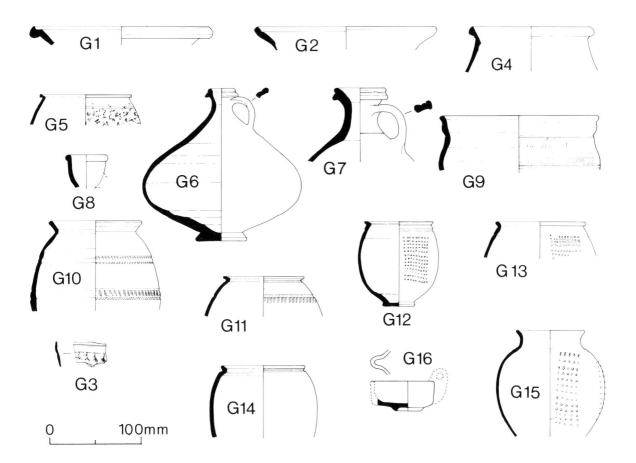

Fig. 13.1    Roman imported and local fine and specialist wares from Greyfriars 1984, nos 1–16. Scale 1:4

G1. (B159) Rim sherd from a large platter, Cam. form 4 in T.N. A rare form not previously recorded at Chichester. Probably Tiberio-Claudian.

G2. (B122A) Rim sherd from a platter, Cam. form 14, in T.N. Fairly common at Chichester, but in a wide range of variants; 20 are recorded in Chichester (Down 1978). AD 50–70.

*(ii) Central Gaulish wares*

(a) Lead-glazed vessels

G3. (C93) Body sherd from a round-bodied vessel, probably a flask or flagon (Greene Type 2). Moulded decoration on the upper frieze: a new motif not represented in Greene 1976. Orange fine sandy-textured ware, green glaze inside and out. The fabric is not typical of Central Gaulish products, but the use of moulded motifs on a round-bodied vessel is not characteristic of British products. Late 1st century AD.

(b) Metallic colour-coated wares

There are sherds from three vessels in typical 'Lyons Ware', a scaled bowl Cam. form 67 and two roughcast beakers Cam. form 94, all pre-Flavian in date. In all, 4 lamps, 10 bowls and 19 beakers have been found at Chichester, usually as very small and abraded sherds.

*(iii) Northern Gaulish butt beakers*

Sherds from three different butt beakers Cam. form 113 have been recorded. All are in typical, more or less iron-free, white ware, tempered with fine quartz sand and occasional grog inclusions. For a detailed discussion of the chronological significance of the various typological characteristics and their likely sources see Rigby 1989.

G4. (B104) Rim sherd from the variant with a cordon beneath the rim and a marked angle inside the neck; typologically one of the earliest examples yet recorded at Chichester (Down 1989, fig. 16.1, 13–16 for the later and definitely post-Conquest versions). Tiberio-Claudian.

*(iv). East Gaulish metallic colour-coated wares*

G5. (B74 and ph.B8) Rim and body sherds from a beaker with a double lip. Micaceous orange ware; thin brown slip over coarse grog rough-casting on the exterior. Probably imported from the Argonne potteries of East Gaul. AD 120–80.
(B122A) Sherd from a second example.

*(v) Fine-grained white ware flagons and lagenae*

(a) White pipeclay and white wares with dark-slipped interior

The finest textured and finished flagon wares have been grouped, although different and unknown production centres in North Gaul and the Rhineland could be involved. One sherd has a grey slip on the inner surface, the others are self-coloured. Five different vessels are represented, two by broad, multi-ribbed handles. The maximum date range may be AD 1–65 (Rigby 1989, 141–5)

(b) Sand-tempered buff 'Mortarium' wares

For the fabric description and range of forms see Down 1989, 118, where examples were very common. Only a single strap-handle is recorded from Greyfriars.

## B. Local specialist wares

*(i) Products of the Chapel Street kilns*

A group of 15 vessels had been manufactured at the early Roman kilns in Chapel Sreet, Chichester (Down 1978, 204–10). They are in fine quartz sand-tempered fabrics, orange or red, with a cream or white slip on the outer surface. The classifiable forms consist of close copies of Gaulish imports—two butt beakers, a barbotine beaker Cam. form 114 and a collared flagon (Down 1978 Types 1, 2 and 10).

*(ii) Fine-grained cream wares*

G6. (Pit A22) Many sherds joining to produce an almost complete vessel. A flanged flagon with an unusual squat body. Even-textured fine cream ware with self-coloured matt finish. Probably a local product. Late 2nd or 3rd century.

*(iii) Coarse-grained gritty Parchment ware*

G7. (B104) Complete neck and 10+ body sherds from a flanged flagon, the handle secured to the body with a tang. Parchment ware, heavily tempered with coarse quartz sand; self-coloured, matt finish, with blob of matt brown slip on the shoulder. Possibly from the Wiggonholt pottery (Evans 1974).

G8. (A26) Three rim sherds from a funnel-mouthed flagon or flask. The fabric is the same as no. 7 above.

*(iv) Fine grained Reduced wares*

(a) Smooth micaceous wares

G9. (A24) Two rims and a sherd from a bowl in soapy, smooth micaceous ware; grey with self-coloured surfaces. Decoration— a single broad band of rouletting. A similar bowl, but with different decoration was found on the Cattlemarket site (Down 1989, Fig. 16.2, 70).
G10. (Pit A25 and A73/80) Two rims and a sherd from a globular beaker in smooth micaceous grey ware. Decoration—at least two zones of rouletting.

(b) Smooth wares

G11. (A58) Rim sherd from a globular beaker in black ware with highly burnished finish. Decoration—rouletted zones.

(c) Slipped wares

G12. (A25) Three rims and 10+ body sherds from a globular beaker in fine quartz sand-tempered grey ware with a whitish-grey burnished slip on the outer surface. Decoration—barbotine spots in dark grey matt slip.
G13. (A25) Two rims and 20+ sherds from a beaker similar to no. 11.
G14. (A25) Twenty+ rims, bases and body sherds from a high-shouldered beaker in a similar fabric to nos 11 and 12, with a highly burnished bluish-white slip.
G15. (B104) Four rims and a sherd from a poppy-head beaker. Grey ware with a darker burnished slip. Decoration—barbotine spots in a dark matt slip.
   (B95) Rim from another in reduced Parchment ware; white ware with blue-grey surfaces.
G16. (Pit A25) Sherds from a lampholder. Quartz sand-tempered ware, grey core, orange undersurfaces and cream slip. Traces of burning inside.


## THEOLOGICAL COLLEGE (Fig. 13.2).

The pottery from the context A52/61 has been catalogued as a single group. Sherds from the remainder of the site have been grouped together at the end of this section. The size and condition of the sherds is better than Greyfriars.

*Context A52/61*

The predominance of vessels in TN yet the absence of late cup and platter forms, particularly Cam. forms 14, 16 and 58, suggest a date of deposition between AD 50 and 60.


## A. The Gaulish imports

*(i) The Gallo-Belgic wares*

T1.   Large platter Cam. form 2, in TN. Rims from three others. Late Augusto-Neronian.
T2.   Platter, Cam. form 15, in TN. Claudio-Neronian.
T3.   Large platter, Cam. form 3, in TN. Stamped CICARV (Fig. 13.3, 1).
T4.   Large platter, Cam. form 3, in TN. Rims and sherds from six others, all in TN. Late Augusto-Neronian.
T5.   Small platter, Cam. form 9, in TN. ( *not illustrated*). Claudio-Neronian.
T6.   Base sherds from two small platters, Cam. form 7 or 8, in TN *(not illustrated)*.
T7.   Small cup, Cam. form 56A in TN. Rims from two others. Tiberio-Neronian.
T8.   Small cup, Cam. form 56A in TR1(C). Rim from a second example. Tiberio-Neronian, possibly pre-Claudian.
T9.   Pedestal cup, Cam. form 74, in TR3. Tiberio-Claudian.
T10.  Girth beaker, Cam. form 82, in apricot TR3. Probably pre-Claudian.
T11.  Girth beaker, Cam form 84, in orange TR3. Tiberio-Claudian.
T12.  Cylindrical beaker in apricot TR3, Tiberio-Claudian possibly pre-Claudian. Sherds from a second example with joining sherds in A2.
T13.  Two rims and 10+ sherds from an ovoid beaker in orange TR3. Tiberio-Claudian. Sherds from a second example.
T14.  Beaker base, form unknown, possibly from vessels 10 or 12, in apricot TR3.
T15.  Barbotine beaker, Cam. form 114 in typical smooth white ware, with mica coating on the rim. Tiberio-Neronian. A single body sherd has chevron barbotine decoration and may be from the same vessel.

*(ii) Central Gaulish wares*

T16.  Platter base, form unknown, in micaceous TN. Probably late Augustan.
T17.  Base from a tazza Cam. form 51 in micaceous TN, burnished spiral on the inner surface. Late Augusto-Claudian.

*(iii) Northern Gaulish butt beakers*

T18. Rim sherd from Variant 1A1 (Rigby 1989, Fig. 56). Typical white ware tempered with fine quartz sand. Probably late Augustan.

T19. Rim sherd from Variant 2B2 ( *op. cit.*, Fig. 56) Typical fabric.

*(iv) Flagons in fine-grained white wares*

T20. Rim sherd from a reeded-rim flagon or lagena, Cam. form 163. Cream ware, probably from a workshop in Gallia Belgica. Tiberio-Neronian.

**B. Local specialist wares**

*(i) Products of the Chapel Street kilns*

T21. Rim sherd from a screwneck flagon in orange ware with thin cream slip. Also 20+ body sherds possibly from the same vessel.

T22. Jar base, form unknown. Orange ware (*not illustrated*).

**Summary**

Tables C–D summarise the finds from all contexts of the Theological College site.

**A. The Gaulish imports**

*(i) The Gallo-Belgic wares*

(a) The potters' stamps

GB1. (A52/61), CICARV, 1 radial; 2 bordered rouletted wreaths. Platter, Cam form 3 (Fig. 13.3, 3). TN—light blue-grey fine sandy-textured ware; dark blue-grey surfaces; abraded.

Cicarvs Die1A1. Stamps from this die and the closely related Die1A2 have been recorded on TN platters at Gatesbury (Braughing) and Camulodunum; on TR platters Cam. forms 5 and 8 at Dalheim, Hofheim (3), Andernach (2), Trier (2), Cologne, Rheims and Vertault; on a TR cup Cam. form 56 at Lebach, Grave 21. The presence of his products at Hofheim and Dalheim confirm that Cicarvs was working in the Claudian period. The predominance of TR implies that he began work in the Tiberian period, but after AD 25, since he included platters Cam. form 8 in his repertoire. Production site unknown; c. AD 30–60.

GB2. (A9), T/R/O/X/ roundel. central; combed wreath of 4 concentric circles. Large platter, form unknown; TN—white fine sandy-textured ware; blue-grey surfaces; polished upper. Troxos Die 1A1. Stamps from this die have been recorded on TN platters, Cam. form 3 and 5, at Camulodunum, Blicquy, Cracouville and Weisenau (2). The vessel forms were produced from the Late Augustan to Neronian period. The absence of TR suggests that Troxos worked after AD 25. Production centre unknown; c. AD 30–60.

**B. The forms**

None illustrated

*(ii) Central Gaulish wares*

(a) Lead-glazed wares

T23. Rim sherd from a carinated bowl cf. Drag. 29 (Greene type 5.2). The upper freize appears to be decorated with the typical arcades (Greene 1978, fig. 3.5). Second half of 1st century AD.

(b) Metallic colour-coated wares

There are body sherds from two vessels with rough-cast decoration, form unknown.

(c) Micaceous TN

Small sherds from three different vessels; a large platter Cam. form 4, a small platter and a tazza Cam. form 51. (For a full description of the fabric-range and discussion of the typology, chronology and sources of micaceous TN, see Rigby 1989, 120–1)

*(iii) Northern Gaulish butt beakers*

Sherds from a minimum of three vessels.

*(iv) Fine-grained white ware flagons and lagenae (Table D)*

T24. (A9) Complete rim circuit and handles from a reeded-rim lagena, Cam. form 163, in white pipeclay ware. Tiberio-Neronian.

## BIBLIOGRAPHY

Down, A., 1978. *Chichester Excavations 3* (Phillimore).

Down, A., 1981. *Chichester Excavations 5* (Phillimore).

Down, A., 1989. *Chichester Excavations 6* (Phillimore).

Evans, K.J., 1974. 'Excavations at a Romano-British Site, Wiggonholt 1964' *SAC* 112.

Greene, K.T., 1978. 'Mould decorated Central Gaulish glazed ware in Britain' in P. Arthur and G.B. Marsh (eds.), *Early fine Wares in Roman Britain, BAR* 57.

Rigby, V., 1973. 'Potters' stamps on Terra Nigra and Terra Rubra found in Britain' in A. Detsicas (ed.), *Current research in Romano-British coarse pottery* CBA Res. Rep. 10, 7–24.

Rigby, V., 1989. In I.M. Stead and V. Rigby, 'Verulamium: The King Harry Lane Site', *HBMC (E) Arch. Rep. 12* 117–145.

**Table A**
**Gallo-Belgic imports, Greyfriars**

| Forms | TN | TR1(A) | TR1(B) | TR1(C) | TR2 | TR3 | Totals |
|---|---|---|---|---|---|---|---|
| Cam. 3 | | | | 2 | 1 | | 3 |
| Cam. 4 | 1 | | | | | | 1 |
| Cam. 5 | | | | 1 | | | 1 |
| Cam. 14 | 1 | | | | | | 1 |
| Cam. 16 | 1 | | | | | | 1 |
| Cam. 56C | 1 | | | | | | 1 |
| Total | 4 | | | 3 | 1 | | 8 |
| Small platters | 3 | | | | | | 3 |
| Total | 3 | | | | | | 3 |
| Beaker sherds | | | | | | 1 | 1 |
| Total | | | | | | 1 | 1 |
| Cam. 74/79 | | 1 | | | | | 1 |
| Total | | 1 | | | | | 1 |

**Table B**
**Flagons from Greyfriars**

| | Imported | | | Local | |
|---|---|---|---|---|---|
| Flagons | Pipeclay/ smooth cream ware | Fine cream | Mortarium cream | Gritty cream | Red ware, white slip. Chapel St. kilns |
| Flanged rim Fish. 298 | | 1 | | 1 | |
| Pulley-mouthed Fish. 297 | | 1 | | | |
| Funnel mouth Grave 138f Chichester 1 | | | | 1 | |
| Even rings Fish. 109 | | 1 | | | |
| Collared Chichester 3 Type 10 | | | | | 1 |
| Bases | | | | 1 | 2 |
| Handles | 2 | 1 | 1 | | |
| Sherds | 11 | | | 10+ | 2 |

**Table C**
**Gallo-Belgic imports, Theological College**

| Forms | TN | TR1(A) | TR1(B) | TR1(C) | TR2 | TR3 | Totals |
|---|---|---|---|---|---|---|---|
| Cam. 2 | 4 | | | | | | 4 |
| Cam. 3 | 9 | | | | | | 9 |
| Cam. 5 | 3 | | | | | | 3 |
| Cam. 7v | | | | 1 | | | 1 |
| Cam. 7/8 | 1 | | | | | | 1 |
| Cam. 9 | 1 | | | | | | 1 |
| Cam. 14 | 1 | | | | | | 1 |
| Cam. 15 | 1 | | | | | | 1 |
| Cam. 16 | 1 | | | | | | 1 |
| Cam. 56 | 3 | | | 2 | | | 5 |
| Total | 24 | | | 3 | | | 27 |
| Large platters | 6 | | | | | | 6 |
| Small platters | 4 | | | | | | 4 |
| Cups | 2 | | | | | | 2 |
| Total | 12 | | | | | | 12 |
| Cam. 82 | | | | | | 1 | 1 |
| Cam. 84 | | | | | | 1 | 1 |
| Cam. 112 | | | | | | 8 | 8 |
| Cylindrical | | | | | | 2 | 2 |
| Beaker sherds | | | | | | 4 | 4 |
| Total | | | | | | 16 | 16 |
| Cam. 74 | | | | 1 | | 1 | 2 |
| Total | | | | 1 | | 1 | 2 |

**Table D**
**Flagons from Theological College**

| | Imported | | Local |
|---|---|---|---|
| Flagons | Pipeclay/smooth cream ware | Mortarium cream | Red ware, white slip. Chapel St. kilns |
| Pulley-mouthed, Fish.297 | | 1 | |
| Reeded cornice Cam. 163 | 2 | | |
| Screwneck | | | 1 |
| Bases | 1 | | 1 |
| Handles | 2 | | 1 |
| Sherds | 23 | 4 | 25+ |

**Table E**
**Consolidated list of cups, platters and bowls in TN and TR**

| Form | TR1(A) | TR1(C) | TR2 | Total TR | Total TN | Total |
|---|---|---|---|---|---|---|
| 2 | | | | | 16 | 16 |
| 3 | 0 | 3 | 1 | 4 | 12 | 16 |
| 4 | — | 0 | 0 | 0 | 1 | 1 |
| 5 | 1 | 10 | 4 | 15 | 16 | 31 |
| 7 | — | 1 | 0 | 1 | 0 | 1 |
| 7A | — | 0 | 0 | 0 | 1 | 1 |
| 7B | — | 1 | 0 | 1 | 0 | 1 |
| 7/8 | — | 1 | 0 | 1 | 0 | 1 |
| 8 | — | 2 | 2 | 4 | 14 | 18 |
| 9 | — | 2 | 2 | 4 | 3 | 7 |
| 12 | | | | | 2 | 2 |
| 13 | | | | | 12 | 12 |
| 14 | | | | | 40 | 40 |
| 15 | | | | | 1 | 1 |
| 16 | | | | | 113 | 113 |
| Hol 81 | | | | | 1 | 1 |
| Platter totals | 1 | 20 | 9 | 30 | 232 | 262 |
| 56 | | 6 | 3 | 9 | 8 | 17 |
| 58 | | 2 | 2 | 4 | 7 | 11 |
| Cup totals | | 8 | 5 | 13 | 15 | 28 |
| 50 | | | | | 5 | 5 |
| Exeter 247 | | | | | 2 | 2 |
| Bowl totals | | | | | 7 | 7 |

161

## Table F
## The consolidated list of potters' stamps on TN and TR

*Abbreviations.*
L, large; S, small; P, platter; R, radial; C, central; B, bordered; I, inverted line
whichever way stamp is orientated; [ ], lost letters; ( ), abbreviated or ligatured letters.

**i. Name stamps**

| | | |
|---|---|---|
| 1. | A[CVTII] | R L TN Acuto 3B2 AD 30–60 V,28 (CH23) |
| 2. | AN]DECO | B R L TR2 Andecos 1A1 AD 30–60 iii, 1 (CH11) |
| 3. | A]SSINO | R L TN Assinos 1A1 AD 20–50 iii, 2 (CHM6) |
| 4. | AEI[ | C 56 TN ?Aetius AD 40–65 vi, 1 (CH21) |
| 5. | ATE (IUS) | C 56 TN Aetius 3G1 AD 40–65 iii, 3 (CH9) |
| 6. | | B C S TN Avelucnios 2A2 AD 30–65 iii, 4 (CH6) |
| 7. | AVCNIᵒ | B C cup TN Benios AD 30–60 vi, 2 (CH15) |
| 8. | CASSICOS | R L TN Cassicos 2A1 AD 40–65 iii, 5 (CHM2) |
| 9. | CICARV | B R 5 TN Cicarus 1A1 AD 30–60 vii, 1 |
| 10. | IVLIO/AVOI | I C S TN Jul(1)ios 1C1 AD 40–65 iii, 7 (CH5) |
| 11. | IVLIVOII/IIOV[ | C P TN Jul(1)ios 601 AD 50–85 iii, 10 (CHM4) |
| 12. | IVIIOII | C P TN Jul(1)ios 2G4 AD 50–85 iii, 9 same (CH4) |
| 13. | IVI[IOII] | C 16 TN ?Jul(1)ios 2G4 AD 50–85 vi, 3 die (CH17) |
| 14. | IVI[IOII] | C 16 TN ?Jul(1)ios 2G4 AD 50–85 vi, 4 (CH20) |
| 15. | MASALLA | R L TN Masala 1A1 AD 30–50 iii, 11 (CHM1) |
| 16. | [M]EÐI | R L TN Medi 1A2 AD 30–65 iii, 12 (CH3) |
| 17. | [SΛ]CIRV | C cup TN Sacirus 1B1 AD 30–65 iii, 13 (CHM3) |
| 18. | SOLLOS | C P TR2 Sollos 1C1 AD 30–50 iii, 14 (CH1) |
| 19. | T/R/O/X/ | C P TN Troxos vii, 2 |

| | | |
|---|---|---|
| 20. VIIBRVS | C P TN Vebrus 1A1 iii, 15 (CH2) | |
| 21. VIIICO[ | R L TN Vilicos 1A1 iii, 16 (CH10) | |
| 22. [VOCAR]A/[FECI]T | C S TN ?Vocara 2G1 AD 30–65 iii, 18 (CH8) | |
| 23. [IOV]A XV | B C 58 TN Ux die AD 50–85 v, 29 (CH24) | |

**ii. Marks**

| | | |
|---|---|---|
| 24. IIIII[ | C P TN AD 50–85 vi, 6 (CH13) | |
| 25. OONO[ | C P TN AD 40–70 vi, 5 (CH14) | |
| 26. IV][V | C 16 TN AD 50–85 vi, 7 (CH18) | |
| 27. Ж˙ΛXΛ | R I TN iii, 19 (CH7) | |
| 28. VI ß | B C cup TN AD 40–65 iii, 20 (CHM5) | } same die |
| 29. V.V.\ ß | B C ?16 TN AD 50–85 vi, 8 (CH16) | |
| 30. V.[ | B C 16 TN AD 50–85 vi, 9 (CH19) | |
| 31. ? | C cup TR1(c) AD 40–65 vi, 10 (CH12) | |
| 32. ? | ? *SAC* 94, 5 (CHM8, not traced) | |

**iii. Unidentified fragments**

| | | |
|---|---|---|
| 33. A[ | B R L TN iii, 17 (CHM7) | |
| 34. ? | B C 7b TR2 AD 10–40 iii, 22 (CH22) | |

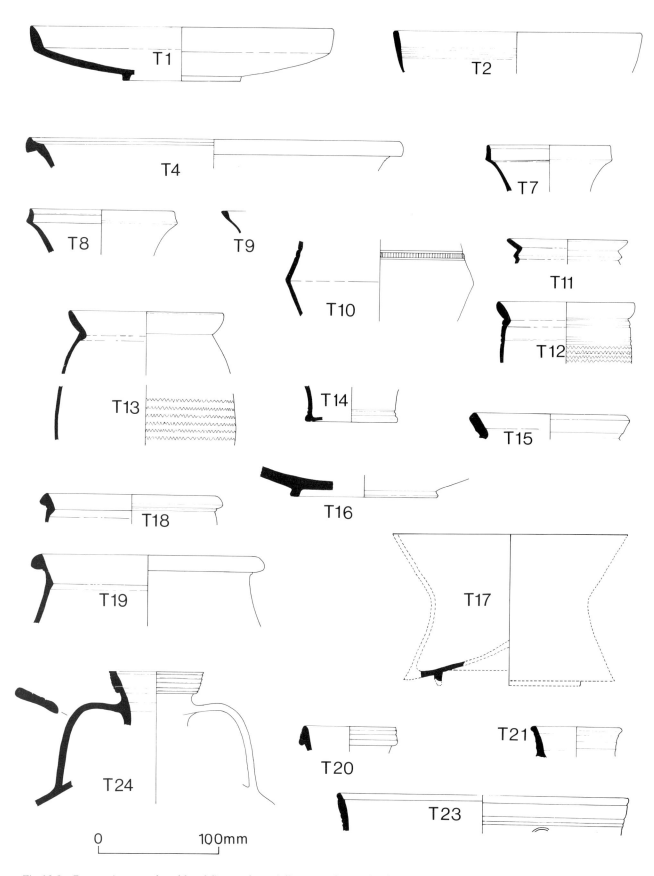

Fig.13.2   Roman imported and local fine and specialist wares from Theological College 1985, nos 1–24. Scale 1:3

GB1                                    GB2

Fig.13.3   Potters' stamps on Gallo-Belgic wares from Theological College 1985. Scale 1:1

# 14

# The amphorae from the sites

## by D.F. Williams

### INTRODUCTION

No complete amphorae were found during the excavations, but a large number of rims, handles and spikes were recovered, together with many featureless bodysherds. The amphorae sherds as a whole were classified by fabric and form. The classification of types is based on Dressel (1899), Pascual (1962), the Camulodunum series (Hawkes and Hull 1947), Pelichet (1946), Laubenheimer (1985) and Peacock and Williams (1986), supplemented by descriptive terms suggested by Peacock (1971; 1977a) and in common usage (Peacock and Williams 1986). The commonest amphora form present is the southern Spanish olive-oil vessel Dressel 20, with lesser amounts of Dressel 2-4, Dressel 1–Pascual 1, Pelichet 47, Camulodunum 185A, Peacock and Williams Class 59, Camulodunum 186A, Camulodunum 186C, Dressel 7-11, southern Spanish, Rhodian style, pseudo-Koan and a small number of unassigned sherds. Brief notes on the origins and chronological span of the amphorae are given below, and a selection of certain forms is published (see below and Fig. 14.1). The unabridged reports by sites are published in the Level 3 archive.

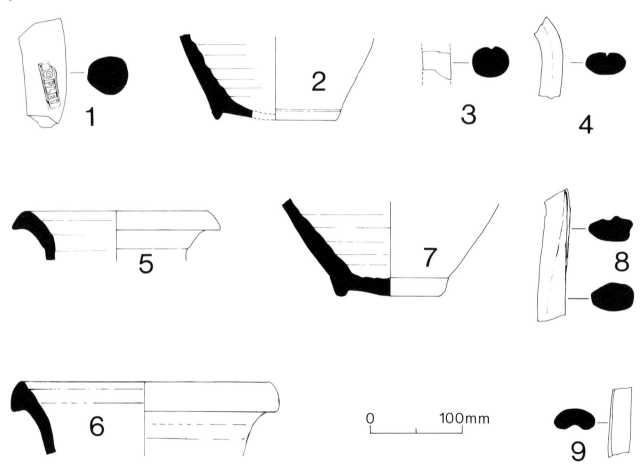

Fig.14.1    Roman amphorae from Greyfriars 1984, nos 1–2; Theological College 1985 and 1987, nos 3–9. Scale 1:4

### GENERAL DESCRIPTION OF FORMS AND FABRICS

#### Dressel 20

This is the commonest amphora form imported into Roman Britain, and was already present in some numbers during the late Iron Age (Williams and Peacock 1983). Dressel 20 amphorae were made along the banks of the River Guadalquivir and its tributaries between Seville and Cordoba in the southern Spanish province of Baetica, where they were used for the long-distance transportation of olive-oil (Ponsich 1974; 1979). This type of amphora has a wide date-range, from the

Augustan proto-type (Oberaden 83) with a fairly upright rim, a short spike and less of a squat bulbous body than the later form, to the well-known globular vessel which, with some typological variation was in use up to at least the late 3rd century AD (Peacock and Williams 1986, Classes 24 and 25). Rim forms of the earlier Oberaden 83 type are known from pre-Roman levels at Prae Wood, Gatesbury Track and Silchester, so that importation of Baetican olive-oil into Britain may have begun as early as the last decade of the 1st century BC. At Fishbourne (Williams forthcoming) the earliest Dressel 20 rim is dated elsewhere to the Tiberian period, with the majority of other rim forms falling in the date-range second half of the 1st century AD to early 2nd century AD. All the Dressel 20 rims from the sites can be paralleled with examples from Augst illustrated by Martin-Kilcher (1983) in her scheme for the development of the Dressel 20 rim.

## Dressel 2-4

This form of amphora has a simple rounded rim, long bifid handles formed from two rods and a solid, slightly flared or knobbed spike (Fig. 14.1, 3–9). Dressel 2-4 amphorae are the direct successors on Italian kiln sites to Dressel 1B amphorae and occur in a wide range of fabrics, dating from the latter half of the 1st century BC to the mid 2nd century AD (Peacock 1977b; Zevi 1966). However, as well as in Italy this form was produced elsewhere in considerable quantity, mostly but not exclusively in the western Mediterranean region. *Tituli picti* suggest that the main content was wine, although on occasion other commodities such as dates, fish sauces and even olive-oil could be carried (Zevi 1966; Sealey 1985; Peacock and Williams 1986, Class 10).

Included in the material are sherds in a dark red to reddish-brown fabric containing conspicuous inclusions of felspar with some granite fragments. It is probable that this vessel represents the Catalonian form of the Dressel 2-4 amphora (*ibid.*). Also at Fishbourne (Williams forthcoming), Greyfriars and Theological College is a rim and a number of handles and body sherds in a distinctive 'black sand' fabric—caused by the inclusion in the clay of frequent dark-coloured grains of augite. This particular fabric was used for the Republican Dressel 1 varieties of amphorae, but the comparatively thinnish walls of the sherds from Greyfriars and Theological College point on balance to the later Dressel 2-4 form (*ibid.*). The 'black sand' fabric is generally thought to indicate an origin in the area around Pompeii and Herculaneum (*ibid.*). The remainder of the Dressel 2-4 material appears to be made up of a majority of Italian fabrics.

## Dressel 1–Pascual 1

This form is characteristic of the Catalonia region of Spain, particularly the area around Barcelona, and probably carried wine (Pascual 1962; Pascual 1977; Keay and Jones 1982). It was made from the late Republican period to AD 79 at Pompeii (Tchernia 1971), although the majority of datable finds from north-western Europe are generally Augustan in date (Deniaux 1980; Williams 1981; 1988; Galliou 1984). The sherds from Fishbourne and Theological College are in my Fabric 1 (see Williams 1981). It is possible that the bodysherds from the Catalan amphora above may in fact belong to this form rather than Dressel 2-4.

In Britain, sherds of Dressel 1–Pascual 1 are usually found on late Iron Age pre-Roman sites, and the distribution tends to be concentrated in the central southern area (Williams 1988).

## Pelichet 47/Gauloise 4

This is a flat-bottomed wine amphora type predominately made in southern France, more particularly around the mouth of the Rhone in Languedoc, where a growing number of kilns have been discovered in recent years (Laubenheimer 1985). This form was produced for many years, from about the middle of the 1st century AD to at least the early 4th century AD (Panella 1973; Laubenheimer 1985). In Britain, Pelichet 47 does not appear to be present in pre-Boudiccan levels (Peacock 1978), with the main concentration of finds appearing to come from 2nd century contexts.

## Camulodunum 185A

This form has its origin in Baetica, southern Spain (Tchernia 1980), the similarity in fabric with the more common Dressel 20 suggesting a source in the region of the River Guadalquivir (Peacock 1971). Amphorae of Camulodunum 185A form (Haltern 70) recovered from the Port Vendres II shipwreck carry inscriptions describing the contents as *defrutum*, a sweet liquid obtained by boiling down the must (Colls *et al.* 1977; Parker and Price 1981). For a more recent discussion of the contents and interpretation of *defrutum* as belonging to the *vins cuits*, see van der Werff (1984). However, fish sauce also appears to have been carried in this form, a recent *titulus pictus* from London reads *mur(ia)* (Rodriguez-Almeida 1981). The date-range for Camulodunum 185A is from about the mid 1st century BC to around the mid 1st century AD (Colls *et al.* 1977; Tchernia 1980).

## Camulodunum 186A

This amphora form was made along the southern Spanish coast, *tituli picti* found on these vessels suggest that fish-based products such as the sauces *garum*, *liquamen* and *muria* were carried, as well as the salted fish themselves (Zevi 1966; Beltran 1970; Peacock 1974). Camulodunum 186A was made from the late 1st century BC to the early 2nd century AD and was widely distributed in the western Roman empire.

## Camulodunum 186C

A similar amphora form to Camulodunum 186A only with a broader neck and hooked rim, while the latter displays a bell mouth and a thickened short rim with a concave outer face. Made in the same region as Camulodunum 186A and carried much the same goods, although appearing at a slightly later date, from about the Flavian period or shortly before to the early 2nd century AD (Beltran 1970; Panella 1973).

## Camulodunum 186sp

This variety of amphora was made along the southern Spanish coast from the late 1st century BC to the early 2nd century AD and seems to have carried fish-based products.

Owing to the similarities of form and fabric in the Camulodunum 186A and C varieties, it is not possible to say whether the sherds listed in Level 3 archive belong to one form rather than the other.

## Southern Spanish

This material probably derives from the coastal regions of southern Spain, in particular between Cadiz and Malaga. The amphorae would have been used to carry fish-based products from around the late 1st century BC to the 2nd century AD (Peacock 1971; 1974).

## Hollow Foot

An amphora type with a high conical neck, tapering body and a tubular, hollowed base with shallow grooves on the exterior, thick broad handles steeply arched above the level of a narrow rim (Peacock and Williams 1986, Class 47). The source of this amphora is uncertain, although an Aegean origin is a possibility (*ibid.*), while the contents carried are unknown. The form is current during the 3rd and 4th centuries AD, although it may begin earlier at the end of the 2nd century AD (Panella 1973). It has occurred sparsely on a number of British sites in late 3rd to early 4th century AD contexts (Peacock 1977c).

## 1. GREYFRIARS

Numbers of individual sherds for each amphora type.

| Type | Number | % by count |
|---|---|---|
| Dressel 20 | 105 | 91.3% |
| Dressel 2-4 | 5 | 4.34% |
| Pelichet 47 | 1 | 0.86% |
| Camulodunum 186sp | 4 | 3.47% |
| Total | 115 | |

A number of Dressel 20 rim fragments were recovered from Greyfriars, all of which can be paralleled with examples from Augst illustrated by Martin-Kilcher (1983) in her scheme for the development for Dressel 20 rim:

## Context no

| | |
|---|---|
| A83 | first part of the second half of the 1st century AD (*ibid.*, no. 11 ). |
| A79 | second half of the 2nd century AD to first half of the 2nd century AD (*ibid.*, nos. 15 and 17). |
| Pit A24, B36 | ditto (*ibid.*, no. 17). |
| Wall B1, A73 | late 1st century AD to early 2nd century AD (*ibid.*, no. 20). |
| A73, A99, Pit A25 | mid 2nd century AD (*ibid.*, no. 27). |

Plus one rim sherd with a broken rim, (A53), one basal wort, (A73), and four handles (A64, A26, A73 and B22/129) were found. B22/129 contained part of a stamp [OPLEI]. This does not appear to be recorded in Callender (1965) or Ponsich (1974; 1979).

## 2. THEOLOGICAL COLLEGE

Numbers of individual sherds for each amphora type.

| Type | Number | % by count |
|---|---|---|
| Dressel 20 | 60 | 66.6% |
| Dressel 2-4 | 13 | 14.2% |
| Dressel 1–Pascual 1 | 1 | 1.0% |
| Pelichet 47 | 8 | 8.7% |
| Camulodunum 185A | 1 | 1.0% |
| Camulodunum 186A | 1 | 1.0% |
| Camulodunum 186C | 1 | 1.0% |
| Hollow Foot | 1 | 1.0% |
| Unassigned | 5 | 5.5% |
| Total | 91 | |

Two fragments of rim were recovered from the Theological College site, both of which can be paralleled with examples from Augst illustrated by Martin-Kilcher (1983) in her scheme for the development of Dressel 20 rim:

**Context no**

F3.85  middle of 1st century AD (*ibid.*, nos 6–8).
65.87  late 1st century AD to early 2nd century AD (*ibid.*, no 23).

## 3. CHAPEL STREET

Numbers of individual sherds for each amphora type.

| Type | Number | % of count |
|---|---|---|
| Dressel 20 | 43 | 68.3% |
| Dressel 2-4 | 2 | 3.2% |
| Pelichet 47 | 13 | 20.6% |
| Camulodunum 186sp | 1 | 1.6% |
| Southern Spanish | 1 | 1.6% |
| Unassigned | 3 | 4.7% |
| Total | 63 | |

The three rim sherds found in X11 and X23 fall within the range of Dressel 20 forms at Augst associated with late 1st century AD to early 2nd century levels (Martin-Kilcher 1983, fig. 2, nos 16–23).

## THE ILLUSTRATED AMPHORAE FROM THE SITES (FIG. 14.1)

*Note:* Numbers in brackets are the context numbers.

### (a) Greyfriars 1984

1. (B22)   Dressel 20, handle stamped [OPLEI]
2. (47)    Pelichet 47

### (b) Theological College 1985 and 1987

3. (A13)   Dressel 1–Pasqual 1
4. (F4)    Camulodunum 185A
5. (C12)   Camulodunum 186A
6. (F4)    Camulodunum 186C
7. (A1)    Pelichet 47
8. (56)    Hollow Foot
9. (F4)    Undesignated; ?Peacock and Williams Class 16.

## BIBLIOGRAPHY

Beltran, M., 1970. *Las anforas romanas en Espana* (Zaragosa).
Beltran, M., 1978. *Ceramica romana: tipologia y classificacion* (Zaragosa).
Callender, M.H., 1965. *Roman Amphorae* (London).
Colls, D., *et al.* 1977. 'L'epave Port-Vendres II et le commerce de la Betique a l'epoque de Claude,' *Archaeonautica* 1.
Cunliffe, B.W., 1971. Excavations at Fishbourne, 1961–69, II, The Finds, *RRSAL* XXVII.
Deniaux, E., 1980. 'Recherches sur les amphores antiques de Basse-Normandie' *Cahier des Annales de Normandie* 12B.
Dressel, H., 1899. *Corpus Inscriptionum Latinarum*, XV, Pars 1 (Berlin).
Galliou, P., 1984. 'Days of wine and roses? Early Armorica and the Atlantic wine trade' in S. Macready and F.H. Thompson (eds.), 'Cross-Channel trade Between Gaul and Britain in the pre-Roman Iron Age' *Society of Antiquaries London* Occasional Paper (New Series) 4, 24–36.
Hawkes, C.F.C., and Hull, M.R. 1947. 'Camulodunum' *RRSAL*, 14.
Keay, S.J., and Jones, L. 1982. 'Differentiation of early Imperial amphora production in Hispania Tarraconensis' in I. Freestone, C. Jones and T. Potter (eds.), 'Current research in ceramics: thin section studies' *B.M. Occ. Paper* 32, 45–61.
Laubenheimer, F., 1985. *La Production des Amphores en Gaul Narbonnaise* (Paris).
Martin-Kilcher, S., 1983. 'Les amphores romaines a huile de Betique (Dressel 20 et 23) d'Augst (Colonia Augusta Rauricorum) et Kaiseraugst (Castrum Rauracense). Un rapport preliminaire' in J.M. Blazquez and J. Remesal (eds.), *Prod. Y Com. del Aceite en la Antiguedad. II Congres* (Madrid) 337–47.
Panella, C., 1973. 'Appunti su un gruppo di anfore della prima, media e tarda eta Imperiale', *Ostia III*, 460–633.
Parker, A.J., and Price, J., 1981. 'Spanish exports of the Claudian period: the significance of the Port-Vendres II wreck reconsidered' *Int. J. Nautical Arch. and Underwater Exploration* 10, 221–28.
Pascual Guasch, R., 1962. 'Centros de produccion y diffusion geographica de un tipo anfore' *VIIe Congreso Nacional de Arqueologia* (Zaragosa), 334–45.

Pascual Guasch, R., 1977. 'Las anforas de la Layetania' *Coll. de l'Ecole Francaise en Rome* 32, 47–96.

Peacock, D.P.S., 1971. 'Roman amphorae in pre-Roman Britain' in M. Jesson and D. Hill (eds.), *The Iron Age and its Hill-forts* (Southampton), 169–88.

Peacock, D.P.S., 1974. 'Amphorae and the Baetican fish industry' *Ant. J.* 54, 232–43.

Peacock, D.P.S., 1977a. 'Roman amphorae: typology, fabric and origins' *Coll. de l'Ecole Francaise de Rome* 32, 261–78.

Peacock, D.P.S., 1977b. 'Recent discoveries of Roman amphora kilns in Italy' *Ant. J.* 57, 262–69.

Peacock, D.P.S., 1977c. 'Late Roman amphorae from Chalk near Gravesend, Kent' in J. Dore and K. Greene (eds.), *Roman Pottery Studies in Britain and Beyond* BAR Int. Series 30, 295–300.

Peacock, D.P.S., 1978. 'The Rhine and the problem of Gaulish wine in Roman Britain' in J. du Plat Taylor and H. Cleere (eds.), 'Roman shipping and trade: Britain and the Rhine provinces' *CBA Res. Rep.* 24, 49–51.

Peacock, D.P.S., and Williams, D.F., 1986. *Amphorae and the Roman Economy* (London).

Pelichet, P.E., 1946. 'A propos des amphores romaines trouvées a Nyon' *Zeit Schweiz Arch. und Kungstesch* 8, 189–209.

Ponsich, M., 1974. *Implantation Rurale Antique sur le Bas- Guadalquivir* (Madrid).

Ponsich, M., 1979. *Implantation Rurale Antique sur le Bas- Guadalquivir* (Paris).

Rodriguez-Almeida, E., 1981. 'Amphora inscription from London' in M. Hassall and R. Tomlin (eds.), 'Instrumentum Domesticum' *Britannia* 13, 417, no 61.

Sealey, P., 1985. 'Amphorae from the 1970 Excavations at Colchester—Sheepen', *BAR* British Series, no 142.

Tchernia, A., 1971. 'Les amphores vinaires de Tarraconaise et leur exportation au début de l'empire', *Archivo Espanol De Arquelogia* 44, 38–85.

Tchernia, A., 1980. 'Quelques remarques sur le commerce du vin les amphores' in J.H. D'Arms and E.C. Kopff (eds.), *The Seaborne Commerce of Ancient Rome: Studies in Archaeology and History* Mem. Amer. Academy in Rome, 36, 305–12.

van der Werff, J.H., 1984. 'Roman amphorae at Nijmegen—a preliminary report' *ROB*, 347–87.

Williams, D.F., 1981. 'The Roman amphorae trade with Late Iron Age Britain' in H. Howard and E.L. Morris (eds.), *Production and Distribution: a ceramic viewpoint*, BAR Int. Series 120, 123–32.

Williams, D.F., 1988. 'The impact of Roman amphorae trade with pre-Roman Britain' *World Archaeological Congress* 142–50.

Williams, D.F., (forthcoming). 'The amphorae from the Fishbourne (A27) 1983/1985–6 excavations' in A. Down *Chichester Excavations* 9.

Williams, D.F., and Peacock, D.P.S., 1983. 'The importation of olive-oil into Roman Britain' in J. Blazquez and J. Remesal (eds.), *Prod. y Com. de Aceite en la Antiguedad. II Congresso* (Madrid), 263–80.

Zevi, F., 1966. 'Appunti sulle anfore romane' *Arch. Classica* 18, 207–47.

Zevi, F., 1967. 'Review of M.H. Callender: "Roman Amphorae"' *JRS* 57, 234–38.

# 15

# Report on the Roman and medieval glass from Chichester sites*

## by H.E.M. Cool and Jennifer Price

### 1. Vessel glass

The Roman glass recovered from the excavations at Chapel Street (CH/84/CS), Greyfriars (CH/84/G) and the Theological College (CH/85-7/T) is summarised below:

|  | Chapel St | Greyfriars | Theological College |
|---|---|---|---|
| Number of fragments | 44 | 25 | 20 |
| Minimum number of vessels | 14 | 8 | 10 |

The assemblages from Greyfriars and the Theological College are primarily of 1st to 2nd century date with mid 1st century material being present in both. No examples of this very early material were found at Chapel Street where the assemblage consists of late 1st to early 3rd century material. Very few late Roman glass vessels have been recorded from sites in Chichester, and this pattern has continued in the assemblages from these three sites, as no examples of late 3rd or 4th century vessels were recovered.

In the discussion which follows, prefixes are used to distinguish the material from different sites as follows: Chapel St, CS; Greyfriars, G; and Theological College, TC.

*Pre-Flavian and early Flavian tablewares*

(Nos G1–3, TC1, 2 and 7.)

At least one vessel from Greyfriars and three from the Theological College may be dated to the pre-or early Flavian periods on typological grounds. The fragment from one of the vessels at the Theological College (no TC1) was found in a Phase 1 context which dates to the early years of occupation after AD 43. Another (no TC2), was found in a disturbed Phase 1 context. A further 6 fragments were found in similar disturbed Phase 1 contexts (nos TC4, 5, 6, 9, 10, 11) but whether these were in contemporary use is open to question as several of the fragments belong to forms which would not normally be dated as early as this. These fragments will not, therefore, be discussed in detail in this section.

No TC1 is a body fragment from a polychrome bowl with a pattern of small opaque red and yellow petalled flowers set in an opaque white ground. It has two wheel-cut lines on the exterior and probably comes from a cast hemispherical bowl with a wheel-cut line on the interior below the rim and one or two pairs of lines on the exterior producing the effect of a shallow rib. These bowls are an early to mid 1st century form which had gone out of use by the Flavian period. They were made in strongly coloured monochrome glass and in polychrome floral mosaic glass as here and at, for example, Vindonissa where a virtually complete example has red and white flowers set in an opaque slate-grey ground (Berger 1960, 13 no 6, Taf.1).

In Britain an increasing number of monochrome examples are being recognised. These are most often made in emerald-green glass such as the example from a Neronian burial at Sheepen, Colchester (Charlesworth 1985, MF1:A6, fig. 15 no 6), but are also known in opaque turquoise from the first pottery shop destroyed during the Boudiccan rising (Harden 1958, 157 no 3, fig. 79), and peacock blue at Trinity St, Dorchester (unpublished). A polychrome fragment from Sheepen, Colchester (see below) probably came from a similar bowl, but other polychrome examples are rare, and this fragment from Chichester appears to be only the second one to have been found in Britain.

The type of millefiori glass used is also unusual in Britain as it consists of opaque elements set in an opaque ground. Opaque millefiori glass has usually only been noted on early sites. From the pre-Conquest site at Braughing, for example, there is a body fragment with an opaque red ground and opaque yellow and translucent brown chips (Price and Cool 1988, 79, 81 no 3, fig. 35). At Sheepen, Colchester, the fragment probably from a similar bowl to no TC1, had opaque yellow and red flowers set in an opaque brown ground and was found in a Claudio-Neronian context (Harden 1947, 293 no 3). No TC1 adds to this pattern as it came from a context dated to the years immediately following AD 43. Other opaque cast polychrome vessels include the lower body and base of a small bowl with base ring made in opaque red glass with green and opaque yellow five petalled flowers from Llandovery (M.G. Jarrett excavations, unpublished). A similar bowl lower body and base fragment was found on the site of the City Baths at Chester. This has an opaque white ground with opaque red, opaque blue and yellow flowers, and opaque yellow oval eyes with opaque red/brown centres set in the bottom of the base ring. At Silchester the handle of a *trulla* with a dark brown ground set with opaque green, red and yellow flowers was found (Boon 1974, fig. 36.1). Body fragments include ones from Brecon (black with green, yellow and red—Wheeler 1926, 249 and frontispiece) and Verulamium (opaque sky blue ground and opaque yellow and red specks—D. Charlesworth 1984, 145 no 4).

The other fragment of cast millefiori glass found at the Theological College (no TC2), is much more typical of the polychrome cast glass found on mid 1st century sites in Britain. It consists of a translucent green ground with opaque yellow spots probably arranged around a central opaque red spot. This colour combination is the commonest one found in Roman

---

* Report submitted in March 1990.

Britain (Cool and Price forthcoming, no 189) and many of the fragments appear to have come from hemispherical bowls of Isings Form 1 such as the example from a Claudio-Neronian rubbish pit at Sheepen, Colchester (Charlesworth 1985, MF3.F2 fig. 80.1). No TC2, however, appears to be a rim fragment from a wide rimmed bowl, perhaps like the polychrome example from late robbing layers at Fishbourne (Harden and Price 1971, 324 no 2, fig. 137). This too had a green ground but with purple and opaque white canes in addition to the yellow and red.

An increasing number of polychrome wide-rimmed bowls have been found on sites not occupied until the early Flavian period or later, for example at Caersws (Cool and Price 1989, 36 No 7, fig. 20), Chester, Carlisle and Catterick (all unpublished). This suggests that polychrome cast glass may have been used to make bowls of this variety in the Flavian period after other cast polychrome vessel forms had gone out of production. No TC2 came from a disturbed Phase 1 context. It could well have been contemporary with Phase 1 but the possibility that it was slightly later in date cannot be ruled out.

The only mould-blown vessel from these three sites, and the first to be recorded from Chichester, was found at Greyfriars (No G3). It is a base fragment, with two moulded rings and a central pellet, from a blue/green vessel. The quality of the vessel is very poor with many large bubbles and the mouldings are in very shallow relief. The surviving fragment is not sufficiently diagnostic to identify the precise form of the vessel, though it may come from a shallow ribbed bowl or a circus cup. The former were in use from the Tiberian/early Claudian period into the Flavian period, and the latter during the third quarter of the 1st century (Price forthcoming). Both varieties are relatively common finds on mid 1st century and early Flavian sites in Britain.

The blue/green handle fragment no TC7 may also have come from a mid 1st century vessel, though the identification has to remain very tentative. It is a fragment from a small rod handle with a pronounced curve towards the top. This is not a common handle form on Roman vessels but has been noted on a two-handled blue/green cup from Wroxeter (unpublished) and a very similar one from an inhumation furnished with many Claudian and early Neronian glass vessels at Saintes, Charente Inferieure (Grasilier 1873, 225 no 8, fig. 22 bis)

### The later 1st to mid 2nd century tablewares

(Nos CS9, CS10, CS13, G1, 2, 4–5, G8, TC7.)
Tablewares datable to the later 1st to mid 2nd century were found on all three sites. A minimum of 8 vessels are represented.

A second cast wide-rimmed bowl is represented by nos G1 and 2 which are almost certainly from the same vessel. Colourless examples of these bowls are the commonest variety of cast vessel found in Britain. In Chichester's neighbouring area, examples have been found at Fishbourne (Harden and Price 1971, 332 nos 25–6, 336 no 33, fig. 138) and Chilgrove (Down 1979, 163 no 8, fig. 57). They occur in both deep and shallow forms and most commonly have an overhang to the wide rim (Cool and Price forthcoming, nos 212–218). No G1–2 is clearly from a small deep bowl with a wide rim without an overhang. A very similar small bowl was found at Wroxeter in a context dated to 'probably not later than the middle of the 2nd century' (Bushe-Fox 1914, 20, fig. 12), and a similar though larger example was found at Castle St, Carlisle in a late Antonine or Severan context (unpublished). The main period of use for cast colourless wide-rimmed bowls is during the last third of the 1st and into the 2nd century. Some clearly remained in use until the mid 2nd century as examples have been found in contexts associated with the Antonine occupation of Scotland at Cramond (Maxwell 1974, 198 nos 6 and 7, fig. 16) and Inveresk (Thomas 1988, Microfiche 2: B7 3.59).

No TC7 is a rim fragment from a large colourless conical beaker or bowl with an externally ground surface. It is very similar in overall form to a rim fragment from an externally ground facet-cut beaker (Isings Form 21; Oliver 1984; Cool and Price forthcoming, nos 395–401), but the wall thickness is less than would be normal on those. In addition to facet-cut beakers, other forms of colourless tablewares with externally ground surfaces and ground-out ribs are known and these tend to have thinner walls (Cool and Price forthcoming, nos 409–10). It seems likely therefore, that no TC7 comes from a beaker with ground-out ribs similar to one from Verulamium found in a make-up layer dated to AD 145–150 (Charlesworth 1984, 156 no 108, fig. 63.59). Externally ground facet-cut beakers are primarily a Flavian form, but the colourless tablewares with ground-out ribs appear to have continued in use until the mid 2nd century. No TC7 was found re-deposited in a Phase 5 context, and cannot be closely dated within the later 1st to mid 2nd century period. Externally ground facet-cut beakers have been found previously in Chichester at the David Greig site (Charlesworth 1974, 134 nos 11–13, fig. 8.13), externally ground vessels with linear ground-out ribs, however, have not been recorded.

Another colourless conical beaker is represented by no G4. It is decorated with horizontal wheel-cut lines and belongs to the range of wheel-cut beakers which were the commonest drinking vessel form of the early to mid 2nd century (Cool and Price forthcoming, nos 426–64). Early examples dating to the end of the 1st century are thin-walled cylindrical beakers with a tubular pushed-in base ring, and during the middle third of the 2nd century there was a great range of body shapes and foot types, see for example one from the St Pancras cemetery, Chichester (Down and Rule 1971, fig. 5.24/144b) and several found in a pit at Harlow dated to AD 160–170 (Price 1987, 188–91, 202–3 nos 8–11, 13–14, fig. 2). This range of beakers includes conical forms such as the one from the 2nd century drain deposit at Housesteads (Charlesworth 1971, 35 no 7; 1975, 24). No G4, which was found in dumped material dating from the pre-Flavian to late Antonine period, is likely to belong to the middle third of the 2nd century.

During the second half of the 1st and the first half of the 2nd centuries, the commonest tablewares other than drinking vessels are tubular rimmed bowls (Isings Form 44/5: Cool and Price forthcoming, nos 630–91), collared jars (Isings Form 67c: *op. cit.* nos 732–806) and globular and conical jugs (Isings Form 52 and 55: *op. cit.*, nos 871–954). With the exception of tubular rimmed bowls which occur in earlier contexts, the forms first appeared during the late Neronian period and were widespread and numerous for the rest of the 1st century. Collared jars and globular jugs disappear during the early 2nd century, but tubular rimmed bowls and conical jugs continued in use into the middle of the 2nd century. This range of vessels has frequently been represented in the glass assemblages from Chichester (for summary see Price and Cool 1989, 133), and additional ones have now been found at Chapel Street and Greyfriars. From the former there are open pushed-in base ring fragments from two different blue/green collared jars or jugs (nos CS9–10), and from the latter a rim fragment from a blue/green tubular rimmed bowl (no G5), the base fragment no G8 may also have come from a bowl of this type. The ribbed blue/green body fragment from Chapel Street (no CS13) is likely to be from one of these varieties of vessels, which often have ribbed decoration. In the case of no CS13 a closer identification may be suggested as there is a horizontal band of wear scratches just below the ribs and such a feature has been noted several times on the lower bodies of collared jars.

*First and 2nd century containers*

(Nos CS1, 5–8, CS11, CS14–17, G6, G9–10, TC6 and TC10–11.)

The majority of the containers discussed in this section are blue/green prismatic and cylindrical bottles, but the sites also produced at least four jars, an unguent bottle and an inkwell.

A total of 29 fragments from blue/green bottles (Isings Forms 50 and 51: Cool and Price forthcoming, 1834–2239) were found on the three sites (nos CS14–17, G9–10 and TC10–11), with the majority (20 fragments) coming from Chapel Street. At that site at least two square bottles (nos CS15–16) and one cylindrical bottle (no 17) are represented. At the other two sites it is only possible to estimate a minimum of one prismatic bottle for each. These bottles are very common on Romano-British sites (for previous ones from Chichester see Price and Cool 1989, 134). They first occur in the Claudian period but do not become very common until the late 1st century. Cylindrical bottles disappear in the early 2nd century but square ones continue in use until the late 2nd or early 3rd century. Nos TC10 and TC11 are recorded as coming from disturbed Phase 1 contexts at the Theological College. It is highly unlikely that either are of Claudian or early Neronian date as they came from large bottles and current evidence suggests that the early bottles were small. These two fragments must, therefore, be regarded as intrusive.

Base fragments with moulded designs were present at Chapel Street and the Theological College. In neither case do they come from bottles with base patterns consisting of concentric circular mouldings which are by far the commonest patterns found on bottles from Roman Britain and hitherto at Chichester (Charlesworth 1978, 267 nos 5 and 6, fig. 10.22; Price and Cool 1989, 140 nos CM50-52, fig. 19.3). No TC11 retains part of one circular moulding close to the edge with at least one and possibly two projections or junctions with other mouldings on its inner edge and part of a corner moulding. Insufficient of the base remains for the pattern to be identified but it may have come from a base similar to ones from Corbridge which have petal designs radiating out from the centre and touching a circular frame (Charlesworth 1959, fig. 9 bottom).

The other base (no CS15) is from a square bottle and retains part of a moulding parallel to the edge. It is not possible to tell if there was additional decoration on the centre of the base. Bases with square moulding are not particularly common and it is therefore interesting to note that this is the second example to have been found at Chichester. The other came from the David Greig site and had two concentric square mouldings with a central diagonal cross (Charlesworth 1974, 134 no 1, fig. 8.13).

The assemblage from Chapel Street includes a rim fragment (no CS11) from a blue/green inkwell (Isings Form 77: Cool and Price forthcoming, nos 862–6). This is not a very common vessel form, though an increasing number are being identified. The precise details of the folding of the rim vary. Most frequently the rim has been folded out, up and in before being flattened into the shoulder. The form of no CS11, where the rim edge is rounded and bent out, is unusual though it has also been found on one from Culver Street, Colchester (Cool and Price forthcoming, no 862). The precise dating of these vessels is uncertain as few have come from securely dated contexts. The form has been found in contexts dating to the middle and later 1st century, but the extent to which it remained in use during the 2nd century or later is unknown. No CS11 was found in a 4th century context where it seems very likely that it was residual.

A lower body and base fragment (no TC6) from a large light-green conical unguent bottle with a relatively tall body, possibly like that from a grave at Colchester (May 1930, pl. LXXIX 32), was found in a disturbed Phase 1 context at the Theological College. Such bottles are commonest in the later 1st and 2nd centuries. They have been found in early Flavian contexts, such as the example from Park Street Verulamium which was found in a pit where the latest pottery was dated to AD 70–80 (Harden 1945, 72 no 22, fig. 11), but a date as early as Phase 1 seems unlikely and no TC6 is probably intrusive.

Jars are well represented at Chapel Street where a minimum of one light green (no CS1) and one blue/green (no CS7) funnel-mouthed jars and one blue/green jar with an out-turned rim (no CS8) were found. All of these had rim edges that were rolled in. It is also possible that the blue/green fire-rounded rim fragments nos CS5-6 could have come from jars, but they are not sufficiently diagnostic for this to be certain. This means that at least three and possibly as many as five of the minimum number of fourteen vessels present at Chapel Street are jars. This is a much higher percentage than is normal but with such a small assemblage its significance is difficult to evaluate. The only other jar is from Greyfriars and has an out-turned tubular rim (no G6).

In general it is not possible to date jars closely within the 1st to early 3rd centuries, though there is some evidence to suggest that ones with fire-rounded rims went out of use in the 2nd century before those with rolled or folded rims. At Chapel Street the examples with rolled rims were from 2nd century contexts (Phase 4).

*The later 2nd and 3rd century tablewares*

(Nos CS2, CS4, CS12.)

A minimum of three vessels are datable to the later 2nd and 3rd century and all were found at Chapel Street.

No CS2 comes from a colourless cylindrical cup with a vertical fire-rounded rim and double-ring base (Isings Form 85b: Cool and Price forthcoming, nos 465–540). These were in use during the last third of the 2nd century and the first third of the 3rd century. During this time they were the commonest glass drinking vessel form in the north-western provinces and examples have been found on several sites in Chichester (for summary see Price and Cool 1989, 134).

No CS4 is difficult to identify as the fragment is small and the rim badly chipped which makes it difficult to ascertain the correct orientation. It is colourless, has an out-turned fire-rounded rim and a horizontal trail around the upper body. These are features that occur on the trailed variant of cylindrical cups (Charlesworth 1971, 34 no 1), but the rim diameter of no CS4 is c. 75 mm which would be small for such a cup. It seems more likely that it could have come from a beaker similar to the one found in the 2nd century drain deposit at Housesteads (Charlesworth 1971, 34 no 6; 1974, 24). This has a double-ring base like cylindrical cups and indents around the side. Such vessels are contemporary with cylindrical cups and have rarely been identified from Romano-British sites, though the rim fragment from what may have been a small example has been found at Culver Street, Colchester, in a context dated to AD 150 to 325 (Cool and Price forthcoming, no 830). The upper body of no CS4 is slightly asymmetrical. This may merely be due to a small area of distortion, but the possibility that CS4 is from a contemporary spouted funnel-mouthed jug cannot be entirely ruled out.

The third late 2nd or early 3rd century vessel is represented by a blue/green body fragment with a cut-out fold (no CS12). This probably comes from a bowl similar in shape to the samian pottery form Dr.38 (Isings Form 69b). This is a relatively rare form. Two securely identified examples from Roman Britain are known from Silchester (Boon 1974, 232, fig. 36.7) and Piercebridge, Co. Durham (unpublished), and body fragments similar to no CS12 are known at Colchester (Cool and Price forthcoming, no 710, Lincoln, Binchester and Old Penrith (all unpublished).

*Miscellaneous vessels*

(Nos G7, TC4–5, TC9, CS6.)
In addition to the vessels already discussed, at least four others are represented by fragments that are not sufficiently diagnostic for the vessel types to be identified. They include folded rim fragments and a cylindrical neck fragment from jugs or flasks (nos G7, G7B, TC5), a handle fragment from a jug (no TC9) and a base fragment from a jug or jar (no TC4). There is also a base fragment with tubular base ring which has been grozed. These fragments are not closely dated but are likely from the colours of the glass to be of 3rd or, in the case of no TC4, 2nd century date or earlier.

## 2. Glass objects

### Beads

Two beads were found in disturbed Period 1 contexts at the Theological College. One of these was a frit melon bead (no TC12). These were in use during the 1st and 2nd centuries, and were most numerous in the 1st century. No TC12 could therefore be contemporary with Phase 1. This is a very common type of bead and several have been recorded from earlier excavations in Chichester (Charlesworth 1978; 273 no 88. fig. 10.24; Charlesworth 1981, 296 nos 27–9, fig. 15.3; Price and Cool 1989, 140 nos CM57-60a, CH5, figs. 19.3–4).

The second bead (no TC13) is most unusual. It is a 'black' barrel-shaped bead with an opaque white zigzag trail marvered smooth. It falls into Guido's Group 5 which are miscellaneous wave-decorated beads (1978, 62). Group 5d beads have the same colour combination as no TC13 but are annular rather than barrel-shaped and are dated to the early post-Roman period (Guido 1978, 135). It seems unlikely therefore that no TC13 is a Group 5d bead. Group 5a beads (Guido 1978, 63) have more varied shapes and though the majority have a translucent blue ground colour, dark opaque examples have been recorded (Guido 1978, 130). This is a very long-lived type with examples being found in contexts that range from the mid 1st millennium BC to the 6th or 7th century AD. Within such a long time-span a large number of variations occurred and it seems likely that no TC13 belongs within this sub-group.

A very small opaque green cylindrical bead was found at Greyfriars (no G11). It cannot be closely dated and may not be of Roman date. Against a Roman date is the fact that it is much smaller than is normal, though the colour of glass that it is made of was often used on late Roman beads such as short disc cylindrical and long hexagonal beads (Guido 1978, 95–6).

### Counters

One example of a 'black' plano-convex counter was found at the Theological College in a Phase 1 context (TC14). Such counters were numerous during the 1st and 2nd centuries and several other monochrome counters have been found during earlier excavations at Chichester (Charlesworth 1978, 272–3 nos 83–6, fig. 10.24; Charlesworth 1981, 296 nos 37–40, fig. 15.3; Price and Cool 1989, 140 nos CM63–4, CH6, fig. 19.3).

## 3. Window glass

Both of the window glass fragments from the Theological College are cast. This type of window glass was primarily in use during the 1st to 3rd centuries. The fragment from Greyfriars, by contrast, is blown and is thus most likely to date to the 4th century.

## CATALOGUE OF GLASS FROM THE SITES

*Note:* The following Catalogue consists of concise descriptions of all the fragments discussed in the text. Those marked with an asterisk * are illustrated in Figs. 15.1–15.3.

*Abbreviations:* PH, present height; RD, rim diameter; BD, base diameter; WT, wall thickness; Dim, dimensions.

All measurements are in millimetres; small find nos are in italics.

**Theological College: vessel glass—cast (Fig. 15.1)**

TC1*  85T A52/61 *61* (Phase 1)
Body fragment of bowl. Polychrome. Mosaic made of multi-angular pre-formed pieces. Opaque white ground with opaque red discs with yellow centres arranged in a ring with central groups of three or four. Convex-curved side. Two shallow horizontal wheel-cut lines. Surfaces ground and wheel-polished. Dim. 27×20, WT 2.

TC2*  85T, F4, *31* (disturbed Phase 1)
Body fragment of bowl. Polychrome. Floral mosaic. Translucent emerald-green ground with opaque yellow and opaque red spots. Yellow spots probably originally arranged around red spots in centre. Convex-curved side bending out to wide rim. Surfaces ground and wheel-polished; exterior still shows irregularities and ? tooling marks. Dim. 25×20, WT 3.

## Blown

*Yellow/green*

TC3*  85T A11, *94* (Phase 4)
Rim fragment of collared jar. Some bubbles. Collared rim first bent in, then folded out and down; top of collar missing. RD c. 100.

TC4  85T A13, *68* (disturbed Phase 1)
Base fragment of jar or jug? Some small bubbles. Side curving into edge of shallow concave base. BD c. 80, WT 2.5.

*Light/pale green*

TC5*  85T F4, *101* (disturbed Phase 1)
Rim fragment from jug or flask. Pale green. Dulled surfaces; strain cracks. Rim bent out, up, in and flattened with edge projecting down inside cylindrical neck. RD 35.

TC6*  85T F4, *99* (disturbed Phase 1)
Lower body and base fragment of conical unguent bottle. Light-green. Many bubbles; black impurities and some dark inclusions; dulled surfaces. Straight side sloping out slightly to thick, slightly concave base. PH 33, maximum body diameter c. 45, WT 4
Also two undecorated light green body fragments
b. . . . . .87T 65, *95* Phase 4
c. . . . . .87T 59, *93* residual

*Colourless*

TC7*  85T F12, *30* (redeposited Phase 5)
Rim fragment of conical beaker or bowl. Occasional small bubbles. Slightly outbent rim, edge cracked off and ground; straight side sloping in. Ground-out rib below rim edge. Exterior ground and wheel-polished. PH 10, RD 115, WT 1.5.

*Blue/green*

TC8*  87T 67, *94* (Phase 4)
Handle fragment of cup? Elongated bubbles; dulled surfaces. D-sectioned curved rod handle. Handle section 5.5×4.

TC9*  85T A13, *95* (disturbed Phase 1)
Handle fragment of jug. Many elongated bubbles. Straight rod handle with central indentation, forming two wide shallow ribs. Section 24×4. Also five undecorated blue/green body fragments
b. . . . . .85T F23, *105* (Phase 5, 2 fragments)
c. . . . . .85T F25, *106* (Phase 5)
d. . . . . .87T 30, *92* (Phase 5 residual)
e. . . . . .87T 59, *93* (residual)

TC10.  85T A13, *96* (disturbed Phase 1)
Part of wide angular reeded ribbon handle from bottle. Handle section 41+ × 9

TC11*  85T F4, *103* (disturbed Phase 1)
Lower body and base fragment of prismatic bottle. Base design—at least one circular moulding with projection or junction with another moulding on inner edge, part of corner pellet. PH 24, diameter of outer circle c. 85, probable width of bottle c. 100.
Also 2 flat body fragments from prismatic bottles
b. . . . . .85T B11, *10* (Period 1, Phase 3)
c. . . . . .87T 62, *97*

## Objects

TC12*  85T A13, *45b* (disturbed Period 1)
Turquoise frit melon bead, complete. Glaze preserved over large parts of the exterior. Grooves on interior of perforation. Length 14, diameter 17.

TC13*  85T A13, *45a* (disturbed Period 1)
     Polychrome barrel-shaped bead. Very dark glass appearing black. Opaque white zigzag trail marvered smooth. Length 11, Diameter 10.5.
TC14*  85T A52/61, *53* (Phase 1)
     Plano-convex counter. Very dark glass appearing black. Base smooth. Some voids on surface. Diameter 17, thickness 6.5.

## Window glass

TC15.  2 fragments of cast matt/glossy window glass
     a. . . . . .85T F4, *104* (disturbed Phase 1, greenish colourless)
     b. . . . . .87T 108, *91* (?Phase 2 or 3, blue/green)

## Greyfriars: vessel glass—cast (Fig. 15.2)

G1*  A73/80, *264* (Phase 2)
     Rim fragment of bowl. Slightly green-tinged colourless; some small bubbles; flaking iridescent surfaces. Wide everted rim with overhang; upper surface ground flat to leave raised ridge by overhang and at rim/body junction; straight side sloping in. Surfaces ground and wheel-polished. PH 16, RD 100, WT 1.5.
G2*  Pit A25, *270* (c. late 1st–2nd century)
     Lower body and base fragment of bowl. Slightly green-tinged colourless; some small bubbles; flaking iridescent surfaces. Slightly convex-curved body sloping in steeply to ground-out base ring; flat base. Surfaces ground and wheel-polished. PH 24, BD 47, WT 1.5.

*Note:* Nos 1 and 2 are probably from the same vessel.

## Mould blown

G3*  B122, *274* (2nd century)
     Base fragment of cup? Blue/green; many bubbles. Moulded base ring in low relief broken at edge of lower body; moulded ring and central pellet on base. BD c. 35, WT 1.

## Blown

*Colourless*

G4*  A73/80, *266* (Phase 2)
     Rim fragment of conical beaker. Occasional small bubbles; iridescent surfaces. Outbent rim, edge cracked off and ground; straight side sloping in. One horizontal wheel-cut line below rim edge: two similar lines on upper body. PH 21, RD 80, WT 1.5.
     Also two undecorated colourless body fragments
     b. . . . . .A41,*250* (destruction layer)
     c. . . . . .B138, *209* (residual) green-tinged

*Blue/green*

G5*  A73/80, *260* (Phase 2)
     Rim fragment of tubular rimmed bowl. Some bubbles; iridescent surfaces. Slightly out-bent rim, tubular edge bent out and down; nearly vertical straight side. PH 21, RD c. 150–160, WT 1.
G6*  B28, *239*
     Rim fragment of jar. Occasional small bubbles; iridescent surfaces. Rim bent out horizontally; tubular edge bent out and up. RD 100, WT 1.
G7*  A73/80, *256* (Phase 2)
     Rim fragment of jug or flask. Small bubbles; iridescent surfaces. Tubular rim edge bent out, up, in and flattened. Neck possibly deliberately grozed. RD c.45.
     Also one cylindrical neck fragment from jug or flask
     b. . . . . .B85, *272*
G8*  A26, *54*, (House 1, Phase 2)
     Base fragment of bowl? Some bubbles; iridescent surfaces. Applied true base ring; slightly convex base. Post technique scars on base ring. Side grozed. BD c. 65.
     Also nine undecorated blue/green body fragments
     b. . . . . .A99, *271* (Flavian)
     c. . . . . .A73/80, *258* (Phase 2)
     d. . . . . .A73/80, *262* (Phase 2)
     e. . . . . .A73/80, *263* (Phase 2)
     f. . . . . .A41, *250* (4th century destruction layer)
     g. . . . . .A53, *254* (residual)

h. . . . . .A83, *267* (residual, 2 fragments)

i. . . . . .Pit B5, *275* (residual)

G9. Unstratified, *269*

Rim and handle fragment of bottle. Rim bent out, up, in and flattened, with inner edge projecting down inside upper part of cylindrical neck, showing vertical tooling marks. Part of folded upper attachment of handle on neck and underside of rim. Neck possibly ground smooth. RD 40.

G10. A95, *268* (2nd century +)

Lower body and edge of base fragment of prismatic bottle. Affected by heat. PH 40.

Also one fragment with 90 degree angle from square bottle

b. . . . . .A41, *250* (4th century destruction layer)

Also three flat body fragments from prismatic bottles

c. . . . . .B122, *274* (2nd century)

d. . . . . .A73/80, *257* (Phase 2)

e. . . . . .A83, *267* (residual)

## Object

G11* B41, *219*

Short cylindrical bead. Opaque green; length 3, diameter 4, perforation diameter 1.

## Window glass

G12. A41, *250* (destruction layer)

One flat fragment of blown, double glossy window glass. Green-tinged colourless; many elongated bubbles.

## Chapel Street 1984: vessel glass (Fig. 15.3)

*Light green*

CS1* X13, *82* (Phase 4)

Rim fragment of jar. Many bubbles; iridescent surfaces. Funnel mouth rim edge rolled in. PH 11, RD 45, WT 1.5.

Also one light-green undecorated body fragment

b. . . . . .X11, *98* (Phase 4)

*Colourless*

CS2* Pit X14B, *76*, (Phase 5)

Rim fragment of cylindrical cup. Slightly green-tinged colourless. Occasional small bubbles; streakily weathered, iridescent surface. Vertical rim, edge fire thickened; straight side. PH 39, RD 75, WT 1.

CS3* Pit X14B, *76* (Phase 5)

Base fragment. Slightly green-tinged colourless. Clouded iridescent surfaces. Tubular pushed-in base ring; slightly convex base with central thickening. Circular pontil scar. Side grozed. BD 45.

CS4* X22, *94* (Phase 5)

Rim fragment of cup? Occasional small bubbles; dulled surfaces. Out-turned rim, edge fire-rounded and now badly chipped; slightly convex-curved side. Horizontal trail on upper body. PH c. 20, WT 1.

Also one undecorated colourless body fragment affected by heat

b. . . . . .X11, *98* (Phase 4)

*Blue/green*

CS5* X23, *85* (Phase 3)

Rim fragment of bowl or jar? Occasional small bubbles; iridescent surfaces. Wide out-turned rim, edge fire-rounded. PH 11, WT 1.

CS6. Pit X14B, *105* (Phase 5)

Rim fragment of jar? Bubbles elongated parallel with edge. Horizontally out-bent and flattened rim, edge fire-rounded. RD c.100.

CS7* X23, *84* (Phase 3)

Rim fragment of funnel-mouthed jug. Small bubbles; iridescent surfaces. Funnel mouth, rim edge rolled in; body beginning to curve out. PH 24, RD 80, WT 1.

CS8* X16, *92*, (Phase 3)

Rim fragment of jug. Many small bubbles; iridescent surfaces. Out-turned rim, edge rolled in. Dimensions 25×16, WT 1.

CS9* X2, *103* (Phase 3)

Lower body and base fragment of jar or jug. Some small bubbles. Side sloping into open pushed-in base ring; concave base. PH 17, BD 50, WT. 3.

CS10. X23, *89* (Phase 3)

Lower body fragment of conical jug. Small bubbles; iridescent surfaces. Fragment broken at carination to lower body which slopes in shallowly to side of open pushed-in base rim. Dimensions 38×35, WT 1.

CS11* Pit X14B, *80* (Phase 5)

Rim fragment of 'inkwell'. Occasional bubbles; flaking iridescent surfaces. Folded rim with rounded edge bent out and flattened into shoulder to produce concave upper surface with small central aperture; shoulder curving over to missing body. Edge of rim and shoulder have scar with small fragment of glass from loop handle. Body diameter c.80, central aperture diameter c.25, WT 5.

CS12* Pit X14B, *78* (Phase 5)

Body fragment of bowl. Small bubbles; iridescent surfaces; dark inclusion. Horizontal cut-out fold with lower body sloping in. Outer diameter fold 120, WT 1.

CS13. X13, *83* (Phase 4)

Body fragment. Occasional bubbles; iridescent surfaces. Convex-curved body. Terminal of 1 vertical rib in high relief and edge of second. Band of horizontal wear scratches below ribs. Dimensions 33×20, WT 3.

Also nine undecorated blue/green body fragments

b. . . . . .X2, *104* (Phase 3)
c. . . . . .X14, *91* (Phase 3, 2 fragments)
d. . . . . .X23, *88* (Phase 3, 2 fragments)
e. . . . . .Pit X24, *74* (Phase 3)
f. . . . . .X11, *102* (Phase 4, 2 fragments)
g. . . . . .X22, *95* (Phase 5)

CS14. Pit X14B, *75* (Phase 5)

Neck fragment of bottle. Cylindrical neck retaining small fragment of upper handle attachment; horizontal shoulder; tooling marks at neck/body junction. Diameter of neck c. 35.

Also 1 other cylindrical neck fragment from bottle, jug or flask

b. . . . . .X11, *100* (Phase 4)

Also the lower part of a reeded bottle handle retaining small part of shoulder.

c. . . . . .Pit X14B, *80* (Phase 5)

CS15* Pit X14B, *77* (Phase 5)

Lower body and base fragment of square bottle. Base design—1 square moulding parallel to base edge. PH 14, dimensions of base 43×43.

CS16. Pit X14B, *80* (Phase 5)

Two joining body fragments forming almost entire side of square bottle; broken at shoulder and edge of base. Height 115, width of bottle 88.

Also twelve body fragments from prismatic bottles

Three fragments with 90 degree angles from square bottles

b. . . . . .X23, *87* (Phase 3)

9 flat body fragments

c. . . . . .X23, *90* (Phase 3)
d. . . . . .X2, *104* (Phase 3)
e. . . . . .X11, *97* (Phase 4)
f. . . . . .X11, *101* (Phase 4)
g. . . . . .Pit X14B, *79* (Phase 5)
h. . . . . .Pit X14B, *80* (Phase 5, 2 fragments)
i. . . . . .X21, *93* (Phase 5)
j. . . . . .X22, *95* (Phase 5)

CS17. X23, *88* (Phase 3)

Two joining shoulder and body fragments of cylindrical bottles with vertical scratch marks.

## Window glass

CS18. Five fragments of cast matt/glossy blue/green window glass

a. . . . . .X20, *81* (Phase 1) (with rounded edge)
b. . . . . .X23, *86* (Phase 3)
c. . . . . .X23, *90* (Phase 3)
d. . . . . .X11, *96* (Phase 4)
e. . . . . .Pit X14B, *80* (Phase 5) (with rounded edge)

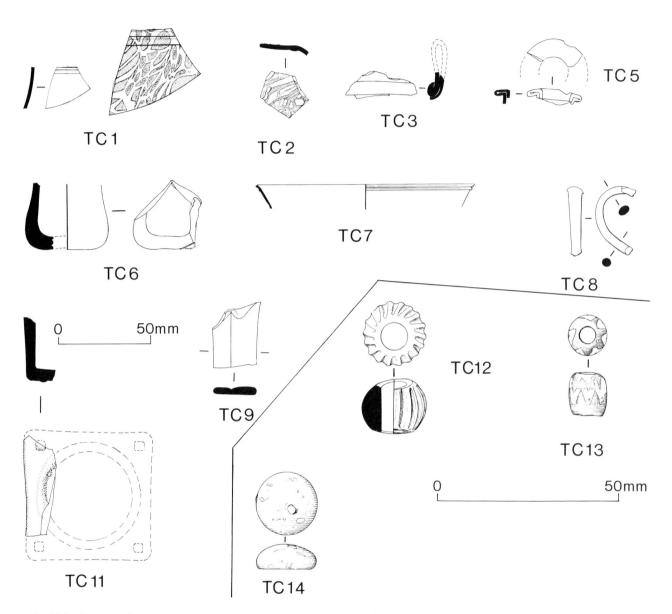

Fig.15.1   Roman glass from the Theological College 1985 and 1987. No TC1 scales 1:2 and 1:1; nos TC12–14 scale 1:1; remainder 1:2

179

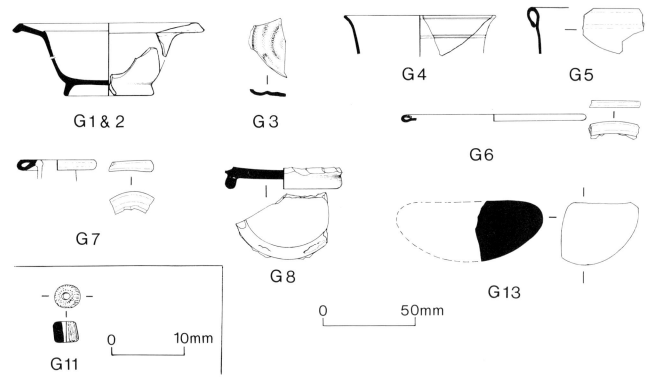

G1 & 2    G3    G4    G5

G6

G7    G8    G13

G11    0    10mm

0    50mm

Fig.15.2   Roman (G1–11) and medieval (G13) glass from Greyfriars 1984. Scales 1:2 apart from G11, 2:1

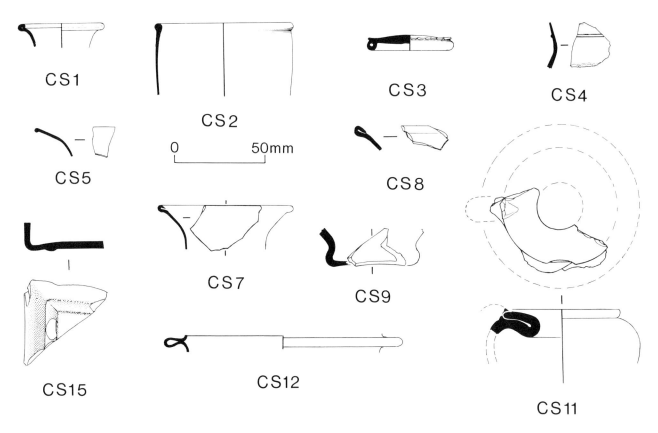

CS1    CS2    CS3    CS4

CS5    0    50mm

CS8

CS7    CS9

CS15    CS12    CS11

Fig.15.3   Roman glass from Chapel Street 1984, nos CS1–CS15. Scale 1:2

## REPORT ON A MEDIEVAL GLASS LINEN SMOOTHER FROM GREYFRIARS BY H.E.M.COOL

G13.* Pit B12 *277* (Fig. 15.2)

> Approximately one-quarter of hemispherical linen smoother. Appearing black with much granular devitrification. Domed upper surfaces; concave base. Diameter c.80, height 33.

Glass linen smoothers are a very long-lived artefact type as they have been found on Viking sites and in contexts dating from the 12th century to the post-medieval period. It is difficult to date individual examples closely although there does appear to be an increase in the diameter with time (R.J. Charlesworth 1984, 37). The example from Greyfriars came from a pit which contained a large amount of 10th to 11th century pottery, and can thus be dated to the period just before or after the Conquest. As such, it is a valuable addition to the corpus of linen smoothers as it is one of the earliest examples to be found in southern Britain, and its diameter of c. 80 mm is further evidence that the early examples were relatively small.

## BIBLIOGRAPHY

Berger, L., 1960. *Römische Gläser aus Vindonissa* (Basel).

Boon, G.C., 1974. *Silchester the Roman town of Calleva* (Newton Abbott and London).

Bushe-Fox, J.P., 1914. 'Second report on the excavations on the site of the Roman town at Wroxeter, Shropshire 1913' *RRSAL* II (Oxford).

Charlesworth, R.J., 1984. *English Glass* (London).

Charlesworth, D., 1959. 'Roman glass from northern Britain' *Arch. Ael. Series 4* XXXVII, 33–58.

Charlesworth, D., 1971. 'A group of vessels from the Commandant's House, Housesteads' *Journal of Glass Studies* XIII, 34–7.

Charlesworth, D., 1974. 'The Roman glass' in A. Down, *Chichester Excavations 2* (Phillimore), 134–7.

Charlesworth, D., 1978. 'The Roman glass' in A. Down, *Chichester Excavations 3* (Phillimore), 267–73.

Charlesworth, D., 1981. 'The Roman glass' in A. Down, *Chichester Excavations 5* (Phillimore), 293–7.

Charlesworth, D., 1984. 'The glass', in S.S. Frere, *Verulamium Excavations III* (Oxford), 146–73.

Charlesworth, D., 1985. 'The glass', in R. Niblett, *Sheepen: an early Roman industrial site at Camulodunum,* CBA Res. Rep. 57 (London), MF1: A6–A9, 3:F1-F11.

Cool, H.E.M., and Price, J., 1989. 'The glass vessels' in J. Britnell, *Caersws Vicus, Powys: Excavations at the old Primary School* BAR British Series 205 (Oxford), 31–43.

Cool, H.E.M., and Price, J., (forthcoming) *Roman Glass from Excavations at Colchester 1971–83* Colchester Arch. Monograph.

Down, A., 1979. 'The Roman Villas at Chilgrove and Upmarden' *Chichester Excavations 4* (Phillimore).

Down, A., and Rule, M., 1971. *Chichester Excavations 1* (Chichester).

Grasilier, P-Th., 1873. 'Memoire sur un tombeau Gallo-Romain decouvert a Saintes en Novembre 1871' *Revue Archéologique* 25, 217–27.

Guido, M., 1978. 'The glass beads of the prehistoric and Roman periods in Britain and Ireland' *RRSAL* XXXV (London).

Harden, D.B., 1945. 'Glass' in H.E. O'Neil, 'The Roman Villa at Park Sreet, near St. Albans, Herts: report of the excavations of 1943–45' *Arch. J.* CII, 68–72

Harden, D.B., 1947. 'The glass' in C.F.C. Hawkes and M.R. Hull, 'Camulodunum' *RRSAL* XIV (Oxford), 287–307.

Harden, D.B., 1958. 'Glass' in M.R. Hull, 'Roman Colchester' *RRSAL* XX 157–8.

Harden, D.B., and Price, J., 1971. 'The glass' in B. Cunliffe, 'Excavations at Fishbourne, 1961–69. II: the finds' *RRSAL* XXVII (London), 317–68.

Isings, C., 1957. *Roman Glass from Dated Finds* (Groningen Djakarta).

Maxwell, G., 1974. 'Objects of glass' in A. and V. Rae, 'The Roman fort at Cramond, Edinburgh, excavations 1954–66' *Britannia* V, 177–9.

May, T., 1930. *Catalogue of the Roman pottery in the Colchester and Essex Museum* (Cambridge).

Oliver, A., 1984. 'Early Roman faceted glass' *Journal of Glass Studies 26*, 35–58.

Price, J., 1987. 'Glass from Felmongers, Harlow in Essex. A dated deposit of vessel glass found in an Antonine pit' in *Annales du 10e Congrés de l'Association Internationale pour l'Histoire du Verre* (Amsterdam), 185–206.

Price, J., (forthcoming). 'Decorated mould blown tablewares in the 1st century AD' in M. Newby (ed.), *Glass of the Caesars: essays in honour of D.B. Harden,* Soc. of Antiquaries Occasional Paper (London).

Price, J., and Cool H.E.M., 1988. 'The glass' in T.W. Potter and S.D. Trow, *Puckeridge-Braughing, Herts: the Ermine Street excavations, 1971–2* Herts. Archaeology 10 (St. Albans), 79–84.

Price, J., and Cool, H.E.M., 1989. 'Report on the Roman glass found at the Cattlemarket, County Hall, East Pallant House sites Chichester' in A. Down, *Chichester Excavations 6* (Chichester), 132–43.

Thomas, G.D., 1988. 'Excavations at the Roman civil settlement at Inveresk 1976–77' *Proc. Soc. Antiquaries of Scotland* 118, 139–76.

Wheeler, R.E.M., 1926. 'The Roman fort near Brecon' *Y Cymmrodorion* XXXVII.

# 16

# The coins from the sites

## by J.A.P. Kenny and R. Lintott

*Note*: Figures in italics are small find numbers, those in brackets are context numbers.

**CHAPEL STREET 1984**

**Roman**

1. *50*. (X23), AE Dup. or As, DOMITIAN (AD 81–96).
2. *32*. (u/s), AE Barb. Rad., 3rd century.
3. *18*. (Pit X8g), AE, illegible.
4. *16*. (u/s), AE, illegible.
5. *7*. (X8), AE Ant., VICTORINUS (AD 268–70).
6. *15*. (Pit X13b), AE Barb., 4th century, Falling horseman type.
7. *10*. (Pit X13b), AE, VALENTINIAN I (AD 364–75).

**THEOLOGICAL COLLEGE 1985/7**

**Roman**

1. *13*. (A36), AE As, CALIGULA (AD 37–41), S.C. Vesta, RIC 30, obv. legend: Caesar Aug. Germanicus.
2. *84*. (85), AE Dup. or As, VESPASIAN (AD 69–79), c. AD 74.
3. *73*. (65), AE Dup. or As, DOMITIAN AUG. (AD 81–96).
4. *69*. (57), AE Sestertius, worn smooth.
5. *47*. (F4), AE As, ANTONINUS PIUS (AD 138–61), Britannia (seated on rock).
6. *44*. (A13), AE Follis, CONSTANTINE I (AD 306–37), Soli invicto comiti, 316–18.
7. *43*. (Gr.15: F16), AE 10mm. Minim, Falling horseman type, 4th century.
8. *72*. (65), illegible

**Post-Roman**

9. *4*. (2), Penny, GEORGE III, Britannia, 1806/7.

**GREYFRIARS 1984**

**Iron Age**

1. *214*. (B115), Ag. Minim of Verica, (Mack 128).

**Roman**

2. *212*. (C41), AE Dup., Nero and Drusus Caesars, S.C. RIC (CAL) 43. Large hole punched in centre of coin. Struck under Caligula (AD 37–41).
3. *126*. (A27 Pit), AE As, CLAUDIUS (AD 41–54), S.C. Minerva, RIC 66.
4. *62*. (A77), AE Dup. or As, VESPASIAN (AD 69–79), S.C. eagle.
5. *225*. (B95), AE Dup. or As, VESPASIAN ? (AD 69–79).
6. *174*. (B84), AE Dup. or As, DOMITIAN (AD 81–96), S.C. Fortunae Augusti.
7. *28*. (u/s), AE Sestertius, ANTONINUS PIUS, (AD 138–61), S.C. figure standing.
8. *160*. (B1), AR Den. illegible, but possibly ELAGABALUS, AD 218–222.
9. *59*. (A46), AE Ant., GALLIENUS (AD 253–68), Dianae Cons Aug., Stag; Rome, RIC 178.
10. *31*. (A55), AE Ant., VICTORINUS (AD 268–70), Invictus., RIC 114.
11. *116*. (B19), AE Ant., VICTORINUS (AD 268–70), Salus Aug.
12. *188*. (Pit C14), AE Ant. VICTORINUS (AD 268–70), Fides standing holding 2 stds, Cologne AD 268–70, RIC 109.
13. *42*. (B1), AE Ant., TETRICUS I (AD 270–3).
14. *118*. (B19), AE Ant., TETRICUS I (AD 270–3).
15. *137*. (B19), AE Ant., TETRICUS I ( AD 270–3).
16. *152*. (B45), AE Ant., TETRICUS I? (AD 270–3).
17. *51*. (A41), AE Ant., TETRICUS II (AD 270–3), Spes.
18. *26*. (u/s), AE Barb. Rad., 3rd century.
19. *34*, (u/s), AE Barb. Rad., 3rd century.
20. *29*. (B1), AE 3, CONSTANTINE I (AD 307–37).

21. *169.* (C14), AE 3, CONSTANTINE I, (AD 307–37), Victoriae Laetae Perp., Trier, AD 319, RIC as 213. No * on altar. Mint condition.
22. *166.* (Pit B6), AE 3, CONSTANTINE 1, 307–37, Gloria Exercitus, 2 soldiers 1 std, Trier AD 337–41.
23. *44.* (B1), AE 3, HOUSE OF CONSTANTINE.
24. *155.* (B3), AE 4 Barb., HOUSE OF CONSTANTINE, Gloria exercitus 1 std., Trier.
25. *162.* (C1), AE 4 Barb., HOUSE OF CONSTANTINE, Virtus Agg., Campgate type.
26. *14.* (A12), AE 4, HOUSE OF CONSTANTINE, Victoriae DD Augg Q NN, 2 Victories, Trier AD 341–6.
27. *52.* (A41), AE 4, HOUSE OF CONSTANTINE, Victoriae DD Augg Q NN, 2 Victories, Trier AD 337–46.
28. *69.* (A78), AE 4, HOUSE OF CONSTANTINE, Pop Romanvs, bridge with 2 towers, AD 330–46.
29. *204.* (Pit C7)(A), AE 4, CONSTANTIUS or CONSTANS, (AD 337–61), Victoriae DD. Augg. Q. NN.; Trier, AD 341–6, LRBC 161/164.
30. *56.* (u/s), AE 3, VALENTINIAN I or VALENS (AD 364–78), Securitas Reipublicae.
31. *36.* (A42), AE 3, VALENTINIAN I (AD 364–75), Securitas Reipublicae; Rome, AD 367–75, R.I.C. 24(A).
32. *75.* (A83), AE 3, VALENTINIAN I or VALENS (AD 364–78), Securitas Reipublicae.
33. *79.* (A83), AE 3, VALENTINIAN I or VALENS (AD 364–78), Gloria Romanorum.
34. *74.* (A83), AE 3, VALENS (AD 364–78).
35. *80.* (A83), AE 3, GRATIAN (AD 367–83), Gloria Novi Saeculi.
36. *27.* (u/s), AE 3, GRATIAN (AD 367–83), Securitas reipublicae; Arelate, AD 375–8, RIC 19 a or b.
37. *12.* (A12), AE 3, GRATIAN (AD 367–83), Gloria novi Saeculi; Arelate, AD 367–75, RIC 15.
38. *2.* (A12), AE 3, GRATIAN (AD 367–83), Securitas reipublicae; Rome, AD 367–75, RIC 24(c).
39. *21.* (A12), AE 3, 4th century.
40. *173.* (C14), AE 4 Barb., 4th century.
41. *20.* (A24), AE 3, Beata tranquillitas.
42. *68.* (A78), AE 4, 4th century.
43. *82.* (A83), AE 3 Barb. Barbarous coin struck on coin.
44. *65.* (A78), AE illegible.

### Post-Roman

45. *172.* (C14), AE Farthing, CHARLES I (1625–49).
46. *9.* (Ditch A1), Token, Chichester 1667, GEORGF IENINGS. of *.
47. *6.* (A12), Halfpenny, GEORGE III, Britannia, 1775.

### WEST WALLS (CH.W.87–88)

#### Roman

1. *104.* (33), As, DOMITIAN, AD 91–6.
2. *134.* (26), AE 4, ?VALENTINIAN II, AD 375–92.

#### Post-Roman

3. *16.* (1), Halfpenny, GEORGE II, 1729–34

### ST PETER'S (CH.P.87)

#### Roman

1. *63.* (42), As, ANTONINUS PIUS, AD 154.
2. *12.* (10), Antoninianus, ?VICTORINUS, AD 268–70.
3. *15.* (u/s), Antoninianus, CLAUDIUS II, AD 268–70.
4. *125.* (u/s), AE 4, ?CONSTANTIUS II, AD 337–64.
5. *35.* (4), AE 3, VALENTINIAN I, AD 364–75.
6. *37.* (4), AE 3, ?VALENTINIAN I, AD 364–75.
7. *45.* (31), AE 4, ?VALENTINIAN I, AD 364–75.
8. *33.* (31), AE 3, ?VALENS, AD 364–78.

### REFERENCE

Mack, R.P., 1964. *The Coinage of Ancient Britain* (London).

# 17

# Small finds from Chapel Street 1984 (Figs. 17.1 and 17.2)

## by Alec Down

*Note:* Context numbers are in brackets; small find numbers are in italics.

### Objects of copper alloy (all Roman unless stated otherwise)

1. (Pit X14B) *12.* Lead-filled ? terminal with a square hole at one end and with traces of iron. It was found in conjunction with a mass of corroded iron to which it was adhering.
2. (X2) *21.* Decorative strip to which another plate has been rivetted at one end, while there are the remains of two rivet holes at the other. This might be part of a narrow belt plate which had been attached to a leather belt.
3. (X 11) *25.* Fragment of a tinned strap hinge.
4. (X 11) *24.* Fragment of thin ribbed sheet 0.25 mm thick
5. (X11) *23.* Fragment of ribbed sheet similar to no 4 and possibly from the same object.
6. (X23) *54.* Spoon.
7. (Pit X14B) *13.* Hairpin.
8. (X13) *34.* Hairpin.
9. (Pit X23) *36.* Ansate, or small, equal-armed brooch. These are broadly datable between the 7th century and the 9th, cf. Capelle 1976, 10–15 and Taf. 2–6, although no close parallel to the Chichester brooch can be cited. (Information from Dr M.G. Welch, to whom thanks are due.)
10. (X16) *51.* A flat circular plate with a central hole. There are two lugs on opposite sides of the plate and there may have been two more at 90 degrees. to these, but damage to the edges of the plate render it impossible to be sure. The object is slightly dished and might perhaps be from a Roman plate brooch.
11. (Pit X5) *3.* Cast 'D'-shaped harness ring; post-Roman.
12. (Pit X13B) *14.* Cast decorative ring with traces of wood inside, probably post-Roman in date.

### Object of stone (Fig. 17.2)

13. (Pit X13D) *68.* Fragment of a Purbeck marble mortar.

### Object of bone (Fig. 17.2)

14. (Pit X14B) *71.* Polished antler workpiece.

### Objects of iron (Fig. 17.2)

15. (Pit X21) *73.* Strapping with a loop at one end. The other end has broken at the point where it appears to be turning through 90 degrees. Possibly a cart fitting.
16. (Pit X13D) *70.* Loop.
17. (Pit X13D) *69.* Staple.
18. (Pit X13C) *9.* Yoke.

### Object of lead (not illustrated)

19. (X 11) *30.* Lead rim.

The lead rim discussed here was found during excavations on the west side of Chapel Street in 1984. When discovered, it appeared to be a fragment from a large-diameter lead bowl or platter but it was noted during conservation that small fragments of red material were embedded in the section. The object was subsequently examined in the Ancient Monuments Laboratory by Justine Bayley who writes:

> The object appeared to be a rim fragment from a large bowl with a very irregular non-rim edge. There was some red material showing at the bottom of the piece which careful examination under a low power microscope showed to be samian ware. It is suggested that the object is a lead patch from a broken samian bowl, the irregular edge following the outline of the fracture. To give this sort of exact fit the lead must have been cast on to the bowl; presumably a temporary mould was fastened to the bowl and the molten lead poured in. When it had solidified the mould would have been broken away and the surface of the metal trimmed and smoothed. The lead is slightly thicker than the pottery, overlapping its edge to provide a positive key between metal and ceramic. When the bowl was finally discarded the lead patch became separated from the rest of it, with the exception of the small fragments still held in the metal.
>
> Lead plugs to fill small gaps or perforations in pottery are relatively well known but this is the first time I have seen evidence for such an ambitious repair. Presumably the large size of the samian bowl (its rim diameter must have been

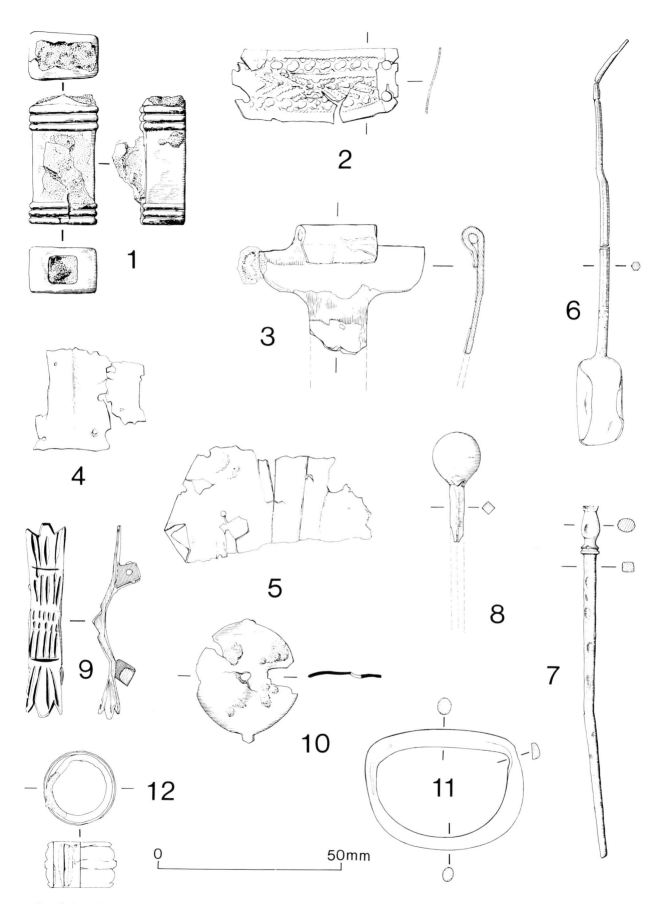

Fig.17.1     Objects of copper alloy from Chapel Street 1984, nos 1–12. Scale 1:1

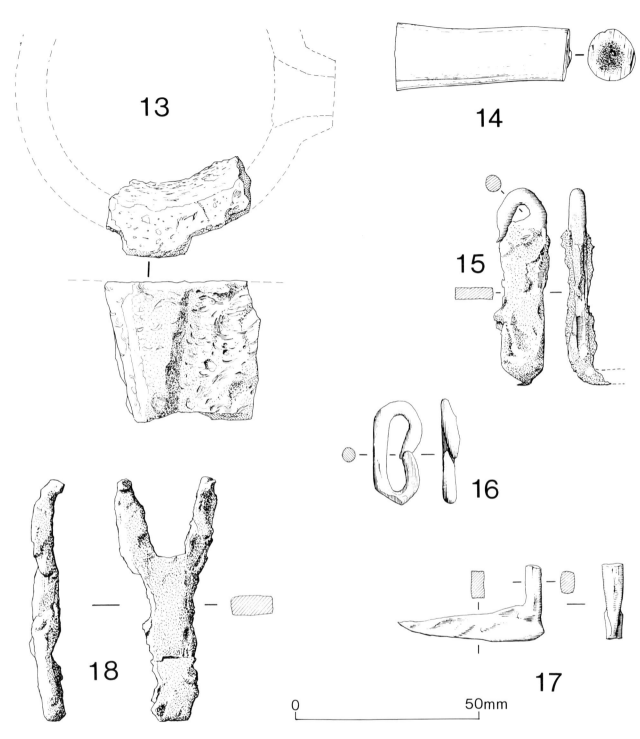

Fig.17.2    Small finds from Chapel Street 1984. No 13, stone; no 14, bone; nos 15–18, iron. All 1:1

of the order of 300 mm) meant it was too precious to discard when all it lacked was a not insubstantial chip from the rim. The lead might originally have been painted (though no evidence of this survives) and would then have been a not too obvious repair.

**REFERENCE**

Capelle, Torsten, 1976. 'Die frugeschichtlichen Metallfunde von Domburg auf Walcheren' in *Nederlandse Oudheden* No 5, ROB, Amersfoort.

# The Iron Age pottery from Chapel Street 1984

## by Alec Down

1. (Pit X14(B)) Two rim fragments, possibly from the same vessel. The fabric is poorly fired, very friable and tempered with flint grits. It is oxidised to a pale buff and is very similar to the sherds found in Chapel Street, Cattlemarket and Fishbourne (Down 1978, p. 187, 1; Down 1989, fig. 21.2 no 31; volume 9 forthcoming). The date of these vessels is uncertain but likely to be earlier than the 1st century BC.
2. (Slot X4) Rim sherd from a hand-made, black burnished ware vessel. The exterior is lightly burnished over the rim, with a zone of heavier burnishing just below the neck. Probably pre-Conquest.

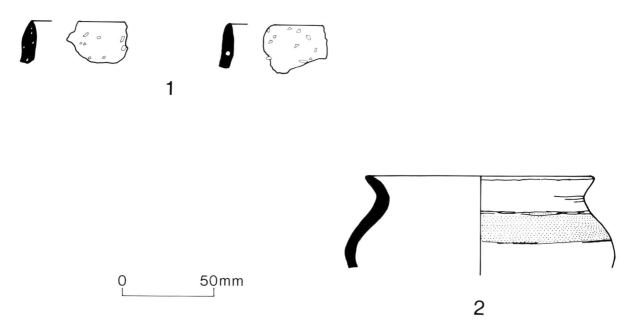

0      50mm

Fig.18.1    Early Iron Age pottery from Chapel Street 1984. Scale 1:2

**REFERENCES**

Cunliffe, B.W., Down, A., and Rudkin, D.J., (forthcoming). 'Excavations at Fishbourne' *Chichester Excavations 9.*
Down, A., (1978). *Chichester Excavations 3* (Phillimore).
Down, A., (1989). *Chichester Excavations 6* (Phillimore).

# Medieval pottery from Chapel Street 1984 (Fig. 19.1)

## by Alec Down

### Saxo-Norman c. 11th–12th century

1. (Pit X10A). Spouted bowl; heavily burnt, dark grey fabric with a few small flint grits (cf. Down 1978, fig. 11.4, 39).
2. (Pit X1A). Shallow dish with finger-impressed rim, similar fabric to no 1, partly oxidised to a dirty brown colour (*Op.cit.*, no68).
3. (Pit X1B). Rim of storage jar; hard grey fabric, flint grogged, oxidised reddish-buff.
4. (Pit X10B). Sherd from the shoulder of a ?cooking pot; hard grey fabric oxidised a reddish-buff inside and out and dimpled decoration applied by a stick-end (see Barton 1974, fig. 7.9, 18, and p. 85 for a similar example).
5. (Pit X10B). Small vessel; hard grey fabric, reduced black exterior, rilled on shoulder.
6. (Pit X1A). Hand-made pottery object. The fabric is a dirty grey/brown and grogged with crushed flint grits. There are faint indications that there may have been a hole right through it, in which case it could be a tuyere. Alternatively it might be part of a crude cresset lamp, although the shape is not quite right.

### Medieval c. late 12th–15th century

*(a) Cooking pots*

· 7 and 8. (Pit X10B). Hard grey fabric, flint grogged. Oxidised reddish-buff in patches.
9 and 10. (Pit X13D). Hard-fired fabric grogged with flint grits of uniform size and oxidised to a bright orange. Both vessels must be from the same production source.
11. (Pit X13D). Bowl; fine light grey sandy fabric, oxidised to dirty reddish-buff. Probably late 15th century.

*(b) Jugs*

12. (Pit X10A). Rim and neck of a large jug or pitcher in a dark grey sandy fabric oxidised a dark reddish-buff. The neck is decorated with a series of shallow horizontal grooves with a band of white painted decoration below a patchy green lead glaze.
13. (Pit X13D). Base of a jug; fine grey sandy fabric oxidised buff.
14. (Pit X13A). Rim sherd from a 'face-on-neck' jug. Fine grey flint grogged fabric, green lead glaze over rim and neck, with a band of white paint inside neck.
15. (Pit X13D). Body sherd from a jug; fine, dark grey sand-tempered ware, oxidised buff and with an exterior dark speckled green lead glaze.
16. (Pit X13D). Hearth tile; 163 × 182 × 37 mm thick.

### REFERENCES

Barton, K.J., 1979. *Medieval Sussex Pottery* (Phillimore).
Down, A., 1978. *Chichester Excavations 3* (Phillimore).

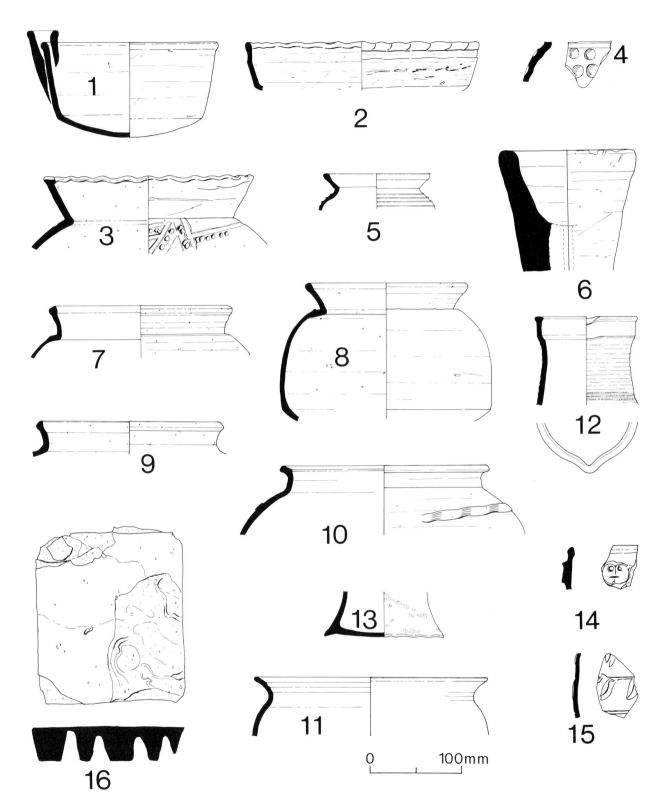

Fig.19.1    Medieval pottery from Chapel Street 1984, nos 1–16. Scale 1:4

# 20

# Small finds from Greyfriars (Figs. 20.1–20.10)

## by Alec Down

*Note:* Figures in brackets are context numbers; those in italics are the numbers in the Finds Register. All finds are Roman except where stated otherwise.

### Objects of copper alloy (Figs. 20.1–20.3)

*Brooches*

1. (A39), *60.* Colchester Derivative, cf. Down 1978, fig. 10.6, 8
2. (B48), *237.* Colchester, *op.cit.* fig. 10.6, 6.
3. (A26), *49.* Nauheim Derivative, cf. Down 1989, fig. 26.1, 18.
4. (C14), *187.* Nauheim Derivative, *op.cit.*

*Roman military objects*

5. (B122), *198.* Part of a rivetted strap from the *lorica* (Phase 2 clay pit).
6. (A83), *81.* Part of a hinged plate from the *cingulum.*
7. (A99), *115.* Scabbard binding, complete with rings to which the baldric would be attached, cf. Down 1978, fig. 10.31, 22 and Down 1981, fig. 8.30, 9, for other, less complete examples.
8. (A73/80), *95.* Dome-headed stud, probably military and possibly from a helmet, cf. *op. cit.*, fig. 8.30, 10. (Phase 2 clay pit).

*Other copper alloy objects*

9. (A52), *38.* ? Lamphook, cf. Hawkes and Hull 1947, pl. C, 33.
10. (A44), *22.* Part of a cast copper alloy belt plate, ?late Roman.
11. (A12), *88.* Cast decorative strip, possibly used as inlay.
12. (A73/80), *106.* Hook with one link of a chain attached, ? from a steelyard weight, cf. Down 1978, fig. 10.38, 114, and Cunliffe 1971, Vol.II, fig. 45, 100 (Phase 2 clay pit).
13. (C110), *221.* Bracelet.
14. (C1), *238.* Fragment of a cast copper alloy vessel with a rim diameter of 180 mm. From the garden soil and may be post-Roman.
15. (B1), *30.* Rivet.
16. (A73/80), *97.* Rod with grooved and flattened ends, function unknown (Phase 2 clay pit).
17. (A12), *4.* Half of a decorated, socketed handle or terminal (post-Roman).
18. (A12), *3.* Pin (post-Roman).
19. u/s, *120.* Child's bangle with chip-carved and punch-dot decoration.
20. (A73), *96.* Part of a flat ring.
21. (B1), *24.* Spoon, stamped inside the bowl with three dots set within circles and enclosed by a larger circle. At the end of the handle and underneath, is stamped a C. The spoon was found in the garden soil and is likely to be post-medieval in date.
22. (Wall, B1), *215.* Spoon, smaller than 21 and lacking part of the handle, (post-medieval).
23. (B47), *180.* Rim of a vessel in copper alloy sheet, probably post-Roman.
24. (A44), *66.* Rim of a copper alloy vessel c. 140 mm external diameter.
25. (B39), *147.* Part of a lock.

### Objects of iron (Figs. 20.4–20.6)

1. (A12), *1.* Buckle, probably post-medieval.
2. (B122), *190.* Part of a square-sectioned bar, possibly part of a punch.
3. (A24), *23.* Knife.
4. (A12), *16.* Key, post-medieval.
5. (A47), *25.* Knife.
6. (A83), *76.* Latch lifter.
7. (A20), *19.* Part of a barrel padlock, made of iron but with a surface coating of bronzing metal (copper + zinc and a little tin). Barrel padlocks are frequently coated with bronzing metal, which sometimes holds the pieces together as well as slowing down corrosion. (Identification by Justine Bayley, A.M. Laboratories, English Heritage, to whom thanks are due.)
8. (B1), *43.* Ring.

9. (B122), *196*. Yoke.
10. (B24), *167*. Iron object, ?spoon.
11. (C68), *178*. Knife.
12. (A64), *225*. Knife.
13. (Pit B6A), *165*. Fragment of a knife blade.
14. (B122), *189*. Iron plate pierced by a nail.
15. (C14), *192*. Adze (cf. Manning 1985, pl. 8, B10 and p. 17).
16. (B3), *146*. Horseshoe, probably post-Roman.
17. (Pit A6), *11*. Carpenter's bit.
18. (C110), *222*. Fragment of strapping, bent double and pierced at one end.
19. (A49), *39*. Blade of a trimming knife.
20. (A99), *117*. Flat bar 192 mm long, 25 mm wide and c. 4 mm thick.
21. (A73), *101*. Iron bar, 560 mm long with an approximate diameter after cleaning of 20 mm, increasing to 30 mm at the head.
22. (B56), *154*. Fragment of iron plate from the *lorica*, with part of a bronze lobate hinge attached.
23. (A73), *231*. Thin iron plate cut away at one corner.
24. (Pit A24), *108*. Knife, with bone handle with ring and dot decoration.
25. (A26), *53*. Knife.
26. (A41), *249*. Iron object, function unknown, possibly some form of graving tool.
27. (C41), *278*. Fragment of curved iron plate.
28. (B26), *142*. Iron object.

## Objects of bone (Fig. 20.7)

1. (B6), *131*. Highly polished bone 'folder', used in folding bed-linen. The context in which it was found suggests it is late or post-medieval in date.
2. (Pit B12C), *161*. Fragment of a single-sided comb, ?early medieval.
3. (C68), *179*. Bone handle, probably from a knife. From a post-medieval context.
4. (Pit B8), *148*. Bone handle, from a 17th century context.
5. (A73/80), *233*. Strip of highly polished bone. The section suggests that it was used as inlay. From the clay pit below the Roman house.
6. (A73/80), *102*. Needle.
7. (B45), *153*. Hairpin.
8. (B3), *125*. Hairpin.
9. (Pit B13), *177*. Hairpin.
10. (B138), *213*. Hairpin.
11. (C53), *224*. Hairpin.
12. (B156B), *218*. Hairpin.
13. (Pit A25), *110*. Hairpin.
14. u/s *90*. Hairpin.

## Objects of stone (Fig. 20.8)

1. (A50), *251*. Fragment of worked masonry in fine-grained limestone.
2. (A41), *100*. Fragment of worked marble.
3. (A52), *252*. Whetstone.
4. (B74), *175*. Small fragment of worked marble.
5. (B31), *139*. Fragment of marble inlay.
6. (A55), *217*. Hone.
7. (A73/80), *261*. Pebble whetstone.

## Objects of lead (Fig. 20.9)

1. (Pit A6), *10*. Fillet for joint sealing. Post-Roman.
2. (B11), *143*. Disc, which has been stamped with a circular punch with the device of a horse. Post-Roman.
3. (A26), *50*. Weight. Post-Roman.
4. (A64), *64*. Stud, with the remains of an iron pin. The head has the device of an elephant in moulded relief. From a late–post-medieval context.

## Objects of fired clay (Fig. 20.10)

1. (B122), *243*. Spindle whorl fashioned from a potsherd.
2. (A52), *253*. Potsherd, trimmed to make a gaming counter.
3. (A60), *254*. Fragment of a small crucible.
4. (A99), *127*. Fragment of a pipeclay figurine of Venus (cf. Down 1989, figs. 27.15, 3 and 29.2, 22).

**Miscellaneous (Fig. 20.10)**

*Objects of shale*

5. (Pit B5), *181.* Fragment of shale measuring 110 × 87 mm and being 10 mm thick. There are traces of burning around the edges and the object has been broken so that only two corners survive. These have been roughly rounded off and it appears likely that the object was re-fashioned from the base of either a large shale platter or perhaps a tray. The pattern of the burning, which follows the edge of the piece, suggests that the re-used fragment had lost very little of the missing side, indicating that the dimension across the short axis would have been c. 95 mm.

6. (A73/80), *265.* Fragment of a shale panel with border decoration. From the Phase 2 clay pit below the Roman house.

*Glass*

7. (B52), *145.* Counter, heavily pitted.

*Gold*

8. (B98), *179.* Ring; from a post-Roman context. The gold is of high quality (in excess of 22 carat) and could be either medieval or Roman in date.

## BIBLIOGRAPHY

Cunliffe, B.W., 1971. 'Excavations at Fishbourne 1961–69' *RRSAL* XXVI.

Down, A., 1978. *Chichester Excavations 3* (Phillimore).

Down, A., 1981. *Chichester Excavations 5* (Phillimore).

Down, A., 1989. *Chichester Excavations 6* (Phillimore).

Hawkes, C.F.C., and Hull, M.R., 1947. 'Camulodunum; first report on the Excavations at Colchester, 1930–39' *RRSAL* XIV.

Manning, W.H., 1985. *'Catalogue of the Romano-British iron Tools, Fittings and Weapons in the British Museum* (British Museum Publications Ltd).

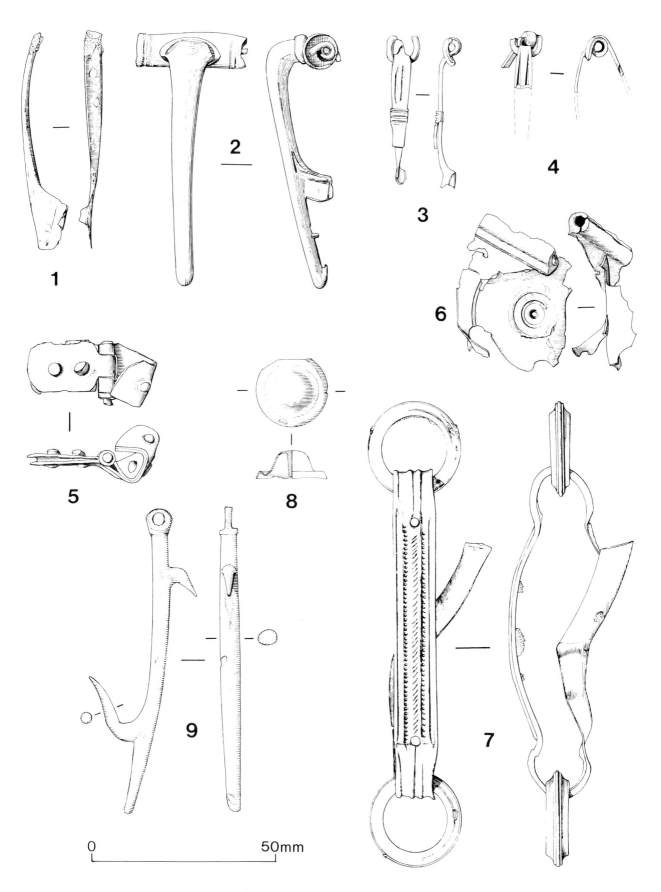

Fig.20.1    Objects of copper alloy from Greyfriars 1984, nos 1–9. All 1:1

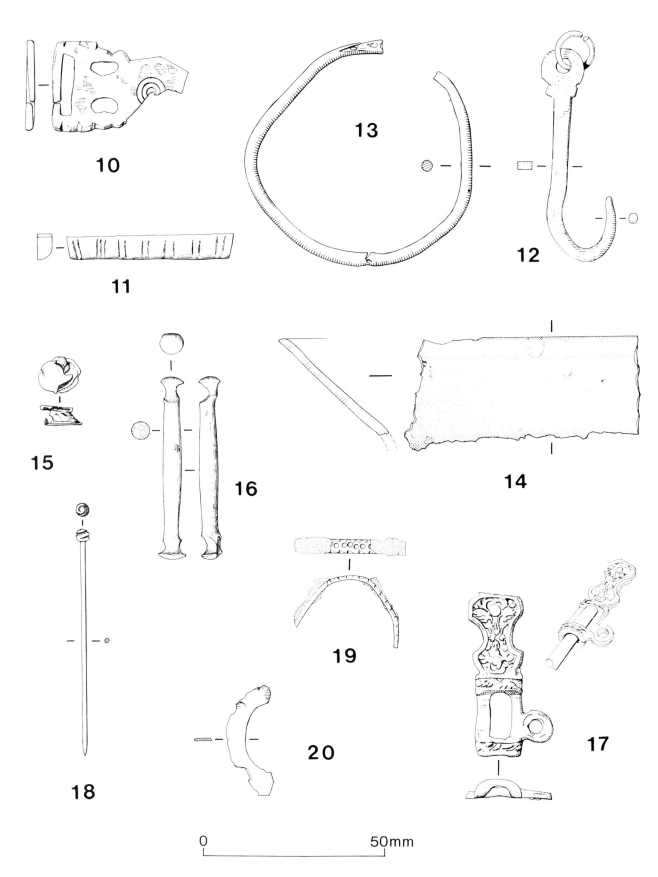

Fig.20.2    Objects of copper alloy from Greyfriars 1984, nos 10–20. All 1:1

194

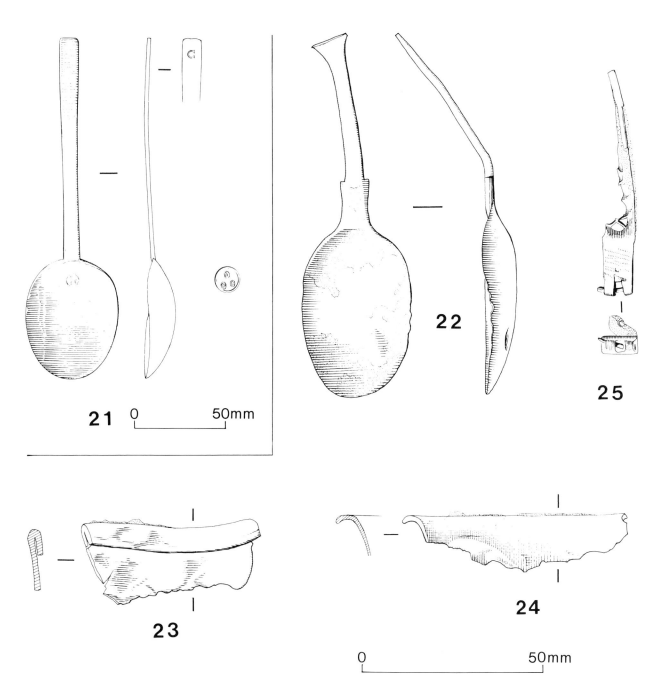

Fig.20.3   Objects of copper alloy from Greyfriars 1984, nos 21–25. Scale 1:1 apart from no 21, 1:2

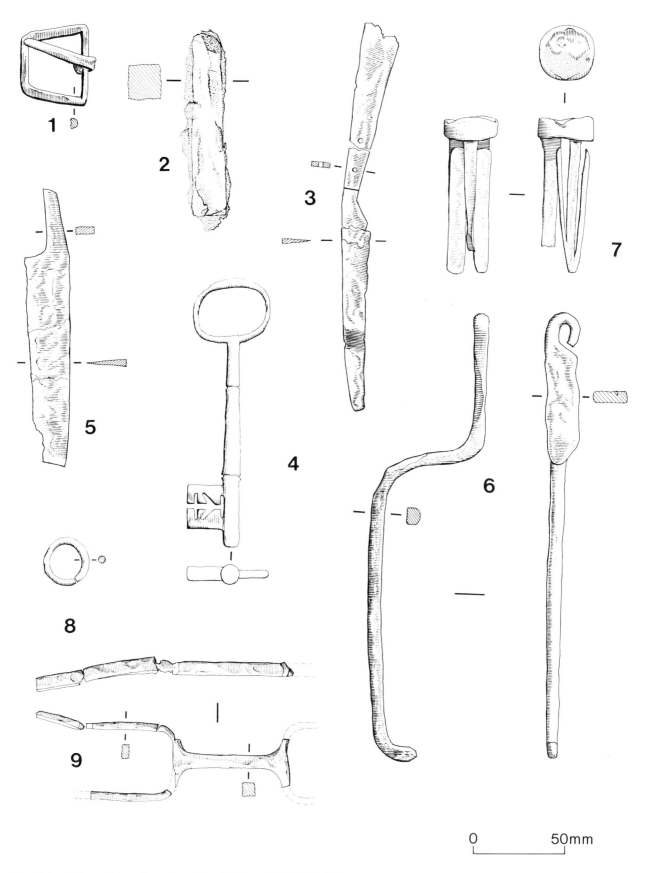

Fig.20.4    Objects of iron from Greyfriars 1984, nos 1–9. Scale 1:2

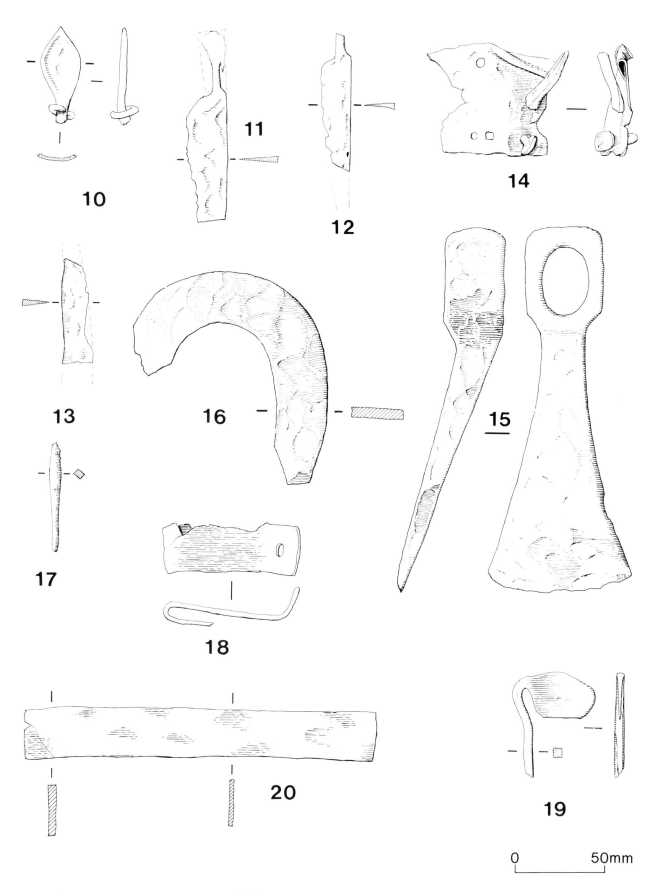

Fig.20.5    Objects of iron from Greyfriars 1984, nos 10–20. Scale 1:2

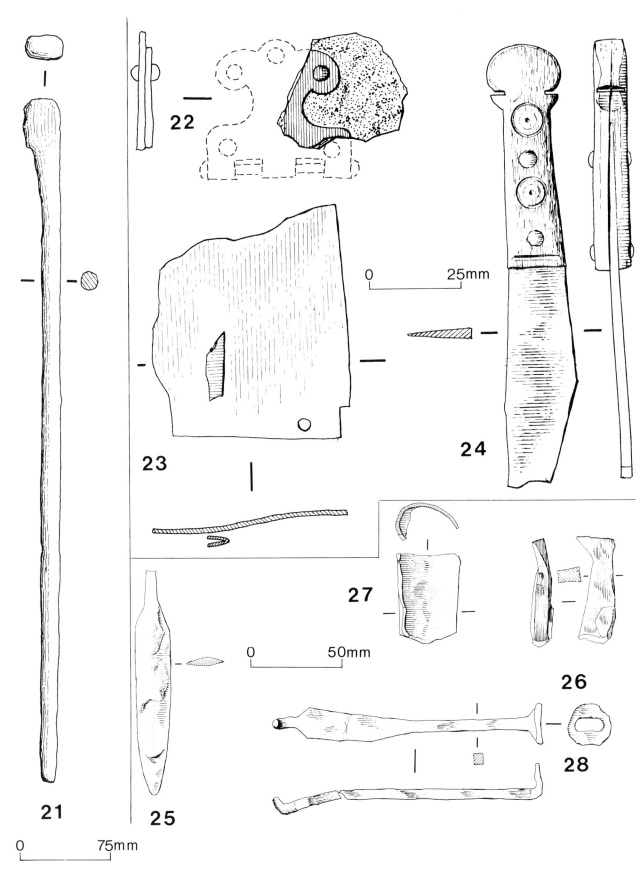

Fig.20.6 Objects of iron from Greyfriars 1984, nos. 21–28. No 21, scale 1:3; nos 22–24, 1:1; remainder 1:2

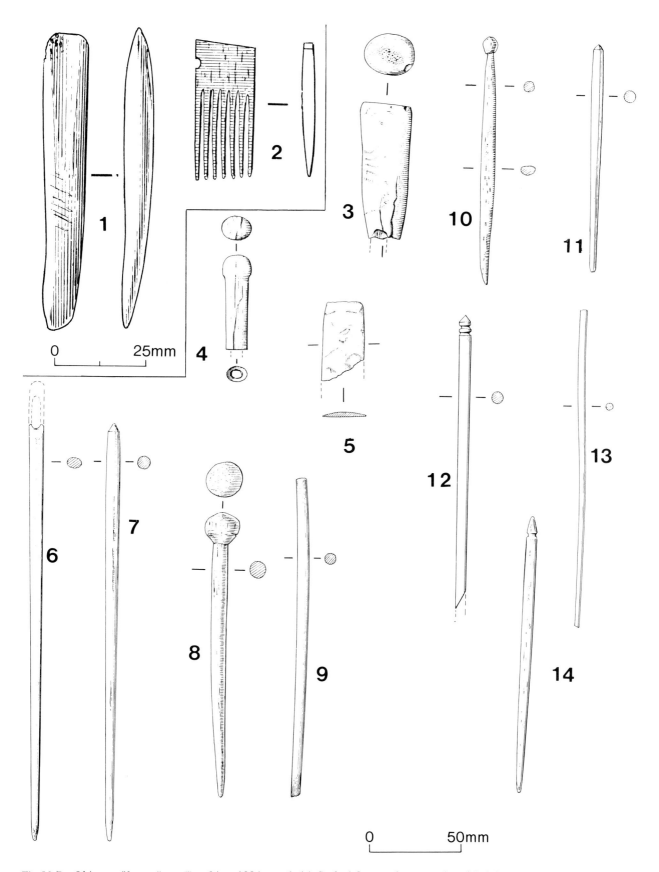

Fig.20.7    Objects of bone from Greyfriars 1984, nos 1–14. Scale 1:2 apart from nos 1 and 2, 1:1

0        25mm

0        50mm

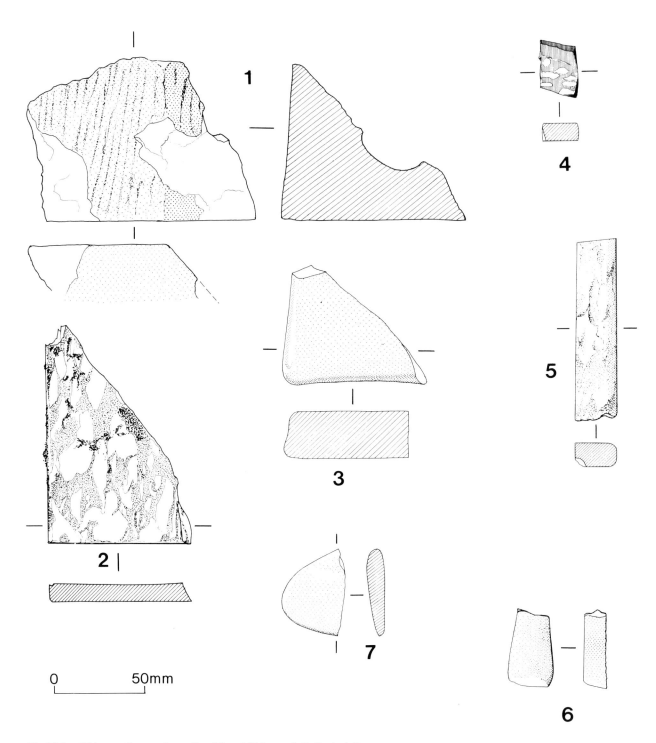

Fig.20.8    Objects of stone from Greyfriars 1984, nos 1–7. Scale 1:2

0    50mm

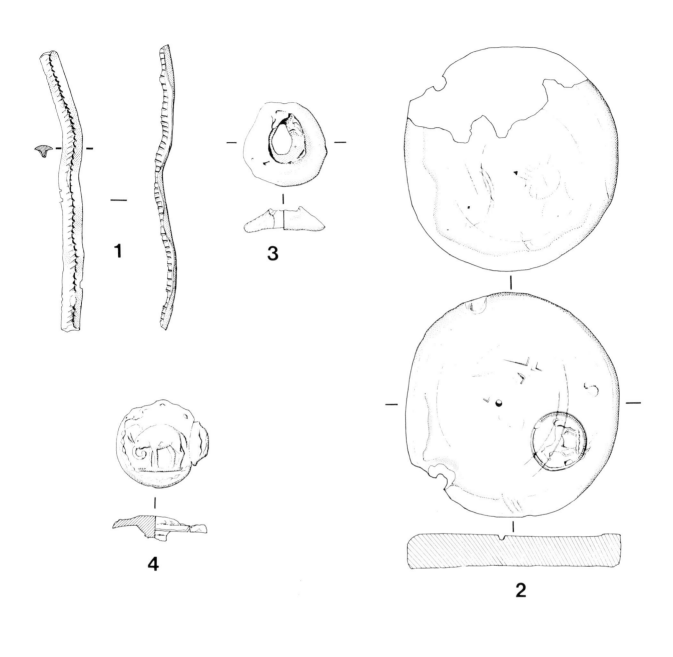

0                           50mm

Fig.20.9   Objects of lead from Greyfriars 1984, nos 1–4. Scale 1:1

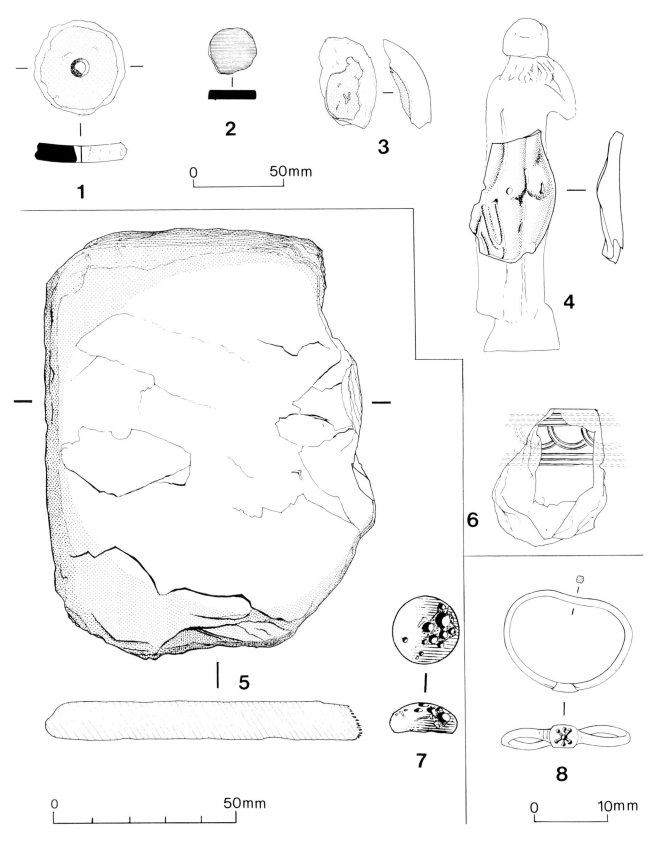

Fig.20.10   Miscellaneous finds from Greyfriars 1984. Nos 1–4, objects of baked clay, scale 1:2. Nos 5–6, shale. No 5 is 1:1. No 6 is 1:2. No 7, glass counter, scale 1:1. No 8, gold ring, scale 2:1

# 21

# Keyed tiles from the Greyfriars site with a note on a tile fragment from Tower Street

## by E.W. Black

Seventeen pieces of keyed tile were examined from the Greyfriars site from ten different contexts. Tiles with a wide range of dates are represented. The contexts are mostly post-Roman and not informative. Fortunately some of the types are well dated at other local sites.

The earliest tiles are four fragments of *parietalis* (keyed flat tiles) used probably in horizontal courses or in flooring. This type was used in the baths of the Period 1C 'proto-palace' at Fishbourne (Black 1985, 372), but these are the first such tiles to be published from Chichester itself. Two individual combs are represented (Fig. 21.1, 1 and 2). The tiles from the post-Roman contexts A12 and A83 had mortar over broken edges and on the back surface as well as the keyed face showing that they had been re-used after being broken. The tile from A79 (a Roman gravel wall-footing) had no proof of such re-use. Two fragments of tile with relief-patterned keying (Lowther's dies 19 and 21), and a third combed piece with part of the central division of a centrally divided box-tile, are perhaps 20–30 years later in date than the *parietales*. Such tiles keyed with 'London–Sussex' dies and by combing were installed in the Period 1C baths at Fishbourne when the Period 2 'palace' was built, and in the earliest period of the excavated public baths in Chichester (Black 1987, 12–13 and 84–86). The fragment from the Greyfriars site is the first occurrence of die 21 from Chichester, but die 19 was found previously in context Y34 in Area 3 at Chapel Street, later than Period 2 (early Flavian) layers and sealed by Antonine gravel metalling (Down 1978, 94–95 and 107 fig. 7.33). At the Greyfriars site two of the contexts (A26 and B31c) are uninformative, but the third (C41) was a layer in which the latest samian was ?Trajanic. The fragment from this context must have come from a tile broken during the installation of London–Sussex tiles in the public baths, and been deposited at that time or not long after. Apart from the two fragments of *parietales*, context A12 contained an undated fragment of combed tile and a fragment stamped with Lowther's die 55. This die is represented by nine other fragments from Chichester, where it was probably used in the public baths, and by two fragments from Fishbourne. Its date is not certain but the elaboration of the pattern compared to other dies known to date before c. 130 suggests that it is probably later than this. One voussoir fragment was present (in context A24: post-medieval) but cannot be dated.

Four pieces of box-tile (two of which join) from context A48 share the same fabric and combing. The type can be reconstructed with a width of 173–4 mm, a height of c. 400 mm, and a depth of c. 120 mm. The face was keyed with three bands of wavy combing running up and down rather than across (Fig. 21.1, 3). The sides were unkeyed and contained rectangular cutaways c. 80 × 40 mm. The tile walls were 16/17 mm thick. The type is a standard box-tile in use from the early 2nd century onwards, but cannot at present be more closely dated. Two of the fragments have mortar over broken edges showing that they have been re-used. A single piece of undated combed tile comes from context B62 and another (with mortar over a broken edge) from A41. Two further fragments of box flue tile from context A41, a late Roman destruction layer, are of considerable interest. One is 25 mm thick and combed with a six-toothed comb 35 mm across (Fig. 21.1, 4). The second is keyed with a comb of three unevenly spaced teeth 34 mm across, with a thickness of 18/21 mm at the end of the tile and 26 mm at the break. The full width (182 mm) survives and the height can be estimated tentatively at c. 360 mm (Fig. 21.1, 5). The sides are unkeyed and contain rectangular cutaways at least 115 mm in length. There is mortar on the keyed surface but not covering any broken edge. Both tiles contain plentiful coarse grog inclusions.

There seems little doubt that most of the specimens of keyed tile from the Greyfriars site reached the site as fragments to be used as hardcore or in some cases as rubble concrete. Some came from tiles used in the public baths in the late 1st/early 2nd century and mid 2nd century, and the fragments of *parietales* perhaps came from a 1st century predecessor of this building. Only the two unusually thick pieces of box flue tile from A41 have a good claim to have been used in hypocausts on the Greyfriars site itself.

## THE CENTRALLY DIVIDED BOX-TILE FROM TOWER STREET

A large part of the central division and parts of the two attached faces of a centrally divided box-tile was retrieved during construction work on the new Telephone Exchange in Chapel Street/Tower Street in 1974. One face is unkeyed and shows dark stains and traces of mortar. It is 22 mm thick. The other face is 19–20 mm thick and is keyed with angular combing measuring 45 mm across four teeth. The central division survives to a height of 255 mm but neither end is present. The division is 23 mm thick splaying out to c. 65 mm at the junction with the faces. The full depth of the tile is 145 mm. A complete box-flue tile was ploughed up on the site of the bath building at Angmering in 1953 and is now in Lewes Museum (Acc. No 1953.16). The full width is 257–260 mm and the height 456–469 mm. It is 140–144 mm deep. The sides of the tile are 17–18 mm thick and the central division 28 mm thick splaying out to c. 69 mm at its junctions with the faces of the tile. There is a semi-circular cutaway at the top of each side and of the central division. In the case of the Angmering tile both sides are stamped with die 19. The front face is stamped with die 21 and the rear face is unkeyed. In the front face at the bottom of each division of the tile there is an 'arched' cutaway, 86–88 mm wide at the base and 140–143 mm high. These would only be found in tiles used in the bottom course of a wall-jacketing which extended below the floor level of a room to the floor of the hypocaust basement. A second type of centrally divided box-tile was found at Eastbourne. One specimen

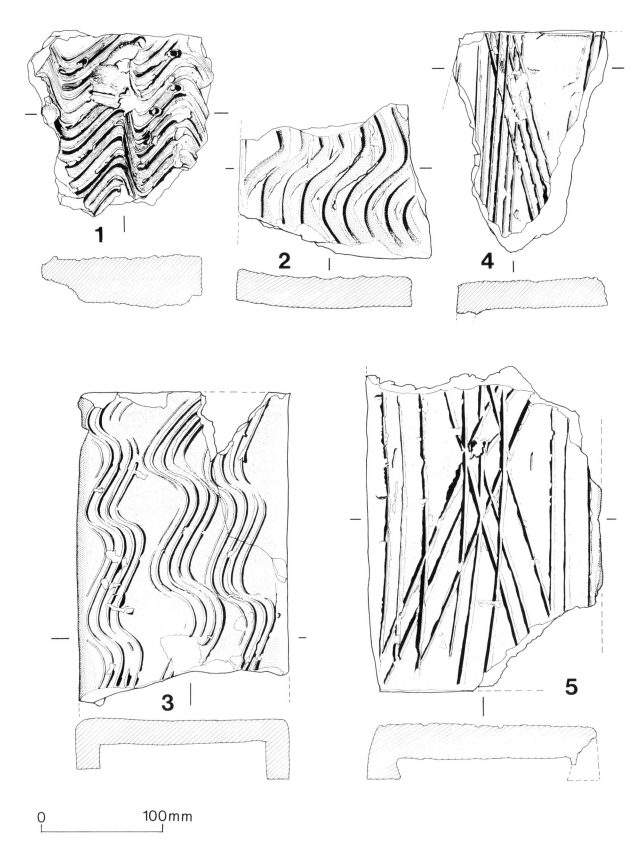

0        100mm

Fig.21.1    Keyed tiles from Greyfriars 1984. Scale 1:3

is in the Towner Art Gallery and Local History Museum in Eastbourne and two others are in the Royal Ontario Museum, Toronto (Cat. Nos 923.49.2 & 3). The specimen in Eastbourne is combed on the surviving face and stamped with the die 19 on one side. The other side is unkeyed. One of the divisions is provided with an oval cutaway in the centre and a triangular cutaway at each end of its combed surface (and these are presumably matched in the corresponding missing face of the tile). These tiles were designed to be substituted at the edge of a floor for the *bipedales* bridging the *pilae* of a hypocaust. It was the division of the tiles with the cutaways which was set next to the wall and allowed heated air from the hypocaust to pass upwards into a jacketing of box tiles placed above.

The fragment from Tower Street is clearly of the Angmering type. The baths at Angmering where such tiles were found *in situ* were excavated in the 1930s and have an early Flavian *terminus post quem* (Scott 1938, 12). The Tower Street tile was presumably one of those installed in the first period of the excavated public baths in Chichester.

## CATALOGUE OF TILES ILLUSTRATED IN THE TEXT

Fig. 21.1  1. Parietalis (A12)
          2. Parietalis (A79)
          3. Box-tile (A48)
          4. Box-tile (A41)
          5. Box-tile (A41)

## BIBLIOGRAPHY

Black, E.W., 1985. 'The dating of relief-patterned flue-tiles', *Oxford Journal of Archaeology*, 4.3, 353–76.
Black, E.W., 1987. *The Roman Villas of South-East England* BAR (British Series) 171 (Oxford).
Cunliffe, B., 1971. 'Excavations at Fishbourne 1961–69' *RRSAL* NoXXVI, Vols. 1 and 2 (Oxford).
Down, A., 1978. *Chichester Excavations 3* (Phillimore).
Lowther, A.W.G., 1976. 'Romano-British chimney pots and finials' *Ant.J.* LVI, 35–48.
Scott, L., 1938. 'The Roman Villa at Angmering' *SAC* 79, 3–44

# 22

# Roman pottery from the Greyfriars site (Figs. 22.1 and 22.2)

## by Alec Down

*Note:* Context numbers are in brackets where quoted; small find numbers are in italics.

1. (C111) Ovoid jar in a hard sandy fabric reduced grey, with a band of lattice decoration and tooling on shoulder.
2. (C111) Wide-mouthed jar; similar fabric to 1, reduced to mid-grey.

*Note:* Both of these vessels were buried complete, dug into the brickearth at the junction of the two slots forming the north-west corner of Structure C1, presumably as a foundation deposit. (See Fig. 2.6).

3. (Ph. A11), *55* Small ovoid jar complete. The fabric is hard and sandy, reduced to a light grey in places. Probably a foundation deposit. See Fig. 2.7 for location.

### The pottery from the sump (B104) (Figs. 22.1 and 22.2)

4. *182* Small lead-glazed beaker with applied white trailed stripes over a base coat of green/brown glaze. The base has been roughly trimmed off at some time after firing (not shown on drawing), and the fabric is a pale orange. See Down and Rule 1971, pl. 14 and fig. 5.24 for a similar vessel.
5. *176* Two joining rim sherds from a similar vessel to 1. The fabric is a slightly darker orange and is much overfired, making the glaze flake. This may have been a waster, and should be compared with another lead-glazed waster found in the St. Pancras cemetery ( *op. cit.*, fig. 5.22, Burial 81F; 77 and 99). The presence of wasters or 'seconds' may be an indication that the kiln producing these wares may be a local one.
6. Wide-mouthed jar, similar fabric to 2, with tooled decoration extending from shoulder to base.
7. Sherd from a wide-mouthed jar reduced to dark grey, with a line of burnishing around the neck and tooled decoration on body.
8. Rim of a large jar; similar fabric to 2.
9. Almost complete pear-shaped jar, reduced black and heavily tooled on shoulder.
10. Bowl, with zone of lattice decoration above carination. The fabric is hard-fired and sandy and reduced to dark grey.
11. Wide-mouthed carinated bowl; fabric similar to 10.
12. Jar in sandy grey fabric; three tally marks below rim.
13. Bowl; tooled above carination, reduced black.
14. Base of ? ovoid vessel. Sandy fabric reduced black.
15. Small, necked bowl in a light grey sandy fabric.
16. Rim of a ? bowl in a slate-grey fabric, with a trace of tooling below neck.
17. Greyware platter; ? variant of Cam. form 26A.
18 and 19. Carinated bowls; similar fabric to 17.
20. Carinated bowl, dirty grey sandy fabric.
21. Part of a vessel with an upstanding, lid-seated rim. Traces of burnishing over and inside rim.
22. *183* Crucible; see report by Paul Wilthew below, and Plate 23A.
23. (B31), *144* Globular beaker with two bands of white slip decoration, from the New Forest kilns (cf. Fulford 1975, fig. 13, Type 30, fabric 1A). c. AD 300+.

### BIBLIOGRAPHY

Down, A., and Rule, M., 1971. *Chichester Excavations 1* (Chichester).
Fulford, M.G., 1975. *New Forest Roman Pottery,* BAR 17.

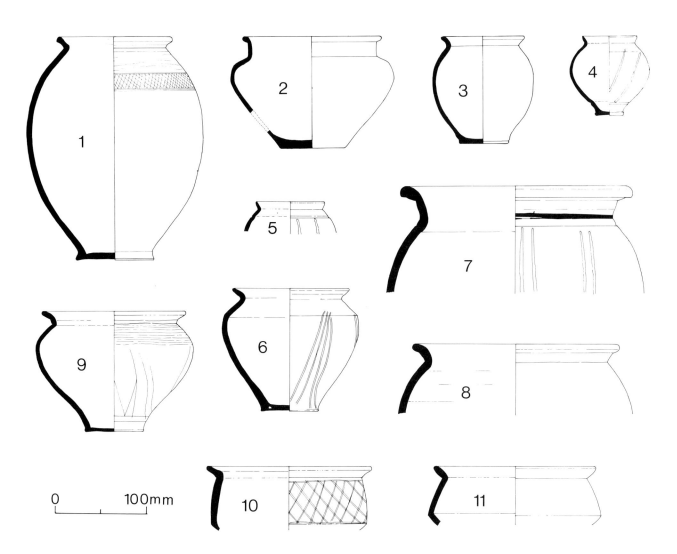

Fig.22.1    Roman pottery from Greyfriars 1984, nos 1–11. Scale 1:4

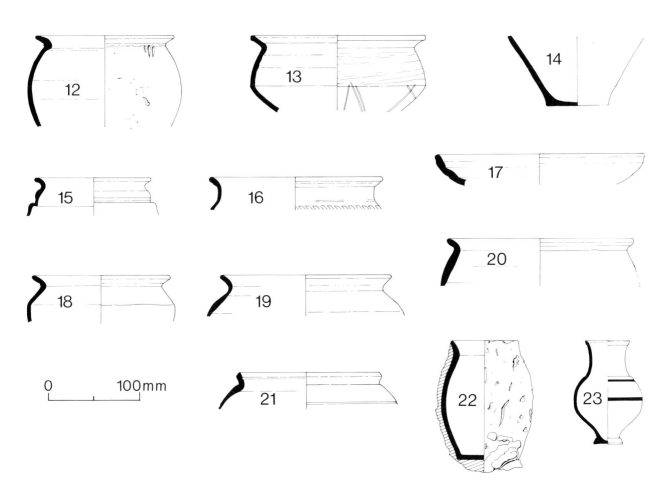

Fig.22.2    Roman pottery from Greyfriars 1984, nos 12–23. Scale 1:4

# 23

# Examination of a crucible from Chichester

## by Paul Wilthew

**Ancient Monuments Laboratory Report No 4451**

One large crucible from the Greyfriars site in Chichester (AM842816) was examined and scrapings of metal deposits from inside the crucible and some areas of its outside surface were analysed qualitatively using energy dispersive X-ray fluorescence. The crucible is illustrated in Fig. 23.1 (sketch by Justine Bayley) and also in Plate 23A. It consisted of a beaker with a refractory, reduced fired fabric surrounded by an outer layer of much less refractory clay. The outer layer was heavily vitrified. There was no evidence from the impressions in the outer layer, which would have been relatively soft at the temperatures reached, to indicate how the crucible was held during the melting and casting process. Similar layers are commonly found on crucibles of the Roman period and later. They would have protected the inner layer from thermal shock and increased the length of time during which the metal inside remained above its melting point and so available for casting.

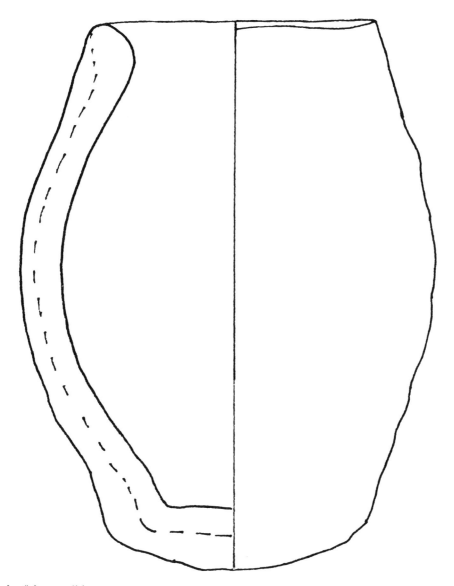

Fig.23.1   A sketch of the crucible

Plate 23   Roman crucibles, A from Greyfriars, Chichester; B from Carlisle

Two volumes were measured for the crucible, its total volume when filled to the brim and the maximum volume of metal which could reasonably have been melted in it. These were 450 ml and about 355 ml respectively. Roman crucibles of similar size and shape have been found, for example, at Carlisle (P. Wilthew, AML Report No 4452), in York (Justine Bayley, AML Report No 4432) and at Baldock (Justine Bayley, AML Report No 3604).

The scraping of metal analysed contained copper, zinc and tin in significant amounts, but no lead was detected. This suggests that a gunmetal (copper–zinc–tin alloy) was being melted. The red colours visible in some vitrified areas of the outer clay layer were due to copper. Similar crucibles from other sites were used to contain various copper alloys including brass (copper–zinc alloy), gunmetal and leaded gunmetal (AML Report Nos 3604, 4432 and 4452).

# 24

# Report on the cattle horn cores from the Greyfriars site, Chichester, 1984

## by Philip L. Armitage

*Note:* Tables 4 and 5 and the Appendix are in the Level 3 archive.

## 1. INTRODUCTION

A total of 118 cattle horn cores were recovered from a post-medieval pit (A50) at the Greyfriars site (Trench A).[1] The date of this assemblage is suggested by the pottery found in association with the cores in the fill of the pit, which is c. late 16th century (Down 1985, *pers. comm.*). However, the presence in the area of a cutler in c. early–mid 18th century may indicate a later date than is suggested by the pottery (see section 3.1, below).

The assemblage of horn cores was sent to The Booth Museum of Natural History, Brighton, in order that a detailed study could be carried out.

## 2. RESULTS OF THE ANALYSIS

### 2.1 State of preservation

Preservation of the majority of the specimens is good but many lack the tip of the core (either broken off in antiquity or during excavation): in some specimens only between one-third and one-half of the basal part of the core has survived attached to portions of the frontal and parietal bones.

All specimens are stained pale yellow.

### 2.2 Evidence for the removal of the hide

Twelve specimens (10.2% of the total) (Table 1) have small superficial cuts on the frontal bone, across the intercornual protuberance or at the base of the skull (Table 2). These marks are recognised as having been made by a skinning knife and provide evidence for the removal of the hide (in this case probably by the butcher prior to disjointing the carcass—see section 3.1, below).

**Table 1**
**Greyfriars, Chichester 1984. Cattle horn cores, evidence of skinning**

| | Age class | Description | No of specimens |
|---|---|---|---|
| 2. | sub-adult (2–3 yrs) | with knife marks | 3 |
| | | without knife marks | 10 |
| | | uncertain[a] | 20 |
| 3. | young adult (3–7 yrs) | with knife marks | 6 |
| | | without knife marks | 13 |
| | | uncertain[a] | 23 |
| 4. | adult (7–10 yrs) | with knife marks | 3 |
| | | without knife marks | 18 |
| | | uncertain[a] | 22 |

[a] in these specimens it is not possible to ascertain whether or not knife marks had originally been present because the horn core only has survived or the frontal and/or parietal bones are poorly preserved.

---

[1] In addition to these 118 complete/partially complete specimens there are 39 small pieces of core and 37 small pieces of frontal/parietal bones. All of these are in a very fragmented condition and so have been omitted from the analysis.

**Table 2**
**Cattle horn cores, detail of specimens showing evidence of skinning**

| | Age class | Side | Length class[a] by knife (per specimen) | No of marks made knife mark(s) | Location of knife marks |
|---|---|---|---|---|---|
| 2. | sub-adult (2–3 yrs) | R | — | 1 | on surface of frontal bone |
| | | R | — | 1 | on surface of frontal bone |
| | | L | — | 1 | on surface of frontal bone |
| 3. | young adult (3–7 yrs) | R | SH/MH | 1 | on surface of frontal bone |
| | | R | SH | 2 | on surface of frontal bone |
| | | R | SH | 2 | on surface of frontal bone |
| | | R | SH | 1 | base of skull |
| | | L | SH/MH | 5 | on surface of frontal bone |
| | | L | SH | 1 | on surface of frontal bone |
| 4. | adult (7–10 yrs) | R | SH | 4 | around base of horn core, anterior surface |
| | | L | SH | 1 | across intercornual protuberance |
| | | L | SH | 2 | on surface of frontal bone |

[a] Length class: SH shorthorned; MH mediumhorned (classification of Armitage, 1982b).

### 2.3 Marks made by cleaver or axe

Almost all the specimens examined show evidence of having been 'hacked off' the skull by means of a cleaver or ?axe. In the majority of the specimens the right and left horns had apparently been removed together (as a single unit) from the head by a sweeping blow directed across the back of the skull—possibly when the animal's head was positioned on the ground (Fig. 24.1). Subsequently (in antiquity) the portion of the cranium bearing the two horn cores broke in two; whether this was done purposely or accidentally during deposition and burial in the pit is, however, unclear—but as no conjoined core was found it may be that separation occurred prior to deposition (?).

A few specimens show evidence of the right and left horns having been removed separately by a blow directed to the side of the head just below the base of each horn in turn (Fig. 24.2).

A third method for detaching the horns is indicated by the core of a young adult shorthorn, in which the blow delivered by the cleaver—or axe—fell across the base of the horn, severing it completely from the parietal and frontal bones (Fig. 24.3). As this method is represented by a single core it was probably the least favoured and would have created problems when the time came to extract the bony core from its outer sheath—in the other two methods (Figs. 24.1 and 24.2) the surviving portions of frontal and parietal bones left attached to the core would have functioned as 'hand-holds' when the horn sheath was being pulled off.

### 2.4 Age of the horn cores

Using the method of Armitage (1982b, 40–3) the specimens can be classified into three age classes on the basis of size, surface texture and appearance of the bone (Table 3). No juveniles (age class 1: 1–2 yrs) or old adults (age class 5: over 10 yrs) were identified (see section 3.2.2, below).

### 2.5 Sex of the horn cores

Tentative determinations of the gender of the young adult and adult specimens (age classes 3 and 4) were made on the basis of a visual appraisal of the shape, curvature and angle of attachment of the core to the frontal bone, after the method of Armitage and Clutton-Brock (1976, 332) and Armitage (1982b, 43). Details of the male, female and castrate cores identified are given in Tables 4 and 5 (in Level 3 archive).

### 2.6 Size of the cores and classification into groups: small/shorthorned, shorthorned, short/mediumhorned and mediumhorned

Measurements taken from the specimens are summarised in Tables 4 to 7. The specimens were measured using a flexible tape-measure (length of outer curve and basal circumference) and dial calipers (Moore and Wright No 1143M, range 150 mm, with dial graduations of 0.02 mm) (maximum and minimum diameters of the base and half the breadth between the horn core bases).

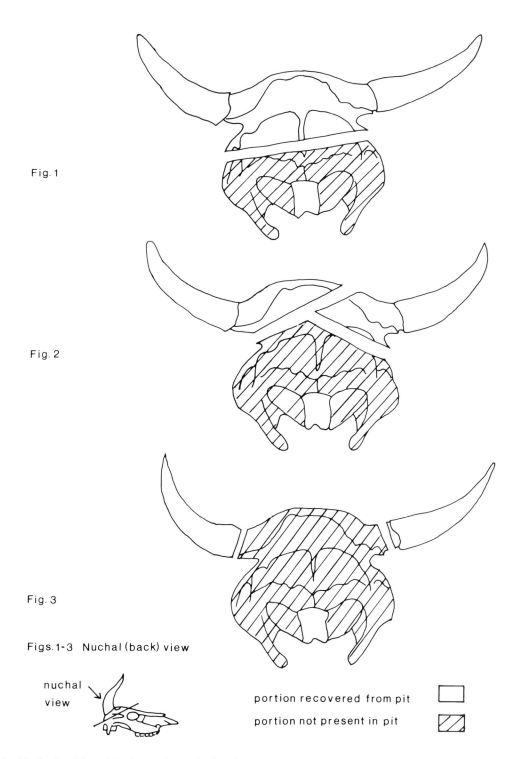

Fig. 1

Fig. 2

Fig. 3

Figs. 1-3  Nuchal (back) view

nuchal
view

portion recovered from pit

portion not present in pit

Figs. 24.1–3   Methods of detaching horns from the head

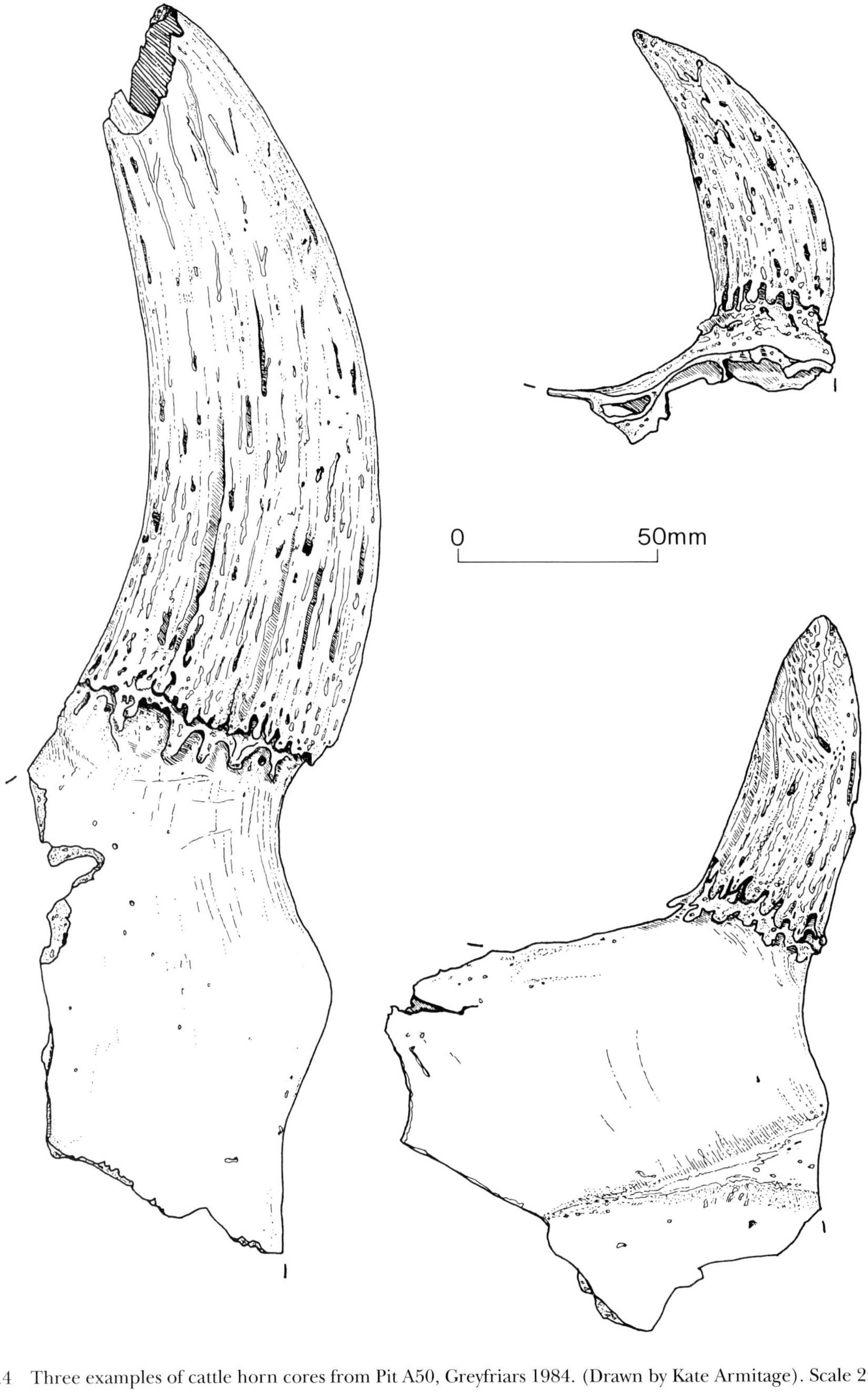

Fig. 24.4   Three examples of cattle horn cores from Pit A50, Greyfriars 1984. (Drawn by Kate Armitage). Scale 2:3

**Table 3**
**Cattle horn cores, summary of the ages of the specimens**

| Age class | Suggested age range (years) | No of specimens | % of total |
|---|---|---|---|
| 1. juvenile | 1–2 | 0 | 0 |
| 2. sub-adult | 2–3 | 33 | 28 |
| 3. young adult | 3–7 | 42 | 35.6 |
| 4. adult | 7–10 | 43 | 36.4 |
| 5. old adult | over 10 | 0 | 0 |

**Table 6**
**Cattle horn cores, summary of the metrical data. All measurements are given in millimetres**

| Age class | Point of measurement[a] | No of specimens | Mean | Range | Standard deviation |
|---|---|---|---|---|---|
| 3. young adult (3–7 yrs) | LOC | 24 | 137.1 | 90.0–205.0 | 40.1 |
| | BC | 41 | 146.8 | 98.0–208.0 | 32.0 |
| | MxD | 41 | 51.3 | 34.0–74.0 | 10.8 |
| | MnD | 42 | 40.5 | 25.3–56.8 | 9.2 |
| | $\frac{1}{2}$BHC | 4 | 85.4 | 82.7–93.1 | — |
| 4. adult (7–10 yrs) | LOC | 23 | 128.7 | 86.0–300.0 | 42.2 |
| | BC | 35 | 130.8 | 83.0–189.0 | 27.1 |
| | MxD | 36 | 47.0 | 34.7–68.5 | 8.7 |
| | MnD | 38 | 37.1 | 23.0–55.5 | 8.8 |
| | $\frac{1}{2}$BHC | 6 | 71.3 | 57.4–105.5 | — |

[a] Point of measurement: LOC, length of outer curve; BC, basal circumference; MxD max. diam. base MnD, min. diam. base; $\frac{1}{2}$BHC, half breadth between horn core bases (see measurement 31, von den Driesch, 1976, 29).

**Table 7**
**Cattle horn cores, frequency distribution for the basal circumference (mm). Young adult and adult cores only (age classes 3 and 4)**

| Basal cicumference. class interval (mm) | | No of cores |
|---|---|---|
| 80–89 | x | 1 |
| 90–99 | xxx | 3 |
| 100–109 | xxxxxxxxxxx | 11 |
| 110–119 | xxxxxxxxxx | 10 |
| 120–129 | xxxxxxxxxxxx | 12 |
| 130–139 | xxxxxxxx | 8 |
| 140–149 | xxx | 3 |
| 150–159 | xxxxx | 5 |
| 160–169 | xxxxxxxx | 8 |
| 170–179 | xxxxxx | 6 |
| 180–189 | xxxx | 4 |
| 190–199 | xx | 2 |
| 200–209 | xxx | 3 |

Number of specimens = 76. Mean = 139.47 mm. Range = 83–208 mm. Standard deviation = 30.72 mm.

As discussed by Martin (1847, 56) it is common to subdivide cattle into the broad categories: 'short', 'medium' and 'longhorned', on the basis of horn length. This is the classification system adopted by Armitage (1982b) to describe cattle horn cores from British post-medieval sites. It should be noted that the method can only be applied to adult cores over 3 years of age (age classes 3 to 5): in younger animals (age classes 0 to 2) it is not possible to determine their potential adult length, and so they are omitted from the analysis.

Using the classification system of Armitage (1982b, 43) the young adult and adult cores (complete and broken) from Greyfriars, Chichester, have been assigned to their respective groups (Tables 4, 5 and 8). Even though many of the Greyfriars' specimens are broken, with only between one-third and one-half of the core remaining intact, it proved possible to derive estimates of the original complete length of the outer curve (measured from the tip to the base) by projecting the dimensions of the surviving basal portion. Although the estimated values so obtained allowed these incomplete specimens to be classified, they are not considered sufficiently accurate for use in metrical analysis with measurements taken of intact specimens and have therefore been omitted from the tables of measurements given in this report. Estimates made from 'virtually' complete cores (i.e. specimens with only the very tip missing), however, are believed to be sufficiently close to the original values to justify their use in metrical analysis and so are included in Tables 4 to 6.

**Table 8**
**Cattle horn cores, summary of the length classes identified. Young adult and adult cores only (age classes 3 and 4)**

| Group (length class) | Length of outer curve (class limits) (mm) | No of specimens | % of total |
|---|---|---|---|
| smallhorned/shorthorned[a] | under 100 | 10 | 11.8 |
| shorthorned | 100–220 | 50 | 58.8 |
| shorthorned/mediumhorned[b] | (200–205) | 11 | 12.9 |
| mediumhorned[c] | 220–360 | 13 | 15.3 |
| longhorned | over 360 | 0 | 0 |
| indeterminate | — | 1 | 1.2 |

[a] Exceptionally small-sized cores but otherwise generally similar in shape and curvature to cores of the shorthorned group.

[b] specimens with LOC less than 220 mm but with larger (more 'robust') bases than the 'true' shorthorned cores.

[c] includes one male core (LOC 205 mm) best classified under the mediumhorned group.

*The problem of classifying late 16th and early 17th century cattle*

As discussed by Armitage (1984, 6) the late 16th century was a time of significant advances in cattle husbandry, which is reflected in the very wide variety of size and general appearance of cattle horn cores found at archaeological sites of this period. In the light of these changes, the existing horn core classification system devised by Armitage (1982b) is proving inadequate to deal with the intermediate forms encountered in deposits of this date and there is clearly a need to revise the system in order to provide a more precise typology which will accommodate *all* late 16th and early 17th century cattle. Until this revision has been carried out, the intermediary types in the Greyfriars sample have had to be assigned to two temporary classes: 'small/shorthorned' and 'short/mediumhorned' (Tables 4, 5 and 8).

## 3. DISCUSSION

### 3.1 Source and dating of the horn core deposit

Deposits of cattle horn cores found at archaeological sites generally derive from one (or combination) of the following three sources:

(i) slaughteryard (butchers' shambles)
(ii) tanyard
(iii) horn-worker's premises

The connection between deposits of cattle horn cores and the crafts of butchery, leather-working and horn-working may be explained as follows.

*(i) Butchery*

During preparation of the carcass for disjointing, the butcher would leave the horns attached to the hide. Occasionally, however, he would remove them for sale directly to the horn-worker, as either complete horns (i.e. outer sheath and bony core) or sheath only (inner core removed). Evidence for this dual practice appears in a late 15th century petition from London horners to the Lord Mayor where mention is made of the purchase by horn-workers of 'hornes in the bones' and horns 'oute of the bones' from the City 'bochers' (Fisher 1936, 23). If the butcher sold the horners horn sheaths only, he soon accumulated large quantities of the inner bony core (horn core) which were then thrown away along with other unwanted slaughteryard waste.

*(ii) Leather-working*

Pictorial evidence showing that tanners bought hides of cattle which still had horns attached is provided by an early 19th century engraving of the 'skinmarket' at Leadenhall, City of London (Wilkinson 1825), and a photograph of a modern leather market (Cooke 1917, 17). As discussed by Prummel (1978, 399–402) this practice is well documented and there is archaeological evidence showing that the tradition is long-established and may be traced back to medieval times. Having purchased hides, the tanner's first task in preparing them for the tanning process was to cut out the horns (see Thomson 1981, 162) which he would sell to the horn-worker either as complete horns (sheath and core) or as outer sheaths only.

If the latter procedure was followed, the tanner soon accumulated large quantities of horn cores, as demonstrated by the excavation of a 16th century tannery site in St Alban's, Hertfordshire, where there was found a pit filled with oak bark and cattle horn cores (Saunders 1977).

*(iii) Horn-working*

If the horner purchased from the butchers and the tanners complete horns, his first task was the removal of the inner bony core (Armitage and Clutton-Brock 1976; Prummel 1978, 409). In this way the horner soon accumulated a large quantity of horn cores which he disposed of with the other horn-working waste. Archaeological evidence for the association between cattle horn core deposits and the horn-working industry was found by Wenham (1964) during excavations at Hornpot Lane in the city of York, which uncovered a 14th century horn-soaking pit containing over 500 cattle horn cores. Further evidence of this comes from Stamford where excavations on the site of a 16/17th century horner's workshop revealed 10 horn-soaking pits filled with cattle horn cores (Cram 1982).

There is no evidence for either tanning or horn-working activity in this part of Chichester in the early modern period (Down *pers, comm.*) and it is very unlikely therefore that the Greyfriars horn cores came from a tanyard or horn-worker's premises. The presence of butchers in the area is, however, well attested: documentary sources examined by R. Morgan (1984) revealed that the Greyfriars site in the 16th and 17th century—then a garden—belonged to the Exton family who were engaged in the butchery trade. It seems very probable, therefore, that the cattle horn cores found in the pit came from a local slaughterhouse run by this family.

There is perhaps one further possible source which needs to be considered. According to the documentary survey carried out by R. Morgan, the owner of the property immediately north of the Greyfriars site, in the 18th century, was Henry Combes, a cutler. This raises the possibility that the horn cores represent waste from his premises. If this assumption is indeed correct then the deposit is therefore of later date than is suggested by the pottery in the fill to the pit (Down *pers. comm.*).

An engraving from the Victorian period (see Reader 1974, 56–57), clearly shows that cutlers handled cattle horns.[2]

The encyclopaedia of early 19th century manufacturing industries by Rees (1819, 226) records that cutlers used the small end of the ox-horn for making handles of table knives and that horn was also used in manufacturing the ornamental 'outer scales' of penknife handles.

Although the illustration of the Victorian cutler in Reader (1974, 57) shows what looks like part of the skull of an ox with the horn attached, it is not known whether it was the *usual* practice of cutlers to buy cattle horns from the butchers in the 'raw' state, i.e. still retaining the bony core, or whether this unwanted (superfluous) part of the horn had already been removed. If the latter was the common practice then the suggestion that the Greyfriars deposit came from the Combes' workshop is untenable. Furthermore, the horn cores themselves do not appear to be of late 17th/early 18th century cattle. There are no cores from the exceptionally large-sized Sussex cattle which would have been expected in a deposit of early 18th century date—according to Defoe (1724 reprinted 1974, Vol.1, pp. 114 and 131) the red Sussex beef cattle could be 'counted the largest breed in England'. The preponderance of small-sized shorthorned cattle in the deposit would seem to substantiate the pottery dates which suggest the cores were deposited in the late 16th century.

## 3.2 Cattle husbandry

### 3.2.1 Evidence of heterogeneity in Sussex cattle

The relatively high values of the coefficient of variation for the length of outer curve in the young adult and adult specimens ($v = 30.8$)[3] indicates that the collection of horn cores from the Greyfriars site is heterogeneous in composition: a 'pure' (homogeneous) sample would be expected to have a coefficient of variation between 4 and 10 (Simpson *et al.* 1960, 91).

The high variability within the Chichester horn core sample can in part be ascribed to the presence of male, female and castrated animals, but it also clearly demonstrates that more than one type of stock is represented. Indeed, the very wide variety of horn cores includes those from exceptionally small shorthorned animals reminiscent of the dwarf 'scrub' cattle of the high middle ages (see Armitage 1980, 406; 1982a, 53) as well as those from individuals of similar size and horn conformation to the modern Sussex breed. (A few of the larger-sized Greyfriars' cores compare very favourably with the horn cores of the two adult Sussex cows in the modern comparative osteological collections of the Booth Museum of Natural History, reg. nos 100026 and 102040).

The very wide variety recorded in the Greyfriars sample is all the more remarkable when one considers that cattle in Sussex in the 16th and early 17th century formed a *single*, geographically isolated population. Although recognised as an important cattle-rearing district, very few Sussex farmers had sufficient capital to fund long-distance movement of breeding stock and they could not therefore afford to import animals from outside the county (Cornwall 1954, 77). All cattle found within the county at this period were therefore 'native' bred. This situation may be contrasted with other farming areas at this period where cattle populations comprised a mixture of local and non-local (sometimes even foreign) stock. The cattle population of Lincolnshire in the 17th century, for example, included recently imported Dutch shorthorned cattle as well as black longhorns from Lancashire and Yorkshire (Markham 1657, 69; Mortimer 1707, 166).

If the variety in the Greyfriars sample cannot be ascribed to the presence of more than one regional 'race' of cattle, the alternative explanation must be that the wide range in size reflects different standards of livestock husbandry practised by Sussex stockmen, i.e. the more progressive farmers reared animals of reasonable size and quality while others, who largely neglected their stock, produced smaller and inferior-quality animals, though even a wealthy landowner such as Sir Thomas

---

[2]  Engraving entitled: 'Graphic illustration of animals showing their utility to man in their services during life and uses after death'.

[3]  $v$ = coefficient of variation (variability) calculated after the method of Pearson (see Simpson *et al.* 1960, 90). Length of outer curve (age classes 3 and 4 combined): $N = 47$; $\bar{x} = 133$ mm; range = 86–300 mm; SD = 40.9 mm.

Pelham of Laughton—who specialised in beef production in the first half of the 17th century—had many runts in his herd; these poor-quality animals (mostly females and castrates) were only half the value of the better sort of cattle, when fattened and sold for meat (Cornwall 1954, 73–4). Fussell (1952, 95) also considered that the majority of Sussex cattle remained little improved until comparatively recent times, and that the Sussex cow was especially 'tiny. . . inspite of the efforts of . . . breeders'.

*3.2.2 Kill-off pattern (age at slaughter)*

Over two-thirds of the Greyfriars horn cores are from animals over three years of age (Table 3). This preponderance of fully grown cattle fits very well the picture of urban centres being principally supplied with culled draught animals. Such animals would not have been sent into the town for slaughter until at least six years of age—draught cattle generally started their working lives when about two or three years of age (Fussell 1952, 63; Cornwall 1954, 73) and after working for a period of between three to five years they were then fattened ready for the meat market (Oschinsky 1971, 162). According to Leonard Mascall (who owned Plumpton Manor, near Lewes), the author of *The Governmente of Cattell* (1587), working oxen could be kept till ten, and then fattened for slaughter (Fussell 1952, 63). In view of Mascall's advice, it is somewhat strange to discover that the sample of horn cores from Chichester does not include at least a few old adults (i.e. animals over 10 years of age); the reason for this discrepancy is unclear.

The presence of immature (sub-adult) horn cores (28%) in the Chichester sample (Table 3) suggests that at least some of the cattle reaching Chichester in the late 16th/early 17th century were supplied by livestock farmers specialising in the rearing of fat cattle (cf. Sir Thomas Pelham of Laughton, referred to above).

Very young veal calves may also have been slaughtered in significant numbers in Chichester in the late 16th/early 17th century but, as the horns of these animals would have been very little developed (i.e. were no more than horn buds), evidence for this is unlikely to be found in excavated horn-core deposits such as that discovered at the Greyfriars site.

## 4. BIBLIOGRAPHY

Armitage, P.L., 1980. 'A preliminary description of British cattle from the late 12th to the early 16th century' *The Ark* VII (No 12), 405–12.

Armitage, P.L., 1982a. 'Developments in British cattle husbandry from the Romano-British period to early modern times' *The Ark* IX (No 2), 50–4.

Armitage, P.L., 1982b. 'A system for ageing and sexing the horn cores of cattle from British post-medieval sites (17th to early 18th century) with special reference to unimproved British longhorn cattle', in B. Wilson, C. Grigson and S. Payne (eds.), *Ageing and Sexing Animal Bones from Archaeological Sites* BAR British Series 109, 37–54.

Armitage, P.L., 1984. *Report on the Cattle Horn Cores from Church Street, West Ham, 1973* (unpublished Level III archival report, Museum of London and Passmore Edwards Museum, 1984).

Armitage, P.L. and Clutton-Brock, J., 1976. 'A system for classification and description of the horn cores of cattle from archaeological sites' *Journ. Archaeol. Science* 3, 329–48.

Cooke, A.O., 1917. *A Day with Leather Workers* (London).

Cornwall, J., 1954. 'Farming in Sussex, 1560–1640', *SAC* 92, 48–92.

Cram, L., 1982. 'The pits and horn cores' in C. Mahany, A. Burchard and G. Simpson *Excavations in Stamford, Lincolnshire 1963–9* Society for Medieval Archaeology Monograph Series No 9, 48–54

Defoe, D., 1724. *A Tour through the Whole Island of Great Britain* (London, reprinted 1974).

von den Driesch, A., 1976. *A Guide to the Measurement of Animal Bones from Archaeological Sites* Peabody Museum Bulletin No 1, Harvard University.

Fisher, F.J., 1936. *A Short History of the Worshipful Company of Horners* (London).

Fussell, G.E., 1952. 'Four Centuries of Farming in Sussex, 1500–1900' *SAC* 90, 60–101.

Markham, G., 1657. *A Way to get Wealth* (London) 9th edition

Martin, W.C.L., 1847. *The Ox* (London).

Mortimer, J., 1707. *The Whole Art of Husbandry* (London).

Oschinsky, D., 1971. *Walter of Henley* (Oxford).

Prummel, W., 1978. 'Animal bones from tannery pits of 's Hertogenbosch' *Berichten van de Rijksdienst voor het Oudheidkundig Bodemonderzoek* 28, 399–422.

Reader, W.J., 1974. *Victorian England* (London).

Rees, A., 1819. *Manufacturing Industry* (London).

Saunders, G., 1977. 'A sixteenth century tannery at St. Albans' *Hertfordshire's Past* 3, 9–12.

Simpson, G.G., Roe, A., and Lowontin, R.C., 1960. *Quantitative Zoology* (New York).

Thomson, R., 1981. 'Leather manufacture in the post-medieval period with special reference to Northamptonshire' *Post-Medieval Archaeology* 15, 161–75.

Wenham, L.P., 1964. 'Hornpot Lane and the horners of York' *Annual Report of the Yorkshire Philosophical Society, York, for the Year 1964*, 25–56.

Wilkinson, R., 1825. *Londina Illustrata* (London).

# The post-Roman pottery from the Greyfriars site (Figs. 25.1–25.4)

## by Alec Down

### Late Saxon–early medieval

1. (Pit B6). Almost complete cooking pot, one of a number from a large late Saxon pit alongside the frontage on to Priory Road. In typical Saxo-Norman heavily gritted dark grey fabric (cf. Down 1978, fig. 11.3 for similar wares, there designated Group 3, c. 11th–early 12th century, although this pit may well date to the late 11th century and be just pre-Conquest).
2. (Pit B6). Small vessel, almost black fabric with some sand filling.
3. (Pit B6). Rim of a small cooking pot. Dirty grey fabric with small flint grits.
4. (Pit B6). Cooking pot rim, hard-fired dark grey ware, flint-tempered.
5. (Pit B6). Spout, probably from a pitcher, in a greyish-brown fabric, partly oxidised to a light brown and with medium flint grits.
6. (Pit A9). Sherd from a large spouted jar. Medium grey fabric oxidised to reddish-buff and heavily flint-tempered, cf. Down 1978, fig. 11.2, no 38.
7. (B26). Base of a vessel in a dark grey fabric very heavily packed with small to medium flint grits.
8. (A12). Sherd from a chimney vent in a hard-fired pale grey fabric with some sand-tempering.

9 and 10. (B36). Two fragments of baked clay daub, probably from a demolished clay oven or possibly from a kiln. The majority of the daub found was tipped into Pit B6, the large late-Saxon cess-pit mentioned above, with the rest being scattered around the vicinity. No trace of the actual oven remained, but it may well have been destroyed by the pit-digging.

### Medieval

11. (Pit A9). Sherd from a vessel or possibly a chimney vent, although the heavy rilling and the barrel-shaped body are untypical. The fabric is hard-fired reddish-brown, with small flint grits.
12. (C1). Handled cooking pot; heavily sooted, reddish-brown sandy fabric.
13. (A24). Lid in a pale grey fabric oxidised to orange/buff.
14. (A58). Jug or pitcher in a fine grey fabric oxidised to a light buff. It has white painted decoration, partly below a 'bib' of green lead glaze, and a deeply slashed rod-sectioned handle, c. late 14th–early 15th century.
15. (B1). Handle and part of the rim from a jug in a fine hard-fired sandy grey fabric oxidised buff. There are traces of a green lead glaze below the handle.
16. (B19). Shallow dish in fine pale grey ware oxidised to reddish-buff.
17. (B19). Sherd from a dish which has been heavily burnt. Fine, sandy grey fabric, internal green lead glaze.
18. (A48). Internally lid-seated rim from a cooking pot. The fabric is mid grey, hard-fired, sand-tempered and oxidised to a pale buff on both surfaces. The seating for the lid is coated with a speckled green lead glaze.

### Tiles

19. (Pit B7). Fragment of a hearth tile in a reddish-buff fabric, heavily flint gritted.
20. (A12). Two fragments of a floor tile with white mortar inlay decoration. Traces of a pale yellow lead glaze remain on the inlay and the sides of the tile.

### Roof furniture, probably late–post medieval

21. (A17[B]). Peg tile 285 × 190 × 13 mm. Reddish-buff sandy fabric.
22. (A17[B]). As no 20 but it can be seen that the peg holes are at 90 mm centres.
23. (Pit B7). Fragment of a peg tile in a sandy, orange-red fabric with sparse flint grits. The thickness is 10 mm; other dimensions are unknown but this is a smaller specimen and might be earlier in date.
24. (A17). Hip tile in similar fabric to nos 20 and 21 but slightly darker in colour.

### The pottery from A47 (Figs. 25.3–25.4)

1. A large fragment from a bung-hole pitcher in a fine mid grey fabric, oxidised to a reddish-buff on both surfaces. It has a horizontal band of white paint around the upper part and an X, underlined, has been incised into the surface after firing. A patch of olive-green lead glaze across the top part of the vessel may have been applied as a 'bib'.
2. Part of a painted ware pitcher in a similar fabric to no 1.
3. The base of a pitcher in identical fabric to no 1 and may in fact be from that vessel. The bottom surface and part of the side has been partially reduced to a black colour in the firing.

4, 5 and 6. Painted ware vessels in identical fabric to no 3. No 4 has been reduced to black over most of the exterior and over the rim, with the inside being oxidised.

7. Part of a crenellated hip tile with a band of greeny/brown lead glaze along the top of the ridge and with white painted cross-banding. The fabric is oxidised to a reddish-buff and has been sand-tempered (cf. Down 1974, fig. 7.12, 45).
8. Painted and glazed ridge tile, similar in fabric to no 7, but much thicker.
9. Peg tile; badly laminated and flaked on the underneath and to some extent on the top surface. The fabric is a pale sandy buff and is slightly underfired.
10. Peg tile; similar fabric to no 7, some flaking on the bottom face due to frost action.

## Imported stonewares (not illustrated)

11. Fragment from a Raeren jug, c. 1475-1525 (cf. Gaimster 1987, fig. 3, no 4).
12. Sherd from a jug or mug, ?Raeren c. 1475–1525.
13. Raeren type jug or mug, c. 1475–1525.

This small group of black and white painted vessels, together with painted ware roof furniture and the associated sherds of imported German stoneware has a date span of c. 95 years from c. 1430 which is the earliest date suggested by Barton for the appearance of the painted wares (Barton 1979, 127), up to 1525 which is the suggested terminal date for the Raeren wares present in the pit (Gaimster 1987). However, Gaimster (*pers. comm.*) is inclined to place the three stoneware sherds discussed above at the earlier end of the date range, so a date of, say, late 15th century for these pieces may be more realistic, and a preferred date range for the whole assemblage could be narrowed to c. 1450–1490.

## Roof slates (Fig. 25.4)

Seven roofing slates came from A47 and others were found as rubbish survivals in later contexts (Fig. 25.4 nos 8–11). The seven examples illustrated from A47 all fall into the category of 'blue' slates. A consignment of these slates, the source of which is unknown, is recorded as being held in stock in the 'Churche's Storehouse' in Tower Street in 1533, some 28,600 of them having been landed at Dell Quay (Morgan 1981). A specimen of slate from A47 was submitted to Dr John Murray, Dept. of Geology, University of Exeter, by the late Mr E.W. Holden FSA. (Mr. Holden *pers. comm.* Murray states that the slate is *not* from south-west England, and it is unfortunate that the Chichester Port Book for that period did not give the source. Certainly the Church would have been well placed to buy in bulk from the cheapest market and the slates may have come by sea from North Wales, Scotland or possibly the Continent.

Having regard to the date brackets proposed for the pottery it seems reasonable to suggest that the large stock of 'blue' slates in the Church's Storehouse in 1533 were by no means the first to have been delivered and that the importation of slates from this particular source may well have had its origins in the preceding century, if not earlier.

## The slates from A47

1. Small, triangular, probably cut to fit around a chimney. 220 mm long by 70 mm at widest point; 7 mm thick, no sign of mortar.
2. As no1, but only 4 mm thick.
3. 186 × 85 × c. 6 mm. Traces of mortar on both faces.
4. 215 × 90 × c. 9 mm at its thickest point. Mortar on bottom surface.
5. 245 × 130 × 6 mm. Mortar traces on bottom face.
6. 260 × 116 × c. 6 mm. The top face has the outline in mortar of the two slates resting on it in the next line down, suggesting a distance between the batten centres of 3 inches (75 mm) (see Holden 1989, 73–88 ). There is another patch of mortar on the underside of the slate, covering the bottom right-hand part as hung.
7. 335 × 192 × 8 mm thick.

## Other late medieval slates from later dated contexts, but probably from the same roof

8. (A24). 186 × 57 × 7 mm thick. ?Re-cut to fit round chimney.
9. (A24). 238 × 72 × c. 3.5 mm thick.
10. (A24). 185 × 82 × 10 mm thick. This is a re-cut older tile and quite different in colour from the others, which are all 'blue' (grey) colour. No 10 is silvery grey in appearance, identical to some of the slates found in earlier medieval cess-pits in Tower Street (Down 1978, fig. 11.9).
11. (A37). 250 × 127 × 9 mm thick. Mortar on both faces.

## Acknowledgements

I gratefully acknowledge the help given by Mr David Gaimster, Dept. of Medieval and Later Antiquities, British Museum, who kindly examined the imported German stonewares and to the late Mr E.W. Holden FSA for much useful discussion on medieval roofing slates.

## REFERENCES

Barton, K.J., 1979. *Medieval Sussex Pottery* (Phillimore).
Cunliffe, B.W., 1973. 'Manor Farm, Chalton, Hants', *Post-Med. Arch.* 7, 31–59.
Down, A., 1974. *Chichester Excavations 2* (Phillimore).
Down, A., 1978. *Chichester Excavations 3* (Phillimore).
Gaimster, D., 1987. 'The supply of Rhenish Stoneware to London 1350–1600' *The London Archaeologist* 5, no 13, 339–47.
Holden, E.W., 1963. 'Excavations at Hangleton' *SAC* 101, p. 157, Fig. 30.
Holden, E.W., 1989. 'Slate roofing in Medieval Sussex—a reappraisal' *SAC* 127, 73–88.
Morgan, R.R., 1981. Chichester Excavations Committee Summary report for 1981.

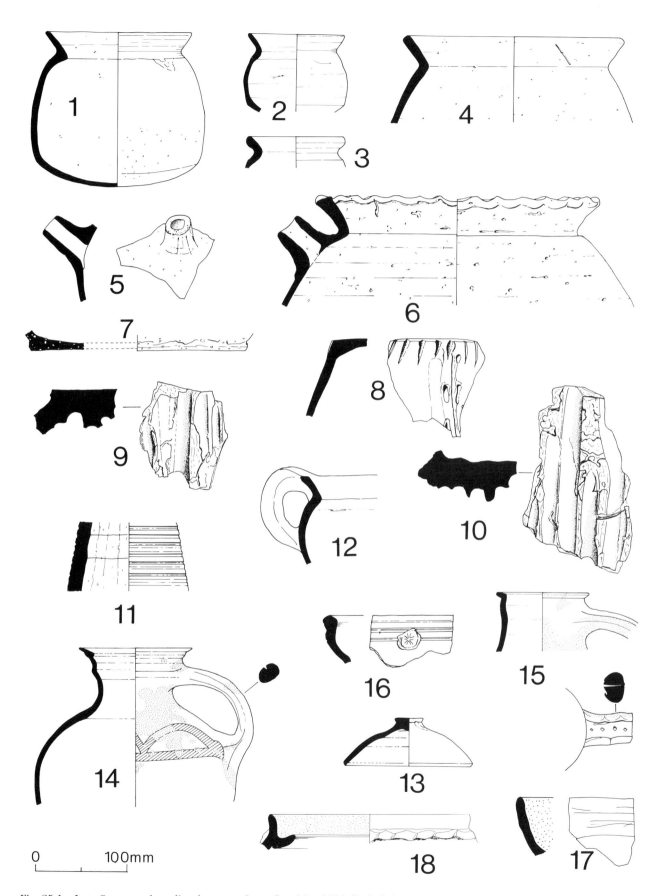

Fig. 25.1   Late Saxon and medieval pottery from Greyfriars1984. Scale 1:4

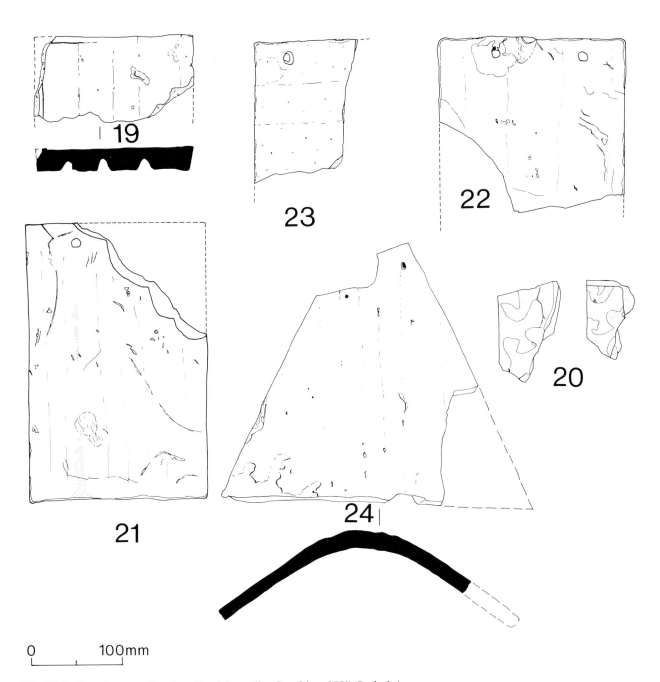

0      100mm

Fig. 25.2    Late/post-medieval roof and floor tiles Greyfriars 1985. Scale 1:4

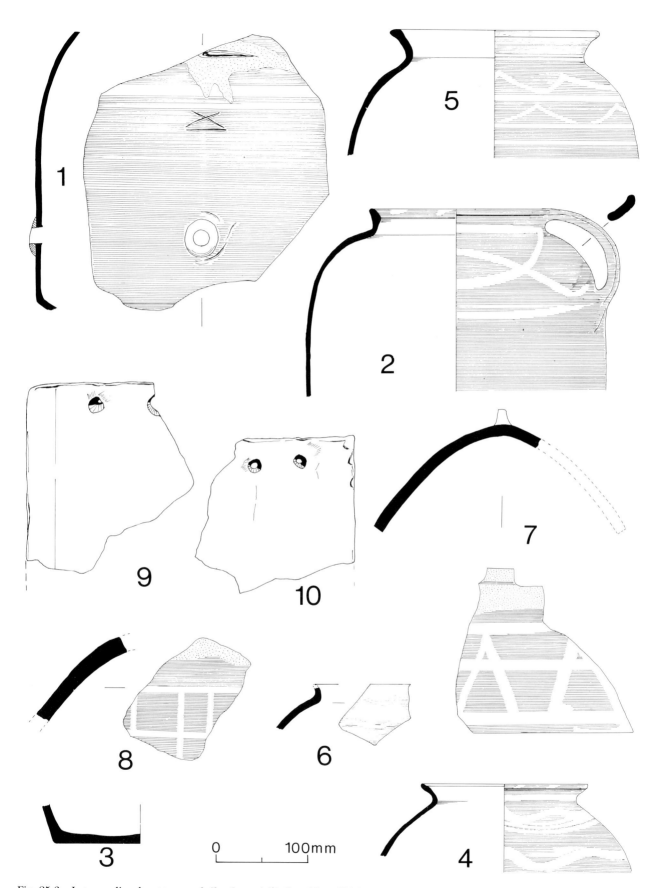

Fig. 25.3   Late medieval pottery and tiles from A47, Greyfriars 1984. Scale 1:4

0       100mm

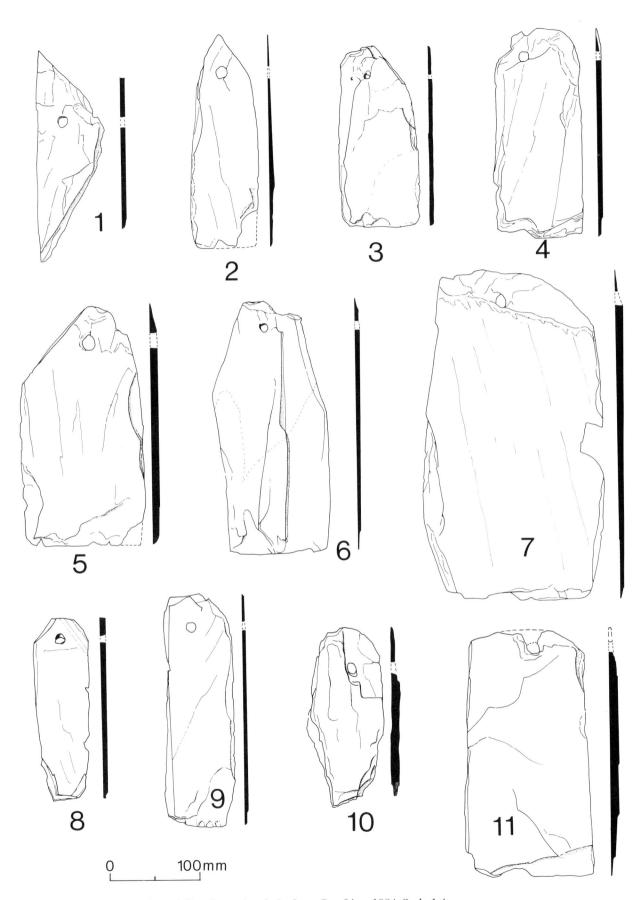

Fig. 25.4  Roofing slates from A47 and associated pits from Greyfriars 1984. Scale 1:4

# 26

# The 18th century wares from Greyfriars (Fig.26.1)

## by Sheila Morgan

### Tin-glazed earthenware

1. Fragments of blue dash charger, dia. 360 mm; decorated in blue, yellow, bright green and manganese. Part of monarch's head, sceptre, sponged foliage on trees; tin-glazed back. 18th century.
2. Fragmentary plate, dia. 230 mm; recessed foot-rim. Blue decoration on grey/blue glaze. Trailing flowers and leaves round the rim; centre design of fence, ?rock and flowers enclosed within a single line. Leaves and flowers are hatched, not solid colour. Similar decoration Garner and Archer (1972, pl. 73B).
3. Fragmentary base and deep foot-rim of ?bowl, dia. 85 mm Grey/blue glaze, crazed, over cream fabric. Decorated in blue with concentric circles surrounded by arcs of decreasing lines, similar to Edwards (1948, illust. 50A).
4. Plate rim fragment. Hard shiny white glaze on cream fabric, dark blue running border pattern as illustrated in Garner and Archer (1972, pl. 66).
5. Very fragmentary plate rim and recessed foot-rim, blue/grey shiny glaze, dark blue single and broad irregular line around cavetto and traces of more decoration round the rim.
6. Two fragments of dish rim and foot-rim; dia. of foot-rim 260 mm; grey/blue glaze on creamy-pink fabric. Dark blue oriental-style decoration, similar to decoration on rim of Garner and Archer (1972, pl. 54A).
7. Fragmentary ?dish rim with slightly everted top, dia. 230 mm Grey/blue glaze, very uneven on the underside, over creamy-pink fabric. Bright blue decoration of debased chinese motif within single and double lines.
8. Fragment of base, grey/blue thick glaze over buff fabric. Decorated in blue, chinese waterweed within double lines.
9. Fragment of thick-walled jar, grey glaze over dull creamy fabric. Bright blue decoration of flowers and leaves within a reserve bordered with stylised leaves and curves.
10. Base fragment, dia. 100 mm. Cream fabric covered externally by greeny-cream glaze, internally by blue and yellow lines on grey/blue glaze.
11. Curved fragment, deep cream fabric, covered internally with buff-coloured glaze and externally with very dark blue lines on creamy glaze. *Not illustrated.*
12. Fragment of a foot-rim, dia. 130 mm; green/grey glaze over deep cream fabric. Sponged blue decoration inside. *Not illustrated.*
13. Small fragment, white interior glaze, sponged blue exterior. *Not illustrated.*
14A and B. Fragment of base, rim and two sherds. Cream fabric covered with varying shades of grey, blue and blue/green glaze. *Not illustrated.*
15A and B. Fragmentary handle and sherds of white glazed hollow ware.
16. Fragmentary rim and fragments of bowl; rim dia. 260 mm. Cream fabric covered in hard white glaze, decorated with dark blue lines and reserves with stylised leaves and flowers, touches of red.
17. Fragment of plate. Cream fabric covered with blue glaze, traces of manganese and dark blue decoration, glaze badly chipped away. *Not illustrated.*
18. Fragment of hollow ware with knob. Creamy fabric covered internally with hard white glaze, externally with mottled manganese glaze. *Not illustrated.*
19. Fragmentary base and rim of ointment pot, dia.of base 55 mm. Light cream fabric, covered by light blue glaze. (Similar to Bloice 1971, fig. 55, no 98.)
20. Nearly complete small ointment pot, height 35 mm. Cream fabric, grey/blue glaze (*Bloice 1971*, no 99).
21. Fragmentary ointment pot, height 55 mm. Cream fabric, blue glaze. Traces of writing in black. Capital letters H or NE and below in script 'erfum'. Similar base to no 19. Date range: First half of 18th century. Probable place of manufacture: London.

### REFERENCES

Bloice, B.J., 1971. 'Norfolk House, Lambeth. Excavation at a Delftware Kiln Site' *Post Medieval Archaeology* vol. 5.

Edwards, R., 1984. 'An early 18th century waste deposit from the Vauxhall Pottery' *English Ceramic Circle Transactions* vol. 12, Pt. 1.

Garner, F.H., and Archer, M., 1972. *English Delftware* Faber and Faber.

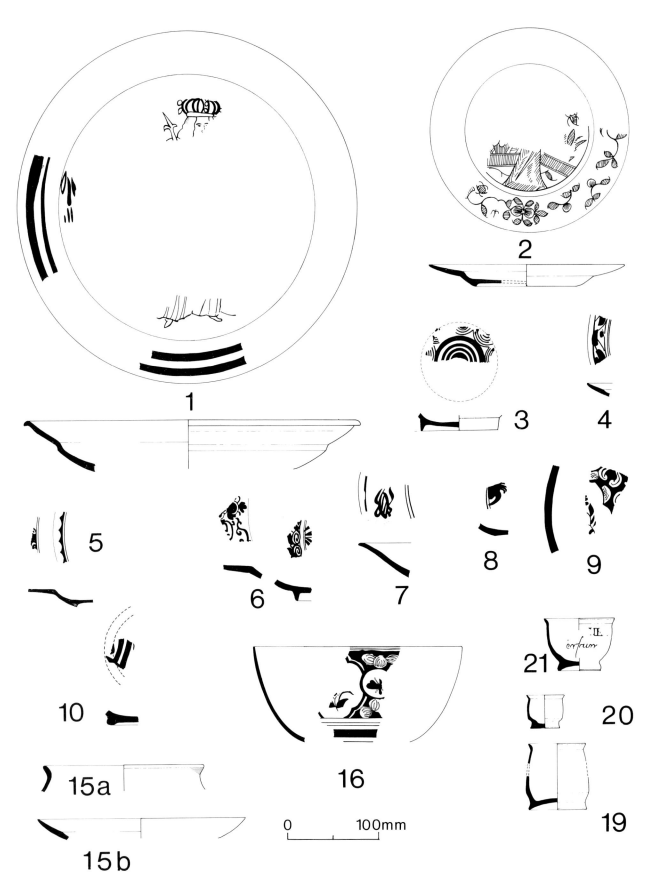

1

2

3

4

5

6

7

8

9

10

15a

15b

16

21

20

19

0        100mm

Fig. 26.1    Eighteenth century tin-glazed earthenwares from Greyfriars 1984. Nos 1–21. Scale 1:4

# 27

# Small finds from St Peter's, North Street

## by J.A.P. Kenny

*Note:* Figures in italics are small find numbers; those in brackets are context numbers.

### Object(s) of pottery (Fig. 27.1)

1. *124* (68)
Two fragments of crucible, probably from the same vessel, found in the top of a complex of late Roman pits. The fragments have been examined by Justine Bayley at the Ancient Monuments Laboratory, whose comments are below:

> The two fragments may be from the same crucible; wall thicknesses are 11–17 mm. The interior and rims of both pieces are vitrified with considerable amounts of copper-rich material adhering. Analysis of these deposits by X-ray fluorescence detected copper, tin, lead and zinc. The metal being melted was almost certainly a bronze; the lead and zinc were not significant components of the alloy.
>
> The fact that the outer surfaces have not been strongly heated and show no sign of vitrification indicates that the crucible was heated from above. The shape of the pieces suggests a fairly shallow triangular form. These observations, when taken together with the composition of the metal being melted, suggest that the crucibles are most likely to be of late Iron Age date. Crucibles of this type are not usually as large as these pieces, though parallels can be found among the crucibles from Fison Way, Thetford (Gregory, forthcoming, East Anglian Archaeology).
>
> The form of the crucible(s) cannot be paralleled among Roman or later examples.

### Objects of copper alloy (Fig. 27.2)

1. *31* (u/s) Chain, c. 145 mm long, heavily worn.
2. *20* (18) Fragment of sheet bronze, function unknown.
3. *25* (14) ?hairpin.
4. *10* (4) Pin.
5. *39* (29) Stud.
6. *82* (46) Stud.
7. *126* (68) Top of a dome-headed stud.

### Objects of iron (Fig. 27.2)

8. *67* (4) Joiner's 'dog'.
9. *92* (87) Hooked iron fitting.
10. *88* (42) Handle, ? of a spoon, with copper alloy bands and rings.

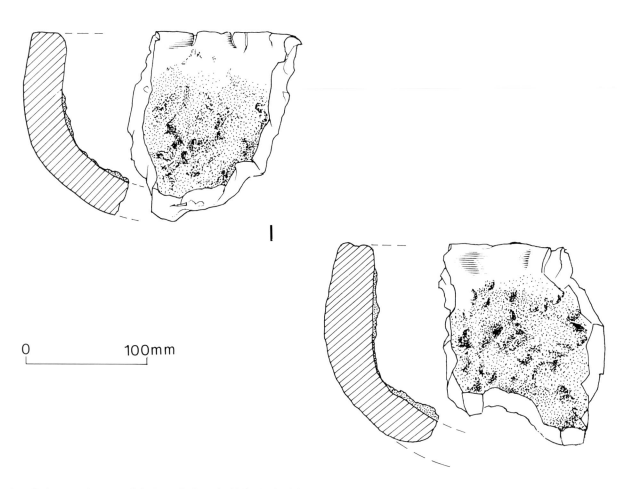

0          100mm

Fig. 27.1     Iron Age crucible from St Peter's 1987. Scale 1:3

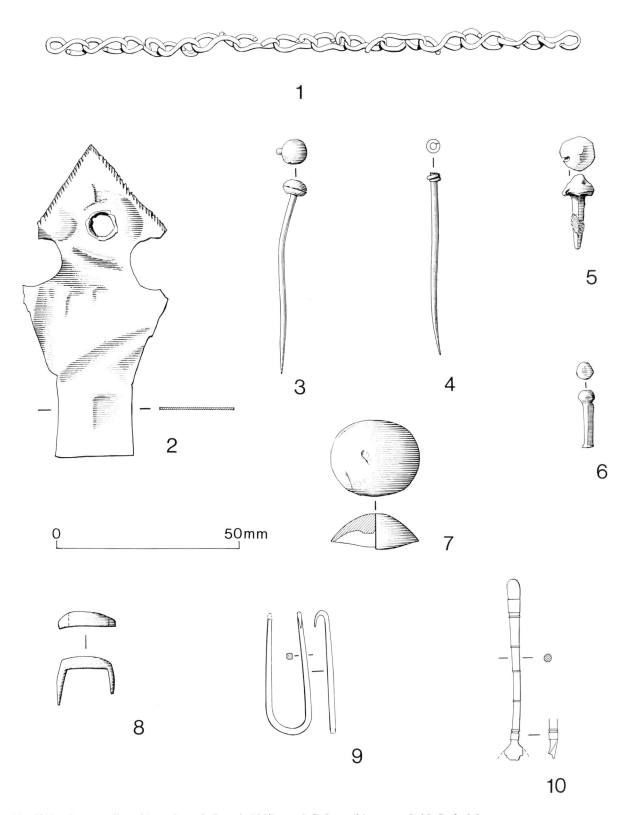

1

2

3

4

5

6

7

8

9

10

0                                    50mm

Fig. 27.2   Copper alloy objects from St Peter's 1987, nos 1–7. Iron objects nos 8–10. Scale 1:1

# Small finds from the Theological College (Figs. 28.1–28.7)

## by Alec Down

*Note:* Context numbers are in brackets, small find numbers are in italics. All objects are Roman or probably so unless otherwise stated. Small finds from the 1987 excavations are prefixed by G.

### a. Objects of copper alloy (Figs. 28.1–28.2)

1. (A13/F4) *80.* Brooch; Nauheim derivative, cf. Mackreth 1978, fig. 10.26, 12–13.
2. (A52/61) *57.* Brooch; Langton Down type. *op. cit.* fig. 10.28.
3. (A35, Gr.3) *22.* Brooch; Aucissa—Hod Hill type. *op. cit.*, fig. 10.28, nos. 42, 43 and 48; Mackreth 1981, fig. 10.2, nos 16–18 and 20.
4. (F9) *49.* Part of the pin from a large brooch. Colchester derivative, cf. Mackreth 1978, fig. 10.28, 1 and 2; Mackreth 1981, fig. 10.1, 1.
5. (A13) *5.* Small decorative boss, cf. Down 1978, fig. 10.39, 120. It may originally have been reinforced with lead behind the central boss but insufficient of the centre remains to be sure.
6. (F18, Gr.17) *73.* Buckle from *lorica segmentata.* For a typical example see Down 1978, fig. 10.30, 19.
7. (A52/61) *78.* Fragment of a cast bronze belt stiffener.
8. (Gr. 40) *83* and (47) *G44.* Studs with punch-dot decoration, probably military. First century AD, (cf. Ritterling 1913,
and 9. *40).*
10. (Gr. 36) *84.* Head of a cast bronze stud, lacking a pin.
11. (A10) *9.* Facetted and domed cap with two rivet holes. One rivet survives, cf. Down 1978, fig. 10.40, 147 for a similar piece although this has eight drilled holes, possibly for decoration. Both objects came from post-Roman levels but may be residual Roman.
12. (38) *G74.* ?Harness ring.
13. (A13) *45.* Three decorative bracelets linked together as found in a group which contained one melon bead and one inlaid glass bead (see below). Although not clearly associated with any burial it is likely that they were originally deposited with an inhumation or a cremation which was subsequently ploughed out or destroyed by pit digging.
14. (A52/61) *52.* ?Finger ring.
15. (F4) *29.* and (A13) *11.* Two large needles possibly used for sailcloth or other coarse fabric, cf. Down, 1978, fig. 10.37,
and 16. *95. Not illustrated.*
17. (A7) *14.* Fragment of edging strip, possibly from a purse or small bag, date uncertain.
18. (u/s) *7.* Fragment of cast decorative open-work.
19. (59) *G71.* Small domed-headed upholstery tack.
20. (2) *G8.* Belt buckle, probably post-medieval.
21. (A6) *16.* Bronze strip.
22. (A55) *75.* Two small fragments of rivetted plate. *Not illustrated.*
23. (A64) *70.* Fragment of bronze strip with rivet hole.
24. (F4) *46.* Flat-headed tack, ?from upholstery.

### b. Objects of iron (Figs. 28.3–28.5)

1. (F9) *27.* Head of large timber spike.
2. (A13) *6.* Timber spike.
3. (F14) *34.* Large nail with remains of wood attached.
4. (F4) *48.* Ring staple, cf. Down 1978, p. 311, 174; Down 1989, p. 221, 31.
5. (A13/F4) *79.* Lock or latch spring, cf. Down 1989, p. 216, fig. 28.3, 28.
6. (A52/61) *64.* Cleaver, cf. Manning (1985), pl. 57, Q102.
7. (A52/61) *66.* Socketed object, probably a cleaver.
8. (A52/61) *77.* Part of ?bucket handle.
9. (A52/61) *54.* Fragment of plate.
10. (F4) *102.* Possibly an iron-ringed saddle fitting for a ?wagon. See Down 1978, fig. 10.42, 175.
11. (A52/61) *69.* Plate.
12. (A52/61) *65.* Tip of ?knife.
13. (F4) *28.* Small knife with ringed handle.
14. (A52/61) *62.* Collar, Manning 1985, pl. 65, 54–S56.
15. (F12) *32.* Stylus.
16. (F1) *21.* Ring.
17. (A52/61) *74.* Tip of a spud, cf. Down 1989, p. 210, fig. 27.12, 66.
18. (A9) *36.* Flat ring or washer.

19. (A13) *98*. Plate. *Not illustrated.*
20. (F3) *23*. Ivory-handled knife, post Roman.
21. (1) *G30*. Curved plate with fixing hole (post-Roman).
22. (45) *G51*. Spur rowel, medieval or later, from a 17th-century context, (cf. Cunliffe 1964, fig. 53, 4; Fox and Barton 1986, fig. 145, 9 and 31).
23. (16) *G120*. Strapping, probably from a cart or large box. From a post-medieval context.
24. (2) *G130*. Part of a bracket, post-Roman.
25. (45) *G159*. Fragment of strapping with a hole drilled through it.

## c. Objects of bone (Fig. 28.6)

1. (F3) *18*. Part of a pin.
2. (F23) *81*. Fragment of a double-sided comb with ring-dot decoration. From Grave 21.
3. (F4) *26*. Gaming counter.
4. (A52/61) *59*. Socketed bone object, probably goat horn, with four holes drilled through the thin end, with a break having occurred in antiquity across the hole nearest the point. The function is uncertain, but the socketed end, which has also partly broken away, gives an indication of which way the forces to which this object was subjected were applied. The broken area, considered together with the four holes drilled through the thin end, suggests that the object may have been part of a stringed instrument, possibly some form of small harp (see Fig. 28.6 for reconstruction). Very little is known of such instruments and this identification must be highly tentative. The deposit in which it was found contained early imported pottery and a few scraps of legionary equipment and it is just possible that this fragment is all that survives of a small, roughly fashioned harp with which some legionary entertained himself and others.

## d. Objects of shale and stone (Fig. 28.7)

5. (B4) *3*. Fragment of shale with scratch marks, possibly the base of a platter.
6. (A52/61) *63*. Large pebble, polished on both sides, which has probably been used for polishing leather equipment. cf. Down 1978, fig. 10.49, 1.
7. (F4) *100*. Fine-grained sandstone hone.
8. (A52/61) *55*. Small fragment of frame moulding in a fine-grained sandstone.

## e. Objects of pottery (Fig. 28.7)

9. (A13/F4) *97*. Part of a pipeclay moulding, probably representing the drapery on a figurine.
10. (A13) *1*. Half of a spindle whorl.

## BIBLIOGRAPHY

Cunliffe, B.W., (ed.), 1964. *Winchester Excavations 1949–60.*

Down, A., 1978. *Chichester Excavations 3* (Phillimore).

Down, A., 1981. *Chichester Excavations 5* (Phillimore).

Down, A., 1989. *Chichester Excavations 6* (Phillimore).

Fox, R., and Barton, K.J., 1986. 'Excavations at Oyster Street, Portsmouth, Hants 1968–71' *Post-Medieval Archaeology* 20, 31–255.

Mackreth, D.F., 1978. 'The brooches' in A. Down, *Chichester Excavations 3.*

Mackreth, D.F., 1981. 'The brooches' in A. Down, *Chichester Excavations 5* (Phillimore).

Manning, W.H., 1985. *Catalogue of the Romano-British iron tools, fittings and weapons in the British Museum* (British Museum Publications Ltd).

Ritterling, E., 1913. 'Das Fruhromische Lager bei Hofheim im Taunus' *Annalen des Vereins fur Nassauische Altertumskunde und Geschictsforschung* 40.

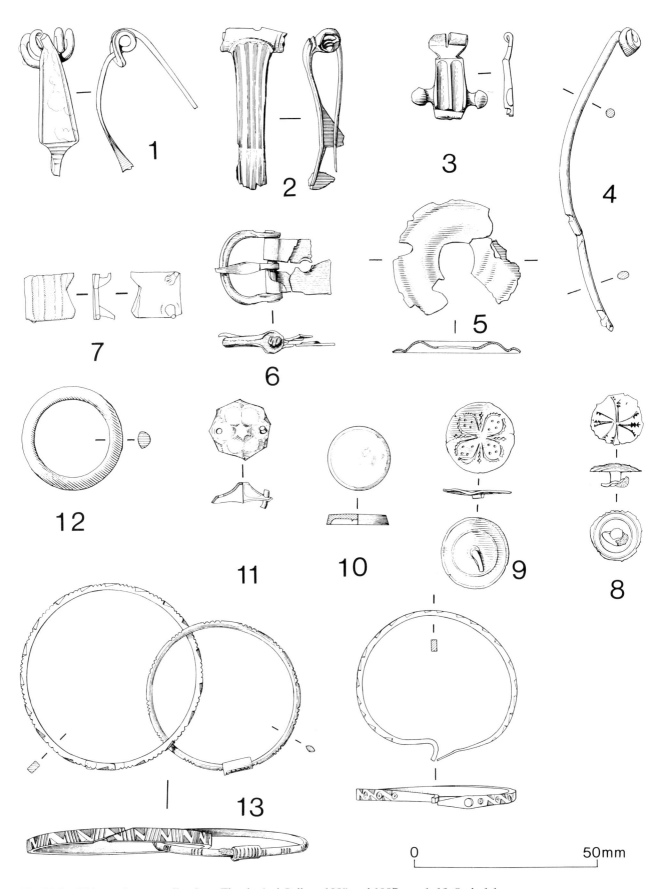

Fig. 28.1    Objects of copper alloy from Theological College 1985 and 1987, nos 1–13. Scale 1:1

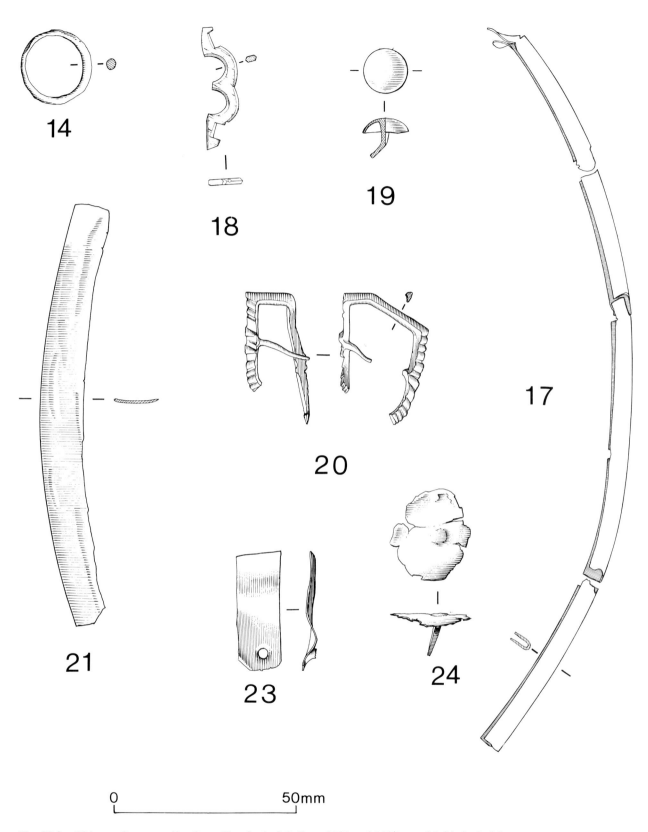

14

18

19

20

21

23

24

17

0    50mm

Fig. 28.2    Objects of copper alloy from Theological College 1985 and 1987, nos 14–24. Scale 1:1

233

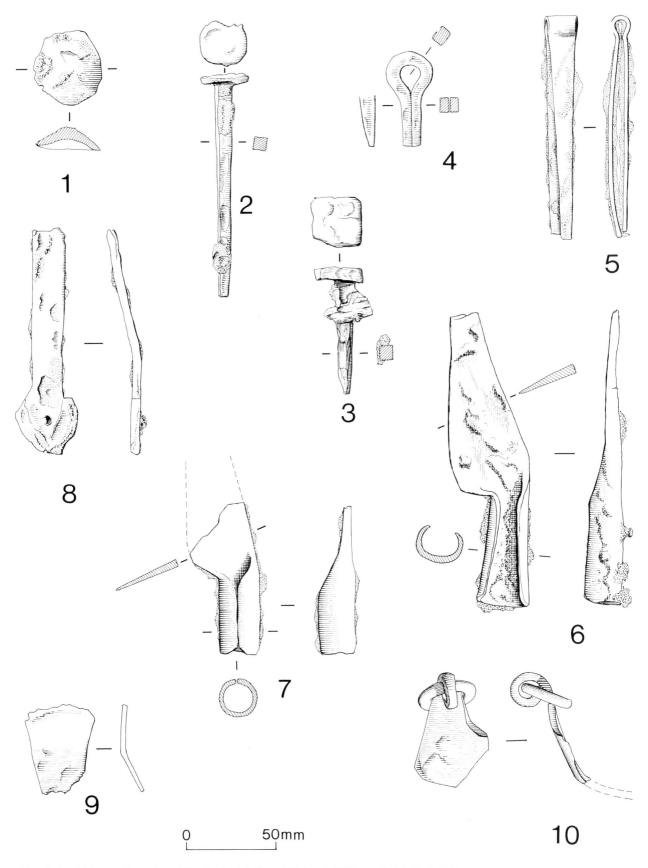

1

2

4

5

3

8

6

7

9

10

0        50mm

Fig. 28.3   Objects of iron from Theological College 1985 and 1987, nos 1–10. Scale 1:2

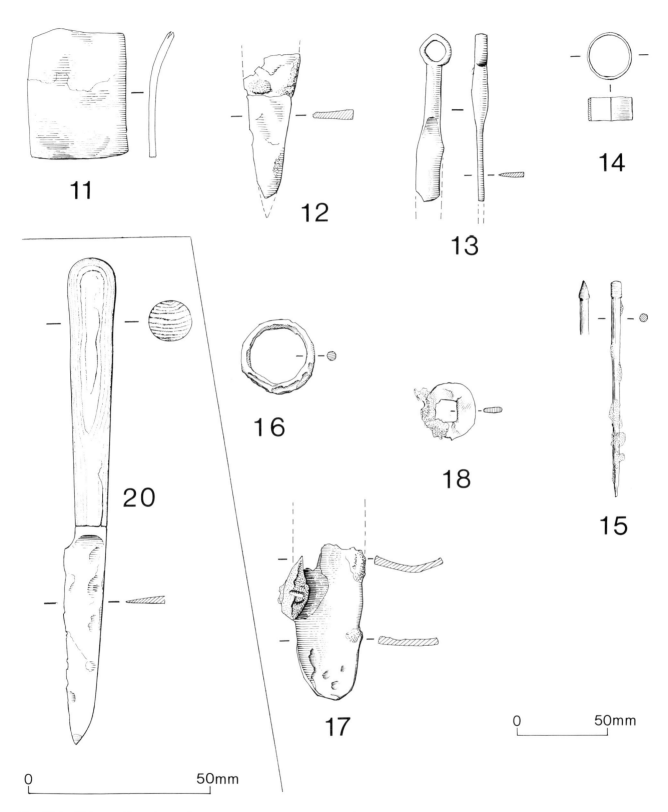

11

12

13

14

20

16

18

15

17

0          50mm

0          50mm

Fig. 28.4   Objects of iron from Theological College 1985 and 1987. All scale 1:2 apart from no 20, 1:1

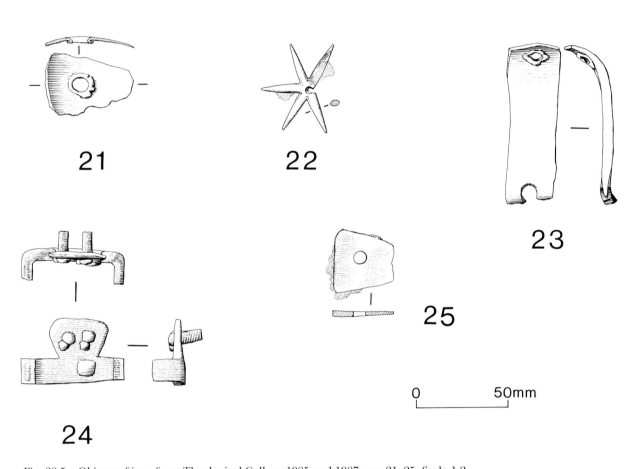

**21**

**22**

**23**

**24**

**25**

0          50mm

Fig. 28.5    Objects of iron from Theological College 1985 and 1987, nos 21–25. Scale 1:2

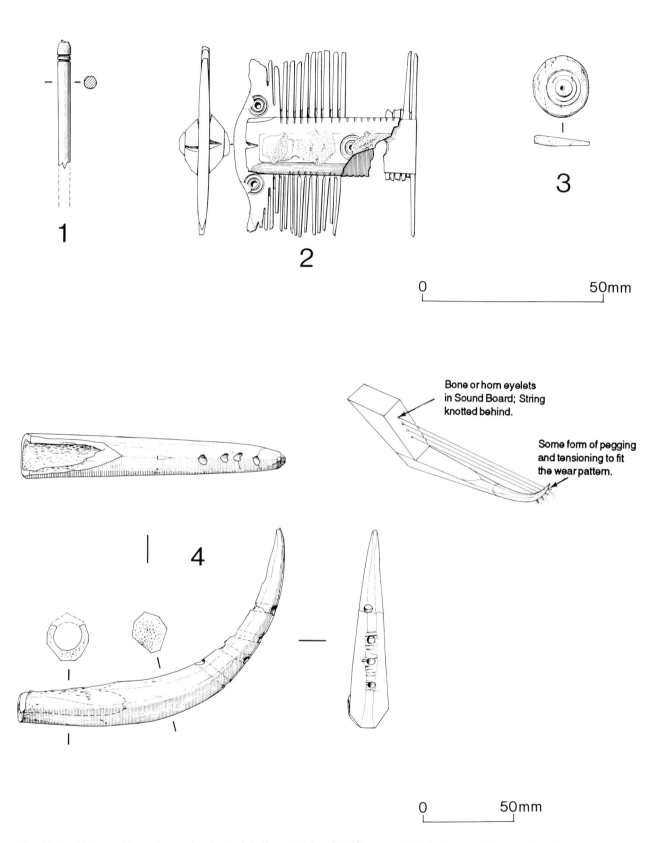

Bone or horn eyelets
in Sound Board; String
knotted behind.

Some form of pegging
and tensioning to fit
the wear pattern.

0                                    50mm

Fig. 28.6   Objects of bone from Theological College 1985 and 1987, nos 1–4. Scale 1:1 apart from no 4, 1:2

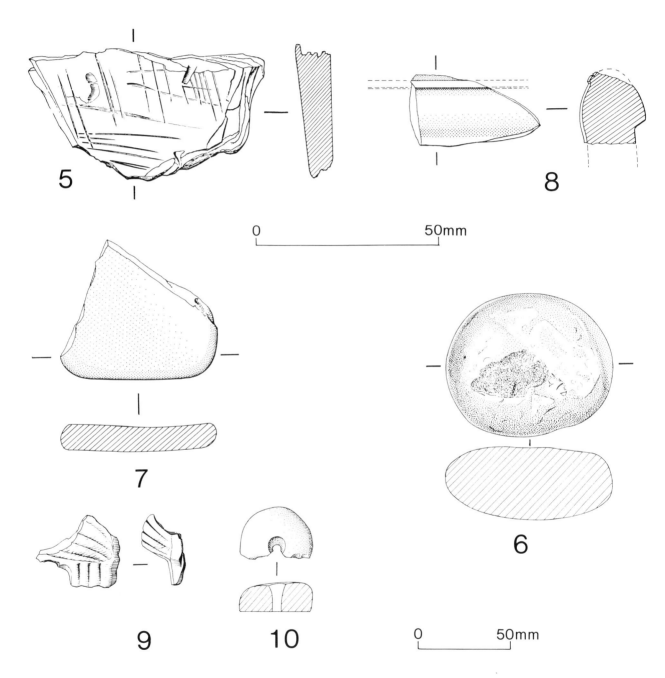

Fig. 28.7    Objects of shale, stone and pottery from Theological College 1985 and 1987, nos 5–10. Scale 1:2 apart from nos 5 and 8, 1:1

# A note on two mortaria stamps from Theological College, Chichester (Fig. 29.1)

## by K. Hartley

*Note:* Numbers in brackets are context numbers, those in italics are small find numbers.

1. (108) *90.* A worn mortarium in pale grey-brown fabric packed with inclusions: mostly quartz with rare red-brown and black material. Trituration grit included flint. The deeply impressed stamp, which reads CAST[, is from one of ten die-types used by Castus, who had at least one workshop at Radlett in the extensive potteries south of Verulamium and adjacent to Watling Street (Page 1898, 261). His activity fell within the period AD 90–140.

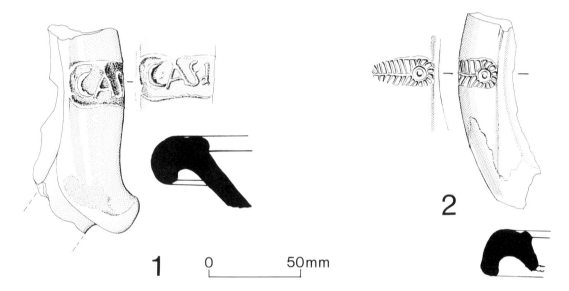

Fig. 29.1    Mortaria stamps from Theological College 1985 and 1987. Scale 1:2

2. (F3) *85.* Orangey cream and grey sandwich fabric, with surface pale grey; frequent, ill-sorted quartz inclusions. The only surviving trituration grit is flint. In texture, the fabric has much in common with that normally associated with the Verulamium region but there are fewer inclusions and they are notably less well sorted. The incompletely impressed stamp is of basically herringbone type but has a circle at one end with a raised central dot and rays round the outside of the circle. No other example of this stamp has been found but it is worth noting that it would be possible for only the herringbone part of the die to be impressed. The fabric and rim form would fit with production at some such local workshop as that at Wiggonholt (Evans 1974, fig. 17, nos 168 and 170); herringbone type dies were also used there (*ibid.*, fig. 17, nos 168–71). The rim and production at Wigginholt would fit a date of AD 110–60.

## BIBLIOGRAPHY

Page, W., 1898. 'Notes on a Romano-British pottery lately found at Radlett, Herts' *Ant. J.* 2nd Ser. XVII, 261–71.
Evans, K.J., 1974. 'Excavations on a Romano-British site Wiggonholt, 1964' *SAC* 112, 1–56.

# Theological College: the coarse pottery from A52/61 and A65 (Figs. 30.1–30.3)

## by Alec Down

### (A) Black Wares

*Note:* All the wares are sand-tempered and most are reduced to a matt black colour.

1. Lid with strap handle.
2. Jar with undifferentiated rim; zone of light burnishing below the rim. Reduced to dark grey/black.
3. High-necked jar, reduced to a patchy dark grey.
4. Small bowl, lightly burnished exterior and over the rim.
5. As no 4
6. Globular jar or beaker, fabric oxidised to a reddish-buff, with a terminal reduction to black.
7. Narrow-necked jar, lightly burnished on neck.
8. Beaker; fabric as no 6.
9. Jar with upstanding rim.
10–14. Jars with everted rims.

### (B) Grey Wares

*Note:* All sand-tempered unless otherwise stated.

15. Bead-rimmed jar, probably from the Chapel Street kilns (Down 1978, fig. 10.3; 7.1).
16. Bead-rimmed jar, different fabric to no 15.
17. Bead-rimmed jar reduced to slate grey on exterior and lightly burnished over rim and shoulder.
18. Small jar in pale grey ware, similar fabric to no 16. There are faint traces of red oxide slip on the shoulder.
19. Small jar or beaker, similar fabric to no 18, with red oxide slip inside and out.
20. Jar with everted rim.
21. Large jar with red oxide slip applied inside and out.
22. Lid: fine grey ware with random flint grits and traces of red slip on both surfaces.
23. Necked vessel, oxidised reddish-buff in patches.
24–26. Vessels in fine pale grey fabric, and probably from the same source.
27. Rim of a storage jar, sand- and flint-tempered and oxidised to a pale reddish-buff colour.
28. Small jar, pale grey, fairly soft fabric, oxidised orange/buff.
29. Cooking pot, black sandy fabric patchily oxidised to a dirty buff colour.
30. Jar, lightly burnished on shoulder and over the rim, reduced to dark grey on exterior.
31. Lid ?, in a hard, dark grey fabric.
32. Rim of large jar with traces of white slip decoration remaining on rim and neck.
33. Jar; fine sandy ware with a few flint inclusions.
34. Small jar in fine pale grey ware, lightly burnished over rim.
35. Sherd from a vessel with vertical combed decoration.
36–40. Grey ware vessels; no 39 is in a fine pale grey/white fabric with slightly mottled slate-grey exterior surface.

### Associated Fine Wares

The following fine wares were found in the pits.

*Note:* The number in brackets refers to the number of sherds.

*Samian ware*

Arretine ware: Tiberian–Tiberio-Claudian (6).
South Gaulish: Tiberio-Claudian (10).
Ritt. 5: South Gaulish (1).
Form 27: Flavian–South Gaulish (1).

*Gallo-Belgic fine wares*

TN  Claudio-Neronian (5)
     pre-Claudian (9)
     late Augustan–Claudian (1)

TR   Tiberio-Claudian (4)
     pre-Claudian (7)
Butt Beakers:  Claudio-Neronian (1)
               Tiberio-Neronian (1)
Fine white Flagons: pre-Flavian (2)

## THE POTTERY FROM THE EARLY DITCH A65 (Fig. 30.3)

A52/61 was a clay pit of irregular shape (see Fig. 4a.3) which cut the probable legionary ditch A65. It is possible that some of the early pottery, reported on above, was derived from a local fill of rubbish originally dumped into the ditch and later re-deposited in the back-filled clay pit. Three additional coarse ware vessels are illustrated here, together with a summary of the imported fine wares.

1. Rim of a pot in a fine sandy ware, oxidised orange/buff.
2. Cooking pot in hard sand-tempered grey ware.
3. Jar in a fine sandy grey fabric with faint traces of a white slip inside rim.

*Samian ware*

Cup. Claudian, South Gaulish.

*Gallo-Belgic fine wares*

Micaceous TN    Cam.4—pre-Claudian.
                Bowl—pre-Flavian.
White ware TN   Cam.3—late Augustan–Claudian.
Pale grey TN    Cam.5—late Augustan–Claudian.
Pale TN         ? —late Augustan–Claudian.

## BIBLIOGRAPHY

Down, A., 1978. *Chichester Excavations 3* (Phillimore).

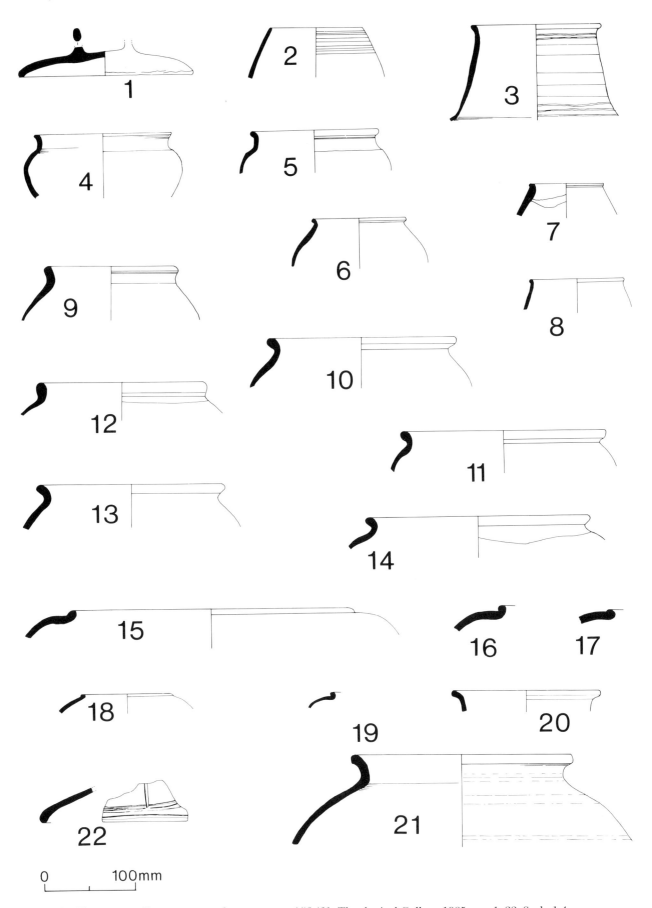

Fig. 30.1    First century Roman pottery from contexts A52/61. Theological College 1985, nos 1–22. Scale 1:4

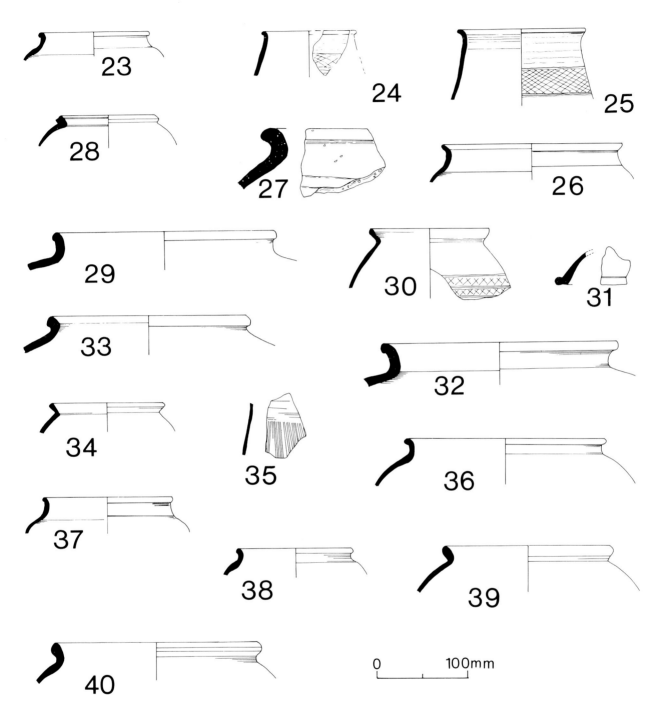

Fig. 30.2   First century Roman pottery from contexts A52/61. Theological College 1985, nos 23–40. Scale 1:4

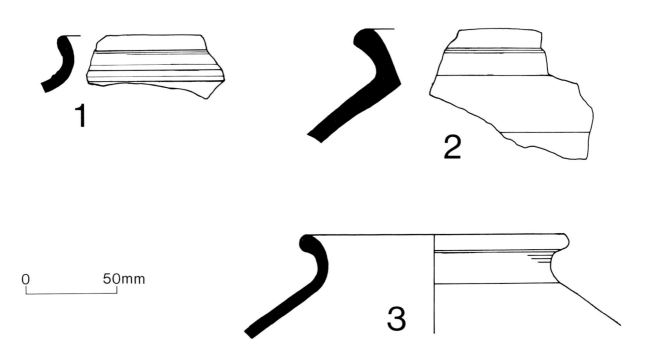

Fig. 30.3  Roman pottery from ditch A65, Theological College 1985, nos 1–3. Scale 1:2

0    50mm

# 31

# Medieval and post-medieval pottery from the Theological College (Fig.31.1)

## by Alec Down

1. (T87/40). Cooking pot; soft dark brown fabric, heavily loaded with small flint grits. The surface is lumpy and uneven. Late Saxon, c. late 10th–11th century.
2. (T87/52). Cooking pot; hard grey fabric with a few flint grits. Oxidised buff c. 14th century.
3. (T87/38). Sherds from curfews; similar fabric to no 2.
and 4.
5. (T87/52). Crudely made shallow bowl; hard grey, sandy fabric oxidised to a pinky-buff and with a green lead glaze on the interior.
6. (T87/38). Cooking pot; fine hard sandy fabric oxidised to a brownish/buff. c. late 14th–15th century.
7. (T87/20). Painted ware jug; fine grey fabric oxidised orange/buff and with white painted decoration on neck and shoulder. c. mid 15th–16th century.
8. (T87/44). ?Cooking pot; similar fabric and decoration to no 7.
9. (T87/21). Handle, deeply slashed, from a jug or pitcher; in typical painted-ware fabric.
10. (T87/58). Shallow bowl; painted-ware fabric and decoration and with a sparse green glaze inside. c. 16th century.
11. (T87/45). Shallow bowl; grey sandy fabric, brown/green glaze inside and over rim. Heavily burnt on outside surface. ?Graffham, c. 17th century.
12. (T87/44). Small dish; fine, off-white fabric, internal yellow glaze. ?Graffham or Crane Street. c. 17th century.
13. (T85/A10). Mug in a sandy grey fabric oxidised to a reddish-buff. Brown lead glaze inside and out, although the inside surface is incompletely covered. Date uncertain.
14. (T87/45). Complete bowl; fine sandy fabric, oxidised pale buff with yellow glaze on the inside. Graffham. c. 17th century.
15. (T87/44). Sherd from a plate, similar fabric to no 12. Sgraffito decoration, brown on white. ?Crane Street. c. 17th century.
16. (T87/45). Peg tile; one of a number from the site. The fabric is typical of the painted wares, being fine, hard-fired grey sandy ware which oxidises to a buff colour. The date for these tiles is likely to be between the mid 15th to the early 17th century.
17. (T87/45). Roofing slate with traces of mortar on the top surface.

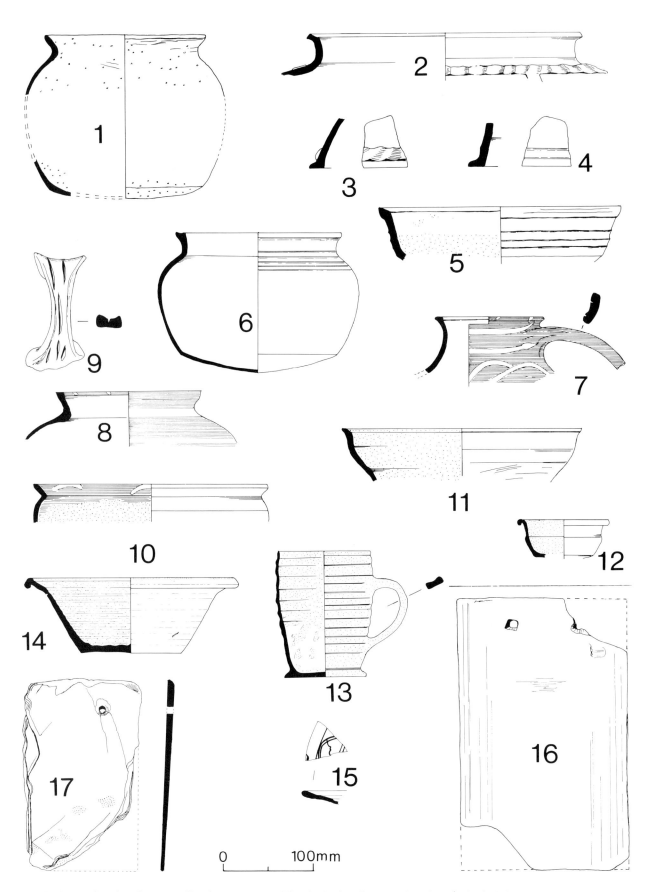

Fig. 31.1   Medieval and post-medieval pottery from Theological College 1985 and 1987. Scale 1:4

# 32

# Comments on the 18th–19th century pottery from the Theological College

## by Sheila Morgan

The pottery covers the whole of the 18th and the first decades of the 19th century. There is a large proportion of practically complete pots and in particular a fine example of a white saltglaze plate (6) with crisp mouldings round the rim, a very popular design in the mid 1700s.

The only two marked pieces date from around the same time: 1780. The Worcester blue and white painted saucer (13) was made for the wealthy who could afford the newly introduced English porcelain, and it must have been cause for concern when it was broken. Not many pieces are found in domestic rubbish pits. The creamware plate (17) made by Turner in Staffordshire is also of high quality, made for the upper end of the domestic market.

The almost complete coffee can of caneware (43) although of later date, c. 1810, is also of fine quality and would have been much more expensive than the contemporary blue and white decorated pearlware.

The pearlware tea bowls, saucers and bowls are decorated with line engravings, with very little stipple. This, together with the dark shade of blue and in some cases the lack of clarity and control of the colour, indicate these products date from the early years of the introduction of blue and white transfer printing, c. 1790–1800.

The practically complete tea bowls (41) with on-glaze painted polychrome decoration also date from about c. 1800–10.

Who owned this relatively expensive pottery and could afford to have the latest products at their table?

Three messuages stood on the Westgate frontage in the early 18th century. These were demolished and a new large house, stable and outbuildings were built on the site in c. 1780. The family connected with the site during most of the 18th century was the merchant/banking family of Diggens. Richard I, a merchant, lived there until his death in 1756; his son Edward, also a merchant, inherited the property in his father's will. He died in 1780 when the property passed to his eldest son Richard II, who may have been the builder of the late 18th century house. He was a banker and died ten years after his father in 1790. Richard's second wife Elizabeth continued to live there and eventually the property passed to her step-son Richard III, a Captain in the Light Dragoons. Richard I and his sons Edward and Francis were important merchants in Chichester and were involved in trade and building a warehouse at Dell Quay. Edward's sons Richard II and John were owners, with their uncle Francis, of the Chichester and Sussex bank in East Street.

By 1827 the property had been sold to another important Chichester family, W. and C. Humphrey, brewers.

It seems possible that the two fragments of delft tiles were part of the three early 18th century messuages on the site, the rest of the pottery relating to the Diggens family. The sale to the Humphreys in the late 1820s would account for the cut-off date of the pottery—a new family in residence would have used another rubbish pit which has not been excavated. All the pottery mentioned in this report has been deposited in the Chichester District Museum.

## CATALOGUE

### Tin glazed earthenware

1. Fragment of blue and white tile; painted with two figures, similar to pl. 96e in de Jonge (1971). Biblical subject—Job I v.14: messenger announcing Job's calamities.
2. Fragment of tile decorated in manganese; serpent's head and forked tongue and trellis-like feature.
3. Fragment of blue and white ridged handle.
4. Fragment of polychrome decorated sherd, blue, iron red and yellow.
5. Fragmentary rim and hollow ware fragments, undecorated.

### White salt glazed stoneware

6. Complete plate, diameter 240 mm; the rim moulded with basket-work panels separating star and diaper and dot and diaper patterns. c. 1760. See pl. 151 in Mountford (1971). This was a very popular form of rim decoration and made by many potters.
7. Fragments of small teapot, base and spout holes etc., undecorated. c. 1750.
8. Fragment of saucer base.
9. Small fragment of hollow ware.

### German stoneware

10. Fragment of grey, blue-banded hollow ware.

### Red stoneware

11. Fragment with mould-applied decoration, c. 1750. Possibly Staffordshire.

## Chinese porcelain

12. Two footrim fragments, painted with underglaze blue decoration.

## English porcelain

13. Fragmentary saucer, decorated with blue underglaze painted flower sprays. Worcester open crescent mark on base. The glassy glaze has deteriorated, turning brown and flaking off. Similar decoration on a coffee pot and milk jug, pls. 104 and 287 in Godden, (1969). c. 1780.
14. Rim fragment of hollow ware; outside underglaze blue-painted flower spray; inside a narrow trellis border.
15. Fragmentary tea bowl; grey/blue glaze full of impurities and bubbling on the base. Pink and iron red scale border inside the rim; pink, orange and green New Hall type flower sprigs on the outside. c. 1800.
16. Fragment of shoulder and rim of hollow ware, undecorated. c. 1820.

## Cream coloured earthenware

17. Fragmentary plate, flat rim, no footrim, diameter 250 mm. Impressed 'TURNER' on the base. c. 1780. Manufactured by John Turner, Lane End, Longton, Staffs.
18. Fragmentary plate, raised edge rim, single footrim, diameter 230 mm.
19. Fragmentary plate, Royal shape rim, single footrim, diameter 240 mm.
20. Fragmentary plate, raised edge rim, single footrim, diameter 250 mm. Impressed mark 'F' (reversed) on the base.
21. Fragmentary plate, raised edge rim, indented footrim, diameter 250 mm.
22. Rim fragment of bowl, diameter 160 mm.
23. Rim fragments of straight-sided tankard, diameter 70 mm.
24. Rounded rim fragment, diameter 200 mm.

## Pearlware with underglaze blue decoration

25. Fragmentary small jug, baluster shape, loop handle, painted with stylised flowers and leaves. Ht. 80 mm.
26. Fragmentary saucer, painted with stylised flower heads, meandering decorated line and dots within single lines around the rim.
27. Fragmentary saucer, transfer print of Chinese family and dog in a garden with pavilion, willow tree and table with large vase of flowers. Border of peonies and leaves.
28. Fragmentary saucer and half a tea bowl, transfer printed with a version of the Malayan Village or Trench Mortar pattern. Several potters used this pattern. c. 1800. See pp. 75–7 in Copeland (1980).
29. Fragmentary saucer and rim sherd from a bowl, both fluted. Transfer print of three sprays of flowers; border decorated with half circles of three rows of petals on a lozenge background.
30. Fragmentary tea bowl and saucer. Transfer print of Chinese landscape with one man on a single-arch bridge. Border inside cup of drapes, fish roe, lozenges and bells. Brown edge to rim of tea bowl. Similar pattern in Miller and Berthoud (1985), pl. 900.
31. Fragmentary fluted cup and slop bowl, cup with ear-shaped handle. Transfer print of floral sprays. Inside and outside rims decorated with a guilloche band. Bowl ht. 70 mm, diameter 120 mm.
32. Fragmentary bowl. Exterior decorated with transfer print of peony bush and two oriental ladies, one with a parasol, sitting on a terrace outside a Chinese house. Inside the rim a complicated border of arcades and bell shapes. A spray of grapes and other fruit in the base. Ht. 65 mm, diameter 135 mm.
33. Fragment of base of small sauce boat, the figure 6 impressed in the base. Interior decorated with bamboo growing on an island. This motif is part of the Buffalo pattern print produced by several potters c. 1800. See pp. 100–16 in Copeland (1980).
34. Fragment of saucer base. All-over pattern of stylised flowers around a central circular motif.
35. Fragment of tea bowl footrim.
36. Two fragments of saucer with Chinese style decoration.
37. Hollow ware fragment decorated with a pattern of Chinese buildings.
38. Fragment of square-shaped tea cup handle—undecorated.
39. Fragment of saucer rim.
40. Fragmentary plate, indented footrim, diameter 250 mm. Printed Chinese landscape, similar to pl. 27 in Coysh (1970). c. 1810, attributed to Davenport, Longton, Staffs.

## Pearlware with polychrome on glaze decoration

41. Two almost complete tea bowls. Flower sprays in pink, orange and green on the outside. Narrow border inside the rim of sprigs between interlaced circles, in brown, yellow amd orange. Fragment of saucer rim with the same border pattern.
42. Fragments of a bowl decorated with orange and brown flower sprigs on the outside. Interior border of rose sprigs in reserves on an orange band with brown enclosing lines.

## Caneware

43. Almost complete coffee can of dry-bodied stoneware, glazed inside, bamboo engine turning around the base, rouletting below the rim. Brown enamel lining to rim, base and sides of loop handle. c. 1810. Ht. 65 mm, diameter 65 mm.

## BIBLIOGRAPHY

Copeland, R., 1980. *Spodes Willow Pattern and Other Designs after the Chinese* (Studio Vista).

Coysh, A.W., 1970. *Blue and White Transfer Ware 1780–1840* (David and Charles).

de Jonge, C.H., 1971. *Dutch Tiles* (London).

Godden, G., 1969. *Caughley and Worcester Porcelains* (London).

Miller, P., and Berthoud, M., 1985. *An Anthology of British Teapots* Micawber Publications.

Mountford, A., 1971. *Staffordshire Salt Glaze Stoneware* (Barry and Jenkins).

## 33

## Small finds from West Walls

### by J.A.P. Kenny

**Brooches of copper alloy from West Walls and St Peter's (Fig. 33.1)**

*Note:* Small find numbers are in italics. Context numbers are in parentheses.
1. *15* (4) Dolphin brooch with hinged pin, second half of 1st century.
2. *84* (22) Enamelled zoomorphic plate brooch (dog), mid 1st–mid 2nd century.
3. *108* (38) Nauheim Derivative, early–mid 1st century.
4. *116* (39) Nauheim Derivative, early–mid 1st century.
5. *52* (18) Nauheim Derivative, early–mid 1st century.

*St Peter's*
6. *68* (42) Thistle brooch, early–mid 1st century.

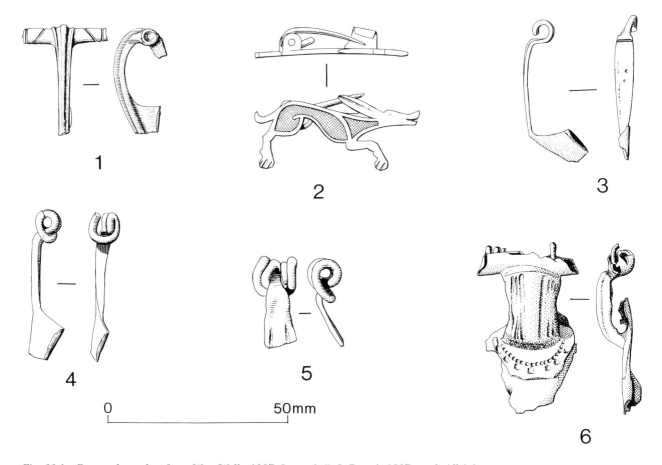

Fig. 33.1    Roman brooches from West Walls, 1987–8, nos 1–5. St Peter's 1987, no 6. All 1:1

**Miscellaneous objects of copper alloy (Fig. 33.2)**

1. *48* (18) Part of a decorative fitting from a horse's harness.
2. *10* (4) Part of a pair of tweezers.
3. *29* (2) Nail.
4. *7* (3) Finger ring.
5. *78* (u/s) Buckle ? post-Roman.
6. *117* (39) Buckle, ? from the *lorica*.
7. *79* (u/s) Ring.

250

8. *44* (8) Stud.
9. *28* (4) Flat-headed stud.
10. *111* (39) Flat-headed stud.
11. *76* (19) Flat-headed stud.
12. *112* (39) Dome-headed stud.

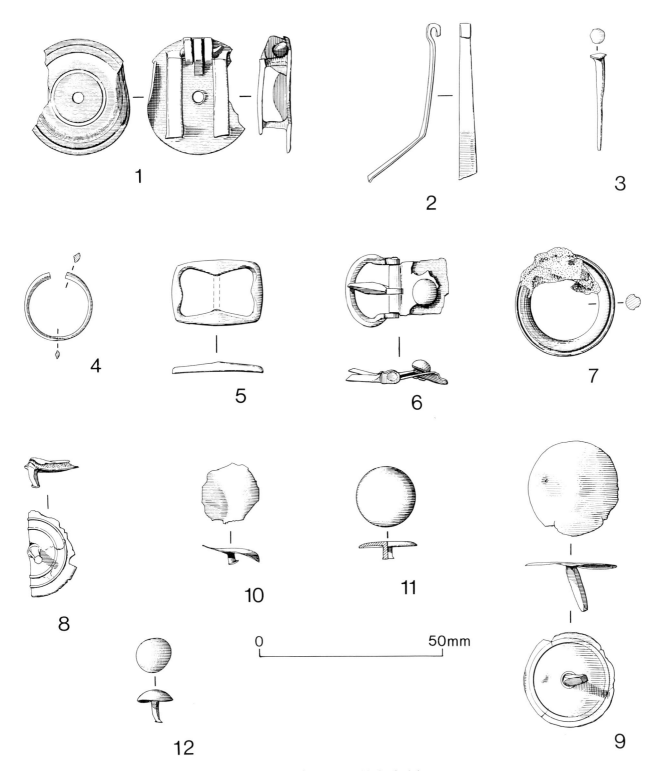

Fig. 33.2   Objects of copper alloy from West Walls 1987–8, nos 1–12. Scale 1:1

**Wall plaster (Fig. 33.3)**

A  *17* (2) Fragment of painted wall plaster with bands of decoration in grey, green and red upon a white background.
B  *32* (11) Fragment of wall plaster with painted decoration in two shades of grey, red and white (see Key to Fig. 33.3).
C  *22* (4) Small fragment of painted plaster with two bands of red and yellow.

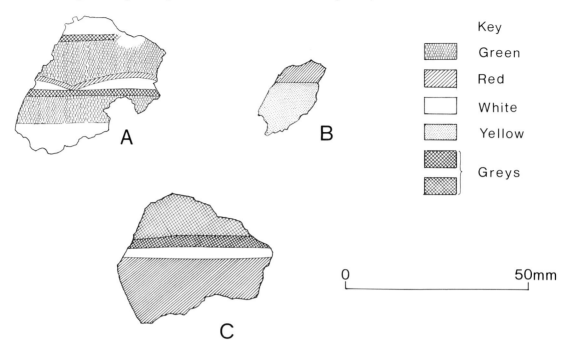

Fig. 33.3   Painted wall plaster from West Walls 1987–8. Scale 1:1

# 34

# Index

**NOTES**: Numbers in bold refer to Figs./Plates. All buildings, locations and streets are in Chichester. Where appropriate sub-headings are arranged chronologically by period, not alphabetically. Pottery references are under following headings: pottery, pottery forms or pottery types. Other finds are listed under their material or form.

    **Bold** page numbers indicate maps, tables and illustrations.

*Abbreviations of archaeological periods*:

| | |
|---|---|
| IA | Iron Age |
| Rom. | Roman |
| Sax. | Saxon |
| Saxo-Norm. | Saxo-Norman |
| med. | medieval |
| post-med. | post-medieval |

hollow ware
  Greyfriars, 225–6
  Theological College, 247–8
pearlware, Theological College, 248
porcelain
  Chinese, Theological College, 248
  English, Theological College, 248
stoneware
  German
    South Street, No 24, 144–6
    Theological College, 247
  red, Theological College, 247
  white salt glazed, Theological College, 247
Price, Jennifer, 171–81

religion
  **Rom.**, Westgate cemetery, 72, 84–5
Residentiary bastion *see* city walls
Rigby, Valery, 155–65
rings *see* copper alloy objects; gold objects; iron objects
roads
  **Rom.**, Westgate, 60
roof furniture *see* slates; tiles

St Peter the Great, West Street, 95–7
  site history, 96
  **Rom.**
    hypocaust, 95, 96
    wall, 96
St Peter's, North Street 1987, 41–51
  **IA**, pottery, crucible, 227, **228**
  **Rom.**, 42–7
    coins, 183
    copper alloy objects, 227, **229**
    hypocaust, 41, 44
    iron objects, 227, **229**
    mosaic, 41, 42, **43**, 46, 48–51
    pits, 42, 44
    potters' stamps, 151–4
    pottery, 42
    wall, 43
  **med.** features, 47–8
  *see also* Greyfriars
samian ware *see* pottery types
shale objects
  **Rom.**
    Greyfriars, 192, **202**
    Theological College, 231, **238**
shells, oyster
  **Rom.**
    city walls, west, 101 48
    St Peter's, 42
  **med.**, St Peter's, 48
slates
  **med.**, Greyfriars, 220, **224**
  **med./post-med.**, Theological College, 245–6
South Street
  No 24, **late post-med.**, pottery, 143–6
  No 74, **med.**, pottery, 141–2
spindle whorls *see* pottery forms
spur rowel *see* iron objects
stamps *see* pottery, potters' stamps
stone objects
  **Rom.**
    Chapel Street, 184, **186**
    Greyfriars, 191, **200**
    Theological College, 231, **238**

stoneware *see* pottery types
strapping *see* iron objects
streets, evidence of
  **Rom.**
    Chapel Street, 3, **5–7**
    city walls, west, 101, **102**, **103**
    Southgate, 124, **125**
structures *see* buildings, evidence of

tableware *see* glass objects
Theological College, 53–94
  site history, 53–4
  **Pre-Conquest**
    mid-late 1st C. BC-AD 43
      claypits, 54, **57**, **67**
      ditch, 54, **57**, **67**
      pits, 54
      pottery, 54
  **Rom.**
    bone objects, 231, **237**
    burials, Westgate cemetery, 72–94
    coins, 182
    copper alloy objects, 230, **232–3**
    glass objects, 171–80
    iron objects, 230, **234–6**
    pottery
      amphorae, **166**, 168–9
      beakers, 240, **242**
      black ware, 240, **242**
      bowls, 158, **161**, 240, **242–3**
      cups, 158, **160**
      fine ware, 240–1
      flagons, **160**
      Gaulish, 157–9, **160–1**, **164**
      grey ware, 240, **242–3**
      jars, 240, **242–3**
      mortaria stamps, 239
      pipeclay moulding, 231, **238**
      platters, Theological College, 158, **160–1**
      potter's stamps, 149–54, 158, **162–3**, **165**, 239
      samian ware, 147–50, 151–4
      spindle whorl, 231, **238**
    shale objects, 231, **238**
    stone objects, 231, **238**
  AD43 plus
    claypits, 57–8
    ditch, 53, 54
    pits, 57–8
    pottery, 54, 58, 59
    timber structure, 57, **58**
  late 1st-2nd C.
    burials, 59–60, **61**
    ditch, 59, **61**, **69**
    pits, 59, **61**, **69**
    pottery, 59
    slots, 58–9
    timber structures, 58, **59**
    wall, 59, **61**, **69**
    well, 58, **59**
  late 3rd-early 4th C., burials, 53, 60, **61**, **61–3**
  **med.**
    ditch, 60, **64–5**
    iron objects, 231, **236**
    pits, 60, **64–5**
    pottery, 60, **246**, 245–6

*Compiled by INDEXING SPECIALISTS, 202 Church Road, HOVE, East Sussex BN3 2DJ.*